1971

# GUIDE TO THE WORKS

# OF John Dewey

*Edited by* JO ANN BOYDSTON

Southern Illinois University Press | *Carbondale and Edwardsville*

Feffer & Simons, Inc. | *London and Amsterdam*

This Guide to the Works of John Dewey is the
result of a co-operative research project at
Southern Illinois University.
Jo Ann Boydston is the General Editor.
The Editorial Advisory Board consists of
Lewis E. Hahn, Chairman; George E. Axtelle,
emeritus; Joe R. Burnett; S. Morris Eames;
Wayne A. R. Leys; William R. McKenzie; and
Francis T. Villemain.
Polly V. Dunn is Staff Assistant.

# CONTENTS

# CONTENTS

# PREFACE

## Purpose and Plan

To the reader relatively unfamiliar with the works of John Dewey, the essays in this volume will offer perhaps surprising evidence that Dewey's thought is immediately relevant to a variety of contemporary philosophical interests, including phenomenological studies, analysis, and dialectic. The reader already acquainted with Dewey's major works will discover lesser-known pieces in which Dewey worked out important points of view; by studying all the Dewey materials in a given field, the essayists have been able to give new insights and new perspectives on Dewey's continuing significance.

John Dewey's impact on America stems largely from his perceptive, creative approach to many different kinds of problems, and his work in one area of specialization was often initiated or foreshadowed in another. To organize the various emphases in his writings twelve categories were selected as the framework for this book. Each section of the book consists of a two-part treatment of one of these categories, composed of an introductory essay and a bibliography. The essayists have given an overview of Dewey's thought in the diverse fields and have suggested directions in which the reader might pursue further studies. Although each of the twelve parts can be used independently, the book as a whole has been designed to emphasize interrelationships among the several areas and to help the reader assess Dewey's total contribution to American thought.

As a dual-purpose volume, this Guide is intended to serve independently as a resource for the study of Dewey's writings and as a complement to the Collected Works which have been initiated with the five-volume series *The Early Works of John Dewey, 1882–1898*. The bibliographical information here was gathered in the course of preparing the collected edition. Publication of the critical, textual edition of all Dewey's writings will require many volumes and many years. Meanwhile, although the search for previously unknown Dewey material continues, scholars will find in this book the most complete and detailed listing of such materials known at present.[1] In addition, the Guide meets a long-standing need for a comprehensive survey of all Dewey's writings, grouping them according to a logical pattern. These groupings will also be useful in conjunction with the Collected Works where the writings are arranged and published in chronological order.

### Principles and Procedures

*Essays*

The contributors conferred about the Guide as a whole, deciding on the proportional length of the essays and assigning varying amounts of space for each. Thus the length of the essays reflects, to a large extent, a combined judgment of the relative importance of the various categories in Dewey's total work.

The two essays which have two authors used different approaches: George Axtelle and Joe Burnett collaborated in the writing of the essay on Education and Schooling, while Herbert Schneider and Darnell Rucker each treated independently a time-period in Dewey's writings on Ethics. Ou Tsuin-chen's essay on Dewey's Lectures in China is not followed by a bibliography because the Lectures are at present available only in Chinese.

Footnotes appear on the essay pages rather than in a separate section, and they refer to Dewey's own published version of the material, whether the original or his revision.

*Checklists*

All the Dewey materials are included in one or more of the listings. The first published version is the main entry. Revisions

1. The earlier bibliographical study of M. H. Thomas, *John Dewey: A Centennial Bibliography* (Chicago: University of Chicago Press, 1962) was indispensable in all the preliminary work for this Guide. The Guide, with its logical rather than chronological arrangement, should serve as a useful supplement to the Thomas bibliography.

of the main entry are indicated in annotations except in the case of *Ethics* and *How We Think*, which Dewey revised so completely that the new "originals" are also listed as main entries. Annotations also direct the reader to collections of Dewey's works in which items were reprinted.

Unpublished items that are clearly authoritative, such as typescripts, syllabi, and transcripts of addresses are included, as well as those that are Dewey's but not written by him—newspaper interviews, stenographic transcriptions of class lectures, reports on lectures, and abstracts of addresses. A number of Dewey's major works appear in several categories and no attempt has been made to single out a category as the primary one. If the work is relevant to that section, it is listed there without cross-referencing.

Materials which are essential to full understanding and use of a Dewey item—articles to which he responded, for example—are also included with the Dewey entry to which they relate. In extended exchanges in which all items pertain to a single main entry, Dewey's replies and rejoinders appear in their proper order in the sequence of intervening items. Within the category bibliographies, works appear in chronological order, except for the exchanges described.

In a section following all the essays and bibliographies, collections consisting entirely of Dewey's writings are listed, with those published under Dewey's name appearing first, followed by collections made and/or edited by others. Collections of articles revised or expanded by Dewey—e.g., *Essays in Experimental Logic*, *Philosophy and Civilization*, *Individualism, Old and New*—are found both in the section bibliographies and in the listing of collections. Thus a distinction is made between collections which are presumably straight reprints and those which represent Dewey's revisions and additions. The latter are considered integral to the category bibliography; the former are primarily of interest as alternate printings.

Bibliographical information is given for currently available sources; for materials published through the year 1892, references are to the volumes in print of *The Early Works of John Dewey, 1882–1898*, and for all others, to the diverse publications in which they appeared. When all volumes of the Collected Works have been published, this Guide is to be revised to key all references to those volumes, making it in that way an integral part of the complete edition of Dewey's work.

*Jo Ann Boydston*

*1 March 1970*

# NOTES ON CONTRIBUTORS

GEORGE E. AXTELLE is Lecturer at United States International University and Professor Emeritus, New York University. Author of articles on Dewey and Dewey's thought; coauthor of *The Discipline of Practical Judgment in a Democracy* (1944), and *The Improvement of Practical Intelligence* (1950). Former teacher and administrator in Oregon, Hawaii, and California; teacher at Northwestern University, New York University, Southern Illinois University; Fulbright Fellow, Cairo, Egypt; former Chairman, Department of History and Philosophy of Education, New York University; Director, Co-operative Research on Dewey Publications, Southern Illinois University, 1961–66. Former President of the Philosophy of Education Society, the John Dewey Society, and the American Humanist Association. B.S., University of Washington; M.A. in Education, University of Hawaii; Ed.D., University of California.

JO ANN BOYDSTON is Director of Co-operative Research on Dewey Publications, Southern Illinois University, and General Editor of *The Early Works of John Dewey, 1882–1898* [Volume I (1969); Volume II (1967); Volume III (1969)]. Author of translations and articles on Dewey, and of *John Dewey: Checklist of Translations, 1900–1967* (1969). Former teacher, Oklahoma State University, University of Mississippi, Southern Illinois University. Editor of the *Dewey Newsletter*; Secretary-Treasurer of the John Dewey Society, 1962–70, President-Elect, 1970. B.A., M.A., Oklahoma State University; Ph.D., Columbia University.

WILLIAM W. BRICKMAN is Professor of Educational History and Comparative Education, Graduate School of Education, University of Pennsylvania, and editor of *School and Society*. Author of *Guide to Research in Educational History* (1949); *Introduction to the History of International Relations in Higher Education* (1960); *Educational Systems in the United States* (1964); coauthor and coeditor of *John Dewey: Master Educator* (1959); *The Changing Soviet School* (1960); *The Countdown on Segregated Education* (1960); *Religion, Government, and Education* (1961); *A Century of Higher Education* (1962); *Education, Automation, and Human Values* (1966); *A History of International and Comparative Education* (1968); editor of *Educational Imperatives in a Changing Culture* (1967). Formerly Professor of Education, New York University; Visiting Professor at Teachers College, U.C.L.A., University of Illinois, University of Hamburg. First President of Comparative Education Society, 1956–59, and President again, 1967–68. B.A., M.S., City University of New York; Ph.D., New York University.

JOE R. BURNETT is Professor of Philosophy of Education, University of Illinois, Champaign-Urbana. Author of articles in *Educational Theory, Harvard Educational Review, School Review*, the *Humanist*, and other journals; coauthor of *Democracy and Excellence in American Secondary Education* (1964). Former teacher at New York City Community College, University of Missouri at Kansas City, New York University, and the University of Puerto Rico. Former President of the John Dewey Society, the Midwest Philosophy of Education Society, and the Philosophy of Education Society. Formerly associate editor of *Educational Theory*, currently an editorial board member of *Studies in Philosophy and Education*. B.A., M.A., University of Tennessee; Ph.D., New York University.

S. MORRIS EAMES is Professor of Philosophy, Southern Illinois University. Author of numerous articles on John Dewey in the *Monist, Educational Theory, Journal of Philosophy, Journal of General Education, Philosophy and Phenomenological Research*, and other journals. Former teacher at Culver-Stockton College, University of Missouri, Washington University. Author of Introduction to Volume III, *The Early Works of John Dewey, 1882–1898*. A.B., Culver-Stockton College; M.A., University of Missouri; Ph.D., University of Chicago.

MAX H. FISCH is Emeritus Professor of Philosophy, University of Illinois, Champaign-Urbana. Author of *Nicolaus Pol Doctor 1494* (1947) and articles and reviews in the history of science, medicine, and philosophy. Coauthor of *Philosophy in America from the Puritans to James* (1939); General Editor, *Classic American Philosophers* (5th printing, rev., 1966); cotranslator of Giambattista Vico's *Autobiography* (1944, 1963), and *New Science* (1948, 1961, 1968). Visiting Research Professor, University of Naples, and Visiting Professor, Keio University, Tokyo, both on Fulbright appointments. Visiting Professor, University of Chicago, State University of New York at Buffalo. Matchette Lecturer, Purdue University; George Santayana Fellow, Harvard University; Honorary Research Associate in Philosophy. Former Chairman of Board of Officers of the American Philosophical Association, and former President, Western Division. Former member, Administrative Board of International Association of Universities. A.B., Butler University; Ph.D., Cornell University.

HORACE L. FRIESS is Emeritus Professor of Philosophy, Columbia University. Author, with Herbert W. Schneider, of *Religion in Various Cultures* (1932). Former Chairman, Department of Religion, Columbia University, and Buttenwieser Professor of Human Relations. Editor of the *Review of Religion*, 1942–58, and former President, Society for the Scientific Study of Religion. A.B., Ph.D., Columbia University, teacher in Department of Philosophy there from 1919 on.

LEWIS E. HAHN is Research Professor of Philosophy, Southern Illinois University. Author of *A Contextualistic Theory of Perception* (1942); contributor to *Value: A Co-operative Inquiry* (1949); author of articles in the *Journal of Philosophy*, *Philosophy and Phenomenological Research*, and other journals; author of "From Intuitionalism to Absolutism," Introduction to Volume I, *The Early Works of John Dewey, 1882–1898*. Teacher, University of Missouri; Visiting Lecturer, Princeton University; Professor and Chairman of Department of Philosophy, Dean of Graduate School of Arts and Sciences, Washington University. Fellow, American Association for the Advancement of Science and International Institute of Arts and Letters; "Man of the Year in Philosophy," 1966–67; Secretary-Treasurer, American Philosophical Association, 1960–66. B.A., M.A., University of Texas; Ph.D., University of California.

GAIL KENNEDY is Henry C. Folger Professor of Philosophy, Emeritus, Amherst College. Author of *The Psychological Empiricism of John Stuart Mill* (1928); coauthor, *Education at Amherst: The New Program* (1955); *Values in American Education* (1964). Editor, *Bacon, Hobbes and Locke: Selected Writings* (1937); *Democracy and the Gospel of Wealth* (1949); *Pragmatism and American Culture* (1950); *Education for Democracy* (1952); *Evolution and Religion* (1957). Coeditor, *The Classic American Philosophers* (1951, 1956); *The American Pragmatists* (1960); *The Process of Philosophy* (1967); *The Transcendentalist Revolt* (1968). Contributor of articles and reviews to various journals. University Fellow, Columbia University; Guggenheim Fellow; Rockefeller Foundation Fellow. Teacher at Columbia University, New School for Social Research, Bennington College, University of Hawaii.

A.B., University of Minnesota; A.M., Columbia University; Ph.D., Columbia University.

WAYNE A. R. LEYS is Professor of Philosophy, Southern Illinois University. Author of *Ethics for Policy Decisions* (1952), and numerous articles on the philosophy of law, politics, and public administration. Formerly Vice-President of Roosevelt University, and formerly Visiting Professor at Northwestern University, Johns Hopkins University, and the University of Michigan. Recipient of research grants from the Rockefeller and other foundations. He has served as an officer of the American Philosophical Association and as a member of the Council for Philosophical Studies. In a recent book, *Gandhi and America's Educational Future* (P. S. S. Rama Rao, coauthor) (1969), he has compared what Dewey and Gandhi thought about moral education. Ph.D., University of Chicago.

BERTRAM MORRIS is Professor of Philosophy, University of Colorado. He is the author of various articles on ethics, æsthetics, and social philosophy, and of *The Æsthetic Process* (1943); *Philosophical Aspects of Culture* (1961); *Institutions of Intelligence* (1968); coauthor of *Science, Folklore and Philosophy* (1966). Teacher at University of Wyoming, Northwestern University, University of Chicago, and California Institute of Technology. Formerly Trustee of the American Society for Æsthetics, and former member of the National Council of the American Association of University Professors. A.B., Princeton University; Ph.D., Cornell University.

OU TSUIN-CHEN is former President of New Asia College, The Chinese University of Hong Kong. He is the author, among other works, of *An Outline of Philosophy of Education* (1934); *La doctrine pédagogique de John Dewey* (1958); *Kiang Kao Chi* (1967). Formerly Professor and Head of the Department of Education, National Peking University; Professor of Education at National Central University; Director of Higher Education of the Ministry of Education, Republic of China; Vice-Minister of Education; Delegate of the Chinese government to the General Conference of UNESCO; Senior Specialist, Institute of Advanced Projects, East-West Center, University of Hawaii. B.A., National Southeastern University, Nanking; Docteur de l'Université de Paris, 1931.

DARNELL RUCKER is Professor of Philosophy at Skidmore College. He is the author of articles on ethics, social philosophy, and education, and of *The Chicago Pragmatists* (1969). He has been a teacher at the University of Chicago, Colorado College, Williams College, Bennington College, and has held fellowships in the Carnegie Program for Internships in General Education at Yale University, and from the American Council of Learned Societies. B.E.E., Georgia Institute of Technology; A.M., Ph.D., University of Chicago.

HERBERT WALLACE SCHNEIDER is Professor Emeritus, Columbia University. Author of *A History of American Philosophy* (1946) and journal articles, especially on Dewey's moral philosophy. Compiler (with M. H. Thomas) of the Dewey bibliography (1929, 1939). Author of Introduction to Volume II, *The Early Works of John Dewey, 1882–1898.* His Ph.D. thesis, supervised by John Dewey, was entitled "Ethics as the Science of Social Progress" and consisted of a critique of French positivist social philosophy. He assisted John Dewey as instructor and then as assistant professor in lecture courses, and took part in all his seminars, 1920–35. He served in the UNESCO Secretariat in Paris, 1953–56, and since his retirement from Columbia in 1957, has continued to teach at Colorado College, Claremont Graduate School, and Oregon State University. B.A., Ph.D., Columbia University; L.H.D., Union College, Baldwin-Wallace, Colorado College; LL.D., Claremont Graduate School.

# GUIDE TO THE WORKS
# OF **JOHN DEWEY**

# 1

## Dewey's Psychology

### HERBERT W. SCHNEIDER

DURING HIS years as a student under George Sylvester Morris, from 1882 to 1886, John Dewey thought of psychology not as a science but as a philosophical method and "standpoint." In part, his studies in Vermont, the influence of Coleridge and the writings of the romantic idealists, and in part, the systematic version of this standpoint as it took shape in the mind of Morris led Dewey to believe that for a "critical" understanding of life-mind-nature as an organic whole, it was necessary to show the identity of psychological, logical, and ontological procedure. Morris had conceived such a "dynamic idealism" as a more adequate "experimental" method than the methods of British Empiricism, which had reduced the idealizing functions of mind to a "hard concretion in the sphere of actual particular fact." [1] The "psychological standpoint" would liberate philosophy and philosophical imagination so that it could "freely work . . . to reach certain intellectual ends." [2]

Morris, under whom Dewey did his Ph.D. research at Johns Hopkins, had worked out this standpoint during his studies in Germany under Adolf Trendelenburg and Hermann Ulrici. Trendelenburg had worked out a biological and Aristotelian reformulation of Hegel's theory of the objectification of mind. He conceived mind as constructive movement (*konstruktive Bewegung*) in the context of natural activity (*Aktivität*)

---

1. *Psychology* (The Early Works of John Dewey, 1882–1898, Vol. II [Carbondale: Southern Illinois University Press, 1967]), p. 175.
2. *Early Works*, II, 175.

conceived as the process of living, and had applied this philosophy to knowing, willing, and feeling by making the category of purpose (*Zweck*) basic for both organic and logical analysis. Ulrici had applied this general method to the interpretation of religious experience and to problems of pedagogy. Morris's version of this philosophical psychology and psychological philosophy reads as follows:

> [The method in which the British Empiricists] put all their trust, and which they style "experimental" is . . . abstract, partial, incomplete, and not commensurate with the whole nature and content of experience; requiring, therefore, to be supplemented by a larger and more liberal, but not less strictly scientific, method, which is not unknown to philosophy and which, not being arbitrarily conceived and forcibly imposed on experience but simply founded in and dictated by the recognition of experience in its whole nature, is alone entitled to be termed fully and without qualification "experimental."
>
> The science of knowledge has nothing to do with unknowable objects. It has no ground on which to posit their existence. It has positive ground for absolutely denying their existence, for *knowing* that they do not exist. . . . The phenomenal object is not a veil or screen effectually to shut out from us the sight of the noumenal object. Nor is the former separated from the latter by an impassable interval. On the contrary, to thought it instrumentally reveals the true object.
>
> In other words, that *is* which is *known*. Knowledge and being are correlative terms. When we know therefore what is the true *object* of *knowledge*, we know what is the final and absolute significance of the terms *being* and *reality*.[3]

Dewey's researches as a student, culminating in his doctor's dissertation in 1884 on "The Psychology of Kant" and in his paper on "Knowledge and the Relativity of Feeling"[4] were preoccupied with a criticism of British Empiricism and of Kant's contrast between feeling and knowing. But when he went in 1884 to the University of Michigan as Instructor under

3. George S. Morris, *Philosophy and Christianity* (New York: Robert Carter and Bros., 1883), pp. 287, 44–45, 70.
4. "Knowledge and the Relativity of Feeling," in *Early Works*, I, 19–33.

Morris [5] he co-operated with his teacher in developing the more positive and philosophical aspects of this psychology, which came to be known as "dynamic idealism."

In his articles in *Mind* in 1886 [6] Dewey referred to "known objects" as "objective consciousness." This use of "consciousness" was attacked at once by Shadworth Hodgson, to whom Dewey replied as best he could, but he was evidently finding it difficult to justify such language and method as empirical and experimental.

Meanwhile, in 1883, Dewey at Johns Hopkins had become acquainted with the more recent trends in experimental psychology as represented by G. Stanley Hall, and had read a paper at a meeting of the Metaphysical Club (presumably in the presence of G. Stanley Hall) on "The New Psychology," later published in the *Andover Review*.[7] On this occasion he discussed "the bearings of the theory of evolution on psychology" and in general showed that he was trying to adapt his ideas and expressions to a more naturalistic biology and to shift his conception of psychology as the philosophical standpoint of "objective consciousness" to that of an experimental science.

Arrived at Michigan in 1884, Dewey devoted himself to developing the "newer" psychology in the framework of an *ethics* of dynamic idealism. A few references to the *Psychology* and to its 1891 revisions will indicate some of the attempts to bring his science up to date. His first revisions in content, for the 1889 printing, centered in an improved analysis of sensation. The more philosophical changes in his revisions for the 1891 printing reveal that the author's thinking was already moving beyond the idealistic theory of self-realization to which his ethical theory was devoted. The reader should consult the context out of which these references are taken if he wishes to get the evidence for the emergence, even in these old-fashioned pages, of doctrines which transformed his theory of mind from "ideali-

---

5. For an excellent account of this Michigan period in Dewey's life and development, see George Dykhuizen, "John Dewey and the University of Michigan," *Journal of the History of Ideas*, XXIII (1962), 512–44.

6. "The Psychological Standpoint," *Early Works*, I, 122–43; "Psychology as Philosophic Method," ibid., 144–67.

7. "The New Psychology," *Early Works*, I, 48–60.

zation" to "reconstruction," and from "objectification" to "adjustment." [8]

*Retention:* Retention is the process by which external, actually-existing material is wrought over into the activities of self, and thus rendered internal or ideal. (1887)
*Conception:* The conception, like every other mental content, is particular in its existence. . . . It is only its meaning that is universal. . . . What is experienced is only the symbolic quality of the image. (1887)

Compare the revision in 1891:

. . . *as to its existence,* every idea must be particular and have more or less sensuous detail. But it is not the existence that we mean by concept. The concept is the power, capacity, or function of the image or train of images to stand for some mode of mental action, and it is the mode of action which is general (p. 179).

*Judgment:* A judgment expressed in language takes the form of a proposition. . . . [It] may either idealize a real thing, by stating its meaning, or it may, so to say, realize an idea by asserting that it is one of the universe of objects. As matter of fact, it always does both. (1887)
*Truth:* Truth is but another name for intelligence. . . . [It is] not only harmony with all intelligences, but harmony with the universal working of one's own intelligence. (1887)

Compare the revision in 1889:

The mind always tests the truth of any supposed fact by comparing it to the acquired system of truth . . . if there is irreconcilable conflict, one or the other must be false. . . . The worth of the criterion will evidently depend upon the degree in which the intelligence has been realized and knowledge acquired (p. 190).

*Reasoning:* There is no such thing as purely *immediate* knowledge. Any cognition is dependent; that is, it is *because of* some other cognition (p. 192).
*Process of Mind in Knowledge:* Fact and law cannot be regarded as anything except two ways of looking at the same

8. See *Psychology* (Early Works, II). All revisions are tabulated in the List of Emendations in the Copy-Text, pp. lix–lxxxvi. Page references are to the *Early Works*, II.

content. . . . Each of these functions is an abstraction; in actual knowledge we always identify and distinguish. . . . All actual knowledge proceeds from the individual to the individual (p. 199).

*Will:* What gives the conflict of desires its whole meaning is that it represents the man at strife with himself. He is the opposing contestants as well as the battle-field. . . . The process of choice is that process by which some one of the conflicting desires is first isolated and then identified with the self to the exclusion of others. . . . Choice is the identification with self of a certain desire (p. 314). We realize the self only by satisfying it in the infinite variety of concrete ways. . . . The self is the end, because it is the organic unity of these various aspects of self-realization (p. 319). The whole process is will (p. 328). The process of our actual life is simply that by which will gives itself definite manifestation, bodies itself forth in objective form. Just what will is, we can tell only so far as it has thus realized itself (p. 330). A man's will is himself (p. 345). Character is the will changed from a capacity into an actuality (p. 352).

The need for reconstructing his psychology more radically did not become critical until 1893 when he began to see that a new ethics as well as a new psychology was forming. In 1893 when Dewey was preparing to get out a revised edition of his 1891 *Outlines of a Critical Theory of Ethics*, in which the language of the *Psychology* had been retained, the old bottles burst, and in 1894 when he published the small *Study of Ethics: A Syllabus*, he explained that the new work was "in no sense a second edition of the previous book." It laid the foundation for his own philosophy and his own terminology.

Dewey's interest and competence in psychology continued to develop throughout his life, and all his works reflect this development. But he abandoned the writing and amending of a textbook on psychology after 1891. Several years after the American Book Company took over the printing of the book, its Editor-in-Chief wrote to Harry Ambrose, then president of the company, "Dewey's *Psychology*: A revision of this book means entirely rewriting it, and when I last wrote to Dr. Dewey on the subject he was not ready to undertake the job." [9] Once, during Dewey's years in Chicago, a friend asked him for information

9. H. H. Vail, handwritten annual report (1906?), quoted by Mauck Brammer, letter of 21 May 1965.

about a certain small college in Michigan. Dewey replied that he knew little about it except that "it is benighted enough still to be using my *Psychology* as a text."

Two radical developments in his thinking during the years 1893 to 1896 gave to Dewey's psychology a new significance and direction. One found expression in his paper presented to the Herbart Society in 1895 at Jacksonville, Illinois, on "Interest as Related to Training of the Will" (published in the Society's *Year Book* for 1895). The other was published as an article in *The Psychological Review* in July 1896, under the title "The Reflex Arc Concept in Psychology." Both essays have been reprinted several times and remain basic expositions of Dewey's contributions to psychology.

The idealistic theory of self-realization through the mediation of desires by the will, with which Dewey had struggled, was now transformed by the theory that the self is the organization of interests. The substitution of "interests" for "desires" enabled Dewey to revise his theory of motivation and emotion in terms of Darwinian biology and social psychology. Interests are not "subjective" feelings or desires, but patterns of overt activity that are objectively directed and socially interrelated. Dewey emphasized these points in his 1894 *Syllabus*: "Interest is active, projective . . . implies an object—the end, or thought, which claims attention, . . . dominates activity, . . . implies the relation . . . to *character*, . . . expresses the *identification* of the object with the subject" (p. 54).[10] The educational implications of this psychological insight for the theories of effort and discipline became obvious at once to Dewey and led directly to his own dominant interest in experimental schools and socialized schoolrooms.

His revision of the reflex-arc concept led directly to his "experimental logic." Developing the psychology which he discovered in William James's treatment of "conception," he pointed out that a response to a stimulus leads not merely to a decision that re-directs activity but also to a re-construction of the environment or the stimulating situation, which reconstruction makes a difference in future stimuli. The human art of adapting the environment to the organism as well as the organ-

10. *The Study of Ethics: A Syllabus* (Ann Arbor: Register Publishing Co., 1894), p. 54.

ism to the environment gave Dewey the psychological analysis
that he needed for a general theory of the reconstructive power
of intelligence. This reconstruction takes place both in the refor-
mation of the habits and character of an individual and also in
the reform of institutions. He now had a psychology that implied a philosophy of science, of education, and of democracy.
The volumes that followed rapidly—*School and Society*, *How
We Think*, *Democracy and Education*—gave systematic expression to his revision of the traditional reflex-arc concept and to his
revision of motivation on the basis of interests.

Dewey had worked out this new psychology with the co-
operation of George H. Mead and James H. Tufts. As a result,
Dewey, during his years at Michigan and Chicago, relied on his
two colleagues to develop the social aspects of the psychology
while he concentrated on the psychology of intelligence in the
individual organism, emphasizing its implications for the theory
of knowledge and the self. He continued to use the term "experience" largely in relation to personal conduct and organic action,
pointing out that he did not limit the concept to *conscious*
experience nor to the process of *experiencing* to the exclusion of
objects-experienced. His method was to insist on "activity" or
"experience" as an operation that implied the co-operation of
organism and environment. The separation of the subjective and
the objective factors in this activity, as if only the organism were
an agent, is useful and valid only for certain technical and
subsidiary operations (logical), and is false or arbitrary if interpreted as a presupposition of psychological science. For this
reason Dewey became a leader in advocating "behavioral"
methods in the human sciences.

The only attempt Dewey made to formulate such a behavioral psychology systematically in both its individual and social
aspects was in his *Human Nature and Conduct* (1922). In the
Preface he stated the theme of this volume concisely:

> The book does not purport to be a treatment of social psychol-
> ogy. But it seriously sets forth a belief that an understanding
> of habit and of different types of habit is the key to social
> psychology, while the operation of impulse and intelligence
> gives the key to individualized mental activity. But they are
> secondary to habit so that mind can be understood in the
> concrete only as a system of beliefs, desires, and purposes

which are formed in the interaction of biological aptitudes with a social environment.[11]

The three parts of the work ("Habit," "Impulse," "Intelligence") were designed to shift the emphasis from the then popular preoccupation in social psychology and ethics with human nature, instincts, moral sentiments and values. Dewey regarded custom and habit as more significant environmental factors than "herd instincts" and universal "drives." Human nature, he thought, is an unorganized mass of reflexes and impulses, which are shaped by custom, habit, institutions, rather than by an order of nature. The changes in the cultural environment necessitate continual re-constructions of habits and impulses through intelligent "deliberation." In the course of such deliberation, ends, values, and ideals are also reformed.

Dewey was thus prepared to accept the growing emphasis in psychology on unconscious factors in motivation. He was especially interested in the discoveries of the physiologists concerning the important functions of the autonomic nervous system, and he discussed critically Sherrington's thesis that the central nervous system is at the service of the autonomic system. He regarded this thesis as an exaggeration, on the ground that no part of man's natural endowment determines fixed ends or values beyond conscious control. For the same reasons he was ready to accept the findings of clinical psychiatry, but rejected the "metaphysical" concepts and construction of the Freudian theory of the subconscious, which he regarded as an inheritance from Schopenhauer's romantic theory of the will. Dewey continued to believe that conflicts tended to generate conscious emotions and that intelligent analysis of the tensions could "sublimate" the emotions into effective interests.

The problem for social psychology that emerged in *Human Nature and Conduct* was that the analysis of the so-called "interaction" between human nature and cultural habits and customs made it increasingly difficult to give a precise content to the natural or inherited endowment of the organism. It became fashionable among social psychologists to read into human nature a variety of instincts ("herd," "moral," "religious," "imitative," etc.) that were clearly in part cultural acquisitions. It

11. *Human Nature and Conduct* (New York: Henry Holt and Co., 1922), p. iii.

was necessary to make a more careful and physiological examination of the distinction between biological and cultural "inheritance." In Dewey's own interests and method, attention shifted
from the analysis of will or of impulses as elements of human
nature to an analysis of social behavior. From the beginning of
his emphasis on "psychological method in philosophy" it was
evident that for Dewey psychology was the handmaiden of
ethics and logic; and the problem of "self-realization" was something he had "inherited" from the idealists. He now consciously
subordinated psychology to more general methods and problems
of human existence as it was exhibited in politics, art, labor, and
in human relations generally; his philosophy became intimately
associated with the social sciences and cultural anthropology.
Accordingly, the problems of self-realization became also problems of cultural reconstruction. He summed up this situation by
saying that "what passed as psychology was a branch of political doctrine," [12] and in more detail:

> Any movement purporting to discover the psychological causes
> and sources of social phenomena is in fact a reverse movement,
> in which current social tendencies are read back into the struc-
> ture of human nature; and are then used to explain the very
> things from which they are deduced. . . . Love of power is put
> forward to play the role taken a century ago by self-interest.
> . . . What are called motives turn out upon critical examina-
> tion to be complex attitudes patterned under cultural condi-
> tions, rather than simple elements in human nature.[13]

For this reason the further developments in Dewey's psychology
will appear best where they should appear in this Guide, as
aspects of broader problems and other sciences. But it may be
well to extract from the other chapters a summary statement of
the general features of Dewey's later psychology.

In *Experience and Nature* he presented a general historical
outline to emphasize the importance of the shift from the classical to the modern concept of mind. He pointed out that in the
classical tradition mind and will were regarded as objective,
cosmic entities, and that even in modern times this classic tradition was kept alive by the Cartesian doctrine of "thinking substance," by Spinoza's "conatus," and by the universalization of

12. *Freedom and Culture* (New York: G. P. Putnam's Sons,
1939), p. 29.
13. *Freedom and Culture*, p. 108.

thought and will in the romantic philosophies of Schopenhauer and Nietzsche and in the Hegelian philosophy of history and *Phänomenologie des Geistes*. In reaction to such speculation, modern scientific psychology drifted into the opposite extreme of subjectivism, taking consciousness in individuals as the essence of mind. The social scientists were tempted to adopt one or the other of these extremes: thus, the Durkheim School interpreted the mind as a collective construct, while Bergson regarded the individual *élan* as a source of creative energy. Dewey conceived his own theory of mind as taking an intermediate position between these extremes: mind, self, and personality are active centers of reconstruction and find themselves realized in intelligent reform.

In his *Logic* he made continual reference to the *process* of inquiry and to the continuity not only between stimulus and responsive inquiry (which he had been emphasizing) but also between natural relationships or "connections" (to use his technical name for them) and the *relations* as they are logically formulated by language and conceptual thought.

His political writings and especially his *Art as Experience* led Dewey to explore the less cognitive dimensions of experience. In addition to the arts of intelligence and inquiry, he analyzed the arts of expression and of "impulsion." He realized that there is an important difference between the scattered raw material of innate impulses and reflexes and urges in human nature and the "impulsion" or propulsion and adventure in the world of objects that is exhibited by sustained imagination and self-expression. These psychical processes are also social and institutional, involving the mind not only in inquiry but also in enjoyments as they are found in the arts and crafts, in politics and sports. The relation of motivation to expression, and of both to culture became an increasing psychological problem to him, especially during the years of war, depression, and revolt. In such a context, he realized how absurd it is to speak of the environment as "external world." To use his own words (taken over in part from his friend Arthur F. Bentley):

> The epidermis is only in the most superficial way an indication of where an organism ends and its environment begins. There are things inside the body that are foreign to it, and there are things outside of it that belong to it *de jure*, if not *de facto*. . . . The need that is manifest in the urgent impulsions that

demand completion through what the environment—and it alone—can supply, is a dynamic acknowledgement of this dependence of the self for wholeness upon its surroundings. . . . But the impulsion also meets many things on its outbound course that deflect and oppose it. In the process of converting these obstacles and neutral conditions into favoring agencies, the live creature becomes aware of the intent implicit in its impulsion. . . . The attitudes of the self are informed with meaning.[14]

Dewey developed in many new ways his central idea that the self is not to be conceived as a metaphysical agent but as an agency of responsibility. The problems of self-control over the imagination and other adventures of the mind in view of the demands made upon them by a particular "human situation" or crisis led Dewey to involve psychology and philosophy continually in "the problems of men" as these become urgent. His responsiveness to such problems and his conception of democratic self-government and responsibility induced him to make continual applications of his psychology to a great variety of cultural problems and interests. He became irritated and worried when he witnessed the fashion among philosophers of dismissing such problems as not a philosopher's business. His activities during the last decades of his life gave eloquent testimony to his own character, for to him the critical concern about such problems was a most "consummatory experience."

These interests and insights led him to co-operate gladly with his friends, especially Albert C. Barnes and Arthur Bentley, and the editors of the *New Republic*, in the critical study of international relations, of the fine arts, and of the behavioral sciences.

During the final decade of his career Dewey was preoccupied with the theory of "transactional" activity which he and Arthur Bentley expounded in joint works. Bentley tried to push Dewey into an extreme behaviorist theory of knowledge. Dewey agreed that the usual conception of the "interaction" of organism and environment failed to do justice to his theory that

14. *Art as Experience* (New York: Minton, Balch and Co., 1934), pp. 58–59. Dewey and Bentley had been discussing "the human epidermis" in connection with the "problem of the external world" before the publication of *Art as Experience*, but Bentley made the point emphatically in an amusing article, "The Human Skin: Philosophy's Last Line of Defense," *Philosophy of Science*, VIII (1941), 1–19.

"activity" is a single process of which organism and environment are merely factors; and he welcomed the term "transaction" as recognizing the "partnership." But he resisted Bentley's suggestion that the concept of "experience" is too ambiguous to be useful. Dewey concluded, on the contrary, that "human experience" in the broad, popular sense that implies nobody's private experience but rather a general process of learning, is still needed in both psychology and philosophy. In this sense, Dewey was quite content to abandon the traditional emphasis on "the subject" and "subjectivity" and to encourage Bentley's pan-objectivism. But he was less willing to agree to the Neo-Positivist doctrine that things are as they are said to be. He continued to the end to think of language as communication and of communication as a kind of manipulation of things for social purposes. This way of thinking about knowledge as endless "inquiry," without ever assuming that any discovery is final, was circumstantial evidence that for John Dewey the most "consummatory experience" or enjoyment was to let things be reconstructing themselves, including his own psychology.

## CHECKLIST

"Knowledge and the Relativity of Feeling," in *The Early Works of John Dewey, 1882–1898*, Vol. I, pp. 19–33. Carbondale: Southern Illinois University Press, 1969.
"The New Psychology," in *Early Works*, I, 48–60.
"The Psychological Standpoint," in *Early Works*, I, 122–43.
"Psychology as Philosophic Method," in *Early Works*, I, 144–67.
   Response by Shadworth Holloway Hodgson, "Illusory Psychology," in *Early Works*, I, xli–lvii.
   Reply by Dewey, " 'Illusory Psychology,' " in *Early Works*, I 168–75.
*Psychology* (The Early Works of John Dewey, 1882–1898, Vol. II). Carbondale: Southern Illinois University Press, 1967. cix, 366 pp.
"Speculative Psychology," [Prof. John Dewey, Feb. 23, 1887]. Class lecture notes, handwritten by C. E. Goddard, University of Michigan. 180 pp. [Michigan Historical Collections.]
"Professor [George T.] Ladd's *Elements of Physiological Psychology*," in *Early Works*, I, 194–204. [Review.]
"Knowledge as Idealization," in *Early Works*, I, 176–93.
"Galton's Statistical Methods," in *The Early Works of John Dewey, 1882–1898*, Vol. III, pp. 43–47. Carbondale: Southern Illinois University Press, 1969. [Review of *Natural Inheritance* by Francis Galton.]
"On Some Current Conceptions of the Term 'Self'," in *Early Works*, III, 56–74.
*The Study of Ethics: A Syllabus.* Ann Arbor: Register Publishing Co., 1894. iv, 151 pp. [2d ed., Ann Arbor: George Wahr, 1897. 144 pp.]

"The Psychology of Infant Language," *Psychological Review,* I (Jan. 1894), 63–66.

Review of *The Psychic Factors of Civilization* by Lester Frank Ward, *Social Evolution* by Benjamin Kidd, *Civilization During the Middle Ages* by George Burton Adams, and *History of the Philosophy of History* by Robert Flint, *Psychological Review,* I (July 1894), 400–411.

"The Theory of Emotion," I. Emotional Attitudes, *Psychological Review,* I (Nov. 1894), 553–69; II. The Significance of Emotions, ibid., II (Jan. 1895), 13–32.

*The Psychology of Number and Its Applications to Methods of Teaching Arithmetic,* with James Alexander McLellan (International Education Series, Vol. XXXIII, ed. William Torrey Harris). New York: D. Appleton and Co., 1895. xv, 309 pp.

    Review by Henry Burchard Fine, *Science,* n.s. III (Jan. 1896), 134–36.

    Reply by Dewey, "Psychology of Number," *Science,* n.s. III (Feb. 1896), 286–89.

Review of *Johnson's Universal Cyclopædia,* I–V, *Psychological Review,* II (Mar. 1895), 186–88.

"Interest as Related to [Training of the] Will," in *Second Supplement to the Herbart Year Book for 1895,* pp. 209–46. Bloomington, Ill.: National Herbart Society, 1896. [Rev. ed., Chicago: The Society, 1899; reprinted in C–16, pp. 260–85, with the title "Interest in Relation to Training of the Will."]

"The Reflex Arc Concept in Psychology," *Psychological Review,* III (July 1896), 357–70. [Reprinted in C–7, pp. 233–48, with the title "The Unit of Behavior."]

Review of *Studies in the Evolutionary Psychology of Feeling* by Hiram Miner Stanley, *Philosophical Review,* V (May 1896), 292–99.

*Educational Psychology: Syllabus of a Course of Twelve Lecture-Studies.* Chicago: University of Chicago Press, 1896. 24 pp.

"The Psychology of Effort," *Philosophical Review,* VI (Jan. 1897), 43–56.

"Some Remarks on the Psychology of Number," *Pedagogical Seminary,* V (Jan. 1898), 426–34. (Reply to: Daniel Edward Phillips, "Number and Its Application Psychologically Considered," *Pedagogical Seminary,* V [Oct. 1897], 221–81.)

"Psychology and Philosophic Method," *University [of California] Chronicle,* II (Aug. 1899), 159–79. [Reprinted separately, Berkeley: University of California Press, 1899, 23 pp.; also reprinted in C–2, pp. 242–70, with the title " 'Consciousness' and Experience."]

*Mental Development.* [Chicago], 1900. 21 pp., mimeographed.

"Psychology and Social Practice," *Psychological Review,* VII (Mar. 1900), 105–24; *Science,* n.s. XI (Mar. 1900), 321–33. [Reprinted separately as University of Chicago Contributions to Education, No. 2. Chicago: University of Chicago Press, 1901. 42 pp.]

"Interpretation of Savage Mind," *Psychological Review,* IX (May 1902), 217–30. [Reprinted in C–7, pp. 173–87.]

Review of *Analytical Psychology* by Lightner Witmer, *School Review,* X (May 1902), 412.

"Report on the Fairhope [Alabama] Experiment in Organic Education," *Survey,* XXXII (May 1914), 199.

*Human Nature and Conduct.* New York: Henry Holt and Co., 1922. [Enl. ed. with Foreword, New York: Modern Library, 1930. ix, vii, 336 pp. Also, Armed Forces ed. (from original plates), 1944.]

*Experience and Nature* (Lectures upon the Paul Carus Foundation, First Series). Chicago, London: Open Court Publishing Co., 1925. xi, 443 pp. [2d ed., with a Preface, New York: W. W. Norton, 1929. ix, 1a–4a, 1–443 pp. 3d. ed., LaSalle, Ill.: Open Court Publishing Co., 1958. xviii, 360 pp.]

"Foreword," in *Human Nature and Conduct,* pp. v–ix. New York: Modern Library, 1930.

"Marx Inverted," *New Republic,* LXX (Feb. 1932), 52. [Review of *The Emergence of Man* by Gerald Heard.]

*Art as Experience.* New York: Minton, Balch and Co., 1934. viii, 355 pp.

*Freedom and Culture.* New York: G. P. Putnam's Sons, 1939. 176 pp.

*John Dewey and Arthur F. Bentley: A Philosophical Correspondence, 1932–1951,* eds. Sidney Ratner and Jules Altman. New Brunswick, N.J.: Rutgers University Press, 1964. ["Means and Consequences— How, What, and What For," pp. 647–54, and "Importance, Significance and Meaning," pp. 655–68, are previously unpublished articles by Dewey.]

# 2

# Dewey's Philosophy and Philosophic Method

## LEWIS E. HAHN

THERE ARE no more crucial topics for an understanding of John Dewey's philosophy than his metaphysical perspective, his conception of philosophic method, and his views on the role of philosophy. His first published article, "The Metaphysical Assumptions of Materialism," which appeared in 1882, and another article, written while a student at Johns Hopkins, "Kant and Philosophic Method," show his early concern with these topics; and for some seventy years he thought and wrote on these themes, working over and rethinking his views on them so that there are significant differences between his early views and his later ones in spite of the fact that some of the dominant motifs of his mature philosophy appeared quite early. For the most part, after his early shift from intuitionalism to Hegelian idealism, he worked his way slowly and almost imperceptibly from one position to another, retaining much of the earlier along with the new. During his last years, as we learn from the Dewey-Bentley correspondence, he worked for a time on another revision of *Experience and Nature* and considered reformulating various of his central ideas. Hence in reviewing Dewey's lengthy productive career we must be prepared to find not simply a single point of view and metaphysical perspective but various perspectives with corresponding conceptions of philosophic method and general philosophy. By contrast with those philosophers "who can write their intellectual biography in a unified pattern, woven out of a few distinctly discernible strands of interest and influence," Dewey admitted that he might appear to be "unstable, chameleon-like, yielding one after another to many diverse and even incompatible influences; struggling to assimilate something from each and yet striving to carry it forward in a way that is logically consistent with what has been learned from its predecessors." [1] But if we note the various phases of his development instead of trying to put everything he wrote in a single simple pattern, we may find that his views at any given time hang together reasonably well with a relatively small number of major strands standing out and that, viewed retrospectively, the broad outlines of his mature pragmatic naturalism were fairly well set by around 1910.

In terms of his metaphysical perspective we find Dewey first holding a form of intuitionalism of a Scotch common-sense or Kantian variety, then Hegelian idealism,[2] which became experimental idealism in the 1890s before turning into instrumentalism, and then, as he spelled out the implications of his outlook, an empirical naturalism, or pragmatic naturalism, or contextualism.

### Intuitionalism and Safeguarding Religion

The first of these perspectives, referred to in his autobiographical essay, "From Absolutism to Experimentalism," as his theological and intuitional phase, is represented by his first two articles, "The Metaphysical Assumptions of Materialism" and "The Pantheism of Spinoza." These articles are concerned with the internal contradictions of materialism and Spinoza's pantheism, respectively, rather than the positive virtues of Dewey's own metaphysics. In each case, taking his cue partly from Kant, partly from the Scotch common-sense realists, he attacked the metaphysical assumptions of the view being considered and attempted to show that they involved fundamental contradictions. He argued that without intuitional or ontological knowledge the materialist could not establish his metaphysics, and

1. "From Absolutism to Experimentalism," in *Contemporary American Philosophy: Personal Statements*, II, eds. George Plimpton Adams and William Pepperell Montague (New York: Macmillan Co., 1930), 22.
2. For a fuller statement concerning his transition from intuitionalism to Hegelian idealism see my essay, "From Intuitionalism to Absolutism," in *The Early Works of John Dewey, 1882–1898*, Vol. I (Carbondale: Southern Illinois University Press, 1969), pp. xxiii–xxxvii.

with such knowledge the materialist brought in a real mind which had no place in his metaphysics.

Philosophy for the intuitionalists was the guardian of religion and values, and its method was that of common-sense observation and deduction from the observations or intuitions. In general the intuitionalists sought to find contradictions in the assumptions of their opponents or to show that the latter's approach led to something contrary to common sense or religion. In terms of their basic intuitions the Scotch common-sense realists combated the sensational empiricism of Locke and Hume which seemed to explain away the reality of the higher objects of religion. Kant's reservations about metaphysics helped strengthen the Scotch common-sense misgivings about speculative systems, especially ones leading to scepticism.

Although Dewey later reacted negatively to much of this phase in his career, and particularly to the many dualisms and sharp separations set up by intuitionalism and New England culture, he retained a belief in the existence of matter and the external world and, like his later mentor, George Sylvester Morris, held that the meaning of this existence rather than the fact of it was the concern of philosophy. Dewey also continued to object to sensationalism, albeit mainly on other grounds, even after abandoning intuitionalism. There is, moreover, an interesting parallel between his mature conviction concerning the contribution philosophy has to make in overcoming the separation of scientific method and morals and the Scotch philosophers' belief concerning the crucial role of philosophy in providing a metaphysics to safeguard values.

### Hegelian Absolutism and the Completed Method of Philosophy

The alacrity with which Dewey adopted Hegelian idealism after he began his graduate work with George Sylvester Morris at Johns Hopkins suggests that he was ready for it. He had been reading W. T. Harris's *Journal of Speculative Philosophy* and Hegel even earlier, and his later reading of such English idealists as John and Edward Caird, T. H. Green, William Wallace, Andrew Seth (Pringle-Pattison), J. S. and R. B. Haldane, F. H. Bradley, and Bernard Bosanquet, spirited participants in the then current reaction against atomic individualism and sensationalistic empiricism, helped convince the young Dewey that absolute idealism was, as he noted in "From Absolutism to Experimentalism," the vital and constructive philosophy of the eighties and nineties. Hegel's idealism as interpreted by Morris, moreover, in addition to furnishing even stronger support than intuitionalism for religion, afforded an intellectual means of satisfying the young philosopher's craving for unification and provided an immense sense of release or liberation from the dualisms and sharp divisions set up by intuitionalism and New England culture–gaps between the self and the world, soul and body, nature and God, subject and object, matter and spirit, the human and the divine, and the finite and infinite. With its treatment of human culture, social institutions, and the arts, this was a philosophy which, at least for a time, satisfied both Dewey's head and heart.

Perhaps even more important for his readiness for Hegel's conception of reality as an absolute organic unity with parts interrelated like those of a biological organism and his notion of reality as a universal consciousness, mind, or life, which differentiates itself into an indefinitely large number of finite consciousnesses, minds, or lives and realizes itself through these finite lives was a short nonlaboratory course in physiology taken in his junior year at the University of Vermont, with a book by Huxley as the text. From this course, Dewey wrote, he derived "a sense of interdependence and interrelated unity" which "created a kind of type or model of a view of things to which material in any field ought to conform," and at least subconsciously he "was led to desire a world and a life that would have the same properties as had the human organism in the picture of it derived from study of Huxley's treatment." [3]

If, indeed, he adopted at that time, at least subconsciously, the model or root metaphor of the organism for his view of the world or life, Hegel's absolute idealism, when subsequently he became acquainted with it under Morris's enthusiastic tutelage, must have seemed made to order for this model though one must add that the organic pattern also found expression in Dewey's major writings long after his abandonment of absolutism. In Hegelian idealism, however, the integrative or organizing proc-

3. "From Absolutism to Experimentalism," p. 13.

ess ties an indefinitely large number of relatively abstract parts or individuals together in a concrete universal, a universal self or consciousness. Viewed from what Dewey called the universal psychological standpoint, the finite experiences in process of becoming, the fragments or parts in transition, are all interrelated, and they move through active diversities, oppositions, conflicts, contradictions, or negations [4] through higher and more inclusive unities to an eternal absolute whole or totality which has never become but which is found to have been implicit all along in the finite experiences or fragments. The more conflicts the better, so long as the conflicting activities can be united in one whole; for this added activity makes for a more complete development of the whole or self.[5] Once the universal consciousness or absolute self is reached, it is found to have been implicit all along in the finite experiences or fragments; and the coherent, harmonious, unified totality transcends the gaps, negations, or contradictions and preserves all the original finite experiences without loss.

At any rate, Dewey espoused the Hegelian philosophy with such expert enthusiasm that his former psychology teacher at Johns Hopkins, G. Stanley Hall, in his review of Dewey's *Psychology*, commented on the latter's skill or cleverness in reading absolute idealism into an amazing range of old and new facts and complained that "the facts are never allowed to speak out plainly for themselves or left to silence, but are always 'read into' the system which is far more important than they." [6] In some ways Dewey's second book, *Leibniz's New Essays Concerning the Human Understanding*, is an even more masterly expression of his absolutistic phase, but his writings from "Knowledge and the Relativity of Feeling" (published in 1883) on up into the 1890s show his commitment to the Hegelian absolute.

Another important factor in Dewey's development stemming from the Johns Hopkins period was the new experimental and physiological psychology of Hall and Wundt. Not merely

4. In his book on *Leibniz's New Essays Concerning the Human Understanding* (*Early Works*, I, 251–435), Dewey complained that Leibniz at times treated negation as a purely formal limitative or privative affair and failed to see with Hegel that it is a constitutive organic element. Cf., e.g., pp. 420, 423.

5. *Psychology* (Early Works, II), 231.

6. *American Journal of Psychology*, I (1887), 157.

did it afford grist for the mill of the organicism of objective idealism, as suggested above, but it also at least initially strengthened the latter's hold on Dewey. Its use of biology's twin explanatory conceptions of the organism and its environment made it impossible to think of experience or the psychical life as "an individual, isolated thing developing in a vacuum" [7] and helped pave the way for Dewey's later naturalistic views of the live creature and its environment. Both its view of experience as continuous rather than as an affair of discrete sensations and ideas and its stress on the importance of specific and concrete, if sometimes confused and unclear, details fitted in with Dewey's idealism and carried over into his mature outlook. He also found in the new physiological psychology of Helmholtz support for his view of knowledge as mediate or inferential,[8] once more a doctrine expressing both his early idealism and his later convictions. From Dewey's early studies of psychology stem also his lifelong belief in the intimate relation between one's views on psychology and one's philosophical perspective and his sense of the importance of a behavioral approach drawing upon the results of biology and the social sciences. In his praise of the new physiological psychology's part in "that organized, systematic, tireless study into the secrets of nature, which, counting nothing common or unclean, thought no drudgery beneath it, or rather thought nothing drudgery," [9] moreover, we find an intimation of his later *Reconstruction in Philosophy* emphasis upon respect for the material conditions of achievement; and in his enthusiastic approval of this psychology's refusal to try to dictate to experience in terms of a scholastic logic or other preconceived abstract system and its willingness "to throw itself upon experience, believing that the mother which has borne it will not betray it," [10] we may have a clue to his eventual abandonment of absolute idealism.

Philosophic method during his absolutistic period Dewey conceived largely in terms of Hegel's logic but with some modifications from the point of view he called the psychological standpoint. He regarded Hegel's essential method as "the quin-

7. "The New Psychology," in *Early Works*, I, 56.
8. "Knowledge as Idealization," in *Early Works*, I, 179–80.
9. "The New Psychology," p. 51.
10. "The New Psychology," p. 60.

tessence of the scientific spirit." [11] His "Kant and Philosophic Method," apparently an early version of his missing doctoral dissertation on "The Psychology of Kant," [12] shows the short-comings of Kant and his predecessors and sketches the way in which Reason, "by differencing itself, or passing into its opposite, its other," allows these differences to "resolve themselves into a higher unity." [13] After stating in the opening sentence of this article that "philosophy comes into existence when men are confronted with problems and contradictions which common sense and the special sciences are able neither to solve nor resolve," [14] Dewey declared that for the deeper view one needs a method or truth-criterion, "some principle which, true on its own account, may also serve to judge the truth of all besides." [15] This method or criterion, the completed "Method of Philosophy," he found in Hegel's logic with its "account of the conceptions or categories of Reason which constitute experience, internal and external, subjective and objective," and its "account of them as a system, an organic unity in which each has its own place fixed." [16] Reason as "both integrating and differentiating" is a unified system of experience in which all things participate, each thing finding its place in the completed system which " 'in its organic wholeness is *the* Truth' " in terms of "its degree of ability to state absolute truth." [17] "And such a system," Dewey concluded, "is at once philosophic Method and Criterion; method, because it shows us not only the way to reach truth, but truth itself in construction; criterion, because it gives us the form of experience to which all the facts of experience as organic members must conform." [18]

In two articles in *Mind*, "The Psychological Standpoint" and "Psychology as Philosophic Method," Dewey, still operating within absolute idealism with its dialectic, held that not

11. "The Present Position of Logical Theory," in *Early Works*, III, 134.

12. See Dewey's letters as quoted in George Dykhuizen, "John Dewey at Johns Hopkins (1882–1884)," *Journal of the History of Ideas*, XXII (1961), 112–13.

13. "Kant and Philosophic Method," in *Early Works*, I, 46.

14. "Kant and Philosophic Method," p. 34.

15. "Kant and Philosophic Method," p. 34.

16. "Kant and Philosophic Method," p. 44.

17. "Kant and Philosophic Method," pp. 45, 46.

18. "Kant and Philosophic Method," p. 46.

logic but "Psychology is the completed method of philosophy, because in it science and philosophy, fact and reason, are one."[19] As he put it, "the nature of all objects of philosophical inquiry is to be fixed by finding out what experience says about them. And Psychology is the scientific and systematic account of this experience."[20] This "infinitely fruitful" psychological standpoint shows that

> all that is, is for consciousness or knowledge. The business of the psychologist is to give a genetic account of the various elements within this consciousness, and thereby fix their place, determine their validity, and at the same time show definitely what the real and eternal nature of this consciousness is.[21]

This involves seeing that "the psychological standpoint is necessarily a universal standpoint and consciousness necessarily the only absolute" and "that it is only because the individual consciousness is, in its ultimate reality, the universal consciousness that it affords any basis whatever for philosophy."[22]

In "Psychology as Philosophic Method" Dewey noted some contradictions in Hegel and insisted that psychology and philosophy, contrary to some of his fellow idealists, cannot be distinguished on the ground that the former is partial and is concerned with the realization of the universe through the individual whereas the latter is complete and deals with the universal self-consciousness and the unity of all being and knowing; for psychology, like philosophy, is a science of the Absolute itself and not simply of a manifestation of the Absolute. Of either psychology or philosophy we may say that "it is not only *a* science, but it turns out to be science as an organic system, in which every special science has its life, and from which it must abstract when it sets up for an independent existence of its own."[23]

These two articles in *Mind* provoked a lively exchange with Shadworth H. Hodgson,[24] an exchange noteworthy as the

19. "Psychology as Philosophic Method," in *Early Works*, I, 157–58.
20. "The Psychological Standpoint," in *Early Works*, I, 123.
21. "The Psychological Standpoint," p. 130.
22. "The Psychological Standpoint," pp. 141–42.
23. "Psychology as Philosophic Method," p. 159.
24. Hodgson, "Illusory Psychology," in *Early Works*, I, xli–lvii; Dewey, " 'Illusory Psychology,' " ibid., I, 168–75; and Hodgson's reply, " 'Illusory Psychology,' a Rejoinder," *Mind*, XII (1887), 314–18.

first of a long series of debates carried on by Dewey with various other philosophers in the journals. Hodgson's vigorous criticism of Dewey's account of both experience and psychology, which reads in part very much like some of the latter's own later views, convinced William James that Hodgson had much the better of the exchange.[25] Hodgson questioned Dewey's identification of individual consciousness and the Absolute Consciousness and contended that he had confused metaphysics and psychology in such fashion as to produce a human and divine psychology valid neither as philosophy nor as psychology.

At any rate, though over the years Dewey drifted away from Hegelian absolutism, his early study of Hegel, as has been suggested above and readily admitted by Dewey, left "a permanent deposit" in his thinking; and almost a half century after his early conversion to Hegel he could still say that "there is greater richness and greater variety of insight in Hegel than in any other single systematic philosopher" except Plato.[26] Determining the proper weight to be given to this deposit, however, is difficult because he also retained long after his abandonment of absolutism traces of the still earlier Huxleyan organismic model described in "From Absolutism to Experimentalism," and deciding in a given instance which is a vestige of Hegel and which is a Jamesian variant of Huxley raises a nice question. There is the further question of how much, if any, of his retrospective tracing of the organismic model to his physiology course and Huxley was made possible by his having viewed these earlier events at least for a time through Hegelian glasses. But it seems clear that some of his characteristic modes of thinking go back to his Hegelian period: for example, his familiar pattern of criticizing objectionable views on the score of their acceptance of a dualism of some sort or his practice of starting with opposite one-sided views, then expanding and comparing them, with the aim of arriving at a more adequate theory or position.

In 1939 in a passage quoted by his daughter Dewey described his Hegelian deposit in this way:

> Hegel's idea of cultural institutions as an "objective mind" upon which individuals were dependent in the formation of their mental life fell in with the influence of Comte and of

25. See George Dykhuizen, "John Dewey and the University of Michigan," *Journal of the History of Ideas*, XXIII (1962), 520.
26. "From Absolutism to Experimentalism," p. 21.

Condorcet and Bacon. The metaphysical idea that an absolute mind is manifested in social institutions dropped out; the idea, upon an empirical basis, of the power exercised by cultural environment in shaping the ideas, beliefs, and intellectual attitudes of individuals remained. It was a factor in producing my belief that the not uncommon assumption in both psychology and philosophy of a ready-made mind over against a physical world as an object has no empirical support. It was a factor in producing my belief that the only possible psychology, as distinct from a biological account of behavior, is a social psychology. With respect to more technically philosophical matters, the Hegelian emphasis upon continuity and the function of conflict persisted on empirical grounds after my earlier confidence in dialectic had given way to scepticism. There was a period extending into my earlier years at Chicago when, in connection with a seminar on Hegel's Logic I tried reinterpreting his categories in terms of "readjustment" and "reconstruction." Gradually I came to realize that what the principles actually stood for could be better understood and stated when completely emancipated from Hegelian garb.[27]

As might be expected, however, Dewey and his critics sometimes have been at odds on the extent of his Hegelian indebtedness. Many scholars—for example, Bertrand Russell and Arthur Murphy, among others—have charged that various aspects of Dewey's mature philosophy spring from and lead directly to Hegelian absolutism; and similarly, Stephen C. Pepper, on the basis of a critical examination of a number of passages from *Art as Experience*, suggested that they express an organismic view and point toward objective idealism rather than toward pragmatism, thus bringing in a confusing eclecticism.[28] Dewey, while admitting his debt to Hegel in the respects indicated in the preceding paragraph, argued that his critics had exaggerated his indebtedness, partly because they had not paid due regard to the context or situation in which he used certain terms, and that, in any event, objective idealism does not have a monopoly on the interpretation of such words as "whole, com-

27. Jane M. Dewey, ed., "Biography of John Dewey," in *The Philosophy of John Dewey* (The Library of Living Philosophers, Vol. I, ed. Paul Arthur Schilpp [Evanston, Chicago: Northwestern University, 1939]), pp. 17–18.
28. See their essays and Dewey's reply in *The Philosophy of John Dewey*.

plete, coherence, integration," and presumably "interrelated unity" or "interdependence."

## Instrumentalism and Reflective Inquiry

Dewey's third stage saw him move from Hegelian absolutism through experimental idealism, the name he gave his view in 1894,[29] or instrumental idealism, to a naturalistic instrumentalism,[30] which eventually became a part of his mature empirical naturalism. In terms of chronology, though a beginning was made at Michigan, the main outlines of his instrumentalism were worked out during his Chicago years, 1894 to 1904, but he continued at Columbia University to add to and develop the view for at least another fifteen or twenty years—some say he spent the rest of his life reworking and refining it. At any rate, the Chicago period was one of dramatic change in his philosophical outlook. During these years he turned his back on absolutism and began seeking an intermediate "viable alternative to an atomism which logically involves a denial of connections and to an absolutistic block monism which, in behalf of the reality of relations, leaves no place for the discrete, for plurality, and for individuals." [31] He moved from an absolutism in terms of which he could hold that "the cause of theology and morals is one, and that whatever banishes God from the heart of things, with the same edict excludes the ideal, the ethical, from the life of man" [32] to a naturalism stemming from a biological-anthropological approach with no resort to supernatural forces or ideals so that in 1939 in a reply to his critics he could say: "For many years I have consistently—and rather persistently—maintained that the key to a philosophic theory of experience must proceed from initially linking it with the processes and functions of life

29. *The Study of Ethics: A Syllabus* (Ann Arbor: Register Publishing Co., 1894).

30. For excellent accounts of the development of Dewey's instrumentalism, see Morton G. White, *The Origin of Dewey's Instrumentalism* (New York: Columbia University Press, 1943), and Richard J. Bernstein, *John Dewey* (The Great American Thinkers Series, eds. Arthur W. Brown and Thomas S. Knight [New York: Washington Square Press, 1967]), Ch. 2.

31. "Experience, Knowledge and Value: A Rejoinder," in *The Philosophy of John Dewey*, p. 544.

32. "Ethics and Physical Science," in *Early Works*, I, 209.

as the latter are disclosed in biological science."[33] From a concern for absolute origins and absolute finalities he turned to a lesson for philosophy he learned from Darwin, a lesson which called for forswearing "inquiry after absolute origins and absolute finalities in order to explore specific values and the specific conditions that generate them."[34] Human values and ideals came to be considered in terms not of God or the Absolute Mind, but rather of the biological and cultural matrices of human behavior. The Universal Consciousness or Mind was replaced by nature, and the central continuity came to be a biological and cultural one between man and his environment rather than a continuity within Universal Consciousness. In like fashion the focal questions came to deal with the interaction of a living organism and its environment as parts of nature instead of with the relation between Universal Consciousness and individual or finite consciousnesses. From viewing thought as constitutive of reality he came to think of it by 1900 as a doubt-inquiry process,[35] as reconstructive reflective inquiry. After having ardently espoused for some years a highly organized system of philosophy with emphasis on completeness and finality, during this third period he tended to deplore systems and system-makers and spoke of metaphysics mainly pejoratively as a way of setting up dualisms, fixed distinctions, or impassable chasms in what for the plain man or the working scientist is fluid, continuous experience.

This is not to say that during his instrumental period his concern with metaphysics was wholly negative. With William Pepperell Montague the monistic realist and Frederick J. E. Woodbridge the Aristotelian realist or naturalist as colleagues he had the challenge and stimulus of their views as well as those of Hegel and the Neo-Hegelians as he sought to work out his own constructive position; and he developed a metaphysics in the sense of a world hypothesis or general perspective on existence or reality. But, retaining his cue from Hegel, he spoke of it as a kind of logic, a Darwinian genetic and experimental logic; and for him this hypothesis or perspective had to be something

33. "Experience, Knowledge and Value," p. 530.
34. "Darwin's Influence upon Philosophy," *Popular Science Monthly*, LXXV (1909), 95.
35. See "Some Stages of Logical Thought," *Philosophical Review*, IX (1900), 465-89.

which could be expressed or defined in terms of experience. This was not experience as described by either the Greeks or the British Empiricists but rather a new conception arising from Huxley's physiology and the biological behavioristic approach of what he had called the New Psychology, a conception for which he found support in the behavioral emphases of William James's *Principles of Psychology*. James, of course, had stressed the continuity of experience whether speaking of "the stream of consciousness" or the behavioral significance of intelligence, and he had defined intelligence or mentality in terms of purposive behavior.[36] One of Dewey's earliest formulations of the new view of experience which was henceforth to occupy a central place in his thinking may be found in his 1896 article on "The Reflex Arc Concept in Psychology." [37] In this article he criticized the reflex arc concept on several counts: *1)* it reflected the ancient dualism between the mental and the physical or mind and matter; *2)* it misdescribed experience as a patchwork of disjointed parts, mechanically related—sensory stimulus, central activity or idea, and motor discharge or response; *3)* it misinterpreted a set of functional or teleological distinctions within an organic co-ordination or circuit as fixed existential ones and mislabeled this circuit as a reflex; *4)* it neglected the prior state or set of the organism, disregarding the fact that an unexpected loud sound may have different values for one depending upon whether one is reading a book, hunting, or performing an experiment in chemistry; *5)* it confused two stages of the teleological process and read a set of considerations holding good only because of the completed process into the set of events conditioning or leading up to this outcome; and *6)* its proponents treated experience as a jerky, unrelated series of arcs instead of as a series of interpenetrating organic co-ordinations or circuits within which the arcs find their appropriate place.

Basic for this view of experience are movement, doing, adaptive courses of action, habits, connections of doing and undergoing, ongoing behavior, organic co-ordinations; and sen-

36. *The Principles of Psychology* (New York: Henry Holt and Co., 1890), I, 8: "*The pursuance of future ends and the choice of means for their attainment are thus the mark and criterion of the presence of mentality* in a phenomenon."

37. "The Reflex Arc Concept in Psychology," *Psychological Review*, III (1896), 357–70.

sations, ideas, and the like are in a sense secondary. A conflict in such a co-ordination, whether due to opposing aims or interests or to environmental changes, provides the problem demanding a new or transformed co-ordination, and alternative possible responses afford various means of reconstructing or reconstituting the co-ordination so as to resolve the conflict or solve the problem. This in brief is the instrumental logic, terminology and all — "conflict," "problem," "reconstitution," "instrument," and the like. Both the logic and the view of experience come out clearly in Dewey's own summary statement concerning the organic co-ordination as the unit of behavior:

> The circle is a coördination, some of whose members have come into conflict with each other. It is the temporary disintegration and need of reconstitution which occasions, which affords the genesis of, the conscious distinction into sensory stimulus on one side and motor response on the other. The stimulus is that phase of the forming coördination which represents the conditions which have to be met in bringing it to a successful issue; the response is that phase of one and the same forming coördination which gives the key to meeting these conditions, which serves as instrument in effecting the successful coördination. They are therefore strictly correlative and contemporaneous. The stimulus is something to be discovered; to be made out; if the activity affords its own adequate stimulation, there is no stimulus save in the objective sense already referred to. As soon as it is adequately determined, then and only then is the response also complete. To attain either, means that the coördination has completed itself. Moreover, it is the motor response which assists in discovering and constituting the stimulus. It is the holding of the movement at a certain stage which creates the sensation, which throws it into relief.[38]

Although Dewey finally concluded late in life that he might have done better to use another term than experience, many of his most important works are concerned with clarifying it — for example, his Carus Lectures, *Experience and Nature*, or his *Art as Experience*, or *Experience and Education*. With William James he recognized that experience is a double-barreled fact including both the experienc*ing* and the experienc*ed*, the experiencing being the province of the psychologist. As he

38. "Reflex Arc Concept," p. 370.

put it in *Experience and Nature* (1925), "Experience denotes what is experienced, the world of events and persons; and it denotes that world caught up into experiencing, the career and destiny of mankind." [39] By experience we mean "something at least as wide and deep and full as all history on this earth, a history which, since history does not occur in the void, includes the earth and the physical relatives of man." [40] It constitutes the entire range of man's relations to, or transactions with, the universe. It is "the peculiar intermixture of support and frustration" afforded man by nature.[41] We experience nature in multiple modes and forms, and things interacting in certain ways make up experience.

In "The Need for a Recovery of Philosophy" Dewey summarized his view of experience by contrasting it with what he called the orthodox view, that accepted by both the traditional empiricists and their opponents.[42] Whereas for the orthodox view experience is primarily a knowledge affair, Dewey spoke of it as intercourse between a living organism and its physical and social environment, a matter of simultaneous doings and sufferings. The traditionalists regarded experience as a subjective inner affair, separate and distinct from objective reality; but Dewey thought of experience as being of a piece with the objective world, which enters into the actions and sufferings of men and which, in turn, may be modified through human responses. Instead of a gulf between disparate inner and outer realms of being, one may move freely from experience to that which surrounds, supports, and maintains it. The proponents of the orthodox view have been preoccupied with what is "given" in a bare present, whereas Dewey was more concerned with what might be done to change what is given or taken, in furtherance of human purposes. The older empiricists thought in terms of what has been or is given, looking toward the past if they went beyond the present. For Dewey the salient trait of experience is its connection with a future. If change is what we are interested in, we look primarily toward the future, and not

39. *Experience and Nature* (Lectures upon the Paul Carus Foundation, First Series [Chicago, London: Open Court Publishing Co., 1925]), p. 28. 2d. ed. (New York: W. W. Norton, 1929).

40. *Experience and Nature* (1925), p. 8.

41. *Experience and Nature* (1929), p. 421.

42. In *Creative Intelligence: Essays in the Pragmatic Attitude* (New York: Henry Holt and Co., 1917), pp. 3–69.

recollection but anticipation is central for the experimental form of experience.

One of the main differences between Dewey's and the orthodox view of experience, however, turns about the latter's particularism, its concern with sense data to the neglect of connections and continuities, and its supposition that relations and continuities are either foreign to experience or are dubious by-products of it. Dewey, like James, emphasized the relations. The contextual, situational, transactional, or field character of experience stands out in his account. The traditional view opposed experience and thought in the sense of inference, but for Dewey experience is full of inference, as might be expected of one who sees the directional and relational character of experience. Where one seeks to control what is to come through employing present environmental supports to effect changes which would not otherwise occur, inference is of vital importance. From the standpoint of the future life-activity of the organism, environmental incidents are favorable or hostile; and if one is to eliminate the latter and insure the former, an imaginative forecast of the future is essential for guidance in this process.

The structure of experience, however, comes out most clearly, on Dewey's view, in æsthetic experience. There, according to *Art as Experience*, we have experience in full, vivified, clarified, organized, and intensified.

Instrumentalism or pragmatism, however, was perhaps better known for its method than for its metaphysics though the two were, of course, intimately interrelated.[43] Looking backward in 1925, Dewey noted that pragmatism's empirical method and concern with future consequences led to "the conception of a universe whose evolution is not finished, of a universe which is still, in James' term, 'in the making,' 'in the process of becoming,' of a universe up to a certain point still plastic." In a world of this sort thought "has a real, though limited, function, a creative, constructive function."[44] Putting ideas into action,

43. Cf. Sidney Hook, *The Metaphysics of Pragmatism* (Chicago, London: Open Court Publishing Co., 1927), for an interesting account of the metaphysics of the instrument and the metaphysical consequences of pragmatic method.

44. "The Development of American Pragmatism," in *Studies in the History of Ideas* by the Department of Philosophy of Columbia Univer-

using them as instruments for reconstructing a problematic situation, does make a genuine difference.

As we have suggested earlier, Dewey's instrumentalism had a gradual development. Starting with objective idealism's insistence that logic, methodology, deals with actual thinking, he came to view that thinking in terms of a Darwinian genetic, experimental logic. Explanation, instead of being primarily an affair of finding the place of something in a system, the absolute totality, came to function in terms of specific concrete problems. Thus the changes taking place in his conception of method during his third or instrumental period were as dramatic as the changes in his general outlook. During this time he became increasingly convinced that through the proper use of intelligence, reflective inquiry, men can come to terms with the problems facing them in a changing world. These problems, he maintained, are specific and concrete, or can be made so; and so long as we can cast our problems in these terms we can deal with them. If we try to make a problem of the universe at large, we have no way of solving it; and escape or despair becomes the answer. But if we can frame our difficulties in specific, concrete terms, we can work at overcoming them.

So in a sense the most important single emphasis of John Dewey is his insistence upon applying reflective or critical inquiry to problems, conflict situations, or indeterminate situations. What, then, is involved in problem solving or thinking through a problem? What is critical inquiry? How does one apply intelligence to human affairs? Dewey's answer to these questions is set forth in its simplest terms in *How We Think* (1910, 1933); and a fuller, more sophisticated version is given in *Logic: The Theory of Inquiry*. Herbert Schneider maintains that the basic insights of *How We Think* may be found in Chapters 8 and 18–20 of the *Psychology*.[45] *The Study of Ethics: A Syllabus* (1894) has the language of experiment, instruments, practice, and conflict, and the fact that thinking or intelligence takes its start from a problematic situation, one involving friction or strain, comes out clearly in a review of articles on social psychology in 1894: "To me it appears as sure a psychological as biological principle that men go on thinking only because of

45. *Early Works*, II, xxv.

practical friction or strain somewhere, that thinking is essentially the solution of tension." [46] The instrumental logic as operative in behavior is reasonably clear in "The Reflex Arc Concept in Psychology" (1896); and in "Some Stages of Logical Thought" (1900), in a manner reminiscent of Peirce, he treated thought as a doubt-inquiry process involving mediation and reconstruction, instrumentalities as organs of thinking, control, discovery rather than proof, and growth of experience, and asked: "Does not an account or theory of thinking, basing itself on modern scientific procedure, demand a statement in which all the distinctions and terms of thought . . . shall be interpreted simply and entirely as distinctive functions or divisions of labor within the doubt-inquiry process?" [47]

The main features of instrumentalism and the instrumental theory of inquiry came out, of course, in the *Studies in Logical Theory* (1903) and in revised and expanded form in *Essays in Experimental Logic* (1916), where in a lengthy introduction and some supplementary notes Dewey tried to clear up some confusing features of the earlier account. In the earlier volume he and his associates acknowledged their indebtedness to William James and his *Principles of Psychology* both for inspiration and the forging of the tools with which they worked out their instrumentalism. They took over his notion that conceptions and theories are instruments which can serve to constitute future facts in a specific manner, but their instrumentalism went beyond his in attempting "to constitute a precise logical theory of concepts, of judgments and inferences in their various forms, by considering primarily how thought functions in the experimental determinations of future consequences," that is, by trying "to establish universally recognized distinctions and rules of logic by deriving them from the reconstructive or mediative function ascribed to reason." [48] In the opening essay of *Studies in Logical Theory* Dewey sketched the stages of scientific theory, anticipating much of his later *How We Think* (1910) five-step analysis of a complete act of reflective thinking; and in the second essay he criticized the transcendental logic he formerly held for viewing thought as an attempt "to represent or state reality once for all, instead of trying to determine some

46. *Psychological Review*, I (1894), 408.
47. "Stages of Logical Thought," p. 489.
48. "Development of American Pragmatism," p. 367.

phases or contents of it with reference to their more effective and significant reciprocal employ—instead of as reconstructive," adding that "the rock against which every such logic splits is that either reality already has the statement which thought is endeavoring to give it, or else it has not. In the former case, thought is futilely reiterative; in the latter, it is falsificatory." [49]

The chapter on "Experience and Thinking" in *Democracy and Education* (1916) sets forth the general features of a reflective experience as contrasted with trial and error behavior. The chapter on "The Significance of Logical Reconstruction" in *Reconstruction in Philosophy* offers another version of what is involved in reflective inquiry, and Part Three of *Human Nature and Conduct* treats the place of intelligence in conduct. Much of *The Quest for Certainty* is devoted to ideas at work, method, the role of intelligence in human affairs, and the pattern of experimental knowing; and his concern for what is involved in reflective thinking is evident in numerous other books and articles. In a sense, moreover, the phases or steps in a complete act of reflective thinking afford an outline of most of his major writings for the last fifty years or so of his life.

A) If inquiry is "the directed or controlled transformation of an indeterminate situation into a determinately unified one," [50] the first step in a complete act of reflective thinking or inquiry is the appearance of the problem or the indeterminate situation. This may be marked by a more or less vague sense of something having gone wrong, a breakdown in habitual responses or modes of action. We begin with an objectively indeterminate situation, one which is perplexing, disturbed, troubled, ambiguous, obscure, or full of conflicting tendencies, and it is distinguishable from other situations by a unique pervasive quality which both makes the situation distinctive and gives direction to the inquiry. One of our beliefs is questioned, or acting upon it leads to a conflict or perplexity.

In view of the misinterpretation of pragmatism as a mani-

49. "Thought and Its Subject-Matter: The Antecedent Conditions and Cues of the Thought-Function," in *Studies in Logical Theory* (University of Chicago, The Decennial Publications, Second Series, Vol. XI [Chicago: University of Chicago Press, 1903]), p. 47.

50. *Logic: The Theory of Inquiry* (New York: Henry Holt and Co., 1938), p. 117.

festation of American commercialism by such distinguished critics as Bertrand Russell and a too common tendency of other
critics to think of instrumentalism as a way of patterning only
low-level organic disruptions, perhaps it should be added that
what we may call the problematic situation in at least a proleptic
or anticipatory sense is not limited to practical difficulties in any
narrow or pecuniary sense but rather includes the full range of
perplexities, intellectual, scientific, moral, political, artistic, and
what have you; and there are situations within which the intellectually curious scientific or scholarly investigator may even
come to seek out the problematic and check his results with the
community of scholars.

B) The second step or phase is clarification of the problem, or what Dewey referred to in *Logic: The Theory of Inquiry*
as the institution of the problem. Through analysis and observation we gather sufficient data to formulate the difficulty or define
the problem. Instead of a felt difficulty we arrive at a clearly
formulated or articulated problem, and this determination is one
of the most important phases of inquiry. If, for example, a belief
is disputed or called into question, further questioning or analysis may indicate precisely what is in dispute.

C) With the problem clearly stated we pass to the stage
of appearance of suggested solutions or hypotheses as to how to
solve the problem. Various ideas occur to us as to how it may be
solved, and these ideas direct further observation and aid in
ascertaining relevant facts. Proper statement of the problem, of
course, facilitates suggestions for solution, and the process of
determining the solution is frequently one of more adequately
specifying the problem.

D) The fourth stage is that of deductive elaboration. We
reason out the implications of the various hypotheses. If we take
the first hypothesis, we may expect such and such consequences;
or we need to make additional observations or gather more
information to see what may be expected. If we take the second
one, we may expect such and such other consequences; and so
on. On the basis of a survey of the various proposed solutions as
elaborated we decide which to test in action.

E) The fifth step is that of verification or disconfirmation. Through observation or experiment we test the hypothesis or hypotheses which looked most promising to us. If one of the hypotheses works out, the indeterminate situation is replaced by a determinate one in which stable lines of action are possible; instead of the problematic situation we have a resolved or clarified one.

These steps or stages do not necessarily come one right after another in the sequence in which I have listed them. For example, the first three stages may be telescoped in such fashion that we do not get a clear indication of the stages, but in general, the more difficult the problem, the more likely the stages are to be clearly outlined before it is solved. Or, again, after we have reached the stage of deductive elaboration, we may discover that we need to go back and further clarify the problem or think of additional ways of trying to solve it.

Although this pattern as I have set it forth is somewhat oversimplified, in fundamentals it is basically accurate. This is what is involved in problem-solving activity whether it is a personal problem, an important social conflict, or a weighty scientific problem. When we solve a problem in this way, moreover, we have not merely a solution to our difficulty but also some descriptive or explanatory statements about how it was solved.

It is interesting to note that there is a certain similarity between what the objective idealist T. H. Green and the instrumentalist Dewey conceived as the main problem of philosophy. Green's main purpose, according to Dewey, was the reconciliation of science and religion through finding one spiritual principle at the basis of science, ordinary experience, ethics, and religion.[51] Dewey found his connecting link or principle of continuity in a method of critical inquiry. Convinced that the deepest problem of any philosophy not isolated from life is that of restoring integration and co-operation between man's beliefs about the world in which he lives, particularly beliefs due to natural science, and his beliefs about the values and purposes which should direct his conduct,[52] he worked to develop his instrumentalism and construct "a logic, that is, a method of

51. "The Philosophy of Thomas Hill Green," in *Early Works*, III, 16–17.
52. "Experience, Knowledge and Value," p. 523.

effective inquiry, which would apply without abrupt breach of continuity" [53] to these two sets of beliefs.

In the first essay in *Studies in Logical Theory* Dewey sketched the function of philosophy as a general logic of experience, offering "an account of the sequence of the various typical functions or situations of experience [for example, the technological or utilitarian, the æsthetic, the religious, the scientific, and the socio-ethical] in their determining relations to one another," [54] as a method of inquiry and interpretation to do for social aims and values what the natural sciences are doing for activity in the physical realm, and as a means of clarifying "the genesis and functioning in experience of various typical interests and occupations with reference to one another"; and he insisted that every system of philosophy reflects and responds to its specific social antecedents. He also raised the question of how the particular functional situation termed the reflective behaves —that is, the question of the role or function of intelligence in human affairs. In his essay on "Darwin's Influence upon Philosophy" he called on philosophy to "become a method of locating and interpreting the more serious of the conflicts that occur in life, and a method of projecting ways for dealing with them: a method of moral and political diagnosis and prognosis." [55] But perhaps his most forceful instrumentalist formulation of the function of philosophy may be found in "The Need for a Recovery of Philosophy." In that essay he declared that philosophy must cease to be "a device for dealing with the problems of philosophers" and become "a method, cultivated by philosophers, for dealing with the problems of men." [56] The problems of men as he saw them, however, cover a range broad enough to include in one way or another most of the traditional problems as well as many others. The method involves treating philosophy as vision, imagination, and reflection; and, though the clarifying process may show that certain epistemological problems are pseudo problems, the fact that they are raised may point to genuine cultural crises. If action at all levels needs to be informed with vision, imagination, and reflection to bring clearly

53. "From Absolutism to Experimentalism," p. 23.
54. "Thought and Its Subject-Matter: The General Problem of Logical Theory," in *Studies in Logical Theory*, p. 19.
55. "Darwin's Influence," p. 97.
56. In *Creative Intelligence*, p. 65.

to mind future possibilities with reference to attaining the better
and averting the worse, there is more than enough for philosophy to do.

Developing an adequate conception of the place of intelligence in human affairs, he maintained, is one important task for
philosophy. How can intelligence which is a creation of a culture
also be a creator or forming influence on that culture? How can
it define the larger patterns of continuity between a stubborn
past and an insistent future? How can philosophy adjust the
body of traditional beliefs to scientific tendencies and political
aspirations which are novel and incompatible? These are tasks
which involve the application of reflective inquiry on the broad-
est scale possible, and in applying it we need to remember, as
Dewey reminded us in the title essay of *Philosophy and Civilization*, that in philosophy we are occupied with meaning rather
than truth.[57] This, of course, is not to deny either the crucial
importance of truths as a subclass of meanings or the relevance
of existence to meanings. It is rather to suggest that imaginative
sweep, values, and significance are our primary concern.

In *Reconstruction in Philosophy* Dewey stressed the social
function of philosophy, holding there that its task is to clarify
men's minds as to the social and moral issues of their day, to
enlighten the moral forces which move mankind, and to contribute to the aspirations of men to attain a more ordered and
intelligent happiness.

Further support for this social function may be found in
*Democracy and Education*, where he defined philosophy as the
general theory of education, or the theory of education in its
most general phases,[58] and saw it as having the double task of
"criticizing existing aims with respect to the existing state of
science, pointing out values which have become obsolete with
the command of new resources, showing what values are merely
sentimental because there are no means for their realization,"
and "interpreting the results of specialized science in their
bearing on future social endeavor." [59] Indeed, what his empirical and experimental philosophy means in practice comes out

57. Cf. *Experience and Nature* (1929), p. 410.
58. *Democracy and Education: An Introduction to the Philosophy
of Education* (Text-Book Series in Education, ed. Paul Monroe [New
York: Macmillan Co., 1916]), pp. 383, 386.
59. *Democracy and Education*, p. 384.

more clearly and simply perhaps in his writings on education than anywhere else. It is to education that we look for "forming fundamental dispositions, intellectual and emotional, toward nature and fellow men," [60] including, of course, the habits of critical inquiry; and it is to education or philosophy that we turn for the vision, imagination, and reflection to guide the reconstruction of customs, institutions, and environmental factors needed to provide the conditions for continued growth.

### Experience, Nature, and Criticism

With the delivery of the Carus Lectures on Experience and Nature in 1922, Dewey's thought moved into its fourth main phase. Though in this period he continued to contrast the theory of inquiry and ontology, using the former to designate his empirical naturalism and the latter for views with which he disagreed, he did develop and defend a contextualistic or naturalistically empirical metaphysical hypothesis, attempting, as he put it, to discover some of the "general features of experienced things and to interpret their significance for a philosophic theory of the universe in which we live"; [61] and he questioned the modern tendency to arrive at theories regarding the nature of the universe by means of theories regarding the nature of knowledge instead of following "the apparently more judicious method of the ancients in basing their conclusions about knowledge on the nature of the universe in which knowledge occurs." [62] He admitted, moreover, as well he might have, after setting forth in *Experience and Nature* one of the great metaphysical systems, that he did have a system in the sense of a cluster of problems and hypotheses hanging together in a perspective determined by a definite point of view.[63] So when he wrote late in life that he "tried the experiment of transferring the old well-known figures from the stage of ontology to the

60. *Democracy and Education*, p. 383.
61. *Experience and Nature* (1929), p. 2.
62. *The Quest for Certainty* (New York: Minton, Balch and Co., 1929), p. 41.
63. "Nature in Experience," *Philosophical Review*, XLIX (1940), 244. In this article he replied to the criticisms Morris Cohen and William Ernest Hocking had made of his account of experience and nature.

stage of inquiry," [64] the contrast is not really between ontology or metaphysics and something free from concern with existential questions concerning experience and nature but rather between different ways of viewing or understanding the things of the world, between the traditional perspectives and categories and his own pragmatic naturalism with its point of view and categories. But the result of his experiment was, indeed, a coherent, highly instructive, and humanly dramatic outlook, an outlook which he vigorously defended against critics but which he also related increasingly to the views of Plato, Aristotle, and the Greeks and to the European philosophical tradition.

Some of his greatest books were written during this period: for example, *Experience and Nature*, *The Quest for Certainty* (his Gifford Lectures), *Art as Experience* (based on his William James Lectures at Harvard in 1931), and *Logic: The Theory of Inquiry;* and during this time he wrote a number of articles significant for his metaphysical perspective and his view of philosophy and philosophic method.[65] Retaining the general view of experience and the method of critical inquiry developed in his instrumental period, during this final stage he gave the method its most systematic treatment in *Logic: The Theory of Inquiry*, provided perhaps his best balanced account of experience in its completeness in *Art as Experience*, showed the place of æsthetic and consummatory experiences in his world view in *Experience and Nature* and *Art as Experience*, and brought out more clearly the implications of his view in such works as *Education and Experience*. Without losing his concern for the specific and the concrete, he showed that his contextualism was not limited to the narrower contexts but rather provided a comprehensive framework within which philosophical problems may be seen in terms of their background in human institutions, cultural patterns, traditions, impelling selective interests, and occupations, and in the broad context of human nature and experience. At the very least he hoped that concern for context would teach a philosopher humility and prevent his freezing

64. [Reply to Letter of Albert George Adam Balz], *Journal of Philosophy*, XLVI (1949), 341. Balz letter, ibid., XLVI (1949), 313–29.

65. For a fine assemblage of articles of this sort with introductory comments, see Richard J. Bernstein, ed., *John Dewey on Experience, Nature, and Freedom* (New York: Liberal Arts Press, 1960).

"the quotidian truths relevant to the problems that emerge in his own background of culture into eternal truths inherent in the very nature of things." [66] For his pragmatic naturalism not eternal static realities or permanent substances but qualitied events, things in time, temporal processes, histories, or historical events, happenings are central. If we accept the testimony of "primary nonreflectional experience" or "the unbiased evidence of experience in gross," things in process or qualitied events are what we find. As he put it, "the denotations that constitute experience point to history, to temporal process," and "in fact anything denoted is found to have temporal quality and reference; it has movement from and towards *within* it; it is marked by waxings and wanings." [67] So when one tries to discover, as the metaphysician on his view does, the generic traits of existence, one seeks the generic traits of qualitied events, histories, or things in process; for "Every existence is an event." [68] And not surprisingly in view of his great stress on diversity, these traits or basic categories are variously listed by Dewey and by some other philosophers. [69]

66. *Context and Thought* (University of California Publications in Philosophy, Vol. XII [Berkeley: University of California Press, 1931]), p. 215.
67. *Experience and Nature* (1925), pp. 28–29.
68. *Experience and Nature* (1929), p. 71.
69. See, for example, my account of contextualism, or pragmatic naturalism, and its categories in *A Contextualistic Theory of Perception* (University of California Publications in Philosophy, Vol. XXII, eds. George Plimpton Adams et al. [Berkeley, Los Angeles: University of California Press, 1942]), pp. 6–19. One item in my account is a note on an early version of the categories given by Dewey in *Essays in Experimental Logic*, pp. 5–7, where he discusses the main traits of primary experience under the headings of 1) internal organization and 2) focus and context.

Stephen C. Pepper gives two alternative statements in "The Conceptual Framework of Tolman's Purposive Behaviorism," *Psychological Review*, XLI (1934), 108–33, especially p. 111, and in his chapter on "Contextualism" in *World Hypotheses* (Berkeley, Los Angeles: University of California Press, 1942). Sidney Hook in *The Metaphysics of Pragmatism* has still another version of the categories; and Elizabeth Ramsden Eames and S. Morris Eames in "The Leading Principles of Pragmatic Naturalism," *Personalist*, XLIII (1962), 322–37, discuss immediacy, connections, and continuity as the basis for Dewey's description of experience and nature.

Useful general background statements on Dewey's philosophy may be found in George R. Geiger, *John Dewey in Perspective* (New York: Oxford University Press, 1958), and Sidney Hook, *John Dewey: An Intellectual Portrait* (New York: John Day Co., 1939).

In "The Subject-Matter of Metaphysical Inquiry" (1915) [70] Dewey sketched a way of conceiving a naturalistic metaphysics of a descriptive, hypothetical sort, holding that its province is ultimate matters in the sense of basic and "irreducible traits in any and every subject of scientific inquiry" and suggesting that three such traits are diversity, interaction, and change. The category of diversity directs attention to what he referred to in another essay as "the boundless multiplicity of the concrete experiences of humanity" [71] and serves notice that this is not a monistic block universe but rather one with a plurality of specifically diverse, heterogeneous existences.

In his mature philosophy, to turn next to the third rather than the second irreducible trait, Dewey focused upon change. If we look closely, he insisted, we can always detect change in this our world—sometimes a very slow rate of change, sometimes very rapid change; but no concrete thing exists apart from temporal process. "A thing may endure *secula seculorum* and yet not be everlasting; it will crumble before the gnawing tooth of time, as it exceeds a certain measure. Every existence is an event." [72] The things that seem to "exclude movement and change" are only "*phases* of things," perhaps legitimate abstractions for certain purposes but not concrete things. [73] We may conclude "that the principle of a developing career applies to all things in nature, as well as to human beings—that they are born, undergo qualitative changes, and finally die, giving place to other individuals." [74] In a changing world unpredictable novelties, qualitatively new things, contingency, incomplete things, things in the making, uncertain, unstable situations are to be expected; and the challenge of the incomplete and the changing is not to be met by attempting to legislate them out of the truly real but rather by intelligent redirection of ongoing affairs—by attempting to stabilize patterns we find good, and by avoiding or finding acceptable ways of living with patterns we find bad. As Dewey argued in *The Quest for Certainty*, the concern of the empirical philosopher is not the pursuit of changelessness but rather finding patterns of change, relations between changes.

70. *Journal of Philosophy*, XII (1915), 337–45.
71. *Context and Thought*, p. 224.
72. *Experience and Nature* (1929), p. 71.
73. *Experience and Nature* (1925), p. 28.
74. "Time and Individuality," in *Time and Its Mysteries*, Series II (New York: University Press, 1940), p. 100.

The second of the irreducible traits of existence mentioned by Dewey in "The Subject-Matter of Metaphysical Inquiry" is interaction, or, as he later called it, especially in his collaboration with Arthur Bentley, "transaction." [75] The idea of interactions, or transactions, in Dewey's thinking goes back at least as far as the organic co-ordinations or organic interactions of his "The Reflex Arc Concept in Psychology" (1896); and it is another way of protesting against dualisms and the notion of insulated atomic elements. Instead, for example, of a knowing subject over against an alien world as object, we have intercourse between a living organism and its physical and social environment, a series of interactions between a live creature and its environment, interactions so integral to the events related that the distinction between them becomes largely a functional one rather than one involving a confrontation between hard and fast, sharply defined, relatively unmodifiable individuals that change in little but position. And, of course, not merely two but commonly many events may interact at a time so that we have a web or complex of relations, connections, referential strands, and vector qualities. As Dewey wrote in an article originally published in 1925, "wherever there is an event, there is interaction, and interaction entails the conception of a *field,*" a field which "extends wherever the energies involved in the interaction operate and as far as any redistributions of energy are effected." [76] In short, nature is an affair of interactions or transactions of varying durations and extents.

This notion is developed in *Experience and Nature* in terms of a series of levels or types of interactions displaying different degrees of complexity, diverse functions, and varied sets of consequences: *1)* the physico-chemical level of mass-energy interactions, the level on which the physical sciences seek to discover the properties and relations of things in terms of which they may serve as means or instrumentalities, *2)* the psychophysical or organic pattern of need-demand-satisfaction activities, and *3)* the level of mind or human experience in which

75. *Knowing and the Known,* with Arthur Fisher Bentley (Boston: Beacon Press, 1949). In this work they distinguished between self-action, interaction, and transaction, giving the second term a narrower meaning than it had for the most part in Dewey's earlier writings and using the third to suggest a more systemic interaction.

76. "The Naturalistic Theory of Perception by the Senses," *Journal of Philosophy,* XXII (1925), 603.

social transactions involving language and meaning come in. Matter, life, and mind accordingly are not separate and distinct kinds of Being but rather are different modes of interconnection and operation, properties characterizing diverse particular fields of interacting events. They are consequences of interactions of varying complexity, scope, and degrees of intimacy.[77] As a matter of irreducible fact, life and mind have evolved from states of affairs in which they were absent, and after the fact we can indicate how potentialities in the former, certain directions of change present there, when taken in conjunction with appropriate occasions or opportunities, pointed toward the state which has evolved. Any given individual is the series of interactions in which he becomes what he is by the way he responds to the occasions with which he is presented,[78] and part of what he is at any given time is his set of potentialities for future change. In Dewey's words,

> Every event as such is passing into other things, in such a way that a later occurrence is an integral part of the *character* or *nature* of present existence. An "affair," *Res*, is always at issue whether it concerns chemical change, the emergence of life, language, mind or the episodes that compose human history. Each comes from something else and each when it comes has its own initial, unpredictable, immediate qualities, and its own similar terminal qualities. The later is never just resolved into the earlier. What we call such resolution is merely a statement of the order by means of which we regulate the passage of an earlier into the later. We may explain the traits of maturity by better knowledge of childhood, but maturity is never just infancy plus.[79]

*Experience and Nature* affords a fuller and more systematic treatment of the generic traits of existence, and at least implicitly Dewey's list of such traits is far longer than the little group he cited by way of illustration in "The Subject-Matter of Metaphysical Inquiry." In what follows I shall comment briefly on seven additional ones I find: *1)* continuity, *2)* texture, *3)* strand, *4)* quality, *5)* fusion, *6)* reference, and *7)* context.

*Continuity*, the first of this group, he recognized as impor-

77. See *Experience and Nature* (1929), pp. 261–62.
78. "Time and Individuality," pp. 103–4.
79. *Experience and Nature* (1929), p. 111.

tant as early as his Hegelian days though he referred to it in *Logic: The Theory of Inquiry* as the primary postulate of a naturalistic theory of logic.[80] This idea precludes complete breaks or gaps and reduction of the "higher" to the "lower" and excludes mere repetitions of identities as well. Intercepting and uniting with the principle of interaction, the lateral aspect of experience, the principle of the continuity of experience affords the longitudinal aspect.[81] It "means that every experience both takes up something from those which have gone before and modifies in some way the quality of those which come after."[82] Or somewhat differently stated, "Every event as such is passing into other things, in such a way that a later occurrence is an integral part of the *character* or *nature* of present existence."[83]

In terms of these two principles, analysis for Dewey as a pragmatic naturalist or contextualist is not a matter of reducing complex transactions to atomic elements but rather is an affair of exhibiting the relational structure of an event. It is an affair of tracing patterns of change, following threads of reference or connection from one situation or transaction to another which affords a convenient instrument of control.

In his instrumentalist phase Dewey recognized that every event has a certain internal organization or structure. With James he saw that experienced events do not have to have relations superimposed from outside. The diverse factors and qualities constituting an event hang together to form a connective or relational pattern, happily described by Pepper in terms of *texture* and *strands*. The latter term helps make clear that the constituent factors are relative to the pattern or whole and not "elements," detachable or independent "entities," "essences," or "realities" occurring in isolation from equally detachable "relations."[84] The terms "texture" and "strand" indicate a

80. *Logic*, p. 23. Cf. *Experience and Nature* (1929), p. 414: "The one cord that is never broken is that between the energies and acts which compose nature."

81. *Experience and Education* (New York: Macmillan Co., 1938), p. 42.

82. *Experience and Education*, p. 27; cf. ibid., p. 16: "Just as no man lives or dies to himself, so no experience lives or dies to itself. Wholly independent of desire or intent, every experience lives on in further experiences."

83. *Experience and Nature* (1929), p. 111.

84. "Interaction and Transaction," with Arthur Fisher Bentley, *Journal of Philosophy*, XLIII (1946), 509.

functional relationship. The strands, moreover, are not "simples" either. Like the texture they have a certain complexity or internal diversity, and what is strand in one transaction may be a texture in its own right in another.[85]

Each texture or affair has its own individual *quality;* [86] and Dewey made much of the "irreducible, infinitely plural, undefinable and indescribable qualities which a thing must *have* in order to be, and in order to be capable of becoming the subject of relations and a theme of discourse," holding that "in every event there is something obdurate, self-sufficient, wholly immediate, neither a relation nor an element in a relational whole, but terminal and exclusive." [87] In a view which insists that "things exist as just what they qualitatively are" [88] and that "every natural existence, in its own unique and brutal particularity of existence, also *has* immediacy," [89] or quality, qualities assume central importance; and by *quality* Dewey understood both the total quality pervading and constituting an affair—a certain cheerful, distressing, or perplexing quality, a Titian or Rembrandt quality—and specific qualities like red, hard, and sweet as distinctions within an affair.[90] Since every quality, whatever

85. "The Subject-Matter of Metaphysical Inquiry," p. 343n.

86. Cf. *Experience and Nature* (1929), p. 97: "Nature is an affair *of* affairs, wherein each one, no matter how linked up it may be with others, has its *own* quality." See *Art as Experience* (New York: Minton, Balch and Co., 1934), pp. 191–92, for a more detailed account of the unique "total and massive quality" which characterizes such an affair as a work of art, or see the chapter in the same book on "Having an Experience" for the role of pervasive quality in constituting an experience. Ch. 6 of *Logic*, pp. 101–19, sketches the role of pervasive felt or had quality in regulating the selection and the weighing of observed facts and their conceptual ordering in an act of inquiry. For one of Dewey's fullest direct accounts of the importance of quality, see "Qualitative Thought," *Symposium*, I (1930), 5–32.

In view of the originality and the complexity of Dewey's account of quality, critics have frequently differed sharply in their interpretations of it, and the last word has not yet been uttered on this important topic. For one recent significant exchange see Richard J. Bernstein, "John Dewey's Metaphysics of Experience," *Journal of Philosophy*, LVIII (1961), 5–14; and Gail Kennedy, "Comment on Professor Bernstein's Paper, 'John Dewey's Metaphysics of Experience'," ibid., LVIII (1961), 14–21.

87. *Experience and Nature* (1929), p. 85.

88. "Time and Individuality," p. 106.

89. "Half-Hearted Naturalism," *Journal of Philosophy*, XXIV (1927), 60–61.

90. *Logic*, pp. 69–71.

the level or type, is an ending or terminus of a natural affair or transaction, the range of qualities is as broad as the range of natural affairs; and since "all qualities, even the tertiary ones and, *a fortiori*, those of color, like red, are 'doings of natural conditions,' " no metaphysical dualism of an inner mental realm and an external physical domain arises.[91] But in Dewey's view there is no quality more fundamental than the felt or had quality of a total texture. This is what gives the texture as a whole its unity. This quality colors and permeates each of the strands.

If, however, one approaches this total quality from the side of the episodes or acts constituting the affair as a whole, it is a *fusion* of the strands.[92] The qualities of the various strands or tendencies which form the pattern of the total affair intercept each other and coalesce so as to give the fused quality of the total texture.[93] Some fusion may be involved in unifying or organizing any event, and the pragmatic naturalist generally interprets whatever seems to be simple in experience as either a product of fusion or something abstracted for a practical purpose.

91. "Experience, Knowledge and Value," p. 598.

92. For a sampling of Dewey's many references to the concept of fusion see *Experience and Nature* (1929), p. v; *Art as Experience*, pp. 36–37, 124 ("any sensuous quality tends, because of its organic connections, to spread and fuse"), 192–93; and *Context and Thought*, p. 211.

93. The following passage from *Art as Experience*, pp. 36–37, gives a good account of quality and fusion and helps make clear the relation which holds between a texture and its strands: "In a work of art, different acts, episodes, occurrences melt and fuse into unity, and yet do not disappear and lose their own character as they do so—just as in a genial conversation there is a continuous interchange and blending, and yet each speaker not only retains his own character but manifests it more clearly than is his wont." It should be noted that there are various degrees of fusion, some of which are much more complete than this one. But, to continue with Dewey's account, "An experience has a unity that gives it its name, *that* meal, that storm, that rupture of friendship. The existence of this unity is constituted by a single *quality* that pervades the entire experience in spite of the variation of its constituent parts. This unity is neither emotional, practical, nor intellectual, for these terms name distinctions that reflection can make within it. . . . Yet the experience was not a sum of these different characters; they were lost in it as distinctive traits. . . . Thinking goes on in trains of ideas, but the ideas form a train only because they are much more than what an analytic psychology calls ideas. They are phases, emotionally and practically distinguished, of a developing underlying quality; they are its moving variations, not separate and independent like Locke's and Hume's so-called ideas and impressions, but are subtle shadings of a pervading and developing hue."

Another generic trait of events or affairs is *reference* (or distance and direction values),[94] and as is the case with the other generic traits, it can provide the central focus for a statement of Dewey's philosophy as a whole. It helps constitute the quality of an event at the same time that it aids in clarifying its *context*. The strands of a texture grow out of and extend into environing textures, and they have varying direction-distance values with reference to these other textures. Since anything denoted has temporal quality and reference, movement from and toward within it,[95] reflection can work out the pattern of connections or relations, the degree of nearness or remoteness of one event to another, and the direction or set of means-objects which need to be taken to move from a given beginning to a desired ending or consummation. Indeed, to guide changes or control the direction of affairs, instruments or means are focal; and accordingly, the whole of the instrumental pattern developed in Dewey's third phase would be appropriate here. His response to the second major problem he saw as controlling the main course of modern thought, "the problem of the relation of physical science to the things of ordinary experience," was to see the objects of physical science as relational patterns, ways of ordering events, means, instruments, or conditions for guiding changes rather than as a second type of reality to compete with qualitied events or common-sense things.[96]

Of any event we may ask: When and where is it? Whence is it? Whither does it go? and How does it go? And the answer to these questions may be given in terms of references or means and *context*. To indicate the context of the event we specify   *1)* its environment,   *2)* the initiations from which it started, and   *3)* the means or instruments through which it moves toward   *4)* consummations or   *5)* frustrations, blocks, jars,

94. As I trust will be evident from what follows, I am not using "reference" here with the meaning Dewey assigned to the term in *Logic*, pp. 54–56: namely, a relation symbol-meanings sustain to existence. In terms of that discussion my usage is closer to what he called connection and involvement.

95. Cf. *Experience and Nature* (1925), pp. 29, 101, 111, and 266. See also *Context and Thought*, p. 211.

96. See, for example, "Experience, Knowledge and Value," pp. 523–24; Ch. 5 of *Experience and Nature* on the instrumental nature of scientific knowing; *The Quest for Certainty*, pp. 237–53 and elsewhere; "Time and Individuality," pp. 95–96; "Nature in Experience," *Philosophical Review*, XLIX (1940), 249–51.

breaks, or hitches. Each event involves an environment of other affairs which sustain, block, or condition its quality, but it is not in its environment like a marble in a box or a Newtonian spatial container. Indeed, it may be more illuminating to say of an organism that it lives by means of its environment than that it is in it.[97] Nature is, moreover, "a scene of incessant beginnings and endings," and they mark ongoing affairs off into unstable individuals.[98] A certain "from which" and a particular "to which" qualify any given affair and make it the distinctive event which it is, showing its special thrust or vector quality. So it is not strange that Dewey, with his concern for causal mechanisms and temporal finalities as phases of the same natural process, should stress initiations, consummations or blockages, and conflicts, and means.

Philosophic method for Dewey in his fourth period remained much what it was in his instrumentalist phase, and his conception of philosophy was also much the same, with the two main new features being his explicit concern with metaphysics as the study of the generic traits of existence and his notion of philosophy as criticism of criticism, which may be considered either as an implication of his earlier account of the theory of inquiry or as a generalization of his previous conception of philosophy as criticism. On this view as set forth in *Experience and Nature*, philosophy is the "critical operation and function become aware of itself and its implications, pursued deliberately and systematically." [99] It becomes a kind of theory of criticism, a consideration of alternative ways of critically evaluating values and beliefs. Meaning and values are focal in this conception of philosophy, and this aspect was not lost when he treated philosophy as general theory of criticism. He was still convinced that

97. Cf. *Experience and Education*, pp. 41–42: "An experience is always what it is because of a transaction taking place between an individual and what, at the time, constitutes his environment, whether the latter consists of persons with whom he is talking about some topic or event, the subject talked about being also a part of the situation; or the toy with which he is playing; the book he is reading (in which his environing conditions at the time may be England or ancient Greece or an imaginary region); or the materials of an experiment he is performing. The environment, in other words, is whatever conditions interact with personal needs, desires, purposes, and capacities to create the experience which is had." See also *Logic*, pp. 25 ff.

98. Cf. *Experience and Nature* (1929), pp. 98, 159.

99. *Experience and Nature* (1929), p. 403.

we criticize for the sake of instituting and perpetuating more enduring and extensive values; and each of the various philosophical disciplines, as he saw it, makes its distinctive contributions to this end, with metaphysics providing "a ground-map of the province of criticism, establishing base lines to be employed in more intricate triangulations." [100]

Philosophic discourse, according to his account, partakes of both scientific and literary discourse. Like literature, he declared,

> it is a comment on nature and life in the interest of a more intense and just appreciation of the meanings present in experience. . . . Its primary concern is to clarify, liberate and extend the goods which inhere in the naturally generated functions of experience. It has no call to create a world of "reality" *de novo*, nor to delve into secrets of Being hidden from common-sense and science. It has no stock of information or body of knowledge peculiarly its own. . . . Its business is to accept and to utilize for a purpose the best available knowledge of its own time and place. And this purpose is criticism of beliefs, institutions, customs, policies with respect to their bearing upon good.[101]

Whereas literature's office is "to perpetuate, enhance and vivify in imagination the natural goods," philosophy has a stricter task with greater responsibility to what lies outside its own products: namely, that of appraising "values by taking cognizance of their causes and consequences," and indispensable for this task are the conclusions of science about matter-of-fact efficiencies. Indeed, granted that "its eventual concern is to render goods more coherent, more secure and more significant in appreciation, its road is the subject-matter of natural existence as science discovers and depicts it." [102] And any philosophy may be tested by whether its conclusions render ordinary life-experiences and their predicaments more significant and luminous to us and make our dealings with them more fruitful.[103]

Some friendly critics feel that Dewey outlined a suggestive, imaginative program for philosophy but failed to spell it out in detailed and rigorous ways, and other less friendly critics regard his philosophy as another addition to the museum of

100. *Experience and Nature* (1929), p. 413.
101. *Experience and Nature* (1929), pp. 407–8.
102. *Experience and Nature* (1929), p. 408.
103. *Experience and Nature* (1929), p. 7.

historical specimens, something to be noted as having perhaps some interest and value for another period but not pertinent for current philosophizing. Though I do not wish to attempt here an assessment of the overall significance of his philosophy, I cannot forego mentioning a few points in connection with the criticisms raised. There is room for further analysis and development of various key notions in his empirical naturalism in spite of the voluminous array of detailed observation and analysis he provided concerning them; but even so he produced a metaphysical perspective which for imaginative sweep and relevance to human predicaments warrants consideration alongside the views of Plato, Aristotle, Democritus, Hegel, Leibniz, and the other great figures of Western philosophy he cited so often in attempting to clarify his own outlook. Acutely aware of the boundless multiplicity and variety of the concrete experiences and problems of men, his strength lay not primarily in detailed analysis but rather in his ability to place these experiences and problems in fresh, meaningful contexts, to see them in the broader framework of the major historical traditions without minimizing or blinking the urgency and reality of the specific problems.

It might be argued that Dewey's method of critical inquiry for resolving indeterminate or problematic situations offers the most important fresh way of tackling relevance since Aristotle's classic formulation in terms of a metaphysics of natural classes. In an age where relevance is the catchword but confusion of tongues, beliefs, and purposes characterizes life, surely Dewey's plea for a philosophy concerned with the problems of men and providing "large and generous ideas in the direction of life" [104] has a special urgency. It seems to me, moreover, that his thesis that through proper use of intelligence, reflective inquiry, men can better come to terms with the problems facing them, still stands as a challenge to renewed endeavor and thought on the part of us all. Though in one sense the main philosophical currents of our time seem to be moving in other directions than Dewey's thought, there is some evidence to indicate that many contemporary philosophers who approach the field from perspectives far removed from his are finding in his writings surprisingly perceptive insights and promising suggestions as to problems they find crucial, and there is even more to show that

104. *The Quest for Certainty*, p. 311.

many others would do likewise if they read him with care. Some Neo-Marxists, somewhat to their surprise, are finding that he saw clearly many features of the economic, social, and cultural setting; and an occasional analytic philosopher has noted his emphasis on logical method and critical inquiry. Finally, I suggest that in spite of the differences in terminology, we may find striking parallels between Dewey and the existential philosophers and the phenomenologists in their concern for problems of decision and the life world and between Dewey and the ordinary language philosophers with their insistence that the use of a word clarifies its meaning and that mind may be best seen as geared to decision-making and action.

## CHECKLIST

"The Metaphysical Assumptions of Materialism," in *The Early Works of John Dewey, 1882–1898,* Vol. I, pp. 3–8. Carbondale: Southern Illinois University Press, 1969.

"The Pantheism of Spinoza," in *Early Works,* I, 9–18.

"Kant and Philosophic Method," in *Early Works,* I, 34–47.

"The New Psychology," in *Early Works,* I, 48–60.

"The Psychological Standpoint," in *Early Works,* I, 122–43.

"Psychology as Philosophic Method," in *Early Works,* I, 144–67.

Response by Shadworth Holloway Hodgson, "Illusory Psychology," in *Early Works,* I, xli–lvii.

Reply by Dewey, " 'Illusory Psychology,' " in *Early Works,* I, 168–75.

"Inventory of Philosophy Taught in American Colleges," in *Early Works,* I, 116–21.

*Psychology* (The Early Works of John Dewey, 1882–1898, Vol. II). Carbondale: Southern Illinois University Press, 1967. cix, 366 pp.

"Ethics and Physical Science," in *Early Works,* I, 205–26.

"Knowledge as Idealization," in *Early Works,* I, 176–93.

*Leibniz's New Essays Concerning the Human Understanding,* in *Early Works,* I, 250–435.

"The Philosophy of Thomas Hill Green," in *The Early Works of John Dewey, 1882–1898,* Vol. III, pp. 14–35. Carbondale: Southern Illinois University Press, 1969.

"On Some Current Conceptions of the Term 'Self'," in *Early Works,* III, 56–74.

"The Present Position of Logical Theory," in *Early Works,* III, 125–41.

"The Scholastic and the Speculator," in *Early Works,* III, 148–54.

"Movements of Thought in the Nineteenth Century." Typewritten class lecture notes by Edwin Peck, University of Michigan, 1891–1892. 36 pp. [Michigan Historical Collections.]

"The Interpretation of Literature," *University Record,* University of Michigan, I (Feb. 1892), ii. [Report and abstract.]

["Thought News"], Detroit *Tribune,* 13 Apr. 1892. [Includes Dewey's statement on the proposed publication.]

*Introduction to Philosophy: Syllabus of Course 5,* in *Early Works,* III, 211–35.

"English Transcendentalism." Typewritten class lecture notes by Edwin Peck, University of Michigan, 1892. 23 pp. [Michigan Historical Collections.]

"The Superstition of Necessity," *Monist,* III (Apr. 1893), 362–79.

*The Study of Ethics: A Syllabus.* Ann Arbor: Register Publishing Co., 1894. iv, 151 pp. [2d ed., Ann Arbor: George Wahr, 1897. 144 pp.]

"Intuitionalism," in *Johnson's Universal Cyclopædia,* IV, 657–59. New York: D. Appleton and Co., 1894.

"The Ego as Cause," *Philosophical Review,* III (May 1894), 337–41.

"Reconstruction," *Monthly Bulletin,* Students' Christian Association, University of Michigan, XV (June 1894), 149–56.

"The Reflex Arc Concept in Psychology," *Psychological Review,* III (July 1896), 357–70. [Reprinted in C–7, pp. 233–48, with the title "The Unit of Behavior."]

"The Metaphysical Method in Ethics," *Psychological Review,* III (Mar. 1896), 181–88. [Discussion of *A Short Study of Ethics* by Archbishop Charles Frederick D'Arcy.]

"Hegel's Philosophy of Spirit." Typescript of lectures by John Dewey, [H. Heath Bawden], University of Chicago, 1897. 103 pp. [St. Louis University.]

"Psychology and Philosophic Method," *University [of California] Chronicle,* II (Aug. 1899), 159–79. [Reprinted separately, Berkeley: University of California Press, 1899, 23 pp.; also reprinted in C–2, pp. 242–70, with the title " 'Consciousness' and Experience."]

Review of *The World and the Individual* (Gifford Lectures), First Series: The Four Historical Conceptions of Being, by Josiah Royce, *Philosophical Review,* IX (May 1900), 311–24; Second Series: Nature, Man, and the Moral Order, ibid., XI (July 1902), 392–407.

"Some Stages of Logical Thought," *Philosophical Review,* IX (Sept. 1900), 465–89. [Reprinted in C–3, pp. 183–219.]

"Modern Idealism." Typescript of class lecture notes, [H. Heath Bawden], University of Chicago, 1902. 49 pp. [St. Louis University.]

"Mind (in philosophy)" [J. M. B. & J. D.], 81–82; "Natural," 133; "Natural Realism," 134; "Naturalism (1)," 137–38; "Naturalism (in art)" [J. H. T. & J. D.], 138; "Nature," 138–41; "Nature (philosophy of)," 142; "Necessity," 143–45; "Neo-criticism," 149; "Neo-Platonism," 150; "Neo-Pythagoreanism," 150; "Nescience," 167; "Nexus," 176; "Nihilism," 177–78; "Nisus," 178; "Noetic," 178–79; "Nominalism," 180; "Non-being," 180–81; "Non-ego," 181; "Noology," 181–82; "Norm and Normative (in the moral sciences)," 182; "Noumenon, and -al," 184–85; "Nous," 185–86; "Nullibrists," 186; "Number (in metaphysics)," 189; "Object (-ive; general and philosophical)," 191–92; "Objectivism," 94; "Occamism," 199; "Occasionalism," 199; "One (the)," 201; "Ontological Argument," 202–3; "Ontologism (2)," 203; "Ontology," 203–4; "Opinion (in philosophy)," 205; "Optimism and Pessimism," 210–12; "Organic," 213; "Organism," 218–19; "Outness," 251; "Oversoul," 252; "Palingenesis," 254; "Panentheism," 255; "Panlogism," 255; "Panpneumatism," 256; "Panpsychism," 256; "Pantheism," 256–57; "Panthelism," 257–58; "Parousia," 263; "Passion and Passive," 266–67; "Peripatetics," 280; "Permanence," 280; "Perseity (1)," 281; "Phase," 288; "Phenomenalism," 288; "Phenomenology," 288–89; "Phenomenon," 289; "Philosophy," 290–96; "Phoronomy," 297; "Plenum," 305; "Pleroma," 305; "Plexus," 305–6;

"Pluralism," 306; "Plurality," 306; "Pneuma," 307–8; "Pneumatology," 308; "Posit," 310–11; "Positive," 311; "Positivism," 312–13; "Possibility, Impossibility, and Possible," 313–14; "Pre-established Harmony," 329–30; "Presentationism (2)," 333; "Primary, Primitive, Primordial," 340; "Primum mobile," 341; "Principle," 341–42; "Property," 359–60; "Psychologism," 382; "Pure (in philosophy)," 401; "Quietism," 412; "Rationalism," 415–16; "Realism," 421–24; "Reals," 424; "Reify (-fication)," 439; "Relation," 439–42, 443; "Same (the) and (the) Other," 484–85; "Scepticism," 489–90; "Schema," 490; "Schematism," 490–91; "Scholasticism (the Schoolmen)," 491–95; "Schopenhauerism (or -eanism)," 499; "Scotism," 503; "Seminal Reasons," 514; "Sensationalism," 515–17; "Sensualism (in ethics)," 520; "Singularism," 533; "Speculation (1)" [J. D. & K. G.], 568; "Speculation (2) and (3)," 568; "Statue of Condillac," 601, [last paragraph, J. M. B. & J. D.], 601; "Subject (-ive)," 607–8; "Subjectivism," 611; "Substance," 612; "Substantiality Theory or Substantialism," 614; "Sui Generis," 620; "Summists," 620–21; "Syncretism (1)," 655; "System," 659; "Tabula Rasa," 661; "Thomism," 696; "Transcendent (-al)," 710–11; "Transcendentalism," 711; "Transient," 712; "Tychism," 721; "Ubication," 723; "Understanding and Reason," 725–26; "Unification of Knowledge," 726; "Unitarianism (1)," 734; "Unity (and Plurality)," 734, 736; "Universal (and Universality) (4) and (5)," 739; "Universal Postulate," 741; "Universe," 742; "Unknowable" [J. D. & J. M. B.], 742; "Unknowable," 743; "Unthinkable," 743; "Vacuum," 747–48; "World," 821, in *Dictionary of Philosophy and Psychology*, II, ed. James Mark Baldwin. New York: Macmillan Co., 1902.

"The St. Louis Congress of the Arts and Sciences," letter in *Science*, n.s. XVIII (Aug. 1903), 275–78. (Discussion of: Hugo Münsterberg, "The St. Louis Congress of Arts and Sciences," *Atlantic Monthly*, XCI [May 1903], 671–84.)
Reply by Münsterberg, *Science*, n.s. XVIII (Oct. 1903), 559–63.
Rejoinder by Dewey, *Science*, n.s. XVIII (Nov. 1903), 665.

"Thought and Its Subject-Matter: The General Problem of Logical Theory," pp. 1–22; "Thought and Its Subject-Matter: The Antecedent Conditions and Cues of the Thought-Function," pp. 23–48; "Thought and Its Subject-Matter: The Datum of Thinking," pp. 49–64; and "Thought and Its Subject-Matter: The Content and Object of Thought," pp. 65–85; in *Studies in Logical Theory* (University of Chicago, The Decennial Publications, Second Series, Vol. XI). Chicago: University of Chicago Press, 1903. [Reprinted in C–3, pp. 75–182, with the titles "The Relationship of Thought and Its Subject-Matter," "The Antecedents and Stimuli of Thinking," "Data and Meanings," and "The Objects of Thought."]

Review of *Humanism: Philosophical Essays* by Ferdinand Canning Scott Schiller, *Psychological Bulletin*, I (Sept. 1904), 335–40.

"Philosophy and American National Life," in *Centennial Anniversary of the Graduation of the First Class, July Third to Seventh 1904*, pp. 106–13. Burlington: University of Vermont, 1905.

"The Realism of Pragmatism," *Journal of Philosophy*, II (June 1905), 324–27. (Reply to: Stephen Sheldon Colvin, "Is Subjective Idealism a Necessary Point of View for Psychology," *Journal of Philosophy*, II [Apr. 1905], 225–31.)

"The Postulate of Immediate Empiricism," *Journal of Philosophy*, II (July 1905), 393–99. [Reprinted in C–2, pp. 226–41.]
Response by Charles Montague Bakewell, "An Open Letter to Pro-

fessor Dewey Concerning Immediate Empiricism," *Journal of Philosophy*, II (Sept. 1905), 520–22.

Reply by Dewey, "Immediate Empiricism," *Journal of Philosophy*, II (Oct. 1905), 597–99.

Response by Frederick James Eugene Woodbridge, "Of What Sort Is Cognitive Experience?" *Journal of Philosophy*, II (Oct. 1905), 573–76.

Reply by Dewey, "The Knowledge Experience and Its Relationships," *Journal of Philosophy*, II (Nov. 1905), 652–57.

Response by Boyd Henry Bode, "Cognitive Experience and Its Object," *Journal of Philosophy*, II (Nov. 1905), 658–63.

Reply by Dewey, "The Knowledge Experience Again," *Journal of Philosophy*, II (Dec. 1905), 707–11.

"The Terms 'Conscious' and 'Consciousness'," *Journal of Philosophy*, III (Jan. 1906), 39–41.

Review of *The Life of Reason*, Vols. I–II, by George Santayana, *Science*, n.s. XXIII (Feb. 1906), 223–25.

"Beliefs and Realities," *Philosophical Review*, XV (Mar. 1906), 113–29. [Reprinted in C–2, pp. 169–97, with the title "Beliefs and Existences."]

"Reality as Experience," *Journal of Philosophy*, III (May 1906), 253–57.

"Experience and Objective Idealism," *Philosophical Review*, XV (Sept. 1906), 465–81. [Reprinted in C–2, pp. 198–225.]

"The Control of Ideas by Facts," I, *Journal of Philosophy*, IV (Apr. 1907), 197–203; II, ibid., IV (May 1907), 253–59; III, ibid., IV (June 1907), 309–19. [Reprinted in C–3, pp. 230–49.]

"Reality and the Criterion for the Truth of Ideas," *Mind*, n.s. XVI (July 1907), 317–42. [Reprinted in C–2, pp. 112–53, with the title "The Intellectualist Criterion for Truth."]

"Pure Experience and Reality: A Disclaimer," *Philosophical Review*, XVI (July 1907), 419–22. (Reply to: Evander Bradley McGilvary, "Pure Experience and Reality," *Philosophical Review*, XVI [May 1907], 266–84.)

Review of *The Life of Reason*, Vols. I–V, by George Santayana, *Educational Review*, XXXIV (Sept. 1907), 116–29.

"Does Reality Possess Practical Character?" in *Essays, Philosophical and Psychological*, in Honor of William James, Professor in Harvard University, by his Colleagues at Columbia University, pp. 53–80. New York: Longmans, Green, and Co., 1908. [Reprinted in C–7, pp. 36–55, with the title "The Practical Character of Reality."]

"What Does Pragmatism Mean by Practical?" *Journal of Philosophy*, V (Feb. 1908), 85–99. [Review of *Pragmatism* by William James.] [Reprinted in C–3, pp. 303–29, with the title "What Pragmatism Means by Practical."]

*The Pragmatic Movement of Contemporary Thought: A Syllabus.* New York, 1909. 11 pp.

"Objects, Data, and Existences: A Reply to Professor McGilvary," *Journal of Philosophy*, VI (Jan. 1909), 13–21. (Reply to: Evander Bradley McGilvary, "The Chicago 'Idea' and Idealism," *Journal of Philosophy*, V [Oct. 1908], 589–97.)

"Realism and Idealism," *Philosophical Review*, XVIII (Mar. 1909), 182–83.

[Discussion on the "Concept of a Sensation"], *Journal of Philosophy*, VI (Apr. 1909), 211–12.

"Darwin's Influence Upon Philosophy," *Popular Science Monthly*, LXXV (July 1909), 90–98. [Reprinted in C–2, pp. 1–19, with the title "The Influence of Darwinism on Philosophy."]

Review of *Anti-pragmatisme* by Albert Schinz, *Philosophical Review,* XVIII (July 1909), 446–49.

*How We Think.* Boston: D. C. Heath and Co., 1910. vi, 224 pp.

*The Influence of Darwin on Philosophy and Other Essays in Contemporary Thought.* New York: Henry Holt and Co., 1910. vi, 309 pp. [Reprints, with revisions, of previously published articles. "A Short Catechism Concerning Truth," pp. 154–68, is the only paper in this collection not published previously.]

"Valid Knowledge and the 'Subjectivity of Experience'," *Journal of Philosophy,* VII (Mar. 1910), 169–74.

"Some Implications of Anti-Intellectualism," *Journal of Philosophy,* VII (Sept. 1910), 477–81.

"The Short-Cut to Realism Examined," *Journal of Philosophy,* VII (Sept. 1910), 553–57. (Discussion of: "The Program and Platform of Six Realists" [Edwin Bissell Holt, Walter Taylor Marvin, William Pepperell Montague, Ralph Barton Perry, Walter Boughton Pitkin, Edward Gleason Spaulding], *Journal of Philosophy,* VII [July 1910], 393–401.)

Response by Edward Gleason Spaulding, "Realism: A Reply to Professor Dewey and an Exposition," *Journal of Philosophy,* VIII (Feb. 1911), 63–77.

Dewey's "Rejoinder to Dr. Spaulding," *Journal of Philosophy,* VIII (Feb. 1911), 77–79.

Edward Gleason Spaulding, "A Reply to Professor Dewey's Rejoinder," *Journal of Philosophy,* VIII (Oct. 1911), 566–74.

"Joint Discussion with Articles of Agreement and Disagreement: Professor Dewey and Dr. Spaulding," *Journal of Philosophy,* VIII (Oct. 1911), 574–79.

"Brief Studies in Realism," I. Naïve Realism vs. Presentative Realism, *Journal of Philosophy,* VIII (July 1911), 393–400; II. Epistemological Realism: The Alleged Ubiquity of the Knowledge Relation, ibid., VIII (Sept. 1911), 546–54. [Reprinted in C–3, pp. 250–80.]

"The Study of Philosophy," *Columbia Monthly,* VIII (Aug. 1911), 367–68.

"A Reply to Professor Royce's Critique of Instrumentalism," *Philosophical Review,* XXI (Jan. 1912), 69–81. (Reply to: Josiah Royce, "The Problem of Truth in the Light of Recent Discussion," in *William James, and Other Essays on the Philosophy of Life,* pp. 187–254. New York: Macmillan Co., 1911.)

"A Reply to Professor McGilvary's Questions," *Journal of Philosophy,* IX (Jan. 1912), 19–21. (Reply to: Evander Bradley McGilvary, "Professor Dewey's 'Action of Consciousness'," *Journal of Philosophy,* VIII [Aug. 1911], 458–60.)

"In Response to Professor McGilvary," *Journal of Philosophy,* IX (Sept. 1912), 544–48. (Reply to: Evander Bradley McGilvary, "Realism and the Ego-centric Predicament," *Philosophical Review,* XXI [May 1912], 351–56; "Professor Dewey's 'Awareness'," *Journal of Philosophy,* IX [May 1912], 301–2; "Professor Dewey's 'Brief Studies in Realism'," ibid., IX [June 1912], 344–49.)

"Perception and Organic Action," *Journal of Philosophy,* IX (Nov. 1912), 645–68. [Reprinted in C–7, pp. 202–32.]

"The Subject-Matter of Metaphysical Inquiry," *Journal of Philosophy,* XII (June 1915), 337–45. (Comments on: Ralph Stayner Lillie, "The Philosophy of Biology: Vitalism *vs.* Mechanism," *Science,* n.s. XL [Dec. 1915], 840–46.)

"The Existence of the World as a Problem," *Philosophical Review,* XXIV

(July 1915), 357–70. [Comments on *Our Knowledge of the External World as a Field for Scientific Method in Psychology* by Bertrand Russell.] [Reprinted in C–3, pp. 281–302.]

*Democracy and Education: An Introduction to the Philosophy of Education* (Text-Book Series in Education, ed. Paul Monroe). New York: Macmillan Co., 1916. xii, 434 pp.

*Essays in Experimental Logic.* Chicago: University of Chicago Press, 1916. vii, 444 pp. [Chs. 2–5 "represent (with editorial revisions, mostly omissions) the essays taken from the old volume (*Studies in Logical Theory*). . . . The other essays are in part reprinted and in part rewritten, with additions, from various contributions to philosophical periodicals." Preface, p. v.]

"The Pragmatism of Peirce," *Journal of Philosophy*, XIII (Dec. 1916), 709–15.

"The Need for a Recovery of Philosophy," in *Creative Intelligence: Essays in the Pragmatic Attitude*, pp. 3–69. New York: Henry Holt and Co., 1917.

"Duality and Dualism," *Journal of Philosophy*, XIV (Aug. 1917), 491–93. (Comment on: Durant Drake, "What Kind of Realism?" *Journal of Philosophy*, IX (Mar. 1912), 149–54; "A Cul-de-Sac for Realism," ibid., XIV [July 1917], 365–73.)

"Philosophy and Democracy," *University [of California] Chronicle*, XXI (Jan. 1919), 39–54. [Reprinted in C–10, pp. 841–55.]

"Dewey's Lectures in Japan," *Journal of Philosophy*, XVI (June 1919), 357–64.

*Reconstruction in Philosophy.* New York: Henry Holt and Co., 1920. vii, 224 pp. [Enl. ed. with a new Introduction, Boston: Beacon Press, 1948. xlix, 224 pp.]

"First Introduction," in *Universe* by Scudder Klyce, pp. iii–v. Winchester, Mass.: S. Klyce, 1921.

"Classicism as an Evangel," *Journal of Philosophy*, XVIII (Nov. 1921), 664–66.

*Types of Philosophic Thought: Syllabus for Philosophy 191–192.* Columbia University, 1922–23. [New York, 1922?]. 67 pp., multigraphed.

"Realism without Monism or Dualism," I. Knowledge Involving the Past, *Journal of Philosophy*, XIX (June 1922), 309–17; II., ibid., XIX (June 1922), 351–61. (Reply to: Arthur Oncken Lovejoy, "Pragmatism *vs.* the Pragmatist," in *Essays in Critical Realism* [1920], pp. 35–81.)

"Notables and Common People," *New Republic*, XXXI (Aug. 1922), 285–86. [Review of *Prime Ministers and Presidents* by Charles Hitchcock Sherrill and *The Rising Temper of the East* by Frazier Hunt.]

"Events and Meanings," *New Republic*, XXXII (Aug. 1922), 9–10. [Reprinted in C–10, pp. 125–29.]

"Tradition, Metaphysics, and Morals," *Journal of Philosophy*, XX (Mar. 1923), 187–92. (Reply to: Daniel Sommer Robinson, "The Chief Types of Motivation to Philosophic Reflection," *Journal of Philosophy*, XX [Jan. 1923], 29–41.)

Review of *Scepticism and Animal Faith* by George Santayana, *New Republic*, XXXV (Aug. 1923), 294–96.

[Statement on Scholasticism], 14 Nov. 1923. Answer to questionnaire of Celestin J. Steiner, St. Louis University.

"Some Comments on Philosophical Discussion," *Journal of Philosophy*, XXI (Apr. 1924), 197–209. (Reply to: Arthur Oncken Lovejoy, "Time, Meaning and Transcendence," I. The Alleged Futurity of Yesterday,

*Journal of Philosophy,* XIX [Sept. 1922], 505–15; and II. Professor Dewey's *Tertium Quid,* ibid., XIX [Sept. 1922], 533–41; and Sterling Power Lamprecht, "A Note on Professor Dewey's Theory of Knowledge," *Journal of Philosophy,* XX [Aug. 1923], 488–94.)

*Experience and Nature* (Lectures upon the Paul Carus Foundation, First Series). Chicago, London: Open Court Publishing Co., 1925. xi, 443 pp. [2d ed., with a Preface, New York: W. W. Norton, 1929. ix, 1a–4a, 1–443 pp. 3d. ed., LaSalle, Ill.: Open Court Publishing Co., 1958. xviii, 360 pp.]

"The Development of American Pragmatism," in *Studies in the History of Ideas* by the Department of Philosophy of Columbia University, Vol. II, pp. 353–77. New York: Columbia University Press, 1925. [Retranslated (by Herbert W. Schneider) from the French "Le développement du pragmatisme américain," *Revue de métaphysique et de morale,* XXIX (octobre 1922), 411–30.] [Reprinted in C–7, pp. 13–35.]

"The Naturalistic Theory of Perception by the Senses," *Journal of Philosophy,* XXII (Oct. 1925), 596–605. [Reprinted in C–7, pp. 188–201, with the title "A Naturalistic Theory of Sense Perception."]

"The Changing Intellectual Climate," *New Republic,* XLV (Feb. 1926), 360–61. [Review of *Science and the Modern World* by Alfred North Whitehead.]

"Events and the Future," *Journal of Philosophy,* XXIII (May 1926), 253–58. [Discussion of *Scientific Thought* by Charlie Dunbar Broad.]

[Statement], in *Present-Day Thinkers and the New Scholasticism, An International Symposium,* ed. John S. Zybura, pp. 29–31. St. Louis: B. Herder Book Co., 1926.

"The Rôle of Philosophy in the History of Civilization," *Philosophical Review,* XXXVI (Jan. 1927), 1–9. [Reprinted in C–7, pp. 3–12, with the title "Philosophy and Civilization"; C–11, pp. 245–55, with the title "Philosophy and Culture."]

"Introductory Word," in *The Metaphysics of Pragmatism* by Sidney Hook, pp. 1–5. Chicago: Open Court Publishing Co., 1927.

" 'Half-Hearted Naturalism,' " *Journal of Philosophy,* XXIV (Feb. 1927), 57–64. (Reply to: George Santayana, "Dewey's Naturalistic Metaphysics," *Journal of Philosophy,* XXII [Dec. 1925], 673–88; and Frank Thilly, "Contemporary American Philosophy," *Philosophical Review,* XXXV [Nov. 1926], 522–38.)

"The Integration of a Moving World," *New Republic,* LI (May 1927), 22–24. [Review of *Purposive Evolution: The Link Between Science and Religion* by Edmund Noble.]

"Philosophy," in *Whither Mankind: A Panorama of Modern Civilization,* ed. Charles Austin Beard, pp. 313–31. New York: Longmans, Green and Co., 1928.

"Body and Mind," *Bulletin of the New York Academy of Medicine,* IV (Jan. 1928), 3–19; *Mental Hygiene,* XII (Jan. 1928), 1–17. [Reprinted in C–7, pp. 299–317.]

"Philosophy as a Fine Art," *New Republic,* LIII (Feb. 1928), 352–54. [Review of *The Realm of Essence* by George Santayana.]

"Social as a Category," *Monist,* XXXVIII (Apr. 1928), 161–77. [Reprinted in C–7, pp. 77–92, with the title "The Inclusive Philosophic Idea"; C–11, pp. 1059–69, with the title "The Social."]

"Things, Thought, Conversation," *Nation,* CXXVI (Apr. 1928), 449–50. [Review of *Possibility* by Scott Buchanan and *Dialectic* by Mortimer Adler.]

"Meaning and Existence," *Journal of Philosophy*, XXV (June 1928), 345–53. (Reply to: Everett W. Hall, "Some Meanings of Meaning in Dewey's *Experience and Nature*," *Journal of Philosophy*, XXV [Mar. 1928], 169–81.)

"Philosophy and Internationalism," in C–10, pp. 831–40. [First publication of "The International Character of Modern Philosophy," from tear sheets found in Dewey's office; source of original printing unknown.]

*The Quest for Certainty*. New York: Minton, Balch and Co., 1929. 318 pp.

Review of *Process and Reality* by Alfred North Whitehead, *New York Sun*, 26 Oct. 1929.

[Lecture], 18 Feb. 1929, at Edward Scribner Ames' University Church of Disciples of Christ, Chicago. [Holograph notes in Southern Illinois University Archives.]

"From Absolutism to Experimentalism," in *Contemporary American Philosophy: Personal Statements*, II, eds. George Plimpton Adams and William Pepperell Montague, 13–27. New York: Macmillan Co., 1930.

"Conduct and Experience," in *Psychologies of 1930*, ed. Carl Murchison, pp. 409–22. Worcester, Mass.: Clark University Press, 1930. [Reprinted in C–7, pp. 249–70.]

"Philosophy and Education," in *Addresses Delivered at the Dedication of the New Campus and New Buildings of the University of California at Los Angeles*, pp. 46–56. Berkeley: University of California Press, 1930.

"Qualitative Thought," *Symposium*, I (Jan. 1930), 5–32. [Reprinted in C–7, pp. 93–116.]

"What I Believe," *Forum*, LXXXIII (Mar. 1930), 176–82. [Rev. statement in *I Believe*, ed. Clifton Fadiman, pp. 347–54. New York: Simon and Schuster, 1939.]

"In Reply to Some Criticisms," *Journal of Philosophy*, XXVII (May 1930), 271–77. (Reply to: William Ernest Hocking, "Action and Certainty," *Journal of Philosophy*, XXVII [Apr. 1930], 225–38; Clarence Irving Lewis, "Pragmatism and Current Thought," *Journal of Philosophy*, XXVII [Apr. 1930], 238–46; and Frederick James Eugene Woodbridge, "Experience and Dialectic," *Journal of Philosophy*, XXVII [May 1930], 264–71.)

*Philosophy and Civilization*. New York: Minton, Balch and Co., 1931. vii, 334 pp. [Reprints, with revisions, of previously published articles.]

*Context and Thought* (University of California Publications in Philosophy, Vol. XII), pp. 203–24. Berkeley: University of California Press, 1931. [Also printed separately.]

"Prefatory Remarks," in *The Philosophy of the Present* by George Herbert Mead, ed. Arthur Edward Murphy, pp. xxxvi–xl. Chicago: Open Court Publishing Co., 1932.

"Introduction," in *Studies in Philosophy* by Theodore T. Lafferty (Lehigh University Publications, Vol. VI), pp. i–ii.

*How We Think*. Boston: D. C. Heath and Co., 1933. x, 301 pp. [Expanded, revised, and rewritten edition of the 1910 *How We Think*.]

"The Adventure of Persuasion," *New Republic*, LXXIV (Apr. 1933), 285–86. [Review of *Adventures of Ideas* by Alfred North Whitehead.]

*Art as Experience*. New York: Minton, Balch and Co., 1934. viii, 355 pp. [Part of Ch. 1 first published as "Art In a Vacuum," *Saturday Review of Literature*, X (Feb. 1934), 501–3.]

"Philosophy," in *Encyclopaedia of the Social Sciences*, XII, 118–28. New York: Macmillan Co., 1934.

"An Empirical Survey of Empiricisms," in *Studies in the History of Ideas* by the Department of Philosophy of Columbia University, Vol. III, pp. 3–22. New York: Columbia University Press, 1935.

"Peirce's Theory of Quality," *Journal of Philosophy,* XXXII (Dec. 1935), 701–8. (Reply to: Thomas A. Goudge, "The Views of Charles Peirce on the Given in Experience," *Journal of Philosophy,* XXXII [Sept. 1935], 533–44.)

Typescript of General Seminar of University in Exile, New School for Social Research, 9 Dec. 1936. [Discussion of "What Pragmatism Means for the Social Sciences," address by Horace M. Kallen. Participants were: Armstrong, Ascoli, Heiman, Dewey, Wertheimer, Kallen.] [In Southern Illinois University Archives.]

"Whitehead's Philosophy," *Philosophical Review,* XLVI (Mar. 1937), 170–77. [Reprinted in C–8, pp. 410–18.]

*Logic: The Theory of Inquiry.* New York: Henry Holt and Co., 1938. viii, 546 pp.

*Experience and Education.* New York: Macmillan Co., 1938. xii, 116 pp.

"Time and Individuality," preprint of text of seventh annual James Arthur Lecture on "Time and Its Mysteries" delivered 21 Apr. 1938. [New York]: New York University, Bureau of Public Information, 1938. [Also published in *Time and Its Mysteries,* Series II, pp. 85–109. New York: University Press, 1940.]

"Experience, Knowledge and Value: A Rejoinder," in *The Philosophy of John Dewey* (The Library of Living Philosophers, Vol. I, ed. Paul Arthur Schilpp), pp. 517–608. Evanston, Chicago: Northwestern University, 1939.

"A Philosopher's Philosophy," New York *Times,* 15 Oct. 1939. [Interview with Samuel Johnson Woolf.]

"Nature in Experience," *Philosophical Review,* XLIX (Mar. 1940), 244–58. [Reprinted in C–8, pp. 193–207.] (Reply to: Morris Raphael Cohen, "Some Difficulties in Dewey's Anthropocentric Naturalism," *Philosophical Review,* XLIX [Mar. 1940], 196–228; and William Ernest Hocking, "Dewey's Concepts of Experience and Nature," *Philosophical Review,* XLIX [Mar. 1940], 228–44.)

Review of *The Human Enterprise: An Attempt to Relate Philosophy to Daily Life* by Max Carl Otto, *Journal of Philosophy,* XXXVII (May 1940), 303–5.

"The Philosophy of Whitehead," in *The Philosophy of Alfred North Whitehead* (The Library of Living Philosophers, Vol. III, ed. Paul Arthur Schilpp), pp. 643–61. Evanston, Chicago: Northwestern University, 1941.

"The Objectivism-Subjectivism of Modern Philosophy," *Journal of Philosophy,* XXXVIII (Sept. 1941), 533–42. [Reprinted in C–8, pp. 309–21.]

"Lessons from the War—In Philosophy." Address in radio series "Lessons from the War," at Cooper Union, 7 Dec. 1941. [Typewritten transcription from copy of wire recording at Cooper Union, in Southern Illinois University Archives.]

"William James as Empiricist," in *In Commemoration of William James 1842–1942,* pp. 48–57. New York: Columbia University Press, 1942.

"Inquiry and Indeterminateness of Situations," *Journal of Philosophy,* XXXIX (May 1942), 290–96. [Reprinted in C–8, pp. 322–30.] (Reply to: Donald Sage Mackay, "What Does Mr. Dewey Mean by an 'Indeterminate Situation'?" *Journal of Philosophy,* XXXIX [Mar. 1942], 141–48.)

# GUIDE TO THE WORKS OF JOHN DEWEY

"By Nature and By Art," *Journal of Philosophy,* XLI (May 1944), 281–92. [Reprinted in C–8, pp. 286–300.]

"The Revolt Against Science," *Humanist,* V (Autumn 1945), 105–7.

"Dualism and the Split Atom," *New Leader,* XXVIII (Nov. 1945), 1, 4.

"Introduction: The Problems of Men and the Present State of Philosophy," in C–8, pp. 3–20. [This section published for the first time in this collection.]

"Interaction and Transaction," with Arthur Fisher Bentley, *Journal of Philosophy,* XLIII (Sept. 1946), 505–17. [Reprinted in C–9, pp. 103–18.]

"Introduction: Reconstruction as Seen Twenty-five Years Later," in *Reconstruction in Philosophy,* pp. v–xli. Boston: Beacon Press, 1948.

[Letter to Albert George Adam Balz], *Journal of Philosophy,* XLVI (May 1949), 329–42. (Reply to: Albert George Adam Balz, "A Letter to Mr. Dewey Concerning John Dewey's Doctrine of Possibility," *Journal of Philosophy,* XLVI [May 1949], 313–29.)

"Experience and Existence: A Comment," *Philosophy and Phenomenological Research,* IX (June 1949), 709–13. (Reply to: Sholom J. Kahn, "Experience and Existence in Dewey's Naturalistic Metaphysics," *Philosophy and Phenomenological Research,* IX [Dec. 1948], 316–21.)

"America's Philosopher Attains an Alert 90," New York *Times,* 16 Oct. 1949. [Interview with Irwin Edman.]

"On Philosophical Synthesis," *Philosophy East and West,* I (Apr. 1951), 3.

"Modern Philosophy," in *The Cleavage in Our Culture: Studies in Scientific Humanism in Honor of Max Otto,* ed. Frederick Burkhardt, pp. 15–29. Boston: Beacon Press, 1952.

*John Dewey and Arthur F. Bentley: A Philosophical Correspondence, 1932–1951,* eds. Sidney Ratner and Jules Altman. New Brunswick, N.J.: Rutgers University Press, 1964. ["Means and Consequences— How, What, and What For," pp. 647–54, and "Importance, Significance and Meaning," pp. 655–68, are previously unpublished articles by Dewey.]

# 3

# Dewey's Logic and Theory of Knowledge

## GAIL KENNEDY

IN THE long reply to his critics, written in 1939, Dewey says: "The actual point of my theory may however be found . . . in a transfer of traits which had been reserved for the function of moral judgment over to the processes of ordinary and scientific knowing." A bit later he adds:

> Were I anonymously to turn critic of my own philosophy, this is the place from which I should set out. I should indicate that after insisting upon the genuineness of affectional and other "tertiary" qualities as "doings of nature," Dewey then proceeds to emphasize in his theory of knowing, as that is manifested in both science and common sense, the operations of transformation, reconstruction, control, and union of theory and practice in experimental activity which are analogous to those involved in moral activity.[1]

Dewey did not arrive easily nor quickly at this conclusion. When, in 1882, he went to do graduate work at the newly established Johns Hopkins University, he found himself confronted by two rival schools of thought: one, the positivism represented preëminently by the writings of Comte and Spencer; the other, philosophers such as his teacher, George Sylvester Morris, and, in England, the group of Neo-Hegelians whose most distinguished member was T. H. Green. "The eighties and nineties," Dewey says, "were a time of new ferment in

1. "Experience, Knowledge and Value: A Rejoinder," in *The Philosophy of John Dewey* (The Library of Living Philosophers, Vol. I, ed. Paul Arthur Schilpp [Evanston, Chicago: Northwestern University, 1939]), pp. 579–80.

English thought; the reaction against atomic individualism and sensationalistic empiricism was in full swing. . . . This movement was at the time the vital and constructive one in philosophy." [2]

The chief concern of these idealists was to demonstrate that the regnant empiricism was hopelessly inadequate because if experience were nothing but an effect of blind collocations of atoms the emergence of life and mind became unintelligible. Only by postulating a spiritual principle in nature correspondent to the structure of society and of the consciousness of individuals could this ultimate inexplicability be avoided. Here, then, was a way of uniting the world of science and the realm of values. Dewey became an adherent to their views. He was not, however, satisfied with a merely speculative resolution of the issue. Like his mentor, T. H. Green, he was also a practical idealist and reformer. "Philosophy," he believed, "should terminate in an art of social control." [3] How, then, can moral progress consist merely in a partial replication in space and time of an infinite Mind? Gradually he acknowledged the paralyzing effect produced by this way of equating value with existence. The result, he says, was that "I drifted away from Hegelianism in the next fifteen years; the word 'drifting' expresses the slow and, for a long time, imperceptible character of the movement." [4]

The direction in which he drifted was towards a biologically and socially oriented naturalism. The forces impelling him were complex and various.[5] The most important were: Darwinism, which he saw was incompatible with the Hegelian conception of evolution as a progressive unfolding of latent potentialities; and, more importantly, he realized that Darwin's conception of evolutionary changes required a "new logic," one that

outlaws, flanks, dismisses—what you will—one type of problems and substitutes for it another type. Philosophy forswears

2. "From Absolutism to Experimentalism," in *Contemporary American Philosophy*, II, eds. George Plimpton Adams and William Pepperell Montague (New York: Macmillan Co., 1930), 18.

3. *Experience and Nature*, 2d ed. (New York: W. W. Norton and Co., 1929), p. 127.

4. "From Absolutism to Experimentalism," pp. 20–21.

5. In addition to Dewey's essay, see the detailed study by Morton G. White, *The Origin of Dewey's Instrumentalism* (New York: Columbia University Press, 1943).

inquiry after absolute origins and absolute finalities in order
to explore specific values and the specific conditions that generate them.[6]

William James's *Psychology* was in many ways an application
of Darwinian principles; the biological strain in that complex
book leads to the conclusion that thinking is one mode, among
others—a peculiarly efficient one—of adapting to an exigent
environment. James says: "*The pursuance of future ends and
the choice of means for their attainment are thus the mark and
criterion of the presence of mentality* in a phenomenon." [7] Finally, his friendship with the journalist, Franklin Ford, helped
convince him that moral progress can be achieved only through
social reform, that the chief obstacles to reform are obscurantist
and reactionary vested interests, and that the only effective
means of overcoming them is development of the sciences, particularly the social sciences, together with a wide dissemination
of the results of scientific inquiry. "*The* duty of the present," he
says, "is the socializing of intelligence—the realizing of its
bearing upon social practice." [8] Most important was Dewey's
own effort to analyze experience, and especially, to determine
how the decision-making process operates. He became convinced, as he was to put it later, that reality, as given in our
experience, has a basically practical character. It is an affair in
which undergoing and doing, rather than knowing, are the
primary traits.[9] This view, stated in earlier writings on ethics, is
fully developed in his essay "The Logical Conditions of a Scientific Treatment of Morality." [10] The usual distinction between
practical and scientific judgments is that the former are supposed to refer to individual cases and to acts. (Peter decides:

6. *The Influence of Darwin on Philosophy and Other Essays in
Contemporary Thought* (New York: Henry Holt and Co., 1910), p. 13.
    7. William James, *The Principles of Psychology* (New York:
Henry Holt and Co., 1890), I, 8.
    8. *Outlines of a Critical Theory of Ethics*, in *The Early Works of
John Dewey, 1882–1898*, Vol. III (Carbondale: Southern Illinois Uni-
versity Press, 1969), p. 320.
    9. Cf. "Does Reality Possess Practical Character?" in *Essays,
Philosophical and Psychological* (New York: Longmans, Green, and Co.,
1908), pp. 53–80.
    10. In *Investigations Representing the Departments: Part II, Philos-
ophy, Education* (University of Chicago: The Decennial Publications,
First Series, Vol. III [Chicago: University of Chicago Press, 1903]), pp.
113–39.

"This evening I shall propose to Joan.") Dewey attempts to show that these two characteristics are found as well in scientific judgments:

> If the use made of scientific resources, of technique of observation and experiment, of systems of classification, etc., in directing the act of judging (and thereby fixing the content of the judgment) depends upon the interest and disposition of the situation, we have only to make such dependence explicit, and the so-called scientific judgment appears definitely as a moral judgment.[11]

The title of the essay is, then, a bit askew—since all judgments have the basic traits of moral ones.

"The attainment of unified method," says Dewey, "means that the fundamental unity of the structure of inquiry in common sense and science be recognized, their difference being one in the problems with which they are directly concerned, not to their respective logics."[12] It also means that the need for an infinite Mind to unite value and existence has evaporated. The requisite unity is supplied within experience itself. For his original metaphysical solution of the problem Dewey has now substituted a methodological one. And, since "experience" is within nature, a part of it, as the live creature is in his environment, he has become a naturalist in his philosophy.

It is for this reason that Dewey was primarily interested in logic as method of inquiry. All of his writings on so many other subjects—ethics, æsthetics, education, social philosophy, and religion—were attempts to apply the method to the solution of problems in those fields. In the conventional sense in which it is true for, say, Spinoza or Leibniz, he did not have a "philosophy." He could say, though,

> I find that with respect to the hanging together of various problems and various hypotheses in a perspective determined by a definite point of view, I have a system. In so far I have to retract disparaging remarks I have made in the past about the need for a system in philosophy.[13]

11. "Logical Conditions of a Scientific Treatment of Morality," p. 126.
12. Logic: The Theory of Inquiry (New York: Henry Holt and Co., 1938), p. 79.
13. "Nature in Experience," Philosophical Review, XLIX (1940), 244–45.

Methods of inquiry are applicable only to real problems, and real problems occur only when the inquirer is in a situation that Dewey calls "indeterminate." A situation which is indeterminate *may* also become problematic when there is not a mere state of confusion but one of doubt. Intelligence is the capacity to doubt, a mode of response to the doubtful as such. This mode of response, as against a merely emotional and impulsive reaction, is indirect. It begins with apprehension that what is doubtful is the *significance* of certain elements within the total situation. These elements no longer are merely given; they now take on the function of signs. All perceived objects are as such qualitatively unique and wholly individual. These simply are what they are. But when an individual object is taken as a sign —a cloud, of rain; a sound, of a ship's foghorn—it acquires intellectual character. In the problematic situation there is a *"characteristic union of the discrete or individual and the continuous or relational."* [14] To take some element as the sign of another is possible only because one perceives certain bonds of relationship between those elements. Inference, says Dewey, "is conditioned upon an existential connection which may be called *involvement."* [15] Inference then proceeds from sign to thing signified through a perception of the way in which elements of the situation are involved with one another. What needs to be known, the "object," that is, the *objective* of knowing is how, by taking some elements of the situation as signs of others one may act in a way that will resolve what is doubtful in the situation. For Dewey there is, then, a crucial difference between knowing and the known. What *is* known is the funded products of previous inquiries, everything that is at hand, as it were, in the way of information and skills that may be used in the solution of the immediate problem. What is *to be* known is eventual: inquiry is directed to what is indeterminate in significance within the problematic situation.

"Thinking" is an imaginative projection of the possible alternate ways of acting in an indeterminate situation which might change that situation into a determinate one. "The heart of the entire theory developed in this work," says Dewey, "is that the resolution of an indeterminate situation is the end, in

14. *The Quest for Certainty* (New York: Minton, Balch and Co., 1929), p. 234.
15. *Logic*, p. 278.

the sense in which 'end' means *end-in-view* and in the sense in which it means *close.*" [16]

It is easy to see how this conception of the role of thought in solving problems might have been carried over from an analysis of the deliberative process which eventuates in a moral decision. In our practical actions we are always dealing with particular situations which require a specific decision. For Dewey all genuine problem solving is of this sort. Each problematic situation is unique and requires its own particular resolution. Even though the problem is one, say, in mathematics or in theoretical physics, yet it is always a specific problem in a particular setting or context that demands a solution. We do not solve problems in general though a solution of the problem may often have general implications, i.e., the solution may be relevant for dealing with similar instances. For Dewey the paradigm of all inquiry would be the way we deal with a case in law. The procedures of the law do not come into operation unless some particular case is brought before the court. It is this concrete instance which is dealt with and about which a decision is reached. The individual case is also treated as an example: it is argued with respect for precedent and with regard to precedent. But judgment "is *individual*, since it is concerned with unique qualitative situations." [17] It is in this sense that all final judgments in *any* field of inquiry are "practical": they are always immediately concerned with individual cases and embody a decision to act in some particular way.

Although the direct object of inquiry is understanding, the outcome—if the inquiry is successful—is a greater measure of control. In both respects action of some sort is involved. In the first phase, that of inquiry itself, the relevant activities are the making of observations, the formulation and reformulation of working hypotheses, the deduction of possible consequences from these hypotheses and the testing of them in various ways. Taken together, these activities involve what Dewey calls an "existential reconstruction" of the situation. The process of inquiry, when it is successful, results in a *judgment*, the "settlement of an *issue* because it decides existential conditions in their bearing upon further activities: the essence of the significance of

16. *Logic*, pp. 157–58.
17. *Logic*, p. 283.

any state of facts." [18] But the judgment is not merely an outcome of inquiry, it also serves to direct future actions. In this way too an existential transformation of the situation will occur. What is *logical* about this total process is the *means* employed to clear up the significance of the situation. This significance is expressed in the final judgment. What is *practical* is the subsequent course of action prescribed by the conclusion drawn from the inquiry, a course of action directed by the final judgment. Every actual case of inquiry has both a theoretical and a practical phase. It is for this reason, that inquiry is "instrumental," that it is a means of control. Inquiry enables us to substitute intelligent for blind or willful behavior; when the perception of future consequences informs present action, what we are doing now becomes meaningful and our future more secure. Because the use of intelligence always imbues present activities with fuller significance it yields a higher degree of understanding and control: control of the *present*, for the inquirer is not a magician who compels the occurrence of events.

These two contentions, that an existential transformation of the situation is involved in the process of inquiry and that the final judgment resulting from an inquiry prescribes some further action of a practical sort, have bothered Dewey's critics no end. Of course, where apparatus is set up and an experiment is performed, an existential transformation has occurred. But are there not many problems of a character such that there is no need for anything of the sort? As for the second kind of activity, that subsequent to the conclusion of an inquiry, why should one always have to do something further about it, why can't one consider the issue settled and let it go at that? Why should a case at law where the "judgment" requires a subsequent "execution" be a paradigm for all inquiry? Isn't it the fact that there are many occasions where problems are solved but no further action is called for?

What Dewey means by an existential transformation has often been misunderstood. Professor H. S. Thayer, for instance, adduces the case of a child placed in a maze. Except for the slight wear and tear caused by the child's walking around in it, nothing whatever has happened to the maze itself and the wear and tear, he rightly concludes, does not seem to have much

18. *Logic*, pp. 120–21.

relevance to a solution of the problem. And he is also right in concluding, "The maze is still a maze, though *we* may have knowledge enabling us to adjust and behave in such a way that the maze does not create a problematic situation for us." [19]

It is true that philosophers have a peculiar talent for falling into absurdities. In the realm of possibility they often become Don Quixotes of the intellectual world. But their absurdities are rarely trivial. Their penchant is for going wrong in a big way. It is fair to assume, then, that the absurdity may not be on Dewey's side. After all, what does he say? What he says—and Professor Thayer quotes this passage—is that inquiry effects an "*existential* transformation and reconstruction of the material with which it deals; the result of the transformation, when it is grounded, being conversion of an indeterminate problematic situation into a determinate resolved one." [20]

Yet, Professor Thayer proceeds to ask:

> Can differences in human response and behavior be rightly said to constitute existential transformation and reconstruction of the *materials* of (in this case) the conditions imposed by the maze? Can the maze conditions be said to have been reshaped or modified? Would not the "transformation" or "reconstruction" rather be exhibited or located in human responses and human behavior in this case? . . . To say that the material of inquiry is human behavior is to start off on the path to subjectivism and Dewey can hardly be accused of wanting to do that.[21]

Here is a nice example of begging the question with a word. Dewey's actual contention is that as such a situation cannot be characterized as either "objective" or "subjective." There is no fixed boundary between an organism and the environment. Transactions are going on in a situation wherein the organism and certain components of the environment are continually interacting. The live creature in his environment is always in a "situation" which is being existentially transformed. In this situation, where the child is in a maze, what is relevant to Dewey's logical theory is only the type of existential transformation that moves in a certain direction. If the situation is indeter-

19. H. S. Thayer, *The Logic of Pragmatism: An Examination of Dewey's Logic* (New York: Humanities Press, 1952), p. 179.
20. Thayer, *Logic of Pragmatism*, pp. 176–77.
21. Thayer, *Logic of Pragmatism*, pp. 179–80.

minate it may become also problematic, that is, indeterminate with respect to its significance. If it is problematic the individual is challenged to *do* something about the problem. What he does or can do depends on what kind of a situation it is. But in any case, something or other has to be changed and one of the things that *always* has to be done is to change one's mind. As a good behaviorist Dewey would say that looking into various alleys before one goes down them for possible clues to the way out, choosing this route as the better thing to try, etc., are existential transformations which differ from the wear and tear in being operational, essential means to a solution of the problem.[22]

Turning now to the second contention, is it true that every problem prescribes some subsequent action? In one sense the answer to this question is obvious because of the way that Dewey describes the doubt-inquiry situation. As he defines it, every judgment involves some sort of execution. To take an example of the simplest kind: in solving a crossword puzzle, having arrived at the conclusion that a certain word would be the correct one to fill a particular gap, we "put it down" or write it in. Whether this is done in one's head or by writing it out makes no difference. There is always an act of some sort which should follow, as its embodiment, a terminal decision. To throw away the completed puzzle and turn to other things is in a different way a terminus of that activity. Like crossword puzzles, so law cases, medical treatments, scientific projects, all come to an end. Whether completed or not, we can speak of them as having a conclusion. Suppose, however, that one is a *regular* solver of crossword puzzles, or a lawyer, a physician, a scientist. What one is now involved in is a continuum of inquiry. A body of funded knowledge and skills is gradually built up. Wherever there is a persistence of interests new problems grow out of funded knowledge that is established. Many communities may be identified in this way—the lawyer, the physicist, the chess expert, the historian and the philatelist—to mention random instances—each belongs to one of these communities. In the sciences, in fields of scholarship, and in the professions this continuum of inquiry reaches its highest development. Here it

22. For a more detailed analysis of Dewey's conception of experience and a reply to some of his other critics see Gail Kennedy, "Dewey's Concept of Experience: Determinate, Indeterminate, and Problematic," *Journal of Philosophy*, LVI (1959), 801–14.

becomes obvious that the results of prior inquiries are necessary means to the solution of certain subsequent problems. This is a second, and most important, way which it is obvious, from Dewey's viewpoint, that subsequent action is prescribed. As Charles S. Peirce once put it, every idea is a little person indefinitely capable of growth.

To engage in the processes of inquiry is, then, the exercise of an art in the generic sense of that term. And corresponding to this art there is a science: "If thinking is the way in which deliberate reorganization of experience is secured, then logic is such a clarified and systematized formulation of the procedures of thinking as will enable the desired reconstruction to go on more economically and efficiently." [23] It would be appropriate to say that Dewey's *Logic: The Theory of Inquiry* (1938) is the lineal successor of John Stuart Mill's *System of Logic: Ratiocinative and Inductive* (1843). Mill professes to discover and describe what is involved in the process of inquiry. Dewey's aim is far more radical and more original: he attempts also to show in detail that logical forms emerge within the continuum of inquiry.

> The theory, in summary form, is that all logical forms (with their characteristic properties) arise within the operation of inquiry and are concerned with control of inquiry so that it may yield warranted assertions. This conception implies much more than that logical forms are disclosed or come to light when we reflect upon processes of inquiry that are in use. Of course it means that; but it also means that the forms *originate* in operations of inquiry. To employ a convenient expression, it means that while inquiry into inquiry is the *causa cognoscendi* of logical forms, primary inquiry is itself *causa essendi* of forms which inquiry into inquiry discloses.[24]

For Dewey, to "inquire" is to act in a certain way when confronted with a problematic situation. Inquiry is a behavior pattern that has developed within a matrix of culture; to some degree it pervades our "common-sense" activities, and in the activities of scientists it has in our own culture taken on the character of an institution. Logical forms have not sprung like Minerva from the brow of Jove, they are not somehow *there* to

23. *Reconstruction in Philosophy* (New York: Henry Holt and Co., 1920), pp. 134–35.
24. *Logic*, pp. 3–4.

be discovered, on the contrary they are themselves products of thought, constructed during the process of inquiry as means of carrying out an inquiry. The logical forms we discover are funded results of prior inquiries. The history of science, then, is not merely a record of the cumulative knowledge obtained through the application of scientific methods, it is also a record of the progressive development *of* those methods.

For Dewey logical theory should be a detailed critical analysis of the actual procedures utilized wherever inquiries are successful. In this respect logic is itself an empirical science. No one else, except Charles S. Peirce, has made so thoroughgoing an effort to state what is logically involved in the concrete processes of inquiry. But he would not consider the creation of a logic a one-man, one-book job. His theory of inquiry should be open to criticism wherever it is inadequate or inaccurate in its description and analysis. And it is also corrigible because our knowledge of what is involved in inquiry will continue to improve as the sciences upon which it depends for its subject-matter are expanded and developed.

The outstanding objection to this theory is that logic is the theory of proof, not an anatomy of the processes of inquiry. Therefore, the title of Dewey's book, *Logic: The Theory of Inquiry*, is a misnomer. He has confused two quite separate things. In fact, by substituting an account of how we think for an analysis of the conditions of valid inference, he has substituted a psychological account of the processes of thinking for logic itself, a study of conditions under which valid conclusions may be drawn from given premises. This is the dread thing Germans call *psychologismus*; and to psychologize logic is to make the irretrievable error of basing logical theory on the genetic fallacy, the confusion of origin with validity—that because people do, in fact, think in certain ways these are the valid ways to do one's thinking.

In answer to the first part of this objection Dewey would say that the theory of proof is a part of logic, not the whole, and should properly be included within the more comprehensive subject-matter denoted by the phrase, theory of inquiry. The second part of the objection rests upon a misconception. While psychology as a behavioral science can of course proffer an objective description of what goes on in actual processes of inquiry this description is merely preliminary to the analytic work of the logician. The logician's task is explanatory, not descriptive. Some methods of inquiry succeed while others fail. The logician's question is, Why does this happen? An adequate logical theory would give the detailed answer.

Dewey's theory has not been as influential as it might have been because his point of view is out of fashion and it is stated in language reminiscent of his Hegelian antecedents instead of the now popular idiom of a formalized system. The dominant group among contemporary logicians has been preoccupied with the exploitation of mathematical logic and the attempt to create formally perfect artificial languages.[25] They have preferred to segregate and constrain their subject-matter by the simple device of presuming the dichotomy, logic *and* methodology. The problems of "methodology" these logicians have relegated to a separate field they usually call the philosophy of science. Dewey's theory is a standing protest against this disjunction and the implied identification of logic with the analysis of formal relations. He believes that here and elsewhere this sort of distinction, one which creates dualisms between "pure" and "applied" in science, "liberal" and "vocational" in education, etc., is the source of pseudo problems which block the progress of inquiry in any field. If logical forms do emerge within the matrix of concrete processes of inquiry, then their full significance is grasped only as we understand their functions in the promotion of inquiry. This is not a derogation of formal analysis. On the contrary, Dewey regards deduction as an essential stage in the process of inquiry. He is arguing against an exclusive preoccupation with what is in fact one part of a larger whole.

> This problem [of the relation of form to matter] is so fundamental that the way in which it is dealt with constitutes the basic ground of difference among logical theories. Those which hold there is no relation between form and matter are formalistic. They differ among themselves; some hold the doctrine that forms constitute a realm of metaphysical possibilities;

25. As an increasing number of philosophers have turned their attention to problems involved in the analysis of ordinary language, there has been a counterreaction to this exclusive preoccupation with formal logic. An example is Stephen Toulmin's book, *The Uses of Argument* (Cambridge: University Press, 1958). See also Alan Pasch, "Dewey and the Analytic Philosophers," *Journal of Philosophy*, LVI (1959), 814–26.

others that forms are syntactical relations of words in sentences.[26]

The basic difficulty, he thinks, with all these radically dualistic
theories is that having begun with a precedent independence of
form and subject-matter, they are immediately confronted with
the factitious and insoluble problems of bringing them together.
It is this dualism which has been the source of those ingenious
and futile epistemological theories (the chief stock-in-trade of
most philosophers) that attempt to answer the gratuitous question, How is knowledge possible? Gratuitous because an *adequate* theory of inquiry would obviate the need for them.[27]

Formal logic is confined to the study of those relations that
enable us to make deductions; the more comprehensive theory of
inquiry since it includes all the arts of investigation within its
scope requires a broader base.

There are, Dewey holds, four basic kinds of relations
which make the process of inquiry possible. The first is the
strictly existential relation he calls connection or involvement.

> The sudden and excessive rise of the customary level of a river
> is involved *in* heavy rain storms and involves *with* its occur-
> rence perils to life and property, impassable roads, etc. An out-
> break of bubonic plague involves a rise *in* death-rate *with*,
> perhaps, a campaign to exterminate rats. There is no need to
> multiply instances. Every case of the causal relation rests upon
> some involvement of existential conditions *with* one another in
> a joint interaction. The entire principle of functional correla-
> tions of changes rests upon involvements, as when, in the case
> of many substances, increase of heat is ground for an inference
> to their expansion; or when the volume of gases is said to be a
> function of pressure and heat. The essential consideration is
> that the relation is a strictly existential one, ultimately a mat-
> ter of the brute structure of things.[28]

26. *Logic*, pp. 371–72.
27. In a brilliant final chapter of the *Logic*, "The Logic of Inquiry
and Philosophies of Knowledge," Dewey argues that each of these types
of epistemological theory has its point of origin "in a one-sided selection"
from the total pattern "of what actually takes place in controlled inquiry."
In an important sense, therefore, the title of this paper is a misnomer;
since, for Dewey, logic, as a theory of inquiry, is autonomous, it does not
need to be supported by a "theory of knowledge" derived from metaphysical presuppositions.
28. *Logic*, p. 278.

When, within a problematic situation, relations of involvement are perceived, it is possible to take one element within the situation as the sign of another. What was originally identified as an object is now treated as a *datum*. When this is done, a new relation has supervened. This he calls inference. The passage from sign to what is signified can take place without language —as when an animal flees when it scents the hunter. In this case the relation is that of a *natural* sign (the scent) to the thing signified, the hunter. With the institution of language, complex inferences based upon the discernment of intricate relations of involvement translated into correspondent symbol-relations become possible. And, with the introduction of discourse, a third level of relationship, that of implication, i.e., the relation which symbol-meanings bear to one another *as* symbol-meanings is also instituted.

The investigation of relations of implication constitutes in itself a field of inquiry. This is the subject-matter of all purely abstract reasoning. When the possible relations among symbol-meanings are investigated on their own account, the subject-matter of the inquiry is formal logic or mathematics. When the possible relations among symbol-meanings are investigated with a view to their eventual application to the solution of existential problems, then the subject-matter is some theory of the kind we designate by terms such as "theoretical physics," "economic theory," etc. There may be theories in this sense about virtually anything: chess or gardening, advertising or foreign policy. Theories, however, are always "abstract," because they deal with universals, i.e., mere possibilities. For inquiries concerned with problems of matters of fact, still a fourth mode of relation is essential, the relation of these symbol-meanings to existence. This relation Dewey calls "reference." The four key types of relation in Dewey's logical theory are, then: *connection* or *involvement*—brute existential relations of existing things; *inference*—the relation of existing things taken as signs to things signified—which is of two sorts, preverbal and as translated into symbol-meanings; *implication*—the relations of symbol-meanings to one another as such; and *reference*—the relation of symbol-meanings to existential subject-matter. It should be noted that *both* involvement and sign-signified are existential relations. These types of relation are the basis for all modes of inquiry. Dewey's logical theory is an attempt to work out in detail the way in which each of them is made use of in the solving of problems.

To attempt an analysis of the nature of inquiry in these terms results in important and, also, controversial conclusions. On this theory, all knowledge wherever an inquiry is instituted is of *relations*; knowledge gained from inquiry is inherently contextual. Things as given in their bare immediacy are what they are. They may arrest our attention and have some emotional impact upon us. They may be recognized or apprehended as familiar objects; but they cannot enter into the process of inquiry, become ingredients of *knowing*, unless they are taken as signs or things signified. Certain qualities of the object will within a given context be significant and others not. When engaged in an investigation, we are not interested in the entire object but only in those qualities or attributes of it that are presumably relevant to a solution of the problem. Certain traits of the object are taken as indicating connections or involvements. In doing this we substitute *data* for objects. Otherwise, any attempted explanation begs the question by an appeal to "occult" qualities: Henry has few colds because he is so healthy; in the United States there is a high standard of living because we are an industrious and enterprising people. We succumb to the fallacy of converting eventual consequences into antecedent existences. Comparably, what is *known* about symbol-meanings is their contextual relations and nothing else. Triangles—when made, say, of wood—can be seen or touched, but the propositions about them are all concerned with the relations—of the sum of their interior angles to right angles, of their areas to those of rectangles, etc. And when symbol-meanings are combined to form theories that may be applied to an existential subject-matter, what is *known* is again a relation. "Reference," as Dewey calls it, is the degree of correspondence between a relational structure of symbol-meanings and a set of sign-signified (inferential) relations which in their turn depend upon a complex of brute existential connections or involvements. What experimental inquiry into matters of fact is concerned with is this threefold correspondence.

In order to express this threefold correspondence certain types of propositions are required. Each of these has its functional role in the process of experimental inquiry. "Propositions of the kind called particular represent the most rudimentary form of propositions of *subject* content. They are propositions which qualify a singular, *this*, by a quality proceeding from an operation performed by means of a sense organ—for example, 'This is sour, or soft, or red, etc.' " [29] Singular propositions are those which "determine *this* to be one of a kind." Examples would be "This is a diamond," or "This is an oak tree," etc. Generic propositions express generalizations about the properties of kinds and their relations to one another, such as "All diamonds will (under condition 'c,' i.e., a scratch test) prove to be harder than any other known substance." Universal propositions divide into two groups, those that have no existential import, mathematical propositions such as $2 + 2 = 4$, and those which *indirectly* do have it, universal hypothetical propositions that are "framed with reference to the possibility of ultimate existential application." For example, the Newtonian law of gravitation is intended to be applicable to physical events; therefore its constituent universals, the abstract characters "mass," "distance," etc., are related to one another within the proposition in the *limited* way that will make them relevant to the investigation of such events.

For lack of space it is necessary to pass over Dewey's intricate account of the genesis and functional interrelationships of these types of propositions—with the exception of one crucial point. That is his distinction between generic propositions and the universal hypothetical propositions that express physical laws. Dewey's case against formalism, it has been noted, is that logical theories of this type postulate an antecedent independence of form and matter which makes any application of logic to a concrete subject-matter unintelligible. Yet, these logicians go on to presume that there is a connection by employing such phrases as "logic *and* scientific method" or "applied logic." "Both expressions serve to beg the issue, or at least to disguise the fact that there is an issue. In the case of the seemingly innocent phrase 'applied logic,' the real issue is whether or not the expression has any meaning at all when logic is defined in terms of forms entirely independent of matter. For the issue is precisely whether such forms *can* be applied to matter. If they cannot, applied logic is a meaningless term." And, he adds: "It

29. *Logic*, p. 289.

is precisely on this fundamental matter of conditions of application that the formalistic theory breaks down." [30]

Unfortunately, our language is systematically ambiguous in the expression of these two sorts of propositions. The same set of words, e.g., "All men are mortal," may in one context express a universal proposition and as such have no reference to existing creatures called men, and in another it may state a generalization based upon biological and other data. A proposition such as that expressing the Newtonian law of gravitation may have a dual meaning: it can be understood as the conclusion of mathematical reasoning from a certain set of postulates and also as a generalization used to describe (in part) and to predict a certain class of events—what in fact has happened and will happen—as, for instance, eclipses of the moon. This becomes clear if the proposition is restated in hypothetical form, "If $x$ is a man then $x$ is mortal." This proposition does not state anything about matters of fact, it has no existential import, but merely expresses a relation of the symbol-meanings "man" and "mortal." These two types of propositions are functionally related: inferential reasoning would hardly get beyond rule of thumb, the empirical lore of the hunter, the sailor or the craftsman, without recourse to the procedures of deduction. Deduction serves as the intermediate process by means of which the possible significance of observed connections or involvements is explored. When successfully employed, it deepens and extends our comprehension of events. A classic illustration is the way in which Newton deduced proofs of Galileo's law for the acceleration of freely falling bodies and Kepler's laws of planetary motion from a basic equation for the determination of gravitational forces. Thus generic propositions based upon inferred connections or involvements may be translated into a set of universal propositions from which deductions can be made; and, in turn, the conclusions from these deductions may be interpreted as a set of corresponding generic propositions which can be subjected to the tests of observation and experiment. What is being tested is the evidential value of certain data taken as signs. The inductive methods used by scientists are essentially devices which attempt to eliminate wrong inferences, i.e., misleading or

30. *Logic*, p. 375.

false ideas of those connections or brute involvements that happen to exist. Inferences are warranted to the extent that, on the evidence, they accurately represent the structural and causal patterns of events. It follows that propositions *as they function within inquiry* are neither true nor false. For Dewey propositions are instrumental to the solution of a problem—a proposition is literally something proposed. It has the sort of meaning indicated by such locutions as, "I've a proposition to make to you" or "What are you going to do about Smith's proposition?" *Within the context of inquiry* propositions are made use of as operative means for solving the problem. But means are efficacious or they are not; it would be misleading to designate them in any other way. Within this context the belief that propositions are true or false is irrelevant to the procedures of inquiry. A proposition might be "true" enough in the sense that it could be validated or warranted if it were itself the conclusion of an inquiry, and yet not be at all helpful, or even be positively misleading when put to use for the solution of the problem at hand. Logically, both kinds of general propositions function within the inquiry process as instruments of investigation, not its subject-matter; "*things and events*," Dewey says, "are the material and objects of inquiry, and propositions are *means* in inquiry, so that as conclusions of a given inquiry they become means of carrying on further inquiries. Like other means they are modified and improved in the course of use." [31]

If means cannot legitimately be called true or false neither can things and events. And universal propositions as the expressions of symbol-meanings have no existential reference. The relation among them is that of implication. When such a relation is asserted as a conclusion from given premises, it should properly be characterized as valid or invalid rather than true or false. What remains is the relation between generic propositions and the objects of knowledge to which they refer. It is to this correspondence that the terms true and false apply. The relation constituting truth or falsity is itself one of correspondence between two other relations: the existential relation of sign and thing signified and the existential relation of connection or involvement to which the inference refers. Inferences, however, are of two sorts. When grounded on merely empirical knowl-

31. "Experience, Knowledge and Value," p. 573.

edge an inference is precarious and unintelligible. It owes its force to the cumulative effect of habit. As previously noted, such inferences do not necessarily require the use of meaning-symbols. They occur wherever any natural object or event is taken as sign of another. This power we call sagacity and to a slight degree animals have it. In human beings sagacity is the parent of common sense—and also of dogma and superstition, since un-guided inference is bound to the cues of habit. Doubtless it never rains but it shines, yet the dog who snaps at his image in the water and loses his bone is following the same principle. Or, as Mark Twain put it, the cat who once sits on a hot stove lid won't do that again, but he won't sit on a cold stove either.

There is a vivid illustration of the difference between un-guided and guided inference in William James's *Psychology*:

> I am sitting in a railroad-car, waiting for the train to start. It is winter, and the stove fills the car with pungent smoke. The brakeman enters, and my neighbor asks him to "stop that stove smoking." He replies that it will stop entirely as soon as the car begins to move. "Why so?" asks the passenger. "It *always* does," replies the brakeman. It is evident from this "always" that the connection between car moving and smoke stopping was a purely empirical one in the brakeman's mind, bred of habit. But, if the passenger had been an acute reasoner, he, with no experience of what that stove always did, might have anticipated the brakeman's reply, and spared his own question. Had he singled out of all the numerous points involved in a stove's not smoking the one special point of smoke pouring freely out of the stove-pipe's mouth, he would, probably, owing to the few associations of that idea, have been immediately re-minded of the law that a fluid passes more rapidly out of a pipe's mouth if another fluid be at the same time streaming over that mouth; and then the rapid draught of air over the stove-pipe's mouth, which is one of the points involved in the car's motion, would immediately have occurred to him.[32]

When an inference is based upon some theory it is complex; in this case certain conclusions from a group of universal proposi-tions are given a reference to existential relations of connection and involvement by means of the corresponding generic proposi-tions. In the illustration cited by James the effect of singling out "of all the numerous points involved in a stove's not smoking

32. James, *Psychology*, II, 342.

the one special point of smoke pouring freely out of the stove-pipe's mouth" is to radically alter the inference. It is no longer the "putting of a car in motion that prevents the stove from smoking" but some consequence of putting it in motion which explains the observed connection. Thus, in simple inference the generic proposition has a one-way reference—to existential relations of connection and involvement. In James's illustration the simple inference leads to the generic proposition: "If the car is put in motion, the smoking of the stove will stop." When, however, some *theory* is involved, the generic proposition has a complex mediatory function. The initially observed connection suggests that there is a body of universal propositions from which a relevant generalization may be deduced. This generalization is then incorporated in a new generic proposition: "When cars are put in motion, the smoking of their stoves will stop, because a fluid passes more rapidly out of a pipe's mouth if another fluid be at the same time streaming over that mouth." The inference now is not: "If the car is put in motion, the smoking of the stove will stop" but "If the law that a fluid passes more rapidly out of a pipe's mouth if another fluid be at the same time streaming over that mouth" is applicable, then, when cars are put in motion, the smoking of the stoves will stop. In this second form of inference generic propositions are the means of referring universal propositions to observed relations of connection or involvement.

In simple inference there is one step, the perception of a connection between starting the car and the fact that the stove ceases to smoke. In complex inference there is an additional step, the perception that starting the car alters the relation between the flow of air over the mouth of the chimney and the flow of smoke up the chimney. It is this step that suggests the relevant physical law. The reference of a generic proposition to things and events is, however, *always* to some degree provisional and tentative—empirical knowledge no matter how well grounded is still fallible. To affirm or deny the reference of a generic proposition is to make a judgment; and when the judgment is based upon sufficient evidence it expresses what Dewey would prefer to call—not "truth"—but "warranted assertibility."

In what sense now can one understand the "reference" of a generic proposition to an existential relation of things or events?

Though able philosophers have said it, the relation of sign and thing signified as expressed in a generic proposition is surely not a mirror-image of some existential relation. If this were so, how would we compare the mirror-image with its original? And why should we choose to "see through a glass darkly"? It is the ambition of those who seek the truth to come out from their cave into the sun where they can clearly perceive things as they are. Sign and thing signified as terms of discourse are different in kind from the existential relation to which they refer.

There are many meanings of the chameleonic term "meaning" in Dewey's writings, each depending on the context in which it is used. But the focal conception of meaning is that of meaning as idea. Professor Wienpahl's statement of it is:

> We come now to the central explication of "meaning" in Dewey's theory: *meaning as idea.* Meaning in this sense is the non-overt or implicit response an organism makes to any other response, overt or implicit, which acts as stimulus. For example, when we say, "What does this mean for this organism?" we might as well say, "What implicit responses is the organism making as a result of this stimulus?" [33]

A meaning is, then, not an image—it is an expectation. As Charles S. Peirce stated it:

> Consider what effects, that might conceivably have practical bearings, we conceive the object of our conception to have. Then, our conception of these effects is the whole of our conception of the object. [34]

Peirce states his "pragmatic" definition of meaning in terms of the behavior of the object of our conception; a correlative definition of meaning by reference to the subject doing the conceiving is the "operational" one offered by P. W. Bridgman:

> In general, we mean by any concept nothing more than a set of operations: *the concept is synonymous with the corresponding set of operations.* If the concept is physical, as of length, the operations are actual physical operations, namely, those by which length is measured; or if the concept is mental,

33. Paul Wienpahl, "Dewey's Theory of Language and Meaning," in *John Dewey: Philosopher of Science and Freedom,* ed. Sidney Hook (New York: Dial Press, 1950), p. 277.
34. "How to Make Our Ideas Clear," in *Collected Papers of Charles Sanders Peirce,* Vol. V, eds. Charles Hartshorne and Paul Weiss (Cambridge: Harvard University Press, 1934), p. 258.

as of mathematical continuity, the operations are mental operations, namely, those by which we determine whether a given aggregate of magnitudes is continuous.[35]

Both definitions, as they are stated, are incomplete since "effects, that might conceivably have practical bearings," implies some anticipatory operation, even if it were merely an act of observing, and to say that "any concept" is "nothing more than a set of operations" would be nonsense, unless the operations were intended to have anticipated consequences.

From this conception of meaning, there follows as a corollary, Peirce says, a definition of what is meant by truth and by reality:

> The opinion which is fated to be ultimately agreed to by all who investigate, is what we mean by the truth, and the object represented in this opinion is the real.[36]

The "truth" as here conceived implies that the processes of investigation, if pushed far enough, will give one certain answer to every meaningful question. In actual practice, however, many inquiries are interminable and the truth value of any particular belief must depend upon the indefinite prolongation of that inquiry. Characteristically, applications of the method of science do not result in certainty but in progressive approximations to an eventual consensus. This is Peirce's doctrine of "fallibilism," that all beliefs, no matter how certain they may seem, are subject to revision as a consequence of the results of further inquiry. If every thought of an object is of "conceivable effects," then every thought is the expression of an expectancy—"what a thing means is simply the habits it involves." The rational purport of a conception lies in the future; implicitly, it is a prediction.

The method of science requires, then, the establishment of a continuum of inquiry, and a continuum of inquiry which is adequate to the purpose of a community of inquirers. No isolated individual, however intelligently he applies "scientific method," can be sure of his results. The objectivity of those

35. *The Logic of Modern Physics* (New York: Macmillan Co., 1932), p. 5.
36. "How to Make Our Ideas Clear," p. 268. Dewey quotes this statement in the *Logic* (p. 345n.), calling it the "best definition of *truth* from the logical standpoint which is known to me."

results depends upon the fact that the methods used are public and can be repeated. The growing consensus of opinion that ensues wherever inquiry is indefinitely prolonged is what establishes the warrantable assertibility of generic propositions.

The "picture" theory, or representational notion of correspondence, is inconsistent with a pragmatic definition of meaning, since operations are distinct from and different from their consequences. On this theory, the meaning of correspondence of an idea to a fact would be, as Dewey says, that "of *answering*, as a key answers to conditions imposed by a lock, or as two correspondents 'answer' each other; or, in general, as a reply is an adequate answer to a question or a criticism—as, in short, a *solution* answers the requirements of a *problem*." [37]

It also follows that the object of knowledge is not antecedent, but eventual. Perhaps the most frequent criticism of his logical theory is based on the objection: If inquiry is a process of discovering existent connections or involvements, does it not follow that the object of knowledge, what is to be known, is already there, is prior to inquiry? How, for instance, can such statements as "Caesar crossed the Rubicon in 49 B.C." or "A supernova has been observed in the extragalactic nebula Andromeda" (whether warrantably assertible or not) *refer* to anything but past events? And if they do, how can what one knows be called "eventual"? This question and the criticism it implies rests upon a misunderstanding of Dewey's theory. [38] First of all, *every* inquiry involves a reference to the past. All inquiries require the use of memory. Every reference to objects or events remote in space involves the past. If one now says, "There are tigers in India" one's conclusion is based on some evidence or other that tigers have been encountered in that country and are presumably not now extinct. And, since inquiry is a temporal process, even a conclusion dealing with something "present" must *now* refer to an immediate past. How, also, is one to understand inquiries concerning the future—is the predicted eclipse of the sun somehow already "there" in the future as Caesar's action is "there" in the past waiting to be known?

37. "Propositions, Warranted Assertibility, and Truth," *Journal of Philosophy*, XXXVIII (1941), 178.

38. For one of Dewey's later efforts to make his position on this point clear see his reply to A. E. Murphy in "Experience, Knowledge and Value," pp. 565–68.

Merely to ask these questions shows that a false analogy is involved. They are based upon the tacit assumption that knowing is like a voyage of discovery, newfound islands drop below the horizon while others rise into view. The perdurability of the islands is here confused with the transiency of the voyage. Of course, what is known may be something about things and events past or future (could they ever be in the present?) but what is it that one knows?

The object of knowledge is the objective, or end-in-view, of the inquiry process, but that "object" is not itself a thing or event; it is the answer to a question, the solution of a problem. The object of knowledge is that which is *to be* known. An assertion may refer to things which exist and events which occur anywhere and at any time. To know whether the assertion is warrantable or not and, if warrantable, to what degree it is warrantable requires a preliminary inquiry; and it is that knowledge which is the object of inquiry. On Dewey's view, this problem is generated by an ambiguity in the use of words. The confusion results because in ordinary usage the word "object" is employed when used as a noun to designate both aim or motive and an event or thing and when used as an adjective to signify both an end-in-view and that which exists independently of the mind. The object of knowledge does not duplicate natural objects or events. To say that is to relapse into the picture theory of meaning. The subject-matter of an inquiry may be, for instance, a man named Caesar who once lived and performed certain actions; whereas the object of knowledge is a warrantable assertion to the effect that one of those actions is that he did (or did not) on a certain date cross a river named the Rubicon. It should be clear that *what* is known is the warrantability of an assertion based, in this case, on evidence drawn from sources—manuscripts, monuments, etc.—of the kind usually employed by historiographers. Dewey does not see that there is a paradox here and if his critics persist in alleging that there is one, all he can do is ask them to examine once more what actually goes on. Whether or not the object of knowledge is "eventual," in Dewey's sense of that term, comes down in the end to a question of fact. As he says,

We know whenever we do know; that is, whenever our inquiry leads to conclusions which settle the problem out of which it grew. This truism is the end of the whole matter—upon the condition that we frame our theory of knowledge in accord with the pattern set by experimental methods.[39]

At this juncture Dewey's formal statement should be recalled:

> *Inquiry is the controlled or directed transformation of an indeterminate situation into one that is so determinate in its constituent distinctions and relations as to convert the elements of the original situation into a unified whole.*[40]

From this statement it follows that every "problematic situation" is a particular event, and every problem is always a specific case. It is some individual inquirer here and now who has *a* problem; and it is *this* individual situation in which he is involved. Hence, the *final* judgment he arrives at is about "a qualitative existential whole which is unique." [41] "Judgment, in distinction from propositions . . . is *individual*, since it is concerned with unique qualitative situations." [42] Of course, the solution of a particular problem may be the proof of a theorem in mathematics, or it may be the discovery of a physical law, but to prove a theorem or to discover a law does not exhaust the work of science. In one sense of the term, scientific knowledge is a funded result of past inquiry: it yields a growing comprehension of the structure and order of nature. This knowledge is a genuine good, but is it the final good? A scientist may enjoy the contemplation of the partial structure but he is not satisfied with that. He is involved in a *continuum* of inquiry—as problems are solved new ones are generated. What is known serves as stimulus and means to further knowing. What is *to be* known always occurs, as a specific problem.

Peirce's statement that "an idea is a little person," it is something capable of growth, follows directly from his definition of meaning: when he says, "our conception of these effects is the *whole* of our conception of the object," he implies, naturally, as that object is *now* conceived; but in the course of experience each new encounter with the object is likely to have new

---

39. *The Quest for Certainty*, p. 198. Dewey quotes this passage in his reply to Professor Murphy.
40. *Logic*, pp. 104–5.
41. *Logic*, p. 122.
42. *Logic*, p. 283.

effects, and experimentation is a deliberate attempt to evoke them. Our conception of the object will develop as the apprehension of its effects is enlarged. Every encounter is for the inquirer a particular experience. Our conception of the object is on Peirce's definition one of conceivable effects having a practical bearing, some or all of which might occur upon any particular occasion. What we *already know* is what in general to expect when the object is encountered. As Dewey says, the "full and eventual reality of knowledge is carried in the individual case, not in general laws isolated from use in giving an individual case its meaning." [43]

The distinction between pure and applied knowledge may be made in two different ways: *1)* between logic and mathematics, which are concerned only with the possible relations of implication between symbol-meanings, and all knowledge which has to do with existential subject-matter; or, *2)* between sciences such as physics, chemistry, biology, etc., and those sciences (or arts) such as engineering, medicine, etc., which deal directly with immediate problems of a "practical" sort. The first of these distinctions is harmless. It is the second which is almost invariably meant when a distinction is made between pure and applied science, and it is with the invidious use of this distinction that Dewey is concerned. The pure sciences it is implied are higher: they are theoretical, they are disinterested and carry with them the aura of certainty whereas practical making and doing is relegated "to a secondary and relatively irrational realm." But this is not a logical distinction between two different kinds of inquiry: there is no essential difference between the methods used by the astronomer and the engineer, the biochemist and the physician; each is trying to solve his problems in the same way. The distinction, when it is invidious, is a moral one. What is being judged is the worth of these inquiries. The distinction is justified only when it is used to enforce the warning against two dangers: the narrow-minded concentration upon immediate "cash" results at the expense of more fundamental types of research—which is an error of judgment; and the perversion of scientific research by using it to serve the exclusive interests of an economic or political interest group. These are ways of impeding or limiting inquiry; they are not reasons for derogating the applied sciences. And, in fact, new suggestions and enlarged perspectives are frequently brought to the pure sciences when they are used as a means of dealing with practical issues.[44] A just view of the moral function of knowledge leads to the conclusion that all science is ultimately applied. What, after all, is the most inclusive humane use of knowledge? Here is Dewey's answer:

> It signifies events understood, events so discriminately penetrated by thought that mind is literally at home in them. It means comprehension, or inclusive reasonable agreement. What is sometimes termed "applied" science, may then be more truly science than is what is conventionally called pure science. For it is directly concerned with not just instrumentalities, but instrumentalities at work in effecting modifications of existence in behalf of conclusions that are reflectively preferred. Thus conceived the characteristic subject-matter of knowledge consists of fulfilling objects, which as fulfillments are connected with a history to which they give character. Thus conceived, knowledge exists in engineering, medicine and the social arts more adequately than it does in mathematics and physics. Thus conceived, history and anthropology are scientific in a sense in which bodies of information that stop short with general formulae are not.[45]

Obviously, our value judgments are affected in many different ways by the growth of scientific knowledge and the impact of technological developments that are rapidly and cumulatively altering our whole mode of life. But there are also a number of ways in which value judgments are involved in carrying on a process of inquiry:   A) every inquiry requires as a necessary part of the means of carrying it out the institution of standards;   B) every inquiry necessitates practical decisions; C) every inquiry to some degree has a moral effect because, like every habit-forming activity, it modifies the character of the inquirer; and   D) every inquiry results in overt consequences, direct and indirect, which may be considered desirable or undesirable.

---

44. The history of science is filled with examples. One of the more recent and important is the "by-products" for pure science of the attempt to produce an atom bomb.

45. *Experience and Nature*, pp. 161–62.

A) No inquiry can proceed without the institution of standards. For example, that "*x* is really red," or that "*x* is approximately one million light years distant from the earth" are not mere statements of fact: *x* may "look" red and not "really" be so; while some time ago, astronomers decided that their calculations of the distances of the extragalactic nebulae required a scale revision factor of rather more than two—the distances are now thought to be over twice as great. The meanings of terms such as "redness" and "distance" are defined through an evaluation of the operational procedures by which the redness of *x* or its distance is determined. The criteria used to formulate these standards may be lax, as they often are in ordinary practical inquiries, or they may, as in the physical sciences, have a high degree of precision; but without these standards of judgment no inquiry could proceed.

In any science the formulation of standards may be complicated by the fact that the terms used are infected with values derived from ordinary language, a language which is loaded with the value judgments of the particular culture. The "conflict of science and religion," which has been going on at least since Anaxagoras described the sun, a "heavenly" body, as a great hot stone, is one between the scientific interpretation of phenomena and the whole pattern of culture. Every science is affected by it—predominantly astronomy and physics in the sixteenth and seventeenth centuries, geology and biology in the nineteenth, psychology and the social sciences today. Such key terms —all used to denote standards within the sciences and all suffused with value judgments derived from the pattern of culture —as "solar system," "geologic time scale," "species," "sex," "race," "social class" are just a few of those around which the conflict of science with society has turned. We associate with them such names (a motley group) as Galileo, Lyell, Darwin, Freud—and Lysenko, Hitler, Stalin. Here is, of course, one of the outstanding impediments to scientific inquiry.

B) Applied science, Dewey says, is concerned with "instrumentalities at work in effecting modifications of existence in behalf of conclusions that are reflectively preferred." Every practical judgment thus expresses a choice among values. If the individual wishes to find out what is wrong with a car that has broken down or the community supports research on poliomyelitis, it is obvious enough that an evaluative judgment instigates and supports the inquiry; what should be equally obvious is that evaluations are present and operative in every inquiry. There is always something or other that an inquiry is supposed to be "good for"; how otherwise could there be a "problem" and what would be one's "purpose" in solving it? Wherever there is a genuinely problematic situation the inquirer is affirming that here is a real problem and preferences will be expressed, such that (under the circumstances) some modes of procedure in attempting to solve it will be better than others. No matter what the context in which the inquiry occurs, whether it be getting a stalled car to go or a problem in theoretical physics, evaluations of this kind constantly occur. In this sense all cases of problem solving are a mode of practical activity and the kind of value judgments Dewey calls "practical" are continually being made.

c) That every inquiry has an effect upon the inquirer follows immediately from Dewey's definition of a problematic situation. Every situation, as we have seen, is a complex set of transactions between the live creature and his environment, a process in which both are continually being transformed. Inquiry is the attempt to deliberately organize an indeterminate situation: "The institution of qualitative individual existential situations consisting of ordered sequences and coexistences is the goal of all existential inquiry." [46] In part it is the self that is reorganized. If the self is a constituent part of the situation it too is put in order. The effort to solve a problem is a choice, and just as each judicial decision contributes to the establishment of a precedent, so every judgment expresses a new habit. If habits are formed, the person is modified.

Is there then no difference between scientific or ordinary practical judgments and those we call moral ones? There is, but it is a relative difference. As Dewey states it:

> The formation of a self new in some respect or some degree is, then, involved in every genuine act of inquiry. In the cognitive situation as such the overt and explicit emphasis falls upon the resolution of the situation by means of change produced in environing conditions, whereas in the distinctively moral situation it falls upon the reconstruction of the self as

46. *Logic*, p. 462.

the distinctively demanded means. But the difference is in any case one of *emphasis*. There are occasions when for the proper conduct of knowing as the controlling interest, the problem becomes that of reconstruction of the *self* engaged in inquiry. This happens when the pursuit of inquiry, according to conditions set by the need of following subject-matter where it leads, requires willingness to surrender a theory dear to the heart of an inquirer and willingness to forego reaching the conclusion he would have preferred to reach. On the other hand, the problem of reconstructing the self cannot be solved unless inquiry takes into account reconstitution of existing conditions, a matter which poses a problem in which scientific knowledge is indispensable for effecting an outcome satisfying the needs of the situation.[47]

D) Finally, every inquiry has overt consequences direct and indirect about which a value judgment may be made. This is obvious. It is a corollary of the statement that every inquiry necessitates practical decisions. Just as one may approve, or disapprove, of the proposal that a research project be established with the end in view of discovering how to produce an atomic bomb, so one may approve a consequence of that inquiry—that new and enormous sources of power for the uses of a peacetime economy are now available.

Science, Dewey tells us, is "the uniquely instrumental art." But this does not mean to him that scientific inquiry is "neutral" and "value-free." On the contrary, the method of intelligence whenever employed is used as a means to the achievement of some end. All purposeful activity is instigated and controlled by an apprehension of what is valuable in that particular situation. Scientific inquiry could hardly be an exception. And scientific inquiry has effects that are constantly modifying our value judgments in every area of human concern. No greater absurdity ever passed itself off as a truism than the remark: Science has nothing to say about values, it merely tells us how things occur.

47. "Experience, Knowledge and Value," p. 587.

## CHECKLIST

"Knowledge and the Relativity of Feeling," in *The Early Works of John Dewey, 1882–1898*, Vol. I, pp. 19–33. Carbondale: Southern Illinois University Press, 1969.

"Kant and Philosophic Method," in *Early Works*, I, 34–47.

Lecture XLII [2 pp.] 1885–1886. [Dewey's holograph, amongst Alice Chipman's lecture notes for Dewey's course in "Real Logic," University of Michigan.]

"Real Logic." Class lecture notes handwritten by Alice Chipman, University of Michigan, 1885–1886. 180 pp. [Columbia University, Special Collections.]

"The Psychological Standpoint," in *Early Works*, I, 122–43.

"Psychology as Philosophic Method," in *Early Works*, I, 144–67.

Response by Shadworth Holloway Hodgson, "Illusory Psychology," in *Early Works*, I, xli–lvii.

Reply by Dewey, " 'Illusory Psychology,' " in *Early Works*, I, 168–75.

*Psychology* (The Early Works of John Dewey, 1882–1898, Vol. II). Carbondale: Southern Illinois University Press, 1967.

"Knowledge as Idealization," in *Early Works*, I, 176–93.

*Leibniz's New Essays Concerning the Human Understanding*, in *Early Works*, I, 250–435.

"Is Logic a Dualistic Science?" in *The Early Works of John Dewey, 1882–1898*, Vol. III, pp. 75–82. Carbondale: Southern Illinois University Press, 1969.

"The Logic of Verification," in *Early Works*, III, 83–89. [Criticism of the position taken earlier in "Is Logic a Dualistic Science," ibid., III, 75–82.]

*Outlines of a Critical Theory of Ethics*, in *Early Works*, III, 239–388.

"The Present Position of Logical Theory," in *Early Works*, III, 125–41.

"How Do Concepts Arise from Percepts?" in *Early Works*, III, 142–46.

"Two Phases of Renan's Life: The Faith of 1850 and the Doubt of 1890," in *Early Works*, III, 174–79. [Reprinted in C–10, pp. 18–23, with the title "Ernest Renan."]

"Renan's Loss of Faith in Science," *Open Court*, VII (Jan. 1893), 3512–15. [Reprinted in C–10, pp. 23–30, with the title "Ernest Renan."]

"Commentary on Logic of Hegel." Class lecture notes, handwritten and typewritten by H. Heath Bawden, University of Chicago, 1894 (?). 75 pp. [St. Louis University.]

"The Reflex Arc Concept in Psychology," *Psychological Review*, III (July 1896), 357–70. [Reprinted in C–7, pp. 233–48, with the title "The Unit of Behavior."]

*The Significance of the Problem of Knowledge* (University of Chicago Contributions to Philosophy, Vol. I, No. 3). Chicago: University of Chicago Press, 1897. 20 pp. [Reprinted in C–2, pp. 271–304.]

"The Sense of Solidity," letter in *Science*, n.s. VIII (Nov. 1898), 675.

"Psychology and Philosophic Method," *University [of California] Chronicle*, II (Aug. 1899), 159–79. [Reprinted separately, Berkeley: University of California Press, 1899, 23 pp.; also reprinted in C–2, pp. 242–70, with the title " 'Consciousness' and Experience."]

"Some Stages of Logical Thought," *Philosophical Review*, IX (Sept. 1900), 465–89. [Reprinted in C–3, pp. 183–219.]

"Thought and Its Subject-Matter: The General Problem of Logical Theory," pp. 1–22; "Thought and Its Subject-Matter: The Antecedent Conditions and Cues of the Thought-Function," pp. 23–48; "Thought and Its Subject-Matter: The Datum of Thinking," pp. 49–64; and "Thought and Its Subject-Matter: The Content and Object of Thought," pp. 65–85; in *Studies in Logical Theory* (University of Chicago, The Decennial Publications, Second Series, Vol. XI). Chicago: University of Chicago Press, 1903. [Reprinted in C–3, pp. 75–182, with the titles "The Relationship of Thought and Its Subject-Matter," "The Antecedents and Stimuli of Thinking," "Data and Meanings," and "The Objects of Thought."]

"Logical Conditions of a Scientific Treatment of Morality," in *Investigations Representing the Departments, Part II: Philosophy, Education* (University of Chicago, The Decennial Publications, First Series, Vol. III), pp. 113–39. Chicago: University of Chicago Press, 1903. [Reprinted separately, Chicago: University of Chicago Press, 1903, 27 pp.; also reprinted in C–8, pp. 211–49; C–16, pp. 23–60.]

"What Do We Mean by Knowledge?" Typescript of Dewey's lectures by H. Heath Bawden, University of Chicago, 1903 (?). 34 pp. [St. Louis University.]

"Theory of Logic," Course 33. Stenographic report of class lectures, [H. Heath Bawden], University of Chicago, 1903–4. 194 pp. [St. Louis University.] [Another copy of the same notes, "Theory of Logic," Course 33, (Dr. W. C. Keirstead), 194 pp. with 9 additional pages of notes. University of New Brunswick.]

"Notes Upon Logical Topics," I. A Classification of Contemporary Tendencies, *Journal of Philosophy,* I (Feb. 1904), 57–62; II. The Meanings of the Term Idea, ibid., I (Mar. 1904), 175–78.

"The Psychology of Judgment," *Psychological Bulletin,* I (Feb. 1904), 44–45.

"The Realism of Pragmatism," *Journal of Philosophy,* II (June 1905), 324–27. (Reply to: Stephen Sheldon Colvin, "Is Subjective Idealism a Necessary Point of View for Psychology," *Journal of Philosophy,* II [Apr. 1905], 225–31.)

"The Postulate of Immediate Empiricism," *Journal of Philosophy,* II (July 1905), 393–99. [Reprinted in C–2, pp. 226–41.]

Response by Charles Montague Bakewell, "An Open Letter to Professor Dewey Concerning Immediate Empiricism," *Journal of Philosophy,* II (Sept. 1905), 520–22.

Reply by Dewey, "Immediate Empiricism," *Journal of Philosophy,* II (Oct. 1905), 597–99.

Response by Frederick James Eugene Woodbridge, "Of What Sort Is Cognitive Experience?" *Journal of Philosophy,* II (Oct. 1905), 573–76.

Reply by Dewey, "The Knowledge Experience and Its Relationships," *Journal of Philosophy,* II (Nov. 1905), 652–57.

Response by Boyd Henry Bode, "Cognitive Experience and Its Object," *Journal of Philosophy,* II (Nov. 1905), 658–63.

Reply by Dewey, "The Knowledge Experience Again," *Journal of Philosophy,* II (Dec. 1905), 707–11.

"Reality as Experience," *Journal of Philosophy,* III (May 1906), 253–57.

"The Experimental Theory of Knowledge," *Mind,* n.s. XV (July 1906), 293–307. [Reprinted in C–2, pp. 77–111.]

"Experience and Objective Idealism," *Philosophical Review,* XV (Sept. 1906), 465–81. [Reprinted in C–2, pp. 198–225.]

"Advanced Logic (J. S. Mill)." Stenographic report of class lectures, [H. Heath Bawden], Columbia University, 1906–7. 60 pp. [St. Louis University.]

"The Control of Ideas by Facts," I, *Journal of Philosophy*, IV (Apr. 1907), 197–203; II, ibid., IV (May 1907), 253–59; III, ibid., IV (June 1907), 309–19. [Reprinted in C–3, pp. 230–49.]

"Reality and the Criterion for the Truth of Ideas," *Mind*, n.s. XVI (July 1907), 317–42. [Reprinted in C–2, pp. 112–53, with the title "The Intellectualist Criterion for Truth."]

"Pure Experience and Reality: A Disclaimer," *Philosophical Review*, XVI (July 1907), 419–22. (Reply to: Evander Bradley McGilvary, "Pure Experience and Reality," *Philosophical Review*, XVI [May 1907], 266–84.)

"Does Reality Possess Practical Character?" in *Essays, Philosophical and Psychological*, in Honor of William James, Professor in Harvard University, by his Colleagues at Columbia University, pp. 53–80. New York: Longmans, Green, and Co., 1908. [Reprinted in C–7, pp. 36–55, with the title "The Practical Character of Reality."]

"What Does Pragmatism Mean by Practical?" *Journal of Philosophy*, V (Feb. 1908), 85–99. [Review of *Pragmatism* by William James.] [Reprinted in C–3, pp. 303–29, with the title "What Pragmatism Means by Practical."]

"The Logical Character of Ideas," *Journal of Philosophy*, V (July 1908), 375–81. [Reprinted in C–3, pp. 220–29.] (Reply to: James Bissett Pratt, "Truth and Ideas," *Journal of Philosophy*, V [Feb. 1908], 122–31.)

"Objects, Data, and Existences: A Reply to Professor McGilvary," *Journal of Philosophy*, VI (Jan. 1909), 13–21. (Reply to: Evander Bradley McGilvary, "The Chicago 'Idea' and Idealism," *Journal of Philosophy*, V [Oct. 1908], 589–97.)

"The Dilemma of the Intellectualist Theory of Truth," *Journal of Philosophy*, VI (Aug. 1909), 433–34.

*How We Think*. Boston: D. C. Heath and Co., 1910. vi, 224 pp.

*The Influence of Darwin on Philosophy and Other Essays in Contemporary Thought*. New York: Henry Holt and Co., 1910. vi, 309 pp. [Reprints, with revisions, of previously published articles. "A Short Catechism Concerning Truth," pp. 154–68, is the only paper in this collection not published previously.]

"Valid Knowledge and the 'Subjectivity of Experience'," *Journal of Philosophy*, VII (Mar. 1910), 169–74.

"The Short-Cut to Realism Examined," *Journal of Philosophy*, VII (Sept. 1910), 553–57. (Discussion of: "The Program and Platform of Six Realists" [Edwin Bissell Holt, Walter Taylor Marvin, William Pepperell Montague, Ralph Barton Perry, Walter Boughton Pitkin, Edward Gleason Spaulding], *Journal of Philosophy*, VII [July 1910], 393–401.)

Response by Edward Gleason Spaulding, "Realism: A Reply to Professor Dewey and an Exposition," *Journal of Philosophy*, VIII (Feb. 1911), 63–77.

Dewey's "Rejoinder to Dr. Spaulding," *Journal of Philosophy*, VIII (Feb. 1911), 77–79.

Edward Gleason Spaulding, "A Reply to Professor Dewey's Rejoinder," *Journal of Philosophy*, VIII (Oct. 1911), 566–74.

"Joint Discussion with Articles of Agreement and Disagreement: Professor Dewey and Dr. Spaulding," *Journal of Philosophy*, VIII (Oct. 1911), 574–79.

"The Problem of Truth," I. Why Is Truth a Problem? *Old Penn, Weekly Review of the University of Pennsylvania*, IX (Feb. 1911), 522–28; II. Truth and Consequences, ibid., IX (Feb. 1911), 556–63; III. Objective Truths, ibid., IX (Mar. 1911), 620–25.

"Brief Studies in Realism," I. Naïve Realism vs. Presentative Realism, *Journal of Philosophy*, VIII (July 1911), 393–400; II. Epistemological Realism: The Alleged Ubiquity of the Knowledge Relation, ibid., VIII (Sept. 1911), 546–54. [Reprinted in C–3, pp. 250–80.]

"A Reply to Professor Royce's Critique of Instrumentalism," *Philosophical Review*, XXI (Jan. 1912), 69–81. (Reply to: Josiah Royce, "The Problem of Truth in the Light of Recent Discussion," in *William James, and Other Essays on the Philosophy of Life*, pp. 187–254. New York: Macmillan Co., 1911.)

"A Reply to Professor McGilvary's Questions," *Journal of Philosophy*, IX (Jan. 1912), 19–21. (Reply to: Evander Bradley McGilvary, "Professor Dewey's 'Action of Consciousness'," *Journal of Philosophy*, VIII [Aug. 1911], 458–60.)

"A Trenchant Attack on Logic," *Independent*, LXXIII (July 1912), 203–5. [Review of *Formal Logic: A Scientific and Social Problem* by Ferdinand Canning Scott Schiller.]

"In Response to Professor McGilvary," *Journal of Philosophy*, IX (Sept. 1912), 544–48. (Reply to: Evander Bradley McGilvary, "Realism and the Ego-centric Predicament," *Philosophical Review*, XXI [May 1912], 351–56; "Professor Dewey's 'Awareness'," *Journal of Philosophy*, IX [May 1912], 301–2; "Professor Dewey's 'Brief Studies in Realism'," ibid., IX [June 1912], 344–49.)

"The Logic of Judgments of Practise," I. Their Nature, *Journal of Philosophy*, XII (Sept. 1915), 505–12; II. Judgments of Value, ibid., XII (Sept. 1915), 512–23; III. Sense-Perception as Knowledge, ibid., XII (Sept. 1915), 533–43. [Reprinted in C–3, pp. 335–442.]

"Types of Logical Theory." Typewritten notes by Walter Veazie, Columbia University, 1915–16. 95 pp. [Southern Illinois University Archives.]

*Essays in Experimental Logic*. Chicago: University of Chicago Press, 1916. vii, 444 pp. [Chs. 2–5 "represent (with editorial revisions, mostly omissions) the essays taken from the old volume (*Studies in Logical Theory*). . . . The other essays are in part reprinted and in part rewritten, with additions, from various contributions to philosophical periodicals." Preface, p. v. The "Introduction," pp. 1–74, and "An Added Note as to the Practical," pp. 330–34, had not been published previously.]

Comments by Daniel Sommer Robinson, "An.Alleged New Discovery in Logic," *Journal of Philosophy*, XIV (Apr. 1917), 225–37.

Dewey's "Concerning Novelties in Logic: A Reply to Mr. Robinson," *Journal of Philosophy*, XIV (Apr. 1917), 237–45.

"The Pragmatism of Peirce," *Journal of Philosophy*, XIII (Dec. 1916), 709–15.

"The Concept of the Neutral in Recent Epistemology," *Journal of Philosophy*, XIV (Mar. 1917), 161–63.

"Duality and Dualism," *Journal of Philosophy*, XIV (Aug. 1917), 491–93. (Comment on: Durant Drake, "What Kind of Realism?" *Journal of Philosophy*, IX [Mar. 1912], 149–54; "A Cul-de-Sac for Realism," ibid., XIV [July 1917], 365–73.)

"Concerning Alleged Immediate Knowledge of Mind," *Journal of Philosophy*, XV (Jan. 1918), 29–35.

"The Object of Valuation," *Journal of Philosophy*, XV (May 1918), 253–58.

(Reply to: Ralph Barton Perry, "Dewey and Urban on Value Judgments," *Journal of Philosophy*, XIV [Mar. 1917], 169–81; Wendell T. Bush, "Value and Causality," *Journal of Philosophy*, XV [Feb. 1918], 85–96.)

"Some Factors in Mutual National Understanding," *Kaizō* [Reconstruction], III (Mar. 1921), 17–28.

"An Analysis of Reflective Thought," *Journal of Philosophy*, XIX (Jan. 1922), 29–38. (Reply to: Laurence Buermeyer, "Professor Dewey's Analysis of Thought," *Journal of Philosophy*, XVII [Dec. 1920], 673–81.)

*Reconstruction in Philosophy.* New York: Henry Holt and Co., 1920. vii, 224 pp. [Enl. ed. with a new Introduction, Boston: Beacon Press, 1948. xlix, 224 pp.]

"Realism without Monism or Dualism," I. Knowledge Involving the Past, *Journal of Philosophy*, XIX (June 1922), 309–17; II., ibid., XIX (June 1922), 351–61. (Reply to: Arthur Oncken Lovejoy, "Pragmatism *vs.* the Pragmatist," in *Essays in Critical Realism* [1920], pp. 35–81.)

"Knowledge and Speech Reaction," *Journal of Philosophy*, XIX (Oct. 1922), 561–70.

Review of *Scepticism and Animal Faith* by George Santayana, *New Republic*, XXXV (Aug. 1923), 294–96.

"Valuation and Experimental Knowledge," *Philosophical Review*, XXXI (July 1922), 325–51.
> Response by David Wight Prall, "In Defense of a *Worthless* Theory of Value," *Journal of Philosophy*, XX (Mar. 1923), 128–37.
> Reply by Dewey, "Values, Liking, and Thought," *Journal of Philosophy*, XX (Nov. 1923), 617–22.

"Some Comments on Philosophical Discussion," *Journal of Philosophy*, XXI (Apr. 1924), 197–209. (Reply to: Arthur Oncken Lovejoy, "Time, Meaning and Transcendence," I. The Alleged Futurity of Yesterday, *Journal of Philosophy*, XIX [Sept. 1922], 505–15; and II. Professor Dewey's *Tertium Quid*, ibid., XIX [Sept. 1922], 533–41; and Sterling Power Lamprecht, "A Note on Professor Dewey's Theory of Knowledge," *Journal of Philosophy*, XX [Aug. 1923], 488–94.)

Review of *The Meaning of Meaning* by Charles Kay Ogden and Ivor Armstrong Richards, *New Republic*, XXXIX (June 1924), 77–78.

Review of *Chance, Love and Logic* by Charles Santiago Sanders Peirce, *New Republic*, XXXIX (June 1924), 136–37.

*Experience and Nature* (Lectures upon the Paul Carus Foundation, First Series). Chicago, London: Open Court Publishing Co., 1925. xi, 443 pp. [2d ed., with a Preface, New York: W. W. Norton, 1929. ix, 1a–4a, 1–443 pp. 3d ed., LaSalle, Ill.: Open Court Publishing Co., 1958. xviii, 360 pp.]

"The Meaning of Value," *Journal of Philosophy*, XXII (Feb. 1925), 126–33. (Reply to: David Wight Prall, "Values and Thought-Process," *Journal of Philosophy*, XXI [Feb. 1924], 117–25.)

"The Naturalistic Theory of Perception by the Senses," *Journal of Philosophy*, XXII (Oct. 1925), 596–605. [Reprinted in C–7, pp. 188–201, with the title "A Naturalistic Theory of Sense Perception."]

"An Empirical Account of Appearance," *Journal of Philosophy*, XXIV (Aug. 1927), 449–63. [Reprinted in C–7, pp. 56–76, with the title "Appearing and Appearance."]

"Types of Logical Theory." Stenographic report by Miss Marion E. Dwight of class lectures, 1927–28, Columbia University. 212 pp. [Added material: Digest of Dewey's Course in Philosophical Theory of Society,

1927–28. 5 pp. Topical outline of course, keyed to lectures and pages of notes.] [Columbiana, Columbia University.]

"Body and Mind," *Bulletin of the New York Academy of Medicine,* IV (Jan. 1928), 3–19; *Mental Hygiene,* XII (Jan. 1928), 1–17. [Reprinted in C–7, pp. 299–317.]

"Social as a Category," *Monist,* XXXVIII (Apr. 1928), 161–77. [Reprinted in C–7, pp. 77–92, with the title "The Inclusive Philosophic Idea"; C–11, pp. 1059–69, with the title "The Social."]

"Meaning and Existence," *Journal of Philosophy,* XXV (June 1928), 345–53. (Reply to: Everett W. Hall, "Some Meanings of Meaning in Dewey's *Experience and Nature,*" *Journal of Philosophy,* XXV [Mar. 1928], 169–81.)

*The Quest for Certainty.* New York: Minton, Balch and Co., 1929. 318 pp.

"Introduction," in *The Organization of Knowledge and the System of the Sciences* by Henry Evelyn Bliss, pp. vii–ix. New York: Henry Holt and Co., 1929.

"The Sphere of Application of the Excluded Middle," *Journal of Philosophy,* XXVI (Dec. 1929), 701–5.

Response by Ernest Nagel, "Can Logic Be Divorced from Ontology?" *Journal of Philosophy,* XXVI (Dec. 1929), 705–12.

Reply by Dewey, "The Applicability of Logic to Existence," *Journal of Philosophy,* XXVII (Mar. 1930), 174–79.

"In Reply to Some Criticisms," *Journal of Philosophy,* XXVII (May 1930), 271–77. (Reply to: William Ernest Hocking, "Action and Certainty," *Journal of Philosophy,* XXVII [Apr. 1930], 225–38; Clarence Irving Lewis, "Pragmatism and Current Thought," *Journal of Philosophy,* XXVII [Apr. 1930], 238–46; and Frederick James Eugene Woodbridge, "Experience and Dialectic," *Journal of Philosophy,* XXVII [May 1930], 264–71.)

*Context and Thought* (University of California Publications in Philosophy, Vol. XII), pp. 203–24. Berkeley: University of California Press, 1931. [Also printed separately.]

"A Philosophy of Scientific Method," *New Republic,* LXVI (Apr. 1931), 306–7. [Review of *Reason and Nature, an Essay on the Meaning of Scientific Method* by Morris Raphael Cohen.]

Response by Cohen, "Reason, Nature and Professor Dewey," *New Republic,* LXVII (June 1931), 126–27.

Rejoinder by Dewey, *New Republic,* LXVII (June 1931), 127.

"A Résumé of Four Lectures on Common Sense, Science and Philosophy," *Bulletin of the Wagner Free Institute of Science of Philadelphia,* VII (May 1932), 12–16.

*How We Think.* Boston: D. C. Heath and Co., 1933. x, 301 pp. [Expanded, revised, and rewritten edition of the 1910 *How We Think.*]

"Logic," in *Encyclopaedia of the Social Sciences,* IX, 598–603. New York: Macmillan Co., 1933.

"Meaning, Assertion and Proposal," *Philosophy of Science,* I (Apr. 1934), 237–38. (Comment on: Rudolf Carnap, "On the Character of Philosophic Problems," *Philosophy of Science,* I [Jan. 1934], 5–19.)

"An Empirical Survey of Empiricisms," in *Studies in the History of Ideas* by the Department of Philosophy of Columbia University, Vol. III, pp. 3–22. New York: Columbia University Press, 1935.

"Nature and Humanity," *New Humanist,* VIII (Autumn 1935), 153–57. [Review of *Philosophy and the Concepts of Modern Science* by Oliver Leslie Reiser.]

"Characteristics and Characters: Kinds and Classes," *Journal of Philosophy,* XXXIII (May 1936), 253–61.

"What Are Universals?" *Journal of Philosophy,* XXXIII (May 1936), 281–88. [This and the preceding article were combined and revised in *Logic: The Theory of Inquiry,* pp. 255–63.]

"General Propositions, Kinds, and Classes," *Journal of Philosophy,* XXXIII (Dec. 1936), 673–80.

*Logic: The Theory of Inquiry.* New York: Henry Holt and Co., 1938. viii, 546 pp.

"Unity of Science as a Social Problem," in *Encyclopedia and Unified Science* (International Encyclopedia of Unified Science, Vol. I, No. 1), 29–38. Chicago: University of Chicago Press, 1938.

*Theory of Valuation* (International Encyclopedia of Unified Science, Vol. II, No. 4). Chicago: University of Chicago Press, 1939. 67 pp.

"Experience, Knowledge and Value: A Rejoinder," in *The Philosophy of John Dewey* (The Library of Living Philosophers, Vol. I, ed. Paul Arthur Schilpp), pp. 517–608. Evanston, Chicago: Northwestern University, 1939.

"Nature in Experience," *Philosophical Review,* XLIX (Mar. 1940), 244–58. (Reply to: Morris Raphael Cohen, "Some Difficulties in Dewey's Anthropocentric Naturalism," *Philosophical Review,* XLIX [Mar. 1940], 196–228; and William Ernest Hocking, "Dewey's Concepts of Experience and Nature," *Philosophical Review,* XLIX [Mar. 1940], 228–44.)

"Propositions, Warranted Assertibility, and Truth," *Journal of Philosophy,* XXXVIII (Mar. 1941), 169–86. [Reprinted in C–8, pp. 331–53.]

"The Objectivism-Subjectivism of Modern Philosophy," *Journal of Philosophy,* XXXVIII (Sept. 1941), 533–42. [Reprinted in C–8, pp. 309–21.]

"How Is Mind to Be Known?" *Journal of Philosophy,* XXXIX (Jan. 1942), 29–35. [Reprinted in C–8, pp. 301–8.]

"Inquiry and Indeterminateness of Situations," *Journal of Philosophy,* XXXIX (May 1942), 290–96. [Reprinted in C–8, pp. 322–30.] (Reply to: Donald Sage Mackay, "What Does Mr. Dewey Mean by an 'Indeterminate Situation'?" *Journal of Philosophy,* XXXIX [Mar. 1942], 141–48.)

"The Penning in of Natural Science," *Humanist,* IV (Summer 1944), 57–59.

"A Search for Firm Names," with Arthur Fisher Bentley, *Journal of Philosophy,* XLII (Jan. 1945), 5–6. [Reprinted in C–9, pp. xi–xiii, as the Introduction.]

"A Terminology for Knowings and Knowns," with Arthur Fisher Bentley, *Journal of Philosophy,* XLII (Apr. 1945), 225–47. [Reprinted in C–9, pp. 47–78, with the title "The Terminological Problem."]

"Are Naturalists Materialists?" with Sidney Hook and Ernest Nagel, *Journal of Philosophy,* XLII (Sept. 1945), 515–30. (Reply to: Wilmon Henry Sheldon, "Critique of Naturalism," *Journal of Philosophy,* XLII [May 1945], 253–70.)

"Postulations," with Arthur Fisher Bentley, *Journal of Philosophy,* XLII (Nov. 1945), 645–62. [Reprinted in C–9, pp. 79–102.]

"Ethical Subject-Matter and Language," *Journal of Philosophy,* XLII (Dec. 1945), 701–12.

"Peirce's Theory of Linguistic Signs, Thought, and Meaning," *Journal of Philosophy,* XLIII (Feb. 1946), 85–95.

Response by Charles William Morris, *Journal of Philosophy,* XLIII (Mar. 1946), 196.

Reply by Dewey, *Journal of Philosophy,* XLIII (May 1946), 280.

"Interaction and Transaction," with Arthur Fisher Bentley, *Journal of Philosophy*, XLIII (Sept. 1946), 505–17. [Reprinted in C–9, pp. 103–18.]

"Transactions as Known and Named," with Arthur Fisher Bentley, *Journal of Philosophy*, XLIII (Sept. 1946), 533–51. [Reprinted in C–9, pp. 119–43.]

"Specification," with Arthur Fisher Bentley, *Journal of Philosophy*, XLIII (Nov. 1946), 645–63. [Reprinted in C–9, pp. 144–69.]

" 'Definition,' " with Arthur Fisher Bentley, *Journal of Philosophy*, XLIV (May 1947), 281–306. [Reprinted in C–9, pp. 170–204, with the title "The Case of Definition."]

"Concerning a Vocabulary for Inquiry into Knowledge," with Arthur Fisher Bentley, *Journal of Philosophy*, XLIV (July 1947), 421–34. [Reprinted in C–9, pp. 287–306, with the title "A Trial Group of Names."]

"Man and Mathematics," *Humanist*, VII (Winter 1947), 121.

"Introduction: Reconstruction as Seen Twenty-five Years Later," in *Reconstruction in Philosophy*, pp. v–xli. Boston: Beacon Press, 1948.

"Common Sense and Science: Their Respective Frames of Reference," *Journal of Philosophy*, XLV (Apr. 1948), 197–208. [Reprinted in C–9, pp. 270–86.]

*4*

# Dewey's Ethics

*Part One*   HERBERT W. SCHNEIDER

THE WRITINGS discussed in this essay cover the period in the development of Dewey's moral philosophy from 1887, when he published in the *Andover Review* an article on "Ethics and Physical Science" [1] in which he ridiculed the then popular attempt to represent man as the crowning creation of the evolutionary process, until his publication in the *Monist* of 1898 of an article on "Evolution and Ethics," [2] which marks the beginning of his attempt to apply genetic method to moral science. This is the revolutionary period in Dewey's development as a moral scientist. It is important, therefore, in reading these writings to note the way in which his "psychological ethics" changed from his early emphasis on self-realization to his "experimental idealism" of 1896, which within two years led him to adopt an evolutionary naturalism.

Both his *Andover Review* article of 1887 and his lecture at the University of Michigan in 1888 on "The Ethics of Democracy" [3] made a radical contrast between the evolutionary process which is based on conflict and competition, and the process of personal development in a social community, which is based on "harmony, unity of purpose and life, community of well-being." [4] Man's spiritual life in society is an essential or natural phase of his organic growth as a person, a process

1. In *The Early Works of John Dewey, 1882–1898*, Vol. I (Carbondale: Southern Illinois University Press, 1969), pp. 205–26.
2. *Monist*, VIII (1898), 321–41.
3. In *Early Works*, I, 227–49.
4. "Ethics and Physical Science," p. 213.

antithetical to the physical struggle for existence. It implies a "democratic" environment in which all must share. Dewey's ethics was clearly against Herbert Spencer and worked out along the lines of T. H. Green.

His first treatise on ethics, *Outlines of a Critical Theory of Ethics* (1891),[5] begins where his revised *Psychology* [6] of the same year left off; it is a continuation of his "psychological method in philosophy." After criticizing the psychologies of hedonism, utilitarianism, evolutionary utilitarianism (Spencer), and Kantianism in the same manner in which he had criticized them in his *Psychology*, he sums up his own psychology in a few sentences:

> The end of action, or the good, is the realized will, the developed or satisfied self. This satisfied self is found neither in the getting of a lot of pleasures through the satisfaction of desires just as they happen to arise, nor in obedience to law simply because it is law. It is found in *satisfaction of desires according to law*. This law, however, is not something external to the desires, but is their own law. Each desire is only one striving of character for larger action, and the only way in which it can really find satisfaction (that is, pass from inward striving into outward action) is *as* a manifestation of character. A desire, taken as a desire for its own apparent or direct end *only*, is an abstraction. It is a desire for an entire and continuous activity, and its satisfaction requires that it be fitted into this entire and continuous activity; that it be made conformable to the conditions which will bring the whole man into action. . . . This "fitting-in" is no mechanical shearing off, nor stretching out, but a reconstruction of the natural desire till it becomes an expression of the whole man.[7]

The structure of this psychological fact is then formulated as the "law of man" or as the "moral faith" and must be accepted as a "metaphysical postulate" as follows:

IN THE REALIZATION OF INDIVIDUALITY THERE IS FOUND ALSO THE NEEDED REALIZATION OF SOME COMMUNITY OF PERSONS OF WHICH THE INDIVIDUAL IS A MEMBER; AND, CONVERSELY, THE AGENT WHO DULY SATISFIES THE COM-

5. In *Early Works*, III, 238–388.
6. (*Early Works*, II).
7. *Outlines*, pp. 300–301.

MUNITY IN WHICH HE SHARES, BY THAT SAME CONDUCT
SATISFIES HIMSELF.

Otherwise put, the postulate is that there is a community
of persons; a good which realized by the will of one is made
not private but public. It is this unity of individuals as respects
the end of action, this existence of a practical common good,
that makes what we call the moral order of the world.[8]

In the detailed exposition of this critique of the "fundamental ethical notions" there appear several ideas which prove
to be prophetic of the revolutionary change in Dewey's views
during the next five years. I mention some of them briefly,
recommending to the reader a careful study of the pages referred to.

1.    Desires are "reconstructed" in moral conduct. No natural desire functions in "isolation": it is a person's desire and
interacts with other desires to form conscience. Obligation,
when thus derived, is not experienced as something external to
desire but as the reconstruction of desires in their interaction.[9]

2.    A personal *function* is Dewey's concept for the union
in action of individual capacities and a specific environment.[10]
This is a way of conceiving the facts of activity as both objective
and subjective. A function is "the skeleton of the moral end
which each clothes with his own flesh and blood." [11]

3.    Interests are generated by functions. They are active,
objective, social, self-satisfying. "[Each] is its own reward." [12]
The analysis of interests now becomes more important for
Dewey than the analysis of desires and motives.[13]

4.    Moral interest is "disinterested," that is, it needs no
"ulterior motives." Deliberate action and decision is both terminal and consummatory.[14]

8. *Outlines*, p. 322.
9. *Outlines*, pp. 300–301, 335, 338.
10. *Outlines*, p. 303.
11. *Outlines*, p. 304.
12. *Outlines*, p. 305.
13. *Outlines*, pp. 304–9, 320, 336, 348–49, 361–62.
14. *Outlines*, pp. 307–8, 324–25, 338–39.

5.    Universals and absolutes have a dynamic context; they are modes of method. Opposite the title page of the book Dewey put Galileo's *e pur se muove*.

> If the physical world is a scene of movement, in which there is no rest, it is a poor compliment to pay the moral world to conceive of it as static and lifeless. A rigid criterion in a world of developing social relations would speedily prove no criterion at all. . . . A truly absolute criterion is one which adjusts itself to each case according to the specific nature of the case; one which moves with the moving world. . . . Universality here, as elsewhere, resides not in a thing, but in a way, a method of action.[15]

Basic to all these doctrines is Dewey's insistence that morality is, from beginning to end, action.

> The whole idea of the separateness of duty from the concrete flow of human action is a virulent example of the fallacy . . . that moral action means something more than action itself.[16]

Part Two, "The Ethical World," which has a central position in the book between Part One, "Fundamental Ethical Notions," and Part Three, "The Moral Life of the Individual," is notable for its brevity, thirteen pages in the original edition. The idea is taken over from Hegel and from Dewey's *Psychology* and is evidently much indebted to Bradley's "My Station and Its Duties."[17] Its subtitle, "The Reality of Moral Relations," is an indication of its central importance for the theory of the "realization" of freedom through institutions. Its brevity, compared with the detailed development of the psychology of the individual life (Part Three), is eloquent testimony to the fact that at this stage Dewey's psychological method was still individualistic, though the social environment is emphasized in general theory:

> The moral world is, here and now; it is a reality apart from the wishes, or failures to wish, of any given individual. It bears the same relation to the individual's activity that the "physical world" does to his knowledge. . . . Moral action is the appropriation and vital self-expression of the values contained

15. *Outlines*, p. 325.
16. *Outlines*, p. 337.
17. F. H. Bradley, *Ethical Studies* (London: Henry S. King and Co., 1876), pp. 145–86.

in the existing practical world.[18] That performance of function which is "the good," is now seen to consist in vital union with, and reproduction of, the practical institutions of which one is a member. The maintenance of such institutions by the free participation therein of individual wills, is, of itself, the common good.[19]

Noteworthy here is the absence of the idea of reconstruction of institutions, later so prominent in Dewey's thought and writing. Here the individual realizes himself in the "reproduction" and "maintenance" of institutions, whereas his desires are undergoing "reconstruction" in the process.

In striking contrast to this conservative idealist doctrine are the pages which Dewey says were inspired by his journalist friend, Franklin Ford. There is here an impassioned rhetoric which reflects the ideas and emotions that animated Ford and Dewey in their plan (never carried out) to publish a periodical to be called "Thought News." [20] It is worth citing a few of these passages on democratic ethics, since they foreshadow Dewey's later development of these ideas:

> We wish the fullest life possible to ourselves and to others. And the fullest life means largely a complete and free development of capacities in knowledge and production—production of beauty and use. Our interest in others is not satisfied as long as their intelligence is cramped, their appreciation of truth feeble, their emotions hard and uncomprehensive, their powers of production compressed. To will their true good is to will the freeing of all such gifts to the highest degree. Shall we say that their true good requires that they shall go to the point of understanding algebra, but not quaternions, of understanding ordinary mechanics, but not to working out an electromagnetic theory of light? to ability to appreciate ordinary chords and tunes, but not to the attempt to make further developments in music?
>
> *Social* welfare demands that the individual be permitted to devote himself to the fulfilling of *any* scientific or artistic capacity that he finds within himself. . . . The new discovery is not yet made. It is absolutely required by the interests of a progressive society that it allow freedom to the individual to

18. *Outlines*, p. 345.
19. *Outlines*, p. 349.
20. For a full discussion of the proposed publication see Willinda Savage, "John Dewey and 'Thought News' at the University of Michigan," *Michigan Alumnus Quarterly Review*, LVI (1950), 204–9.

develop such functions as he finds in himself, irrespective of any *proved* social effect. Here, as elsewhere, morality works by faith, not by sight.

Indeed the ordinary conception of social interests, of benevolence, needs a large over-hauling. It is practically equivalent to doing something directly for others. . . . But this is only negative morality. A true social interest is that which wills for others freedom from dependence on our *direct* help, which wills to them the self-directed power of exercising, in and by themselves, their own functions.

As society advances, social interest must consist more and more in free devotion to intelligence for its own sake, to science, art and industry, and in rejoicing in the exercise of such freedom by others. Meantime, it is truth which makes free.

Where, finally, does the social character of science and art come in? Just here: they are elements in the perfection of individuality, and they are elements whose very nature is to be moving, not rigid; distributed from one to another and not monopolistic possessions. . . . To complete their scientific and artistic character is to set these facts in motion; to hurl them against the world of physical forces till new instruments of man's activity are formed, and to set them in circulation so that others may also participate in their truth and rejoice in their beauty.

It makes it one of the pressing duties that every man of intelligence should do his part in bringing out the public and common aspects of knowledge. *The* duty of the present is the socializing of intelligence.[21]

Such preaching is rare in the pages of this otherwise academic treatise. These passages reflect the influence not only of Franklin Ford but also of Mrs. Dewey. Dewey himself acknowledged this fact; but the reading references in this section are to Bradley's *Ethical Studies* and Spencer's *Data of Ethics*! [22]

Dewey's own copies of this textbook are graphic witnesses to the new interests and ideas which were reconstructing his philosophy during the years 1891 to 1894. In one copy (which the publisher had prepared especially for Dewey's use by inserting blank pages between all the printed pages) his revisions fill almost all the blank pages and show why he finally gave up the

21. *Outlines*, pp. 318–20.

22. F. H. Bradley, *Ethical Studies* (London: Henry S. King and Co., 1876); Herbert Spencer, *Data of Ethics* (New York: D. Appleton and Co., 1882).

idea of a new edition. The book that emerged—*The Study of Ethics: A Syllabus*—was "in no sense a second edition." [23] In the other copy he cut out certain pages for use in the new book and marked with an *x* certain paragraphs which he thought still good.

*The Study of Ethics: A Syllabus* (1894) was hurriedly printed, composed in outline style, making a poor appearance, but full of excitement and fresh insights. The Prefatory Note is decidedly programmatic:

> Amid the prevalence of pathological and moralistic ethics, there is room for a theory which conceives of conduct as the normal and free living of life as it is. The present pages . . . undertake a thorough psychological examination of the process of active experience, and a derivation from this analysis of the chief ethical types and crises—a task, so far as I know, not previously attempted.[24]

The book contained frequent and enthusiastic references to William James's *Psychology* and his "The Moral Philosopher and the Moral Life"; to Samuel Alexander's *Moral Order and Progress;* to Thomas Davidson's *Aristotle and Ancient Educational Ideals;* to A. T. Hadley's "Ethics as a Political Science"; [25] and to recent articles in the *Journal of Speculative Philosophy* and the *Psychological Review.* James and Alexander were evidently major influences in Dewey's reorientation, but there were many others. Dewey's own article in the *International Journal of Ethics* (1891) on "Moral Theory and Practice" [26] became increasingly important to him. He had referred to it in the *Outlines* in connection with the theory of practical judgment and had said very emphatically even then:

> It is the very essence of theoretical judgment, judgment regarding fact, to state the truth—what is. And it is the very

23. *The Study of Ethics: A Syllabus* (Ann Arbor: Register Publishing Co., 1894), p. iii.

24. *Syllabus*, p. iii.

25. William James, *The Principles of Psychology*, 2 vols. (New York: Henry Holt and Co., 1890), "The Moral Philosopher and the Moral Life," *International Journal of Ethics*, I (1891), 330–54; Samuel Alexander, *Moral Order and Progress: An Analysis of Ethical Conceptions* (London: Trübner and Co., 1889); Thomas Davidson, *Aristotle and Ancient Educational Ideals* (New York: Charles Scribner's Sons, 1892); Arthur T. Hadley, "Ethics as a Political Science," I, *Yale Review*, I (1892), 301–15; II, ibid., I (1893), 354–67.

26. *Early Works*, III, 93–109.

essence of practical judgment, judgment regarding deeds, to state that active relation which we call obligation, what *ought to be*.

The judgment as to what a practical situation *is*, is an untrue or abstract judgment.

The practical situation is itself an *activity;* the needs, powers, and circumstances which make it are moving on. At no instant in time is the scene quiescent. . . . And it is on the basis of this movement that conscience declares what ought to be.[27]

This "logic of judgments of practice" now began to loom large in Dewey's philosophy and became the point of departure for the new *Syllabus*. The difference in formal structure between the two volumes indicates the scope of the changes.

| THE OUTLINES (1891) | THE SYLLABUS (1894) |
|---|---|
| I. Ethical Concepts (Good, Duty, Freedom) (In *The Syllabus* these become: Value, Control, Freedom) | I. Relation of Theory to Practice<br>1. Historical introduction<br>2. The factors of moral conduct: Agent and Sphere of Action The Ethical Postulate |
| II. The Ethical World (Institutions) | II. Psychological Ethics (the Agent) Chs. 3-9 [28] |
| III. The Moral Life of the Individual (Psychological Ethics) | III. Social Ethics (Sphere of Action) postponed (see p. 12) [29] |

The structure of the *Syllabus* is not clearly indicated; it does not appear in the Table of Contents. After an introductory two chapters (referred to later as Part One) in which the new theory is outlined, the remainder of the volume is devoted to

27. *Outlines*, pp. 360–61.
28. *Syllabus*, Chs. 3–9.
29. *Syllabus*, p. 12.

"Psychological Ethics," which corresponds roughly to Part Three of the *Outlines*. Part Two of the *Outlines*, "The Ethical World" becomes a projected Part Three (unwritten) of the *Syllabus*, entitled Social Ethics and dealing with "the sphere of action." Part One of the *Outlines*, devoted to a critique of ethical concepts, is covered in much shorter form in the concluding chapters of the *Syllabus*. Both volumes close (as part of the discussion of "Freedom") with an analysis of the virtues. In the *Outlines* virtue is conceived as "realized morality" and the two cardinal virtues are "wholeness" and "disinterestedness." In the *Syllabus*, virtue is defined as "wholeness of self" and the cardinal virtues are named and treated on the basis of Aristotle's *Ethics*.

The following themes, suggested incidentally in the *Outlines*, become central to what Dewey now calls his "experimental idealism":

*1*. Critique of the psychology of self-realization. The substance of this major departure had been published in two articles: "Green's Theory of the Moral Motive" [30] and "Self-Realization as the Moral Ideal." [31] Dewey now turns Green's critique of hedonism against Green's own, too abstract, conception of the ideal self as the moral end. Morality need not be self-conscious, in this sense, any more than it need seek happiness consciously. Green's Kantian separation of will and desire is false psychology. The "identity of choice, deed and will" as forms of self-realization is "the culmination of psychology, as well as the supreme moral lesson." [32] His polemic here is directed even more sharply at Martineau, Lotze, and all theories which transform interests into motives, thus turning action "outside in," or which conceive the self as transcending action, thus turning action "inside out." [33]

*2*. The process of "mediation of impulse" by reflective interest takes the place of the former "dualism of will and desire." This process of mediation (later developed as *How We*

30. *Early Works*, III, 155–73.
31. *Philosophical Review*, II (1893), 652–64.
32. *Syllabus*, p. 129.
33. *Syllabus*, p. 42.

*Think*) culminates in acts or decisions which as *acts* are also value judgments or norms. Preference is the "normal outcome of the process of will." [34]

3. Moral *functions* are distinguished from physiological functions by being *conscious*. Values are consciously experienced in acts of preference. Dewey relates his theory of value judgment to Josiah Royce's "appreciation" [35] and refers back to his own treatment of appreciation and retention on page 131 in his *Psychology*.[36] In his relating the psychology of appreciation to mediation process Dewey sees the basic difference between his "instrumental" theory of judgment and the idealistic theory of Royce. Ideals are made, not given.[37] They are principles of change, not of fixity. "We steer *by* them [the stars], not *towards* them." [Italics added.] [38]

4. The Ethical Postulate is retained, but it is no longer "metaphysical faith." It is an hypothesis which is empirically verified. The reformulation is significant:

> The conduct required truly to express an agent is, at the same time, the conduct required to maintain the situation in which he is placed; while, conversely, the conduct that truly meets the situation is that which furthers the agent.
> The word "truly" in this statement means with reference to the exercise of function.[39]

This is merely a restatement of the basic idea of his psychology that conduct involves the two factors of agent and sphere of action. The whole postulation of the "common good" of T. H. Green, which is contained in the Postulate of 1891, drops out.

The thoroughly analytic and behavioristic method adopted in the *Syllabus* is not only stated, almost dogmatically, at the very outset of the treatise, but it is immediately applied to education:

> Every act (consciously performed) is a judgment of value: the act done is done because it is thought to be *worth while*, or valuable. Thus a man's real (as distinct from his nominal or

34. *Syllabus*, p. 126; see also p. 25.
35. *Syllabus*, pp. 36–37.
36. *Syllabus*, p. 10.
37. *Syllabus*, p. 37.
38. *Syllabus*, p. 41.
39. *Syllabus*, p. 11.

symbolic) theory of conduct can be told only from his acts. Conversely, every judgment about conduct is itself an act; it marks a practical and not simply a theoretical attitude. That is, it does not lie outside of the matter judged (conduct), but constitutes a part of its development; conduct is different after, and because of the judgment. Ill[ustration] in education, where the main point is not so much to get certain acts done, as to induce in the child certain ways of valuing acts, from which the performance of the specific deeds will naturally follow. That is, the best education aims to train *conscience*. Ethical theory is only a more conscious and more generalized phase of conduct.[40]

This application to education implies in Dewey's interpretation that acts of punishment, if they are to be educative, must reveal to the person that is being punished the intrinsic quality of the act to which the punishment is a consequence, and punishment should not be an object of fear. This psychology obviously has far-reaching implications for educational practice as for theory. Dewey worked out some of these in an important 1894 article (to which he refers) entitled "The Chaos in Moral Training." [41] This article marks a dramatic turning point in Dewey's practical interests as well as in his philosophical system.

In the *Psychological Review* for 1896 Dewey published a review of Archbishop Charles Frederick D'Arcy's *A Short Study of Ethics*.[42] With his own short study of ethics in the background, this gave him a good opportunity to make the contrast. He entitled the review "The Metaphysical Method in Ethics" and used the occasion to say farewell in public to the whole classical tradition in ethics.

The subsequent development of Dewey's moral philosophy can be summarized here. During the years 1898 to 1904 he was preoccupied with genetic method and substituted in his expositions an anthropological account of the evolution of morals for his former critique of ethical concepts and systems. At the same time he worked out in more detail "the logical conditions for a scientific treatment of morality" which culminated in 1915 with a series of articles on "The Logic of Judgments of Practise," [43]

40. *Syllabus*, pp. 1–2.
41. *Popular Science Monthly*, XLV (1894), 433–43.
42. *Psychological Review*, III (1896), 181–88.
43. *Journal of Philosophy*, XII (1915), 505–12, 512–23, 533–43.

the substance of which was included in his major work, *Logic: The Theory of Inquiry* (1938).[44]

Meanwhile, the publication of Dewey and Tufts's *Ethics* (1908) [45] made explicit what he and his friends knew in 1894 when he published only the "Psychological Ethics" half of his *Syllabus* as projected theoretically, namely, that there was a division of labor between Dewey and his colleague, James Hayden Tufts, according to which the "Social Ethics" and the historical introductions would be supplied by Tufts. Throughout his teaching career at Columbia University, Dewey alternated, teaching Psychological Ethics one year and Social Ethics (later called Moral and Political Philosophy) the next. Dewey did not integrate his individual and his social psychologies in published form until 1922, when he published his *Human Nature and Conduct*,[46] based on lectures delivered at Stanford University in 1918. In the Preface to this notable volume, which is the most inclusive formulation of his social psychology and ethics, Dewey indicates that he is supplementing his former "psychological ethics" by a "social psychology."

> An understanding of habit and of different types of habit is the key to social psychology, while the operation of impulse and intelligence gives the key to individualized mental activity. But they are secondary to habit so that mind can be understood in the concrete only as a system of beliefs, desires and purposes which are formed in the interaction of biological aptitudes with a social environment.[47]

Late in life, and with the co-operation of Arthur F. Bentley, Dewey used the term "transaction" for what he here describes as "interaction." This terminological change calls attention to the basic thesis of his work of 1894 in which he was already insisting that individual agent and social sphere of action are not two separate agents interacting but two co-operating "factors" in conduct.

In the second edition of Dewey and Tufts's *Ethics* (1932) [48] Dewey rewrote his "psychological" part along the lines of his *Human Nature and Conduct*. In his own courses at

44. New York: Henry Holt and Co., 1938.
45. New York: Henry Holt and Co., 1908.
46. New York: Henry Holt and Co., 1922.
47. *Human Nature and Conduct*, p. iii.
48. New York: Henry Holt and Co., 1932.

Columbia University, however, he continued to separate, by teaching them in alternate years, the theory of "impulse and intelligence" and the theory of habit, custom, and moral institutions. It should be evident to the reader that the development of Dewey's psychology and of his ethics is a single story, and that it illustrates his conviction that the two are inseparable.

# Dewey's Ethics

## *Part Two*   DARNELL RUCKER

THE CHANGES Dewey's philosophy underwent in his early writing as he developed his own distinctive brand of thought are perhaps less obvious in his ethical writings than they are in the other works. Two reasons for this lack of apparent change are the degree of continuity in the content of his ethical writings and the similarity of language and approach between earlier and later works. The shifts which do take place appear to be largely shifts in emphasis, the working out and strengthening of the underlying theoretical analysis taking place in the psychological and logical investigations. An important factor in the ethics is the continuing role of a general point of view deriving from Hegel. In a monograph of a public lecture Dewey gave at Columbia in 1908, he said of Hegel's philosophy:

> In intellectual and practical effect, it lifted the idea of process above that of fixed origins and fixed ends, and presented the social and moral order, as well as the intellectual, as a scene of becoming, and it located reason somewhere within the struggles of life.[1]

The analysis of this process which encompassed the social and the intellectual transformed Hegel's dialectical *"aufheben"* into Dewey's own biological "growth" and gave birth to his instrumentalism. The beginning of this transformation is exemplified in the change from the institutional concern of the *Outlines of a Critical Theory of Ethics* to the psychological concern of *The Study of Ethics: A Syllabus*, as pointed out in Herbert Schnei-

1. *Ethics* (New York: Columbia University Press, 1908), p. 19.

der's essay. However, the social side is never absent from Dewey's ethics; it is merely subordinated at times to the working out and exposition of the psychological side.

In his 1904 article "Ethics" in *The Encyclopedia Americana*,[2] Dewey points out that ethics has been regarded as a branch of philosophy, as a science, and as an art. It is evident that he considers scientific ethics central, since it will relieve philosophic ethics from its dependence upon fixed values and standards and relieve ethics as an art from its search for specific rules of conduct, replacing both set ideals and rules with *methods* for analysis of moral problems. Scientific ethics, he says, has two divisions: social, or sociological, ethics, and individual, or psychological, ethics. The interaction of these two divisions remains paramount for Dewey throughout his ethical writings, no matter what happens to be the particular subject of investigation.

The peculiarly ethical writings reflect, more than they comprise, the analyses that form the basis for the scientific ethics. For the technical analyses of action, the reader should go to the psychological and logical works, especially "The Reflex Arc Concept in Psychology" (1896), "Logical Conditions of a Scientific Treatment of Morality" (1903), *How We Think* (1910), *Essays in Experimental Logic* (1916), *Logic: The Theory of Inquiry* (1938), and *Theory of Valuation* (1939). And for Dewey's explicitly sociological analyses, see *Human Nature and Conduct* (1922), *The Public and Its Problems* (1927), *Individualism, Old and New* (1930), and *Liberalism and Social Action* (1935).

While there is, as Herbert Schneider says, a permanent shift marked by the empirical statement of the ethical postulate in the *Syllabus* in contrast to the metaphysical statement of the postulate in the *Outlines*, the social *content* of the 1891 formulation returns in the definition of virtue in Dewey and Tufts's 1908 *Ethics*:

> The habits of character whose effect is to sustain and spread the rational or common good are virtues; the traits of character which have the opposite effect are vices.[3]

2. Vol. VII (New York: Scientific American, 1904).
3. *Ethics*, with James Hayden Tufts (New York: Henry Holt and Co., 1908), p. 399.

And this concern with the social side becomes even more pronounced in the second edition of the *Ethics* (1932). Dewey's statement, in the *Encyclopedia Americana* article mentioned above, of the moral problem he inherited is illuminating:

> The problem of 19th century ethics was to get back from the individual to the social whole which includes him and within which he functions; but to do this in a way which should take due account of the deepened significance given to individual initiative and freedom—without, that is, a return to pure institutionalism, or to arbitrary external authority.[4]

The interrelations of the free individual and institutions of increasing size and complexity remain Dewey's (and our) central moral problem.

Dewey makes no distinction between ethics and morals, pointing to the common meaning of the Greek word *ethos* and the Latin word *mores*, both of which meant customs or approved usages. He defines ethics as the science of conduct which we judge as good or bad, right or wrong, virtuous or vicious. Conduct, in turn, is action that involves purpose, intention, motive, and relations to others and to society. Not all action is conduct, since, for Dewey, any process of change whether animate or not may be called action. Neither is all conduct moral; there are deliberate actions about which we do not make value judgments. But, in keeping with Dewey's pervasive insistence upon the continuity of action, he maintains that *all* conduct is potentially moral, since every act affects habits and habits constitute character. Dewey defines moral conduct as taking place within what he calls the moral situation, a situation involving deliberation, desire, and choice. Moral acts contain an idea of an end to be attained, an expenditure of energy in attaining it, and a selection of the end from among two or more incompatible ends.[5] These same criteria serve to distinguish reflective morality from customary morality. And while "moral" derives from the Latin for custom, there is no room for moral *theory* so long as social usage determines judgments of right and wrong. Moral theory is a systematization of what is involved in reflecting upon

4. "Ethics," *Encyclopedia Americana.*
5. *Ethics*, with Tufts (1908), pp. 201–11.

questions of conduct, such reflection necessarily calling into question moral custom itself.[6]

The business of ethics is to study the interactions of the individual and his environment in order to discover principles of conduct. Principles, however, are not the same thing as rules. Principles are general ideas arising out of experience as guides for experience; they are tools for dealing with new situations, methods for solving problems. A rule, on the other hand, is like a recipe, a set of specific steps to follow to attain a fixed end; and ethics cannot provide moral rules because each concrete problem is different from every other, and all moral problems are concrete ones. Moral theory, just as any theory for Dewey, is an intellectual tool, not a body of achieved knowledge in which we can rest.

The fact that Dewey deals with historic moral theories to such an extent in developing his own theory frequently serves to obscure just what *Dewey* is saying. He does this because he is always a problematic philosopher, in the sense that philosophy arises out of and must be referred to specific problems that confront men. There are no moral problems in general. Theoretic problems arise out of specific theoretic contexts. So Dewey starts with explicit theoretic statements that have had some impact on men's thinking about moral problems and proceeds from the difficulties he finds in those statements. His use of these theories is to indicate both truths upon which he can build and failures which he can set right. In particular, critiques of hedonism and Kantianism run through most of his moral works. In the *Outlines* he contrasts hedonism's abstraction of the consequences of action with Kant's abstraction of the will of the agent, his task being to show the concrete relation of the two. The same contrast is carried through the *Syllabus* and appears in the first edition of the *Ethics* as the contrast between teleological and jural theories. This classification of theories is expanded in the second edition to include approbational theories; ends (teleological), law (jural), and virtue and vice (approbational), emerging as what Dewey calls the three independent variables in morals. (The distinction of the three factors first

6. *Ethics*, rev. ed., with Tufts (New York: Henry Holt and Co., 1932), pp. 171–76.

appears in a lecture Dewey gave before the Société Française de Philosophie and which was published in their *Bulletin* as "Trois facteurs indépendants en matière de morale" in 1930.) In every case, what Dewey does is to show that the separations that occur in other theories are artificial and serve to conceal the fundamentally organic nature of the moral situation. The various aspects of action cannot be erected into distinct entities, since none of them can exist or be given meaning apart from the other aspects. The good, the right, and virtue and vice are useful moral concepts only as they are used as means for dealing with existing desires, interests, habits, relations, institutions, and societies. Although the three variables cannot be reduced to a single factor, they remain simply three distinct standpoints from which the single act situation can be viewed as moral.

Dewey's ethics is teleological, but his is the biological teleology required by the concept of growth. His ethics is jural in the sense that habits and principles are requisites for coherent action. It is approbational in that judgment makes intelligent action possible. But in opposition to most moral theorizing since the Greeks, for Dewey there are no fixed ends, either psychological, sociological, or theological; no authoritatively decreed moral laws; and no eternally specified virtues or vices. He insists that goals, laws, and judgments be balanced and related to each other in any account of ethics and that the account be given in terms of actual moral experience and not in terms of a divine plan, an isolated feeling, or casuistic categories of behavior.

Dewey states in a variety of places that the job of philosophy is to restore the long-broken connection between the realms of science and value. Hence his insistence upon a science of ethics: the procedures of the natural sciences are the procedures of any search for knowledge and understanding. The analysis of the act of reflective thought yields the ground for science and for ethics, the distinction between them being one of the primary interest at the time: knowledge or action, truth or goodness. Dewey early insists that morality is not a separate compartment of life:

> Moral insight, and therefore moral theory, consist simply in
> the every-day workings of the same ordinary intelligence that

measures dry-goods, drives nails, sells wheat, and invents the telephone.[7]

And, correspondingly, he insists that science as value-free is a useful abstraction which must be referred to the same act situation from which moral and other value judgments derive. (See especially "Logical Conditions of a Scientific Treatment of Morality," 1903.)[8]

One way to grasp what Dewey is about in his ethics is to look at how he deals with certain key moral concepts. Among others, freedom, responsibility, character, virtue, and good indicate what is characteristic in Dewey's moral theory. These terms also serve to demonstrate the continuing relevance of Dewey's thought for present problems; the problems denoted by the terms are perennial, and Dewey was aware of the importance and complexity of those problems as few philosophers in this century have been. The one-sidednesses Dewey found in past philosophizing have certainly been repeated in different guises by his contemporaries, and his consciousness of this fact colors his presentation of his moral ideas and keeps them pertinent in the face of current intellectual and practical trends.

Freedom remains the primary controversial concept in ethics. It is indispensable in the explanation of conduct; yet its meaning continues to escape moralists and antimoralists alike. Dewey rejects both the conception of freedom as reason, knowledge, or any other internal state of the individual and that of freedom as the absence of external obstacles to whatever movement a man may be launched upon. Typically, Dewey sees both the subjective and the objective explanations as abstractions which point out essential elements but which fail in their incompleteness to make sense of the fact of conduct and learning. The two sides must be brought together to make freedom intelligible. Freedom means the realization of satisfactory ends,[9] the

---

7. "Moral Theory and Practice," in *The Early Works of John Dewey, 1882–1898*, Vol. III (Carbondale: Southern Illinois University Press, 1969), pp. 94–95.

8. In *Investigations Representing the Departments, Part II: Philosophy, Education* (University of Chicago, The Decennial Publications, First Series, Vol. III [Chicago: University of Chicago Press, 1903]), pp. 113–239.

9. *Outlines of a Critical Theory of Ethics*, in *Early Works*, III, 343.

unification of the self and the act, the will and the deed,[10] the control of the material resources for satisfying desires and the effective powers of initiative and reflection necessary for choice and foresight,[11] an awareness of and an active interest in growth, learning, and modification of character,[12] and a trend of conduct leading to more diversified and self-aware choices and to enlarged areas of unimpeded action.[13] All of these formulations point to freedom as a special kind of interaction between an organism and its environment in which experience becomes the basis for the conscious modification of further experience in accordance with emerging goals. But this conception of freedom, of course, is the foundation of all learning, scientific as well as moral. And so Dewey has no trouble in answering the determinists who make man a moral puppet while granting him the power of acquiring knowledge. The evaluations of true and false rest on the same grounds as do those of good and bad, and if one set is thrown out, the other goes with it. Learning is a matter of control; and control constitutes freedom:

> It is assumed sometimes that if it can be shown that deliberation determines choice and deliberation is determined by character and conditions, there is no freedom. This is like saying that because a flower comes from root and stem it cannot bear fruit. The question is not what are the antecedents of deliberation and choice, but what are their consequences. What do they do that is distinctive? The answer is that they give us all the control of future possibilities which is open to us. And this control is the crux of our freedom. Without it, we are pushed from behind. With it we walk in the light.[14]

In addition to providing a reply to those who recurrently want to make man a pawn of external conditions, Dewey's analysis also provides a reply to the opposite extreme called out by determinism:

10. The Study of Ethics: A Syllabus (Ann Arbor: Register Publishing Co., 1894), p. 129.
11. Ethics (1908), p. 438.
12. Ethics (1932), p. 340.
13. "Philosophies of Freedom," in Freedom in the Modern World, ed. Horace Meyer Kallen (New York: Coward-McCann, 1928), p. 261.
14. Human Nature and Conduct (New York: Henry Holt and Co., 1922), p. 311.

When freedom is conceived to be transcendental, the coercive restraint of immediate necessity will lay its harsh hand upon the mass of men.

In the end, men do what they can do. . . . They do what their own specific powers in conjunction with the limitations and resources of the environment permit.[15]

Morality is coextensive with the capacity of freedom; that capacity is actual only in deliberate control of the self and the environment.

Control gives rise to responsibility. Just as with freedom, Dewey insists that the reference of responsibility is to the future, rather than to the past. To call a man to account for what he *has* done serves no useful purpose except as that calling to account can serve to alter what he *will* do. It is, again, a matter of such control as we can exercise over future possibilities and not a matter of some peculiarity in the precedent conditions:

A human being is held accountable in order that he may learn; in order that he may learn not theoretically and academically but in such a way as to modify and—to some extent—remake his prior self. The question of whether he might when he acted have acted differently from the way in which he did act is irrelevant. The question is whether he is capable of acting differently *next* time; the practical importance of effecting changes in human character is what makes responsibility important.[16]

There are two meanings of responsibility corresponding to the social and the individual aspects of ethics: negatively, responsibility means liability to answer for an act and to suffer disfavor or punishment if the answer is not a satisfactory one; positively, responsibility means the appropriation by the individual into his activities of an active awareness of the rights of others and of the connection of his acts with those rights. The social aspect of responsibility is negative because it is initially just an external force on the agent, as is most obvious in the discipline inflicted upon a child. This externally imposed responsibility Dewey calls legal or political. But the legal role of responsibility is a necessary prerequisite for the coming into being of the moral role exercised by the individual:

15. *Ethics* (1908 monograph), p. 25.
16. *Ethics* (1932), p. 337.

Liability is the beginning of responsibility. We are held accountable by others for the consequences of our acts. . . . The individual is *held* accountable for what he *has* done in order that he may be responsive in what he is *going* to do.

These two facts, that moral judgment and moral responsibility are the work wrought in us by the social environment, signify that all morality is social; not because we *ought* to take into account the effect of our acts upon the welfare of others, but because of facts.[17]

Responsibility, in its positive meaning, lies in the desires, interests, and character of the individual agent. But that responsibility depends for its very being upon the prior existence of mores, laws, and judgments of others; upon *others* holding the agent to account before he can develop that capacity of holding himself to account. And beyond its inception, individual responsibility takes its content and its manner of operation primarily from the social situation in which it functions. Hence Dewey's functional conception of human action cannot be classified as either an individualism or a socialism. All acts are individual, but all acts require a social context. All values must be valued by individuals, but those values function effectively only as they are propagated and preserved and made available in institutional structures.

Character is the inner side of the act situation, with conduct being its outer manifestation. From his early writings on, Dewey points out that character and conduct are correlative. Character is the individual's orientation toward his world which is both formed and manifested in conduct. Character is "the abiding unity in which different acts leave their lasting traces"; [18] and it is "attitudes of participative response in social affairs." [19] The whole set of habits which are operative in the conduct of an individual constitute his character, habits of emotion, desire, interest, concern, action.

The more detailed analysis of the function of character yields a discussion of virtue. Yet virtue, like character, cannot be dealt with apart from the other basic moral categories:

Virtue may be considered either as a case of substantial freedom, of solid, thoroughly unified action, or as a case of sub-

17. *Human Nature and Conduct*, pp. 315–16.
18. *Ethics* (1932), p. 182.
19. *Democracy and Education* (New York: Macmillan Co., 1916), p. 370.

stantial responsibility, of flexible, properly adjusted, interaction
—the adequate intellectual recognition of, and adequate emotional interest in, the demands of the situation.[20]

Most frequently, virtue is defined as an interest, with the result
that the traits of genuine interest must be set forth as part of the
definition. In the sense that "the genuine principle of interest is
the principle of the recognized identity of the fact or proposed
line of action with the self," [21] virtue is, then, the consciousness
of the identity of self and act. A genuine interest is wholehearted, persistent, and pure or impartial; thus these are aspects
of virtue.[22] Dewey rejects attempts to list particular virtues,
because such lists are inevitably made up of those modes of
behavior approved at a particular time and place. Rather, he
divides virtues into two categories, specific and cardinal. The
specific virtues are excellences (in the Greek sense) of particular abilities or skills, as those of a musician or a carpenter; these
capacities are virtues when they are "turned to account in
supporting or extending the fabric of social values." [23] The
cardinal virtues are simply the traits of a genuine interest referred to character. As wholehearted, interest involves justice;
as persistent, it is courage; as impartial, it is temperance; and
since to be any of these things a habit or interest must be
reasonable, interest involves wisdom.[24] Once more, it is worth
noting that there is a continuity in Dewey's treatment of the
virtues, throughout the shifts of emphasis. The cardinal virtues
remain the same, although virtue is defined psychologically in
the *Syllabus* [25] as "the adequate mediation of impulse" and
consequently the virtues are distinguished in terms of habits
with relation to impulse; whereas in the second edition of the
*Ethics*, virtue is defined as social awareness, and the virtues are
distinguished by reference to interest and the overwhelming
emphasis is upon wisdom and justice, the peculiarly socially
oriented excellences of character. But the distinction of four
cardinal virtues is, of course, itself one of emphasis. The vir-

20. *Syllabus*, p. 139.
21. "Interest as Related to [Training of the] Will," *Second Supplement to The Herbart Year Book for 1895*, rev. ed. (Bloomington, Ill.:
The Society, 1899), p. 9.
22. *Ethics* (1908), pp. 403–4; (1932), pp. 281–82.
23. *Ethics* (1908), p. 400.
24. *Ethics* (1908), pp. 404–5; (1932), p. 283.
25. p. 141.

tuous man is a man of wholeness, integrity, unity. Psychology makes clear what such integrity involves from the side of the individual; logic sets forth the grounds for our judgments with relation to a possible wholeness; sociology looks at this same unity from the standpoint of the social environment of virtuous action; ethics attempts to show the organic interrelationship of these aspects with a view to our moral lives. Dewey's persistent return to the concept of wholeness even as he develops the process by which wholeness is approximated is one of the more obvious signs of his debt to Plato (which he explicitly owns in the case of the cardinal virtues in the *Syllabus*,[26] and acknowledges more generally in "From Absolutism to Experimentalism" in *Contemporary American Philosophy*, 1930).[27]

Dewey's concept of the good is that of the total actualization of that wholeness which in virtue is viewed with respect to the individual. Good lies in the successful carrying out into the world of those habits and attitudes we call virtues. A good is a satisfaction, satisfaction of a desire or an interest. But a satisfaction becomes a good only as the result of reflection upon the consequences of the satisfaction and the relation of those consequences to other desires and interests and as a result of its incorporation into an organization of activity. The good is growth; and from the moral standpoint growth consists in

> ends of action, desirable in themselves, which reënforce and expand not only the motives from which they directly spring, but also the other tendencies and attitudes which are the sources of happiness.[28]

Thus Dewey's idea of good is opposed both to that idea of good as some remote ideal and to that as fleeting enjoyment. The good has to be in the present: "good is now or never"; but it is good precisely in being both now and in the future. Not in the future as the same good, but as promoting further goods of the same and of different kinds. Present satisfactions can, and sometimes must, be postponed for some future good, but unless there are sufficient present satisfactions in any course of activity, desire for future goods is weakened and warped. Action is

26. p. 141.
27. *Contemporary American Philosophy: Personal Statements*, II, eds. George Plimpton Adams and William Pepperell Montague (New York: Macmillan Co., 1930), 13–27.
28. *Ethics* (1908), p. 284.

toward an end, an ideal in the sense of some consequence that exists originally only in idea; yet that ideal must grow out of the present situation, an experienced good to be preserved or expanded or improved upon. In ethics, as elsewhere, Dewey is concerned that goals not be erected into fixed ends, rigid criteria. Our ends always project something from the past into the future. The future, however, is never like the past. New situations, new characters, new environments require new goods, and a viable conception of the good will be one that takes account of the changes taking place and of the ever-present fact of change itself. The good is always a process, not the Good as some fixed state to which we aspire. There are no absolutes in ethics any more than there are in any other realm of consideration. There is no good in itself apart from judgment of the thing in question in relation to a particular problematic situation, and correspondingly no evil in itself.

> The better is the good; the best is not better than the good but is simply the discovered good. . . . The worse or evil is a rejected good. In deliberation and before choice no evil presents itself as evil. Until it is rejected, it is a competing good. After rejection, it figures not as a lesser good, but as the bad of that situation.[29]

The early distinction Dewey made between goodness as a doing and badness as a having in the *Outlines* is indicative of the active nature of the good. Good is not a possession, not an attainment. That which is good in the present act situation, if clung to in the face of changes in that situation, will become bad, for the simple reason that it no longer serves as a means to genuine satisfactions in the existential situation.[30]

The fact that Dewey is so concerned to deny that there is *a* Good or *an* Ideal does not mean that he denies all ideals and standards. True, after the early writings, he does play down the role of the conception of the whole or any other formulation of the moral ideal. For one thing, he leaves behind that conception of the state as something to which the moral individual must accommodate himself [31] for the more fruitful conception of mutual interchange and adjustment between the individual and social organizations. Yet, although there are no eternal ends or

29. *Human Nature and Conduct*, p. 278.
30. *Ethics* (1932), p. 302.
31. *Outlines*, pp. 345–46.

values in any concrete sense, there are general ideals or principles for Dewey which condition everything he says about morality. Three general criteria operate for him, harmony, variety, and expansion. He states them succinctly in *Human Nature and Conduct*:

> Sufficient unto the day is the evil thereof. Sufficient it is to stimulate us to remedial action, to endeavor in order to convert strife into harmony, monotony into a variegated scene, and limitation into expansion. The converting is progress, the only progress conceivable or attainable by man. Hence every situation has its own measure and quality of progress, and the need for progress is recurrent, constant.[32]

Moral action is, first of all, action in the direction of harmony, co-operation, elimination of discord, restoration of fluidity.

> To be good is to be better than; and there can be no better except where there is shock and discord combined with enough assured order to make attainment of harmony possible.[33]

The moral-psychological problem is one of trying to organize the impulses and desires of the organism into a coherent self; the moral-social problem one of the working together of groups and institutions; and the moral-philosophic problem is that of showing the possibility of the harmonious interworkings of individual desires and social orders. Harmony, however, is a principle, not a rule. It supplies no content for action; it supplies a guide that must be filled in by reflection upon the particularities of the actual situation. It gives no answers, merely supplying a general framework for posing hypotheses whose value can be determined solely by their consequences. Similarly, the criterion of variety within harmony precludes in a general way any confusion of harmony with homogeneity. Variety means more opportunities for action, more possibilities for development of coherences, more color and vivacity in action itself. Again, the principle gives no specific instructions; it is a tool for analysis. And the criterion of expansion is almost a synonym for growth; except that growth includes also organization and variety. The expansion of the possibilities of action constitutes the definition

32. p. 282.
33. *Experience and Nature* (Chicago, London: Open Court Publishing Co., 1925), p. 62.

of good quoted above. The end of action is action itself, action of a quality such that it opens up new and various potentialities and harmonies in the lives of the agents involved.

The role of ideals for remedial action has been stressed because one recurrent criticism of Dewey's ethics has been that he provides no guides beyond the disruption of the immediate situation which calls forth action, that for him anything that gets rid of the current obstacle is *per se* good, that because he refuses to recognize an overarching good he must call any expedient that removes the agent from his present dilemma moral. In reply to such criticisms, it can be pointed out that from start to finish, Dewey has set forth and utilized ideals that are general because they grow out of the general analyses of action. Corresponding to the criteria of the consequences of action just mentioned (harmony, variety, and expansion) are the criteria for genuine interest: wholeheartedness, impartiality, and energy; and the criteria for a good agent: justice, temperance, and courage. And in the same sense that wisdom is the nurse of the other virtues, so is reasonableness a characteristic of all genuine interest and increased understanding or sense of significance a consequence of all moral conduct. But however Dewey uses these general ideas, they remain ideas applicable to the *process* of human activity, not to some state of affairs to be achieved or even to be striven for as a stable goal. Our notions of the good and of virtue will evolve in the process of their realization. Ethics, like everything else for Dewey, is a search, not a prize, and we are moral or immoral men as we do or do not consciously apply our intelligences to that search.

The purpose of this essay has not been to set forth a concise statement of Dewey's ethics. Dewey's ethics is nothing more or less than the application of his method of reflective thought to problems of human behavior, problems of good and bad, right and wrong, virtue and vice. That method can be appreciated only by reading what Dewey wrote as he developed that method and applied it to a variety of problems from a variety of standpoints. But the methodological unity of Dewey's philosophy means that whatever you read, you will increase your insight into his attempt to understand the world. The concepts discussed above are some of the central moral ideas that run through Dewey's moral works. Because they are traditional concepts, the attempt has been made to show the sense in which they operate for Dewey. But the discussion is intended as no more than a guide to the reading of Dewey himself.

The traditional language of Dewey's moral philosophy makes an additional problem in getting at what is peculiarly Dewey's in his theory, but that same language, once understood in Dewey's vernacular, makes it even clearer than it sometimes is in some of his other writings that Dewey's philosophy is still relevant to our problems. The theoretic problems of moral philosophy in this century are all dealt with one way or another by Dewey. And one sign of the enduring quality of his thought in this area is that he has been so influential without falling into the extremes that so frequently characterize the theories that catch the public or academic fancy. By extremes, I mean those disproportionate views which startle us into attention but which also betray moral theories into destroying all meaningful grounds for the very morality they set out to explain. Dewey's behaviorism stands, despite technical advances, as a corrective to the inhuman behaviorisms from John B. Watson to the present. (See Dewey's "Conduct and Experience" in *Psychologies of 1930* [34] for a discussion of this issue.) His empiricism restores the balance between science and ethics upset by positivism and its claim that science is cognitive but ethics not. (Explicitly, in *Theory of Valuation*.) [35] Dewey's functionalism remains an answer to the separation of thought and feeling by a variety of emotivisms. (A good example is Dewey's "Ethical Subject-Matter and Language," 1945.) [36] And, finally, his instrumentalism puts into proper perspective some of the existentialists' claims for man's moral independence of his environment.

Almost all of Dewey's major ethical writings remain of interest and of value when read in relation to the problems to which he was addressing himself. Most of these problems, theoretic or practical, remain problems, although we may have changed our formulations of them. For instance, the *Outlines* provides a better answer to Bradley's problem of the conflict between a man's duties to his society as a citizen and his duties

34. Ed. Carl Murchison (Worcester, Mass.: Clark University Press, 1930), pp. 409–22.
35. (International Encyclopedia of Unified Science, Vol. II, No. 4 [Chicago: University of Chicago Press, 1939]).
36. *Journal of Philosophy*, XLII (1945), 701–12.

to himself as an artist or scientist, even though Dewey's theory in that book is to a considerable extent derived from Bradley. And his reply to Thomas Huxley in "Evolution and Ethics" (1898) [37] is still pertinent to such popular notions as that civilized men interfere with the natural process of selection to the detriment of the species.

The major *practical* problem of our day is that of the preservation and expansion of individuality in a world of increasingly impersonal and increasingly pervasive institutions. And a primary part of that problem is the very divergence Dewey pointed out between the moral norms we profess and those upon which we act. There are no better sources for our beginning to understand the current situation than Dewey's treatments of these difficulties in *Human Nature and Conduct; The Quest for Certainty; Individualism, Old and New;* and *Ethics* (1932). His statement of the problem remains a good one:

> What is needed is intelligent examination of the consequences that are actually effected by inherited institutions and customs, in order that there may be intelligent consideration of the ways in which they are to be intentionally modified in behalf of generation of different consequences.[38]

A philosophy is always of its time. A good philosophy transcends its time, as well. We are still of Dewey's time, and his philosophy so far holds promise of serving both us and our posterity.

37. *Monist*, VIII (1898), 321–41.
38. *The Quest for Certainty* (New York: Minton, Balch and Co., 1929), p. 273.

## CHECKLIST

*Psychology* (The Early Works of John Dewey, 1882–1898, Vol. II). Carbondale: Southern Illinois University Press, 1967. cix, 366 pp.
"Ethics and Physical Science," in *The Early Works of John Dewey, 1882–1898*, Vol. I, pp. 205–26. Carbondale: Southern Illinois University Press, 1969.
*The Ethics of Democracy,* in *Early Works,* I, 227–49.
*Outlines of a Critical Theory of Ethics,* in *The Early Works of John Dewey, 1882–1898*, Vol. III, pp. 239–388. Carbondale: Southern Illinois University Press, 1969.
"Moral Theory and Practice," in *Early Works,* III, 93–109.

"[Thomas Hill] Green's Theory of the Moral Motive," in *Early Works*, III, 155–73.

"Self-Realization as the Moral Ideal," *Philosophical Review*, II (Nov. 1893), 652–64.

*The Study of Ethics: A Syllabus*. Ann Arbor: Register Publishing Co., 1894. iv, 151 pp. [2d ed., Ann Arbor: George Wahr, 1897. 144 pp.]

Review of "On Certain Psychological Aspects of Moral Training" by Josiah Royce, *International Journal of Ethics*, III (July 1893), 413–36; "Moral Deficiencies as Determining Intellectual Functions" by Georg Simmel, ibid., III (July 1893), 490–507; and "The Knowledge of Good and Evil" by Josiah Royce, ibid., IV (Oct. 1893), 48–80; *Psychological Review*, I (Jan. 1894), 109–11.

"The Chaos in Moral Training," *Popular Science Monthly*, XLV (Aug. 1894), 433–43.

"Ethics and Politics," *University Record*, III (Feb. 1894), 101–2. [Report of an address made to the Philosophical Society in Dec. 1893.]

"Several Lectures in Anthropological Ethics, '94." Handwritten by Charles H. Cooley, University of Michigan. 158 pp., 2 pp. typewritten. [Michigan Historical Collections.] [Handwritten copy by Winifred Higbee Rose, 120 leaves, in private collection of Edward Rose, University of Colorado.]

*Educational Ethics: Syllabus of a Course of Six Lecture-Studies*. Chicago: University of Chicago Press, 1895. 12 pp.

"Logic of Ethics." Stenographic report of class lectures, [H. Heath Bawden], University of Chicago, 1895–96. 48 pp. [St. Louis University.]

"Interest as Related to [Training of the] Will," in *Second Supplement to the Herbart Year Book for 1895*, pp. 209–46. Bloomington, Ill.: National Herbart Society, 1896. Rev. ed., Chicago: The Society, 1899. [Reprinted in C–16, pp. 260–85, with the title "Interest in Relation to Training of the Will."]

"The Metaphysical Method in Ethics," *Psychological Review*, III (Mar. 1896), 181–88. [Discussion of *A Short Study of Ethics* by Archbishop Charles Frederick D'Arcy.]

"Evolution and Ethics," *Monist*, VIII (Apr. 1898), 321–41.

Review of *Social and Ethical Interpretations in Mental Development* by James Mark Baldwin, *Philosophical Review*, VII (July 1898), 398–409. Response by Baldwin, *Philosophical Review*, VII (Nov. 1898), 621–28. Rejoinder by Dewey, *Philosophical Review*, VII (Nov. 1898), 629–30.

Review of *Social and Ethical Interpretations in Mental Development* by James Mark Baldwin, *New World*, VII (Sept. 1898), 504–22.

"Political Ethics." Stenographic report of class lectures, [H. Heath Bawden], University of Chicago, 1898. 175 pp. [St. Louis University.] [Another copy, Grinnell College; a third copy, labeled "Lectures in Psychology at the University of Chicago," Duke University.]

"Psychology of Ethics." Stenographic report of class lectures, [H. Heath Bawden], University of Chicago, 1898. 120 pp. [St. Louis University.]

"Logic of Ethics." Stenographic report of class lectures, [H. Heath Bawden], University of Chicago, 1900. 85 pp. [St. Louis University.]

"The Psychology of Ethics," Course 35. Stenographic report of class lectures by Mary L. Read, [H. Heath Bawden], University of Chicago, 1901. 125 pp. [St. Louis University.]

"The Historical Method in Ethics." Typescript from notes, [H. Heath Bawden], of an address before the Philosophical Club, 4 Dec. 1901, University of Chicago, 5 pp. [St. Louis University.] [Another copy, 6 pp., in the Henry Waldgrave Stuart Papers, Stanford University.]

"Social Ethics," Course 44. Stenographic report by Mary L. Read, [H. Heath Bawden], University of Chicago, 1901. 129 pp. [St. Louis University.]

"The Evolution of Morality." Stenographic report of lectures, University of Chicago, 1901. 111 pp. [Henry Waldgrave Stuart Papers, Stanford University.]

"The Evolutionary Method as Applied to Morality," I. Its Scientific Necessity, *Philosophical Review,* XI (Mar. 1902), 107–24; II. Its Significance for Conduct, ibid., XI (July 1902), 353–71.

"Sociology of Ethics." Stenographic report of class lectures, [H. Heath Bawden], University of Chicago, 1902–3. 355 pp. [St. Louis University.] [Another copy in the papers of Dr. W. C. Keirstead, University of New Brunswick Library, lacks pp. 180–89.]

"Logical Conditions of a Scientific Treatment of Morality," in *Investigations Representing the Departments, Part II: Philosophy, Education* (University of Chicago, The Decennial Publications, First Series, Vol. III), pp. 113–39. Chicago: University of Chicago Press, 1903. [Reprinted separately, Chicago: University of Chicago Press, 1903, 27 pp.; also reprinted in C–8, pp. 211–49; C–16, pp. 23–60.]

"Psychological Method in Ethics," *Psychological Review,* X (Mar. 1903), 158–60.

"Ethics," in *Encyclopedia Americana,* VII. New York, Chicago: Americana Co., 1904.

Review of *World Views and Their Ethical Implications* by Wayland Richardson Benedict, *International Journal of Ethics,* XIV (Apr. 1904), 389–90.

*Ethics.* New York: Columbia University Press, 1908. 26 pp. [Reprinted in C–2, pp. 46–76, with the title "Intelligence and Morals."]

*Ethics,* with James Hayden Tufts (American Science Series). New York: Henry Holt and Co., 1908. xiii, 618 pp.

*Moral Principles in Education* (Riverside Educational Monographs, ed. Henry Suzzallo). Boston: Houghton Mifflin Co., 1909. xii, 61 pp.

"Objects, Data, and Existences: A Reply to Professor McGilvary," *Journal of Philosophy,* VI (Jan. 1909), 13–21. (Reply to: Evander Bradley McGilvary, "The Chicago 'Idea' and Idealism," *Journal of Philosophy,* V [Oct. 1908], 589–97.)

"The Logic of Judgments of Practise," I. Their Nature, *Journal of Philosophy,* XII (Sept. 1915), 505–12; II. Judgments of Value, ibid., XII (Sept. 1915), 512–23; III. Sense-Perception as Knowledge, ibid., XII (Sept. 1915), 533–43. [Reprinted in C–3, pp. 335–442.]

*Democracy and Education: An Introduction to the Philosophy of Education* (Text-Book Series in Education, ed. Paul Monroe). New York: Macmillan Co., 1916. xii, 434 pp.

*Human Nature and Conduct.* New York: Henry Holt and Co., 1922. vii, 336 pp. [Enl. ed., with Foreword, New York: Modern Library, 1930. ix, vii, 336 pp. Also, Armed Forces ed. (from original plates), 1944.]

*Social Institutions and the Study of Morals: Syllabus for Philosophy 131–32,* Columbia University, 1923–24. [New York, 1923?]. 57 pp., multigraphed.

"Tradition, Metaphysics, and Morals," *Journal of Philosophy,* XX (Mar. 1923), 187–92. (Reply to: Daniel Sommer Robinson, "The Chief Types of Motivation to Philosophic Reflection," *Journal of Philosophy,* XX [Jan. 1923], 29–41.)

*Experience and Nature* (Lectures upon the Paul Carus Foundation, First Series). Chicago, London: Open Court Publishing Co., 1925. xi, 443 pp. [2d ed., with a Preface, New York: W. W. Norton, 1929. ix, 1a–4a,

1–443 pp. 3d ed., LaSalle, Ill.: Open Court Publishing Co., 1958. xviii, 360 pp.]

"The Ethics of Animal Experimentation," *Atlantic Monthly*, CXXXVIII (Sept. 1926), 343–46; also published by Government Printing Office, Washington, 1926, in the report of a hearing before a subcommittee of the 69th Congress, 1st Session, on Senate Bill No. 2975.

"Philosophies of Freedom," in *Freedom in the Modern World*, ed. Horace Meyer Kallen, pp. 236–71. New York: Coward-McCann, 1928. [Reprinted in C–7, pp. 271–98.]

*The Quest for Certainty*. New York: Minton, Balch and Co., 1929. 318 pp.

"Foreword," in *Tolstoi and Nietzsche, a Problem in Biographical Ethics* by Helen Edna Davis, pp. ix–xiv. New York: New Republic, 1929.

"Foreword," in *Human Nature and Conduct*, pp. v–ix. New York: Modern Library, 1930.

"Conduct and Experience," in *Psychologies of 1930*, ed. Carl Murchison, pp. 409–22. Worcester, Mass.: Clark University Press, 1930. [Reprinted in C–7, pp. 249–70.]

*Ethics*, with James Hayden Tufts. New York: Henry Holt and Co., 1932. xiii, 528 pp. [Rev. ed., with Preface to the 1932 Edition. The 1908 edition has been completely revised, with "about two-thirds of the present edition . . . newly written, and frequent changes in detail . . . in the remainder."]

"Means and Ends," *New International*, IV (Aug. 1938), 232–33. (Discussion of: Leon Trotsky, "Their Morals and Ours," *New International*, IV [June 1938], 163–73.)

*Theory of Valuation* (International Encyclopedia of Unified Science, Vol. II, No. 4). Chicago: University of Chicago Press, 1939. 67 pp.

"Religion and Morality in a Free Society." Typescript of an address by John Dewey for Hollins College Centennial, 18 May 1942. 16 pp.

"Ethical Subject-Matter and Language," *Journal of Philosophy*, XLII (Dec. 1945), 701–12.

"William James' Morals and Julian Benda's: It Is Not Pragmatism That Is Opportunist," *Commentary*, V (Jan. 1948), 46–50. (Reply to: Julian Benda, "The Attack on Western Morality," *Commentary*, IV [Nov. 1947], 416–22.)

"Three Independent Factors in Morals," trans. Jo Ann Boydston, *Educational Theory*, XVI (July 1966), 197–209. [First published as "Trois facteurs indépendants en matière de morale," *Bulletin de la société française de philosophie*, XXX (octobre–décembre 1930), 118–27, (Discussion, 127–35).]

# 5

# Dewey's
# Social, Political, and Legal Philosophy

### WAYNE A. R. LEYS

DEWEY'S MAJOR contributions to political, legal, and social philosophy were made during the 1920s and 1930s. It was during that period that he diagnosed the tensions and wastes of modern institutions. It was then that he became well known as an advocate of "scientific method" in the *reconstruction of society*. This was the period in which his objections to moral and theological "absolutes" were most explicit in relation to *social policy*. This was also the time in which he rejected the Soviet conception of public planning (because it depended too much upon coercion and too little upon the participation of all concerned in the give-and-take of an educative process).

Readers who skim hurriedly through *Human Nature and Conduct* and the later writings can get the impression that Dewey was a latter-day Jeremy Bentham, a Utilitarian who had turned to mild socialism, an eighteenth-century Empiricist grappling with twentieth-century issues. To some critics, who have seen only fact-finding and troubleshooting in his "experimentalism," Dewey has seemed to lack solid moral footing for his political opinions.[1] But such a reading is a distortion, a distortion for which Dewey himself was partially responsible.

When, after the First World War, Dewey gave more and more attention to political institutions, he used much of the

1. See, for example, Lewis Mumford, "The Pragmatic Acquiescence," in *The Golden Day* (New York: Horace Liveright, 1926), reprinted in Gail Kennedy, *Pragmatism and American Culture* (Boston: D. C. Heath and Co., 1950), pp. 36 ff. See also A. E. Murphy's review of Morton White's *Social Thought in America*, *Philosophical Review*, LX (1951), 582.

vocabulary of the British Empiricists. For casual readers this was misleading for the same reason that his use of Hegelian language had been misunderstood in his Michigan period. Whatever sectarian terminology Dewey employed, he was always trying to unsettle well-established definitions and thus convey meanings and insights that had been neglected by the sectarians. So it was with the Empiricist language in which Dewey wrote his mature social and political philosophy.

Dewey wrote several critiques of British Empiricism.[2] He carefully distinguished his viewpoint from both ancient and modern empiricists. But the meanings of "experience," "consequences," "control," etc., had been so firmly fixed by the British Empiricists that Dewey's texts were frequently misread as echoes of Bacon, Locke, and Mill. When, in his old age, Dewey found a reader (Arthur F. Bentley) with the time and patience to expose the inappropriateness of his Baconian and Benthamite phrases, Dewey collaborated in the writing of a series of articles that, hopefully, would provide a vocabulary without built-in Empiricist errors. The result was, eventually, a book, *Knowing and the Known* (Boston, 1949), abounding in hyphenated barbarisms, such as, "search-research," "distinguishing-connecting," "knowings-knowns," "perceptive-manipulative," and "event-fact."

What new kind of wine did Dewey pour into the old Empiricist bottles? Dewey himself mentioned the lasting influence of Hegelian thought, to which G. S. Morris introduced him in the 1880s. There is some evidence that Morris brought to Dewey the insights of another German philosopher, the biologically oriented F. A. Trendelenburg,[3] and still other German points of view seem to have been brought home by Dewey's colleagues Mead and Tufts, who had studied in Germany. What these German influences did for Dewey was to impress him with the relatedness of things, which many of the British philosophers neglected or took for granted. Life and the world were not, in the more organismic German philosophies, a set of

2. "An Empirical Survey of Empiricisms," in *Studies in the History of Ideas* by the Department of Philosophy of Columbia University, Vol. III (New York: Columbia University Press, 1935), pp. 3–24; and *Human Nature and Conduct* (New York: Henry Holt and Co., 1922), Pt. III, Sec. 4.

3. Gershon George Rosenstock, *F. A. Trendelenburg, Forerunner to John Dewey* (Carbondale: Southern Illinois University Press, 1964).

isolated, disconnected facts. When, therefore, Dewey came to employ Empiricist language in his institutional critiques, he accepted none of the atomistic assumptions that, rightly or wrongly, may have been associated with that vocabulary.

In autobiographical statements Dewey mentioned his temperamental disposition to formulate ideas in "schematic form," with "logical consistency" a dominant consideration.[4] It was apparently this hankering for unity that made him, as an undergraduate, responsive to the Positive Philosophy of Auguste Comte, not to Comte's Positivism, but Comte's picture of the disorganization of society and the possible role of science in overcoming anarchy and chaos. Of his Neo-Hegelian period, Dewey recalled his appreciation of Hegel's idea of cultural institutions as an "objective mind" upon which individuals were dependent in the formation of their mental life.

The adoption of an Empiricist vocabulary was evidently a reflection of Dewey's persistent efforts to correct his schematic unities in the light of stubborn facts. He has testified to the influence of friends and events that forced him to modify his preconceptions. His repeated urging of "scientific study of the facts" and "evaluation in terms of consequences," then, do not prove him to be an antitheoretic empiric or a piecemeal reformer. They represent the mature concessions that are implicit in Dewey's conclusion that order, unity, and community are not "given"; they need to be achieved, and precisely what they can or ought to be will only be discovered in the achieving. In his last years Dewey was contemplating the abandonment of the word "experience": he had long been trying to establish an account of "experience" "which would include the relational along with the 'sensible.'"[5] It was a difficult effort, for he was convinced that the relational aspects of experience, especially of institutional experience, should not be regarded as an alien fact, somehow mirrored in a passive mind.

4. "From Absolutism to Experimentalism," in *Contemporary American Philosophers: Personal Statements*, II, eds. George Plimpton Adams and William Pepperell Montague (New York: Macmillan Co., 1930), 19. See also "Biography of John Dewey," Jane M. Dewey, ed., in *The Philosophy of John Dewey* (The Library of Living Philosophers, Vol. I, ed. Paul Arthur Schilpp [Evanston, Chicago: Northwestern University, 1939]), pp. 44–45.

5. *John Dewey and Arthur F. Bentley: A Philosophical Correspondence, 1932–1951*, eds. Sidney Ratner and Jules Altman (New Brunswick, N.J.: Rutgers University Press, 1964), p. 454.

## An Unprejudiced Concept of Maladjustment

In his social philosophy Dewey was moving, during the twenties and thirties, to a point of view which he finally called "transactional." The view was foreshadowed in a famous sentence in *Human Nature and Conduct*: " 'It thinks' is a truer psychological statement than 'I think.' " [6] In describing the conflicts and malfunctionings of society, Dewey was trying to get away from a conception of human beings as entities with a fixed nature that were adjusting to or manipulating an environment, another set of entities with a fixed nature. What he was talking about was a process, an interaction, a transaction, in which nouns referred to the changing features of a partially indeterminate situation.

Hence, when Dewey talked about the maladjustment of economic and political institutions, he was only in partial agreement with a man like Harold Laski. He agreed that economic activities had developed into complex, large-scale, corporate enterprises, and that many political practices remained as they had been in the days of small farmers and local markets. But Dewey did not regard either pole of the contrast as necessarily fixed. The problem was not one of adjusting everything else to a certain form of economic technology.

When Dewey talked about "the lost individual" and a loss of freedom, his diagnosis of the malaise was not to be confused with the diagnoses of Herbert Spencer and William Graham Sumner. Dewey tried not to think of "the individual" as a being whose freedom depended upon a given condition. For him "freedom" and "democracy" were terms that indicated "the participation of every mature human being in formation of the values that regulate the living of men together." [7]

Similarly, "planning" and "control" were words that did not imply the subordination of men or materials to unchanging ends. To the extent that associated activities were intelligent, ends might adjust to means no less than means adjust to ends. The crucial question was whether there was any awareness of

6. *Human Nature and Conduct*, p. 314.
7. "Democracy and Educational Administration," *School and Society*, XLV (1937), 457.

the relation of "ends" and "means" and whether there was any deliberate direction.

In his endeavor to avoid unnecessary limitations upon the socio-political process, Dewey was particularly anxious to liberate the social sciences from a "stultifying" isolation. In one of his last long articles he noted the tendency of sociologists and economists to think of themselves as technicians who applied certain methods to certain problems. Dewey quarreled with the notion that "*the* problem" of a scientist is to get *the* facts and find out what is true of the existing social order. Intelligent scientists, he thought, have a good deal to say about what will be considered as a problem, and that requires inquiry into what ought to exist. Otherwise, scientific inquiry is subordinated to predetermined ends.[8]

I am not asserting that in his later essays Dewey always succeeded in avoiding dualisms of "subject" and "object," "human" and "environment," "ends" and "means," etc. But I do assert that he made a heroic effort in this direction. To the extent that intelligible language permitted, he talked about social processes as actual disharmonies and discontinuities and as potential harmonies and unities, without prejudice as to what was out of tune or what the tune should be.

### Relation to Early Educational Theory

It is obvious that I have spoken of the last thirty years of Dewey's political philosophizing without reference to the pedagogical work that made him famous during the second thirty years of his life. I cannot find evidence in Dewey's early treatises on the philosophy of education that he had already achieved his later conception of human society. In *Democracy and Education*, no less than in *The School and Society*, he has a great deal to say about the school as a social institution. There is much comment on the problem of relating the child to the activities of home and community. Social progress is seen as depending upon the regulation of the process in which the child comes to share in the social consciousness. In "My Pedagogic Creed" (1897) Dewey wrote that "education is the fundamental method of social

8. "Liberating the Social Scientist: A Plea to Unshackle the Study of Man," *Commentary*, IV (1947), 385.

progress and reform. . . . All reforms which rest simply upon the enactment of law, or the threatening of certain penalties, or upon changes in mechanical or outward arrangements, are transitory and futile." [9] This is certainly an opinion that remained unaltered forty years later. But the reader will look in vain for early expressions of that fluid notion of what is adjusting and what is adjusted to, so characteristic of Dewey's political writing from 1920 to 1950.

### Beginnings of Mature Political Philosophy

I may have overlooked some earlier trace of political transactionism, but I believe that it is first evident in what Dewey wrote during the First World War. In many respects *German Philosophy and Politics* is the worst book of his career. Yet, it was in this unsympathetic study of a modern nation and its philosophers that Dewey began to use his instrumental logic in a critique of political beliefs and practices. He was treating philosophical ideas as something that may have an influence upon practical affairs, but he concluded that German politics "has rather been the controlling factor in the formation of philosophic ideas." [10] Dewey then speculated on what might happen if Hegel's dictum were ignored and social constitutions were regarded as objects of choice.

> That such an experimental philosophy of life means a dangerous experiment goes without saying. It permits, sooner or later it may require, every alleged sacrosanct principle to submit to ordeal by fire—to trial by service rendered. . . . An experimental philosophy differs from empirical philosophy as empiricism has been previously formulated. Historical empiricisms have been stated in terms of precedents; their generalizations have been summaries of what has previously happened. . . . They were perforce lacking in directive power except so far as the future might be a routine repetition of the past. In an experimental philosophy of life, the question of the past, of precedents, of origins, is quite subordinate to prevision, to guidance and control amid future possibilities. . . . Our country is too big and too unformed, however, to enable us to trust

9. "My Pedagogic Creed," *School Journal*, LIV (1897), 80.
10. *German Philosophy and Politics* (New York: G. P. Putnam's Sons, 1915), p. 123.

to an empirical philosophy of muddling along, patching up here and there some old piece of machinery which has broken down by reason of its antiquity. We must have system, constructive method, springing from a widely inventive imagination, a method checked up at each turn by results achieved.[11]

Some of the articles published in the *New Republic* and the *Nation* during and after the First World War testify to Dewey's growing convictions: *1)* that the tragic conflict could not have been avoided in 1914 by good, moral intentions alone, and another war would not be prevented without new institutional apparatus, better suited to a rapidly changing civilization. Noble attitudes and motives, apart from suitable social organization, were dismissed as ineffective sentimentalism.[12]  *2)* Within the limited objectives of nations at war there was now a demonstration of the extent to which societies can be reconstructed. ("War has revealed the possibilities . . . of intelligent administration — administration which will raise and maintain on a higher level the general standard and scale of living.") [13]

These themes are not prominent in all of Dewey's reflections upon the First World War. His essay, "Force and Coercion," for example, showed a rather slight development toward Dewey's later conception of an experimental social philosophy.[14] But a full-blown programmatic announcement of "cooperation between philosophy and the course of events" was contained in the last lecture which Dewey delivered in Tokyo in 1919. He called for efforts to make coherent the meaning of daily detail, with resulting interpenetration of practice and imagination.[15] He was recommending a point of view that would avoid the atomistic empiricism of British liberal social philosophy and the dangerous rigidity of German political thought.

In concluding that Dewey's social and political experimentalism took shape as he thought about nations at war, I do not want to deny the importance of Dewey's educational theories in

11. *German Philosophy*, pp. 125–27, 129.

12. "Morals and the Conduct of States," *New Republic*, XIV (1918), 232. See also, "A New Social Science," *New Republic*, XIV (1918), 293.

13. "Internal Social Reorganization After the War," *Journal of Race Development*, VIII (1918), 397.

14. "Force and Coercion," *International Journal of Ethics*, XXVI (1916), 359–67.

15. *Reconstruction in Philosophy* (New York: Henry Holt and Co., 1920), Ch. 8, pp. 187–213.

his political philosophy. When he had caught his vision of an open-ended society (in which nothing was properly exempt from criticism and nothing could be *assumed* to be unchanging), the insights of his Laboratory School years fitted neatly into the picture. Government, business, and religious institutions were not limited to their most typically routine services. They also had an educative function, which might be discharged wittingly or unwittingly, intelligently or stupidly, generously or selfishly.

> The moral function of law and institutions, as well as of freedom of inquiry and expression, is in last analysis educative. Their final test is what they do to awaken curiosity and inquiry in worthy directions; what they do to render men and women more sensitive to beauty and truth; more disposed to act in creative ways; more skilled in voluntary coöperation.[16]

This passage from the 1932 *Ethics* is, significantly, not found in the original 1908 edition.

### Early Political Teaching

In arguing the relatively late appearance of Dewey's political experimentalism I do not imply that he was not thinking about politics prior to 1915. Almost from the beginning of his teaching career Dewey was giving instruction in the history of political and social thought. He offered, usually at the graduate level, many topical courses on such subjects as "The Development of English Utilitarianism," "Contemporary Theories regarding the Ethical Relations of Individual and Society," and "The History of Political Ethics."[17] At Columbia he collaborated with Professor Patterson in a course on "The Philosophy of Law." However, the political and social topics on which Dewey first published seem to have been the normal by-products of a young instructor's reading and course preparation. The twenty-one-page article on "Austin's Theory of Sovereignty," published in the *Political Science Quarterly* in March 1894, was critical of any theory that tried to understand government with-

16. *Ethics*, rev. ed., with James H. Tufts (New York: Henry Holt and Co., 1932), p. 405.
17. The Grinnell College Library transcript of Dewey's 1898 course on Political Ethics, in my opinion, confirms the view that his political experimentalism was a relatively late development.

out reference to "the whole social activity, the entire play of social life." [18] But we have already noted Dewey's self-confessed disposition to seek some kind of unity. While that disposition was an ingredient in his mature political philosophy, it was not the experimental transactionism to which he eventually came.

The Instrumentalist political philosopher advocated experimentation on the ground that conflicts between individuals and institutions are transactions, none of whose elements can safely be assumed to be unchanging or unrelated. Although Dewey rejected the Hegelian and Marxist belief that there was one fundamental direction in the changing transactions, it was important for him to inquire into the directions of social change. Such inquiry he undertook in a serious way, especially during the 1920s.

Dewey's investigation of the need for political and economic reconstruction was undoubtedly affected by his sojourns in China, Japan, Turkey, and the Soviet Union. (His observations on the turbulent and far-reaching changes in these countries are discussed in William W. Brickman's chapter in this volume.) It was against the background of these international experiences, as well as the experience of the First World War, that Dewey achieved something like a systematic theory of politics in his Kenyon College lectures, later published as *The Public and Its Problems* (1927). Dewey's theory was remarkable because it was an eloquent plea for an expansion of the services of government beyond the narrow peace-keeping functions recognized by nineteenth-century liberalism, but yet, at the same time, an even more eloquent plea for the restoration of local community life. The impact on thoughtful officials and political scientists was especially noticeable in the decade of the Great Depression and the equally disturbing decade of the Second World War. Events inside the United States then combined with Dewey's 1926 comments to shake up long-established ideas about what was public and what was private. The effect was not a new "philosophy of government" in the sense of a new set of dos and don'ts, but rather a way of relating thoughts about government to changing conditions of life, on the one hand, and the persisting need of human beings for meaningful participation as well as for specified goods and services. In Dewey's view

18. "Austin's Theory of Sovereignty," *Political Science Quarterly*, IX (1894), 31–52.

there were no fixed and immutable boundaries for the State. The limits of governmental action fluctuated from time to time, as publics were created by "extensive and enduring indirect consequences" of "conjoint behavior" (p. 47). Precisely what was creating public needs and where government should intervene or withdraw: these were matters to be determined by broad inquiry.

### Some Tentative Conclusions

As mentioned above, Dewey had some beliefs about the directions of social change. Among the tentative conclusions of this inquiry Dewey asserted the truth of several rather sweeping generalizations: *1)* Human life was no longer isolated in one locality or in one nation. In the multiplying international transactions it was obvious that "national sovereignty" created more problems than it solved. However, Dewey did not accept pacifist movements or international organizations (such as the World Court) as adequate responses to the new situation. From 1915 on he encouraged reconstruction efforts that dealt with international anarchy, although he was not plumping for any panacea. *2)* Economic life was being organized on a widening scale, and Dewey came to believe that some sort of socialism ("private" or "public") was inevitable.[19] In *The Public and Its Problems* and in numerous occasional pieces, Dewey was calling for countercyclical measures and the planned use of resources. Although his prescriptions were often vague, the fiscal and monetary policies of the Roosevelt administration in 1933 were steps in a direction that Dewey had advocated in the preceding decade. *3)* New forms of human association and communication were being invented which, in Dewey's opinion, gave promise of "meaningful" participation in policy determination, despite the size of organizations. "The great community" was, in his view, emergent democracy. General suffrage, representative government, and majority rule were the crude beginnings of a more adequate relating of parts to the whole human enterprise. Dewey seemed confident that war and wasteful litigation would be reduced as social skills and better machinery were developed.

19. "The Crisis in Culture," *New Republic*, LXII (1930), 123–26.

Much of the existing politics he condemned as deception and intimidation, anachronistic hangovers from the time when the largest part of the population consisted of illiterate peasants.

In view of Dewey's Instrumentalism the foregoing descriptions could hardly be advanced as truths independent of the particular context and practical values of the author. In the *Encyclopaedia of the Social Sciences* (1934), Dewey's article on "Philosophy" treated philosophies as cultural phenomena, always involving valuation and preferential attachment to special types of objects and courses of action.[20]

## Dewey's "We"

It will be, therefore, an unsympathetic reader who tries to distinguish some eternal truths in Dewey's social philosophy from his controversial positions in the debates of his time. On the other hand, the sympathetic reader, who tries to understand this social philosophy by identifying Dewey's personal involvement in historical situations, will discover that Dewey's texts are not very helpful. Dewey talked about "liberals" and "those who believe in the method of intelligence," but a historian would have a hard time finding any group, class, or movement for which Dewey was the spokesman when he used (as he frequently did) the personal pronoun "we." In his frequent employment of the normative word "need," there was seldom a definite reference to an action-group from whose point of view the "needs" of society were being outlined.

The reader can, of course, identify the organizations which claimed Dewey's support: the Progressive Education Association, the League for Industrial Democracy, the American Federation of Teachers, the People's Lobby, etc. But these organizations were not characterized by the unified direction of Dewey's thoughts. Nor did their changing memberships include more than a small fraction of Dewey's "public," the students and adult readers who found his ideas challenging.

20. Dewey admits that after philosophical beliefs receive formal articulation they begin a secondary career without reference to the cultural conditions of their origin (thanks to the professors and other antiquarians who keep alive the memory of what were once living philosophies). See "Philosophy," *Encyclopaedia of the Social Sciences*, XII (New York: Macmillan Co., 1934), 124.

The reader, still looking for Dewey's "we," may identify the opposition to the organizations that Dewey condemned. In *Liberalism and Social Action*, Dewey expressed his dissatisfaction with the major American political parties and the system of party government. In the same volume are Dewey's reasons for rejecting the invitations of the Communists to join in a violent revolution. The faith in the major American parties and the faith in a Communist revolution are both branded as Hegelian dialectic magic. The method of the two-party system has nothing in common "with the procedure of organized co-operative inquiry which has won the triumphs of science in the field of physical nature." And the method of revolution is an incredible use of brute force by one class, claiming "all of a sudden" to transmute itself into a democratic classless society.

After rejecting the major parties and the Communist party, Dewey went on to lament the divisions among "liberals" and their inability to use organized social effort as a means to desirable ends. Then he added: "It is no part of my talk to outline in detail a program for renascent liberalism."

Although Dewey stood up to be counted on numerous occasions (when Gorky was refused lodging in New York hotels, when Russell's teaching contract was broken by the New York School Board, when Communists captured control of the Teachers' Union in New York City, etc.) he was not a partisan in the sense of making long-term commitments "for better or for worse." This, of course, was the basis of Reinhold Niebuhr's objection to Instrumentalism (in *Moral Man and Immoral Society*, 1932). Such commitments and such partisanship were, in Dewey's view, the negation of experimentalism and "intelligence." They assumed that the running battles of society had a fixed nature. Dewey, recalling the many surprises in history, believed that such an assumption could lead to the missing of opportunities for problem solving.

### The Problem of Individuality

Despite this freethinking independence, Dewey steadfastly refused to assert the kind of personal autonomy that rationalized for Kant any morally political program. Nor was there an appeal, as there had been in William James, to a "dumb turning of the will." Horace Kallen, partial to James in this regard, noted that, while Dewey showed a persistent concern for individuality and its growth, he conceded the lack of a satisfactory theory of personality.[21] Kallen and Dewey were unable to complete a proposed collaboration because, as Kallen put it, individuality for Dewey was only a variable social product and "all an individual's life, his impulses, and his passions" were " 'agencies for transfer of existing social power into personal ability.' " [22] In 1939 Dewey did write:

> I should now wish to emphasize more than I formerly did that individuals are the finally decisive factors of the nature and movement of associated life. . . . It has been shown in the last few years that democratic *institutions* are no guarantee for the existence of democratic individuals. The alternative is that individuals who prize their own liberties and who prize the liberties of other individuals, individuals who are democratic in thought and action, are the sole final warrant for the existence and endurance of democratic institutions.[23]

But, Kallen observed, Dewey's *Freedom and Culture* (1939) resumed the advocacy of the situational conception, which Kallen took to be a "blindness to the sheer individuality of individuals" and a lack of deep sensitivity "of the evil that flows from the inexpugnable warfare of irreconcilable goods." [24]

### Does Philosophy Solve Problems?

Some of Dewey's Chicago colleagues once commented on his matter-of-factness, a kind of selfless and impersonal quality in his thinking. Contrasting Dewey's characteristic posture with the agonizing of Existentialists and Phenomenologists in the early years of the Atomic Age, we might dismiss the matter as the effect of temperament upon philosophy. But such a post-

21. "Experience, Knowledge and Value: A Rejoinder," in *The Philosophy of John Dewey*, p. 555.
22. Horace M. Kallen, "Individuality, Individualism, and John Dewey," *Antioch Review*, XIX (1959), 303.
23. "What I Believe," in *I Believe*, ed. Clifton Fadiman (New York: Simon and Schuster, 1939), pp. 347–48. Revision of "What I Believe," *Forum*, LXXXIII (1930), 176–82.
24. Kallen, "Individuality, Individualism, and John Dewey," p. 313.

script would overlook a disclaimer which Dewey occasionally inserted into his texts. He did not assert (at least in 1948) that philosophy can solve problems. The theoretical work, represented by a philosophy, does not stand or fall on its achievement of a good life. "But that achievement is the work of human beings as human, not of them in any special professional capacity." [25] The reconstruction Dewey attempted was a reconstruction of theory, a clarification and a criticism that might enable men to proceed to problem-solving efforts without obstruction on the part of their clashing social purposes and aspirations, "the things to which they are most deeply and passionately attached." [26]

If these comments are taken at face value, Dewey's writings on social, political, and legal philosophy were not conceived as attempts to solve political problems. They were thought of as an inquiry into inquiry and were directed primarily toward the reconstruction of ideas that kept men from finding out what the problems were that occasioned thought and action.[27]

It is possible that Dewey had at times meant that "philosophy solves practical problems." It is possible that "philosophy removes theoretical obstacles to problem solving" was a position to which he retreated. It may be that the latter view was what he had in mind all the time, and that the contrary impression was created by ax-grinding students who misinterpreted him as making the sort of claims that Comte, Marx, and Bentham had made for their intellectual formulas.

In either case, I believe that "philosophy removes theoretical obstacles to problem-solving" was the defensible opinion for a social and political philosopher. Far from minimizing the importance of political instrumentalism or transactionism, this conception of philosophy identified the target. It was all those sophomoric and pedantic definitions of blind critics and investi-

---

25. *Reconstruction in Philosophy*, enl. ed. (Boston: Beacon Press, 1948), p. xli.
26. *Reconstruction in Philosophy* (1948), p. 25.
27. See *Logic: The Theory of Inquiry* (New York: Henry Holt and Co., 1938), Ch. 24, pp. 487–512. Dewey's 1938 statement was anticipated in *How We Think* (Boston: D. C. Heath and Co., 1910), in which he argued that thinking begins with difficulties that are not well defined, and that it is the course of wisdom to explore and define the problem before proposing solutions for the ill-defined problem.

gators. The target also included neat, rigid conceptions of "heredity," "environment," "government," "economy," etc., and all those cocksure opinions about the nature of the problems that scientists, lawyers, and officials are paid to solve.

From this point of view Dewey's quest for unity and community in an imperfectly apprehended social experience loses whatever appearance of apriorism that it may sometimes have had. Dewey was asking his readers to look for possibilities of ordering the disorderly. He was not telling them that some particular kind of order must be achieved. He repeatedly denied that order is *given*, found, or discovered. It is "achieved."

### Objections to Adversary Procedures

The only persistent prejudice that I detect in Dewey's social and political philosophy, thus interpreted, is a presumption that adversary procedures and "propaganda" are *never* the best possible methods for attacking certain problems. It seems to me that Dewey was misled by a temporary condition. In his day, lawyers often used the skills of courtroom and commercial negotiation in industrial relations, family relations, and international relations. They were in the presence of problems which would yield, if they yielded tolerable order at all, to other kinds of skill. Similarly, politicians were using the skills of the old-fashioned political campaign in the presence of problems that could more effectively be met by new types of consultation.

The neglect, in Dewey's middle years, of the skills of psychologists and economists did not, in my opinion, prove that the traditional skills of the lawyer and the political office seeker were useless. It merely indicated that these skills had a more limited usefulness than was generally supposed. Dewey, however, appears to have formed a permanent objection to the procedures of advocacy and oratorical persuasion. If one takes seriously Dewey's advice to explore and define problems before trying to solve them, one should sometimes expect to take the psychologists and economists off the case and bring in the lawyers and politicians, just as one should be ready to do the reverse.

With that amendment, Dewey's social and political philosophizing does not seem to be, in any important way, superseded by the linguistic analysts or the phenomenologists of the 1950s and the 1960s. Indeed, the followers of Wittgenstein and Jaspers, among others, continue the effort to loosen up men's thinking to cope with the complexities and surprises of institutional experience and anarchy. If they do not quote Dewey very often, and if they use expressions that would have been repugnant to his style, nevertheless they share his conviction that "systems" of philosophy can blind men as readily as they can enlighten them. The best of the post-Deweyan philosophers have returned to what Dewey regarded as the primary task of philosophy, that of Socratic criticism and midwifery.

### Controversial Positions

It is, of course, possible to catalogue the positions that Dewey took with reference to the controversial issues of his time. He

Opposed American imperialism at the turn of the century,

Supported American participation in the two wars against Germany,

Urged American participation in the League of Nations,

Rejected the claims of Marxism that a better world order could be established by world revolution,

Opposed American isolationism.

Dewey came to strong convictions about needed changes in American politics. He believed that:

The power of well-organized industrial and financial interests should be countered by organized labor and improved organization of interests that were relatively inarticulate;

Government, responding to a wider range of needs, should be characterized by more publicity, greater use of scientific resources, less dependence on litigation and propaganda, and more deliberate and comprehensive planning;

Old "philosophies" should be re-examined; and that neither ancient religious beliefs nor the new totalitarian programs should be used as a justification of censorship or any restriction of inquiry (whether conducted in the schools or under other auspices).

## Concept of Democracy

It was not these particular positions, however, that led Joseph Leighton (Dewey's adversary in technical philosophy) to assert that Dewey had done more than any other single thinker to prepare men for the political crises of the twentieth century.[28] What Leighton appreciated was Dewey's awareness of the instability and problematic nature of society, the inadequacy of any "external" plan, the need for eternal Jeffersonian vigilance and intelligent problem solving. Dewey was able to take democratic ideals seriously and, at the same time, avoid believing that any particular democratic practice was a final solution of the political problem. The way in which he retained an awareness of the precariousness of institutional life is exemplified by his 1927 statement concerning democracy:

Regarded as an idea, democracy is not an alternative to other principles of associated life. It is the idea of community life itself. It is an ideal in the only intelligible sense of an ideal: namely, the tendency and movement of some thing which exists carried to its final limit, viewed as completed, perfected. Since things do not attain such fulfillment but are in actuality distracted and interfered with, democracy in this sense is not a fact and never will be. But neither in this sense is there or has there ever been anything which is a community in its full measure, a community unalloyed by alien elements. The idea or ideal of a community presents, however, actual phases of associated life as they are freed from restrictive and disturbing elements, and are contemplated as having attained their limit of development. . . . Only when we start from a community as a fact, grasp the fact in thought so as to clarify and enhance its constituent elements, can we reach an idea of democracy which is not utopian. The conceptions and shibboleths which are traditionally associated with the idea of democracy take on a veridical and directive meaning only when they are con-

28. I heard Leighton make this assertion on 15 April 1938, when he was delivering his presidential address during the meeting of the American Philosophical Association. The comment was a departure from his prepared text and does not appear in the 1938 Addresses and Proceedings (*Philosophical Review*, XLVIII [1939]).

strued as marks and traits of an association which realizes the defining characteristics of a community.[29]

## A Problem Thinker

As he dealt with the issues of political and legal philosophy Dewey was what the Existentialists have called a "problem thinker" rather than a philosopher of systems. Yet, he did not become disoriented and dizzy. His starting point was always an admittedly imperfect orientation in the facts and generalizations of the social sciences. His *terminus ad quem* was never whimsical and arbitrary; his goals, however tentative, were always in the direction of an ordering, a unification of conflicting desires and sentiments.

In the terms of analytic philosophy, Dewey usually sensed the difference between an evaluation of action and a study of the criteria which may be employed in evaluations. But he never thought that the study of criteria either necessitated or permitted abstention from normative evaluations. Practical evaluation and the clarification of theory could, in his opinion, become intelligent only as they interacted upon each other. The analysts who tried to clarify criteria and methods (rules) in complete independence of the political controversies of the day seemed to him as unreliable as the old system builders who spin out their systems from uncriticized assumptions.

29. *The Public and Its Problems* (New York: Henry Holt and Co., 1927), pp. 148–49.

## CHECKLIST

"Anthropology and Law," *Inlander* (University of Michigan), III (Apr. 1893), 305–8.

"[John] Austin's Theory of Sovereignty," *Political Science Quarterly*, IX (Mar. 1894), 31–52.

Review of *Philosophy and Political Economy in Some of Their Historical Relations* by James Bonar, *Political Science Quarterly*, IX (Dec. 1894), 741–44.

"Interpretation of the Culture-Epoch Theory," *Public-School Journal*, XV (Jan. 1896), 233–36.

"My Pedagogic Creed," *School Journal*, LIV (Jan. 1897), 77–80. [Reprinted in C–12, pp. 3–17; C–15, pp. 19–32; C–16, pp. 427–39.]

"Academic Freedom," *Educational Review*, XXIII (Jan. 1902), 1–14.

"Interpretation of Savage Mind," *Psychological Review*, IX (May 1902),

217–30. [Reprinted in C–7, pp. 173–87, with the title "Interpretation of the Savage Mind."]

"The Battle for Progress," *Journal of Education,* LVI (Oct. 1902), 249.

*Ethics,* with James Hayden Tufts (American Science Series). New York: Henry Holt and Co., 1908. xiii, 618 pp.

*How We Think.* Boston: D. C. Heath and Co., 1910. vi, 224 pp.

"Nature and Reason in Law," *International Journal of Ethics,* XXV (Oct. 1914), 25–32. [Reprinted in C–10, pp. 790–97; C–7, pp. 166–72.]

*German Philosophy and Politics.* New York: Henry Holt and Co., 1915. 134 pp. [Reset and reprinted with "verbal corrections," a Foreword and new Introduction, New York: G. P. Putnam's Sons, 1942.]

Comments by William Ernest Hocking, "Political Philosophy in Germany," *New Republic,* IV (Oct. 1915), 234–36.

Dewey's "In Reply," letter in *New Republic,* IV (Oct. 1915), 236.

"Force, Violence and Law," *New Republic,* V (Jan. 1916), 295–97. [Reprinted in C–10, pp. 636–41.]

"Progress," *International Journal of Ethics,* XXVI (Apr. 1916), 311–22. [Reprinted in C–10, pp. 820–30.]

"Force and Coercion," *International Journal of Ethics,* XXVI (Apr. 1916), 359–67. [Reprinted in C–10, pp. 782–89.]

"Our Educational Ideal in Wartime," *New Republic,* VI (Apr. 1916), 283–84. [Reprinted in C–10, pp. 493–97, with the title "Our Educational Ideal"; C–12, pp. 87–91.]

"The Need for Social Psychology," *Psychological Review,* XXIV (July 1917), 266–77. [Reprinted in C–10, pp. 709–20, with the title "Social Psychology and Social Progress."]

"Conscience and Compulsion," *New Republic,* XI (July 1917), 297–98. [Reprinted in C–10, pp. 576–80.]

"The Future of Pacifism," *New Republic,* XI (July 1917), 358–60. [Reprinted in C–10, pp. 581–86.]

"Fiat Justitia, Ruat Cœlum," *New Republic,* XII (Sept. 1917), 237–38. [Reprinted in C–10, pp. 592–95.]

"The Principle of Nationality," *Menorah Journal,* III (Oct. 1917), 203–8.

"Social and Political Philosophy," Course 31. Handwritten notes by James Gutmann, with typewritten syllabus, Columbia University, 1917–18. 97 pp. [Private collection of James Gutmann.] [Another set, "Social and Political Philosophy," handwritten notes by Ethel Cornell, 1917–18. 30 pp. (Cornell University Library).]

"Morals and the Conduct of States," *New Republic,* XIV (Mar. 1918), 232–34. [Reprinted in C–10, pp. 645–49; C–11, pp. 508–11, with the title "Preconditions of the Security of Nations."] (Reply to: Salmon Oliver Levinson, "The Legal Status of War," *New Republic,* XIV [Mar. 1918], 171–73.)

"Internal Social Reorganization After the War," *Journal of Race Development,* VIII (Apr. 1918), 385–400. [Reprinted in C–10, pp. 745–59, with the title "Elements of Social Reorganization."]

"A New Social Science," *New Republic,* XIV (Apr. 1918), 292–94. [Reprinted in C–10, pp. 733–38, with the title "The New Social Science."]

"Political Science as a Recluse," *New Republic,* XIV (Apr. 1918), 383–84. [Reprinted in C–10, pp. 728–32.]

"Creative Industry," *New Republic,* XVII (Nov. 1918), 20, 23. [Review of *Creative Impulse in Industry* by Helen Marot.]

"On the Two Sides of the Eastern Sea," *New Republic,* XIX (July 1919), 346–48. [Reprinted in C–4, pp. 3–9, with the title "On Two Sides of the Eastern Sea"; C–10, pp. 170–76.]

"The Discrediting of Idealism," *New Republic*, XX (Oct. 1919), 285–87. [Reprinted in C–10, pp. 629–35, with the title "Force and Ideals."]

*Reconstruction in Philosophy.* New York: Henry Holt and Co., 1920. vii, 224 pp. [Enl. ed. with a new Introduction, Boston: Beacon Press, 1948. xlix, 224 pp.]

"Freedom of Thought and Work," *New Republic*, XXII (May 1920), 316–17. [Reprinted in C–10, pp. 522–25.]

"Social Absolutism," *New Republic*, XXV (Feb. 1921), 315–18. [Reprinted in C–10, pp. 721–27.]

*Human Nature and Conduct.* New York: Henry Holt and Co., 1922. vii, 336 pp. [Enl. ed. with Foreword, New York: Modern Library, 1930. ix, vii, 336 pp. Also, Armed Forces ed. (from original plates), 1944.]

"Pragmatic America," *New Republic*, XXX (Apr. 1922), 185–87. [Reprinted in C–10, pp. 542–47.]

Review of *Public Opinion* by Walter Lippmann, *New Republic*, XXX (May 1922), 286–88.

"Events and Meanings," *New Republic*, XXXII (Aug. 1922), 9–10. [Reprinted in C–10, pp. 125–29.]

"Industry and Motives," *World Tomorrow*, V (Dec. 1922), 357–58. [Reprinted in C–10, pp. 739–44.]

"Mediocrity and Individuality," *New Republic*, XXXIII (Dec. 1922), 35–37. [Reprinted in C–10, pp. 479–85; C–12, pp. 164–70.]

"Individuality, Equality and Superiority," *New Republic*, XXXIII (Dec. 1922), 61–63. [Reprinted in C–10, pp. 486–92; C–12, pp. 171–77.]

"Racial Prejudice and Friction," *Chinese Social and Political Science Review*, VI (1922), 1–17.

"Culture and Professionalism in Education," *Columbia Alumni News*, XV (Oct. 1923), 31–32; *School and Society*, XVIII (Oct. 1923), 421–24. [Reprinted in C–12, pp. 178–83.]

"Ethics and International Relations," *Foreign Affairs*, I (Mar. 1923), 85–95. [Reprinted in C–10, pp. 804–14; C–11, pp. 474–86.]

"Political Combination or Legal Cooperation?" *New Republic*, XXXIV (Mar. 1923), 89–91. [Reprinted in C–10, pp. 666–71, with the title "Why Not Outlaw War?"]

"What Outlawry of War Is Not," *New Republic*, XXXVI (Oct. 1923), 149–52.

"War and a Code of Law," *New Republic*, XXXVI (Oct. 1923), 224–26. [Reprinted with "What Outlawry of War Is Not," as *Outlawry of War: What It Is and Is Not*, Chicago: American Committee for the Outlawry of War, 1923, 16 pp.; also reprinted in C–10, pp. 677–84, 685–90.] (The two articles are in answer to: Walter Lippmann, "The Outlawry of War," *Atlantic Monthly*, CXXXII [Aug. 1923], 245–53.)

"Science, Belief and the Public," *New Republic*, XXXVIII (Apr. 1924), 143–45. [Reprinted in C–10, pp. 459–64.]

"Logical Method and Law," *Philosophical Review*, XXXIII (Nov. 1924), 560–72; *Cornell Law Quarterly*, X (Dec. 1924), 17–27. [Reprinted in C–7, pp. 126–40.]

"Highly-Colored White Lies," *New Republic*, XLII (Apr. 1925), 229–30. [Reprinted in C–10, pp. 312–16, with the title "The White Peril."]

"Practical Democracy," *New Republic*, XLV (Dec. 1925), 52–54. [Review of *The Phantom Public* by Walter Lippmann.]

"The Historic Background of Corporate Legal Personality," *Yale Law Journal*, XXXV (Apr. 1926), 655–73. [Reprinted in C–7, pp. 141–65, with the title "Corporate Personality."]

Review of *The Art of Thought* by Graham Wallas, *New Republic*, XLVII (June 1926), 118–19.

*The Public and Its Problems.* New York: Henry Holt and Co., 1927. vi, 224 pp. [Reprinted as *The Public and Its Problems: An Essay in Political Inquiry,* with a new Introduction, Chicago: Gateway Books, 1946. xii, 224 pp.]

"Anthropology and Ethics," in *The Social Sciences and Their Interrelations,* eds. William Fielding Ogburn and Alexander Goldenweiser, pp. 24–36. Boston: Houghton Mifflin Co., 1927.

"Introductory Note," in *Inside Experience: A Naturalistic Philosophy of Life and the Modern World* by Joseph Kinmont Hart, pp. xxi–xxvi. New York: Longmans, Green and Co., 1927.

"Foreword," in *The Outlawry of War: A Constructive Policy for World Peace* by Charles Clayton Morrison, pp. vii–xxv. Chicago: Willett, Clark and Colby, 1927.

"Foreword," in *Primitive Man as Philosopher* by Paul Radin, pp. xv–xviii. New York: D. Appleton and Co., 1927.

"The Pragmatic Acquiescence," *New Republic*, XLIX (Jan. 1927), 186–89. [Reprinted in C–10, pp. 435–42, with the title "Philosophy and the Social Order."] (Reply to: Lewis Mumford, *The Golden Day.* New York: Horace Liveright, 1926.)

"Politics and Human Beings," *New Republic*, L (Mar. 1927), 114–15. [Review of *Man and the State* by William Ernest Hocking and *The Science and Method of Politics* by George Edward Gordon Catlin.]

"The Fruits of Nationalism," *World Tomorrow*, X (Nov. 1927), 454–56. [Reprinted with the title "Nationalism and Its Fruits," in C–10, pp. 798–803; C–11, pp. 467–74.]

"Science, Folk-lore and Control of Folk-ways," *New Republic*, LII (Nov. 1927), 316–17. [Review of *Science: The False Messiah* by Clarence Edwin Ayres.]

"Psychology and Justice," *New Republic*, LIII (Nov. 1927), 9–12. [Reprinted in C–10, pp. 526–36.]

*Readings in Legal Philosophy,* with Edwin W. Patterson. Prepared for the exclusive use of students in the course in Columbia University known as "Logical and Ethical Problems of the Law: An Introduction to Legal Philosophy," Philosophy 130. New York: Columbia University, 1927. 153 pp., mimeographed.

"Philosophy," in *Whither Mankind: A Panorama of Modern Civilization,* ed. Charles Austin Beard, pp. 313–31. New York: Longmans, Green and Co., 1928.

"Philosophies of Freedom," in *Freedom in the Modern World,* ed. Horace Meyer Kallen, pp. 236–71. New York: Coward-McCann, 1928. [Reprinted in C–7, pp. 271-98.]

"An Appreciation of Henry George," in *Significant Paragraphs from Henry George's "Progress and Poverty,"* ed. Harry Gunnison Brown, pp. v, 1–3. Garden City, N.Y.: Published for the Robert Schalkenbach Foundation by Doubleday, Doran and Co., 1928.

"Justice Holmes and the Liberal Mind," *New Republic*, LIII (Jan. 1928), 210–12. [Reprinted in C–10, pp. 100–106, with the title "Oliver Wendell Holmes."]

Review of *The Origin of the State* by Robert Harry Lowie, *Columbia Law Review*, XXVIII (Feb. 1928), 255.

Review of *Law in the Making* by Carleton Kemp Allen, *Columbia Law Review*, XXVIII (June 1928), 832–33.

"Philosophy and Internationalism," in C–10, pp. 831–40. [First publication of "The International Character of Modern Philosophy," from tear sheets found in Dewey's office; source of original printing unknown.]

"Philosophy," in *Research in the Social Sciences*, ed. Wilson Gee, pp. 241–65. New York: Macmillan Co., 1929.

"The House Divided Against Itself," *New Republic*, LVIII (Apr. 1929), 270–71. [Reprinted in C–6, pp. 9–18.]

"'America'—by Formula," *New Republic*, LX (Sept. 1929), 117–19. [Reprinted in C–6, pp. 19–34.]

"Individualism, Old and New," I. The United States, Incorporated, *New Republic*, LXI (Jan. 1930), 239–41; II. The Lost Individual, ibid., LXI (Feb. 1930), 294–96; III. Toward a New Individualism, ibid., LXII (Feb. 1930), 13–16; IV. Capitalistic or Public Socialism? ibid., LXII (Mar. 1930), 64–67; V. The Crisis in Culture, ibid., LXII (Mar. 1930), 123–26; and VI. Individuality in Our Day, ibid., LXII (Apr. 1930), 184–88. [Reprinted in C–6, pp. 35–171.]

*Individualism, Old and New.* New York: Minton, Balch and Co., 1930. 171 pp. ["Material that originally appeared in the columns of (the *New Republic*) . . . now incorporated in connection with considerable new matter, in this volume." Prefatory Note.]

"What I Believe," *Forum*, LXXXIII (Mar. 1930), 176–82. [Revised statement in *I Believe*, ed. Clifton Fadiman, pp. 347–54. New York: Simon and Schuster, 1939.]

"Psychology and Work," *Personnel Journal*, VIII (Feb. 1930), 337–41.

"Foreword," in *Human Nature and Conduct*, pp. v–ix. New York: Modern Library, 1930.

"Conduct and Experience," in *Psychologies of 1930*, ed. Carl Murchison, pp. 409–22. Worcester, Mass.: Clark University Press, 1930. [Reprinted in C–7, pp. 249–70.]

"From Absolutism to Experimentalism," in *Contemporary American Philosophy: Personal Statements*, II, eds. George Plimpton Adams and William Pepperell Montague, 13–27. New York: Macmillan Co., 1930.

"Social Change and Its Human Direction," *Modern Quarterly*, V (Winter 1930–31), 422–25.

"Science and Society," *Lehigh Alumni Bulletin*, XVIII (July 1931), 6–7. [Reprinted in C–7, pp. 318–30.]

"Social Science and Social Control," *New Republic*, LXVII (July 1931), 276–77. [Reprinted in C–11, pp. 949–54.]

*Ethics*, with James Hayden Tufts. New York: Henry Holt and Co., 1932. xiii, 528 pp. [Rev. ed., with Preface to the 1932 Edition. The 1908 edition has been completely revised, with "about two-thirds of the present edition . . . newly written, and frequent changes in detail . . . in the remainder."]

"Human Nature," in *Encyclopaedia of the Social Sciences*, VIII, 531–36. New York: Macmillan Co., 1932.

"The Collapse of a Romance," *New Republic*, LXX (Apr. 1932), 292–94.

"Politics and Culture," *Modern Thinker*, I (May 1932), 168–74, 238.

*How We Think.* Boston: D. C. Heath and Co., 1933. x, 301 pp. [Expanded, revised, and rewritten edition of the 1910 *How We Think.*]

"Unity and Progress," *World Tomorrow*, XVI (Mar. 1933), 232–33. (Reply to: Reinhold Niebuhr, "After Capitalism—What?" *World Tomorrow*, XVI [Mar. 1933], 203–5.)

"Why I Am Not a Communist," *Modern Monthly*, VII (Apr. 1934), 135–37.

"New Worlds for Science," *Modern Thinker*, IV (Apr. 1934), 323–25.

"Philosophy," in *Encyclopaedia of the Social Sciences*, XII, 118–28. New York: Macmillan Co., 1934.

"Intelligence and Power," *New Republic*, LXXVIII (Apr. 1934), 306–7.

"American Ideals (I)," The Theory of Liberty *vs.* the Fact of Regimentation, *Common Sense*, III (Dec. 1934), 10–11.

*Liberalism and Social Action.* New York: G. P. Putnam's Sons, 1935. viii, 93 pp.

"An Empirical Survey of Empiricisms," in *Studies in the History of Ideas* by the Department of Philosophy of Columbia University, Vol. III, pp. 3–22. New York: Columbia University Press, 1935.

"The Crucial Role of Intelligence," *Social Frontier*, I (Feb. 1935), 9–10. [Reprinted in C–8, pp. 80–82, with the title "The Teacher and His World."]

"The Future of Liberalism," *School and Society*, XLI (Jan. 1935), 73–77; *Journal of Philosophy*, XXXII (Apr. 1935), 225–30. [Reprinted in C–8, pp. 133–40.]

"Nature and Humanity," *New Humanist*, VIII (Autumn 1935), 153–57 [Review of *Philosophy and the Concepts of Modern Science* by Oliver Leslie Reiser.]

"Liberty and Social Control," *Social Frontier*, II (Nov. 1935), 41–42. [Reprinted in C–12, pp. 316–19; C–8, pp. 111–14.]

"The Meaning of Liberalism," *Social Frontier*, II (Dec. 1935), 74–75. [Reprinted in C–8, pp. 121–25, with the title "Liberty and Social Control."]

"Liberalism and Equality," *Social Frontier*, II (Jan. 1936), 105–6. [Reprinted in C–8, pp. 114–17, with the title "Liberty and Social Control."]

"Liberalism and Civil Liberties," *Social Frontier*, II (Feb. 1936), 137–38. [Reprinted in C–8, pp. 118–21, with the title "Liberty and Social Control."]

"A Liberal Speaks Out for Liberalism," New York *Times Magazine*, VII (Feb. 1936), 3, 24. [Reprinted in C–8, pp. 126–33, with the title "The Future of Liberalism."]

"The Social Significance of Academic Freedom," *Social Frontier*, II (Mar. 1936), 165–66. [Reprinted in C–12, pp. 320–24; C–8, pp. 76–80, with the title "The Teacher and His World."]

"Class Struggle and the Democratic Way," *Social Frontier*, II (May 1936), 241–42. [Reprinted in C–11, pp. 696–702, with the title "Educators and the Class Struggle"; C–12, pp. 325–30.]

"Characteristics and Characters: Kinds and Classes," *Journal of Philosophy*, XXXIII (May 1936), 253–61.

"What Are Universals?" *Journal of Philosophy*, XXXIII (May 1936), 281–88. [This and the preceding article were combined and revised and appear in *Logic: The Theory of Inquiry*, pp. 255–63.]

"Authority and Resistance to Social Change," *School and Society*, XLIV (Oct. 1936), 457–66. [Reprinted in C–8, pp. 93–110.]

"Democracy Is Radical . . . As an End, and the Means Cannot Be Divorced from the End," *Common Sense*, VI (Jan. 1937), 10–11.

"Democracy and Educational Administration," *School and Society*, XLV (Apr. 1937), 457–62. [Reprinted in C–11, pp. 400–404 and 716–21, with the titles, "The Democratic Form" and "Democracy in the Schools"; C–12, pp. 337–47; C–8, pp. 57–66.]

"Liberalism in a Vacuum: A Critique of Walter Lippmann's Social Philosophy," *Common Sense*, VI (Dec. 1937), 9–11. [Comments on *The Good Society*.]

*Logic: The Theory of Inquiry.* New York: Henry Holt and Co., 1938. viii, 546 pp.

"Foreword," in *Scientists Are Human* by David Lindsay Watson, pp. vii–xi. London: Watts and Co., 1938.

"Does Human Nature Change?" *Rotarian*, LII (Feb. 1938), 8–11, 58–59.

"Education, Democracy, and Socialized Economy," *Social Frontier*, V (Dec. 1938), 71–72.

"The Economic Basis of the New Society" and "The Unity of the Human Being," in C–11, pp. 416–33, 817–35. [Two sections published for the first time in this collection.]

"Experience, Knowledge and Value: A Rejoinder," in *The Philosophy of John Dewey* (The Library of Living Philosophers, Vol. I, ed. Paul Arthur Schilpp), pp. 517–608. Evanston, Chicago: Northwestern University, 1939.

"Introduction," in *Problems of Ageing—Biological and Medical Aspects*, ed. Edmund Vincent Cowdry, pp. xxvi–xxxiii. Baltimore: Williams and Wilkins Co., 1939.

*Freedom and Culture.* New York: G. P. Putnam's Sons, 1939. 176 pp.

"A Foreword to This Issue," *Educational Trends*, VII (Nov.–Dec. 1939), 5.

" 'Contrary to Human Nature,' " *Frontiers of Democracy*, VI (May 1940), 234–35.

"Creative Democracy—The Task Before Us," in *The Philosopher of the Common Man: Essays in Honor of John Dewey to Celebrate His Eightieth Birthday*, ed. Sidney Ratner, pp. 220–28. New York: G. P. Putnam's Sons, 1940. Also in *Bulletin of the Association of American Colleges*, XXVI (May 1940), 198–203.

"Thomas Jefferson and the Democratic Faith," *Virginia Quarterly Review*, XVI (Winter 1940), 1–13.

"The Meaning of the Term: Liberalism," *Frontiers of Democracy*, VI (Feb. 1940), 135.

[Quotation from a Letter to Nelson Prentiss Mead, Acting President of City College, Defending the Appointment of Bertrand Russell], New York *Times*, 12 Mar. 1940.

"The Techniques of Reconstruction," *Saturday Review of Literature*, XXII (Aug. 1940), 10. [Review of *Men and Society in an Age of Reconstruction* by Karl Mannheim.]

["My Philosophy of Law"], in *My Philosophy of Law: Credos of Sixteen American Scholars*, pp. 73–85. Boston: Boston Law Book Co., 1941.

"Foreword to Revised Edition" and "The One-World of Hitler's National Socialism," in *German Philosophy and Politics*, 2d ed., pp. 5–7, 13–49. New York: G. P. Putnam's Sons, 1942. [New Foreword and Introduction to 1915 edition, which was "reprinted without change, save for a few verbal corrections."]

"The Penning in of Natural Science," *Humanist*, IV (Summer 1944), 57–59.

"Challenge to Liberal Thought," *Fortune*, XXX (Aug. 1944), 155–57, 180, 182, 184, 186, 188, 190. [Reprinted in C–8, pp. 143–59.]
Response by Alexander Meiklejohn, *Fortune*, XXXI (Jan. 1945), 207–8, 210, 212, 214, 217, 219.
Rejoinder by Dewey, *Fortune*, XXXI (Mar. 1945), 10, 14.
Further reply by Meiklejohn, *Fortune*, XXXI (Mar. 1945), 14.
Letter from Dewey, *Fortune*, XXXI (Mar. 1945), 14.

"Democratic Versus Coercive International Organization: The Realism of Jane Addams," in *Peace and Bread in Time of War* by Jane Addams, Anniversary Edition, 1915–1945, pp. ix–xx. New York: King's Crown Press, 1945. Also published as "Peace and Bread," *Survey Graphic*, XXXIV (Apr. 1945), 117–18, 138–39.

"Dualism and the Split Atom," *New Leader*, XXVIII (Nov. 1945), 1, 4.

"Introduction: The Problems of Men and the Present State of Philosophy," in C–8, pp. 3–20. [This section published for the first time in this collection.]

"Introduction," in *The Public and Its Problems: An Essay in Political Inquiry*, pp. iii–xii. Chicago: Gateway Books, 1946.

"The Crisis in Human History: The Danger of the Retreat to Individualism," *Commentary*, I (Mar. 1946), 1–9.

"Liberating the Social Scientist: A Plea to Unshackle the Study of Man," *Commentary*, IV (Oct. 1947), 378–85.

"Introduction: Reconstruction as Seen Twenty-five Years Later," in *Reconstruction in Philosophy*, pp. v–xli. Boston: Beacon Press, 1948.

"Has Philosophy a Future?" in *Proceedings of the Tenth International Congress of Philosophy (Amsterdam, August 11–18, 1948)*, pp. 108–16. Amsterdam: North-Holland Publishing Co., 1949.

*John Dewey and Arthur F. Bentley: A Philosophical Correspondence, 1932–1951*, eds. Sidney Ratner and Jules Altman. New Brunswick, N.J.: Rutgers University Press, 1964. ["Means and Consequences— How, What, and What For," pp. 647–54, and "Importance, Significance and Meaning," pp. 655–68, are previously unpublished articles by Dewey.]

# 6
## Dewey's Theory of Art

**BERTRAM MORRIS**

> Consummation is not rare or occasional, but accompanies
> the whole orchestration of life, often discordant and dis-
> tressful, sometimes pure and harmonious.
>
> *George Santayana*

DEWEY'S PHILOSOPHY is one of experience, and his philosophy of art is one of experience in an emphatic way. Our task is
therefore twofold: to observe how he analyzes art and to see
how it connects with the bulk of human activities. The subject-
matter contains pitfalls at every turn and it is important to learn
how he avoids them, both when he copes with the intricacies of
absorbing enjoyments and when he spells out their connections
with the grosser aspects of human life. El Greco and Matisse,
the Parthenon and Shakespeare, no less than politics and war or
religion and industry, figure in the discussion of how art gets
manifested in experience. In this essay I propose, after giving a
rough characterization of Dewey's theory of art, to show its
philosophical orientation. From there I shall exhibit two strands
of his analysis, together with his method of braiding them
together. Then after raising a number of critical questions, I
shall conclude with an acknowledgment of what I regard as his
fundamental contributions to the philosophy of art.

The genius of art is the joy one takes in immediate experience of things. The art-experience entails absorption in things
without our yielding to pressing business or ulterior aims. Such
experiences enliven and enrich, liberate and fulfill. They are in a
way ultimate, and they call for a sense of "natural piety" in that

they exist as irreducible facts of the world. They are finalities, even if there are innumerable such finalities. The shape of a leaf, the waltzing sunbeams on a branch, the umbrellas walking in the rain, the mountainside pines etched in snow, the stride of the track runner, the crane swinging an I-beam into place—these are the kinds of things Dewey regards as constituting immediate experience, which partakes of art. Unlike Kant, he finds that such experience is to be had at every turn, if only we are not hurried or dulled in ways that destroy the birthright of perceptual fulfillment. Yet, though these are artlike, they are not quite art.

Art involves a making, a shaping or moulding, of a thing so that experience is less casual and more concentrated and coherent. Art is thus regarded as the clarification, intensification, and vivification of experience. It is capable of sustaining attention, and therefore appreciation, to an extent rarely found in things not especially designed to arrest experience and to permit our hovering over its object and our exhausting the rhythmic internalities of its being. Art requires not only an amplification and extension of the perceptual processes but also built-in restraints in order that experience can develop its own momentum in arriving at immediate satisfaction. Consequently, it is always more than a first impression gained upon noticing a total effect of instantaneous observation. It has to be seen in its "elements" as well as to be fused into a satisfactory form. But more of this later.

The boldness of Dewey's approach lies in his resistance to getting sentimental about art by lingering over the "mysteries" of enjoyment that transport one to another realm. If art is a transfixion, it is because it has its origins in the encounters within a common life. Were there not impulses to create works of art outside of the fine arts, he insists, there would be no fine art. Art is not a transcription of reality even though it grows out of and is conditioned by reality. Dewey's naturalism thus manifests itself, first, in admitting everything discernible in experience of art and, second, in exploring the relations that art bears to the rest of human activities, past, present, and possible. He writes:

Ultimately there are but two philosophies. One of them accepts life and experience in all its uncertainty, mystery, doubt, and half-knowledge and turns that experience upon itself to deepen and intensify its own qualities—to imagination and art. This is the philosophy of Shakespeare and Keats.[1]

This is acknowledgment of experience, not limited to cognition in its thinness, but rather inclusive of all that it has to offer, thin or thick, narrow or broad, and as high as the sky. Even if there are conditions that dictate what art will include, we cannot know these conditions until after we have learned from it what they are. At this point we can begin to see naturalism full-blown, and to recognize its most taxing problem.

*The* problem of a naturalistic philosophy of art is "that of recovering the continuity of esthetic experience with normal processes of living."[2] Hence, it is necessary to go "back to experience of the common or mill run of things to discover the esthetic quality such experience possesses."[3] So far from being based upon the fine arts, this notion is an explication of what can be found whenever experience fulfills its potential in an intense and clarified form. Such fulfillment involves man in his profoundest relations to nature and in his variegated unions with other men. Nature as it manifests itself in matter, life, and mind is the raw material of art. The artist's task is to embody meanings in objects such that they reflect their source luminously, even when they are, paradoxically, nonluminous. Nature cannot but be reflected in the material—wood, stone, pigments, sound, and all the other physical things that enter into experience. In art this aspect of naturalism signifies the exploitation of the medium by transforming mechanical relations into expressive qualities, emotionally engendered and climactically formed. Yet, in order to realize this end, there must be still other layers of naturalistic meanings which absorb and transform physical properties into æsthetic qualities—the biological and the cultural. Darwinism shows its jealous tenacity in the "biological commonplaces . . . [that] reach to the roots of the esthetic in experience."[4] Perception is selective, and it involves the total organism, and its rhythms are one with the whole of animal

1. *Art as Experience* (New York: Minton, Balch and Co., 1934), p. 34.
2. *Art as Experience*, p. 10.
3. *Art as Experience*, p. 11.
4. *Art as Experience*, p. 14.

nature.[5] The play between organism and environment provides substance for the "life" that art as memorable experience contains. And if art is an adumbration of "biological commonplaces," it is also an adumbration of cultural attainments, which are the social context within which man moves and has his being. Dewey insists that a prime source of meaning in art is the cultural activities of men. However much art is a transvaluation of other cultural values, it unmistakably contains relics of man's past. Somewhat flamboyantly he insists, "the history of human experience is a history of the development of arts." [6] Art revivifies the elements of experience that tend to get lost in the chaos of human affairs. But it is nevertheless experience at its best—clarified and intensified.[7] Hence, we turn to the terms in which it is to be analyzed.

Traditional empiricism has treated experience as constituted by discrete data—sensa, qualities, ideas, occurrents—as having separate existences. Dewey does not deny that reflective thought can discern such discreta, but he does repudiate this kind of analysis when the intent is to recover the integrity of experience—i.e., common-sense or gross experience with which all analyses must begin and to which they should return.[8] He insists upon pointing to experience in its total richness, for it includes not just knowings, but also sufferings, envyings, searchings, questionings, doubts, as well as anything else that can be denoted. He resists exclusion of the fugitive aspects of experience and condemns those who read it basically in terms of sense-data, especially color, sound, and touch. A truly empirical philosophy does not play fast and loose with experience; either it acknowledges all that is to be found, or it is a cheat.

Herbert Schneider has shown [9] that this conception of ex-

5. Cf. in this volume the essay on "Dewey's Psychology" by Herbert Schneider. Dewey's early criticism of the Reflex Arc is directly relevant, as is also his "functional psychology," which is an outgrowth of it.

6. *Experience and Nature*, 2d ed. (New York: W. W. Norton, 1929), p. 388.

7. Edna Shearer's comment is worth pondering: "For him [Dewey] the naturalistic basis is not something to make the best of, but something to make the most of." "Dewey's Esthetic Theory," *Journal of Philosophy*, XXXII (1935), 663.

8. Cf. *Experience and Nature*, Ch. 1.

9. In the opening of the aforementioned essay on "Dewey's Psychology" in this volume.

perience is prefigured in Dewey's early essays, and especially in what he borrowed from Trendelenburg and George Sylvester Morris as constituting the proper psychological standpoint. The union of knowing, willing, and feeling contained in "purpose," constantly acknowledged by Dewey, serves to ready his philosophy for inclusive æsthetic analysis. And the reason is not far to seek: Dewey's account of art and æsthetic appreciation is a reading of experience, rich and purified, condensed and clarified. There remains only the invention of a technique for analyzing it without losing its integrity or distinctive quality. Employing Darwinian Empiricism, disabused of its limited psychology, he seizes upon the temporal character of moving experience to lay bare the structure of art-experience. The terms of analysis thus become clear: process and product. And the latter can be had only as a fulfillment of the former. The temporal process establishes expressive movement that is consummated in the object as expressed. Such is the least arbitrary kind of analysis possible, because it avoids the disastrous dualisms of subject and object, emotion and physical thing, liking and art, form and matter, in all their multitudinous varieties. His terms are meant to avoid the fracturing of experience in unrecoverable ways.

Experience is a process, because whatever is psychical is a process. Whatever appears as immediate is selective—selective because perception is itself a process of responding to something distinctive in the environment. No living thing can respond to the whole environment; it "picks out" things to which to respond; it "makes" its environment. Art is unmitigatedly perceptual; it is sensuous, moving experience; therefore its essence is process. The argument is simple—and convincing. Yet Dewey is not interested in argument; he insists upon showing what art is by directly analyzing experience, or, if it must be secondhand, by going to the artist—certainly not to the æsthetician or the philosopher.[10] *Art as Experience* is a long exercise the purpose of which is to convince the reader that there is no substitute for direct sensitivity to art-works, and that appreciation entails the active response of an appreciator to an art-object if it is to contain a fresh, yet final meaning. There is no shortcut to the

10. Cf. his reply to Croce's comments on *Art as Experience*. "A Comment on the Foregoing Criticisms," *Journal of Æsthetics and Art Criticism*, VI (1948), 207–9.

end. One cannot discern the "end" of *King Lear* by skipping to the death scene of Lear and reading:

> *A plague upon you murderers, traitors all!*
> *I might have sav'd her; now she's gone forever.—*
> *Cordelia, Cordelia! stay a little. Ha!*
> *What is't thou say'st? Her voice was ever soft,*
> *Gentle, and low—an excellent thing in a woman.—*
> *I killed the slave that was a'hanging thee.*

One must either establish a whole continuity from Lear's pronouncement that "we shall express our darker purpose" to its final outcome or else forego any realization of what the drama is. Art is exacting before it will yield its rewards.

The pursuit of æsthetic value is a process, exciting and engaging, and usually pleasurable; for it is an activity of a "live creature" fully responding to an object. At its highest the response is total, involving all the human faculties and exhausting all there is of the object. But the amalgamation is so complete that the transaction of faculties and the relations within the object are discernible only afterwards from the point of view of reflective thought. There must be a factor of selectivity which guides creative effort, both in creation and in appreciation, and the corresponding object needs to facilitate perception in order to yield consummatory experience. Emotion proves to be both the moving and the guiding agent.

> Emotion is the moving and cementing force. It selects what is congruous and dyes what is selected with its color, thereby giving qualitative unity to materials externally disparate and dissimilar. It thus provides unity in and through the varied parts of an experience.[11]

> [Art is selective] because of the role of emotion in the act of expression. Any predominant mood automatically excludes all that is uncongenial with it. . . . [Emotion] reaches out tentacles for that which is cognate, for things which feed it and carry it to completion.[12]

Æsthetic emotion Dewey defines as one which "adheres to an object formed by an expressive act."[13] And the process of

11. *Art as Experience*, p. 42.
12. *Art as Experience*, pp. 67–68.
13. *Art as Experience*, p. 76.

expression then turns out to be one that clarifies turbid emotion. Emotion so wrought avoids gushy sentiment, one of the enemies of art. "When people," he writes, "begin to enjoy their own feelings instead of enjoying the scene or the material of their experience" [14]–this is sentimentality. Consequently, those are sentimental who admit, "I don't know anything about art, but I know what I like." [15] Emotion may not be severed from its object without loss of æsthetic quality. Yet the cultivation of emotion which nevertheless remains æsthetic lies in spontaneity. And spontaneity is not explosive, but on the contrary consists in absorption in subject-matter which is fresh and which is the result of long periods of activity.

Æsthetic emotion then cannot be divorced from perception, which is always serial and thus never devoid of movement. Dewey rejects the assertion that perception is instantaneous. It grows and moves in an ordered way. Not merely is there movement involved in every art, but if the "motor response, even in observation, were taken away from us, we would not have an esthetic observation. We would not have even a perception that would mean anything to us." [16] Motion–ordered motion–is intrinsic to all art, even painting.

Motion comes to æsthetic fulfillment in rhythm, and there is no art without rhythm. Clearly, this is so in the temporal arts, music, song, the dance, drama, and literature. But it is no less so in sculpture, architecture, and painting. Even a sculptured vase is not just a curved line but a lifted and moulded shape that supplies vitality and movement to a self-contained form. Architecture is so obviously a structure, not just of gravity and levity, stresses, thrusts and counterthrusts, but of a play of lights and shadows, and above all a form recognizable only as one moves from place to place in order to construct its organic wholeness. And painting: Dewey takes enormous delight in analyzing Barnes's paintings–especially Renoir, Cézanne, and Matisse–

14. "The Philosophy of the Arts," typescript of lecture given before the Washington Dance Association at the Phillips Memorial Gallery, Washington, D.C. (23 Nov. 1938), p. 10.

15. As for those who don't know anything about art, Dewey complains, "The chief trouble . . . [is that their admission] implies a certain . . . finality [and that they] do not propose to learn to see anything different or to like in any new way." *Construction and Criticism* (New York: Columbia University Press, 1930), p. 19.

16. "The Philosophy of the Arts," p. 12.

to show balanced rhythms in design, color placement, repetition of lines and shapes, as well as the play of lights and darks. Even symmetry turns out to be, in his reading of art, a correlate of rhythm.

> Symmetry and rhythm are the same thing felt with the difference of emphasis that is due to attentive interest. When intervals that define rest and relative fulfillment are the traits that especially characterize perception, we are aware of symmetry. When we are concerned with movement, with comings and goings rather than arrivals, rhythm stands out. But in every case, symmetry, since it is the equilibrium of counteracting energies, involves rhythm, while rhythm occurs only when movement is spaced by places of rest, and hence involves measure.[17]

Both in their making and in their appreciation, all the arts take time, and their æsthetic value gets expressed in the rhythmic organization of energies.

Dewey observes that nature is rhythmic and art is rhythmic, but they are not the same. Nature gets expressed in art, but it undergoes a transformation in the process. Nature's rhythms are mechanical and repetitive and are therefore best described by modular mathematics. Æsthetic recurrences "sum up and carry forward." They are cumulative in that they contain a "progressive massing of values." Dewey seems to suggest that art engenders a kind of syncopated rhythm, with breaks and stops that catch up the preceding and carry it forward with unexpected yet congruous novelties. The rhythms of nature, including the seasons and the biological recurrences in man and animal, life and death—these "somehow" get caught up in the art-process. He tells us that the "esthetic effect is due to art's unique transcript of the energy of the things of the world." [18] The biological metaphor is helpful for distinguishing the mechanical rhythms of physical nature from the cumulative rhythms characteristic of a live creature.[19]

17. *Art as Experience*, pp. 178–79.
18. *Art as Experience*, p. 185.
19. I trust that my remarks are merely suggestive in regard to Dewey's position. The reader should not take them as a substitute for Dewey's own discussions, especially those of Chapter 7, "The Natural History of Form," and Chapter 8, "The Organization of Energies," *Art as Experience*, pp. 134–61, 162–86.

The biological metaphor gets explicit mention in the dynamic organization that Dewey deigns to call "growth."

> Time as organization in change is growth, and growth signifies that a varied series of change enters upon intervals of pause and rest; of completions that become the initial points of new processes of development.[20]

> I call the organization dynamic because it takes time to complete it, because it is a growth. There is inception, development, fulfillment.[21]

The metaphor signifies a cumulative process in which even the repetitions are altered because they include what has gone before. They are in Dewey's language "funded," that is, carried over from the past and incorporated in the present. No wonder then that he makes the process all-important, for the end is reached only through the development of the theme. In the words of the poet, Roethke, "I learn by going where I have to go." The art-process easily becomes the paradigm of the educational process. And indeed Dewey defines them both in the same way. "This cumulative movement of action toward a later result is what is meant by growth." [22] The only difference is that whereas art has an end, a finality, education has none, since "there is nothing to which education is subordinate save more education." [23] In art the funding of meanings has an end as its product.

The product of the process is form; that is, subject-matter come to its fulfillment. Matter and form are, Aristotelian-like, two ways of looking at the same thing; hence, matter is not to be confused with the subject with which a statue or painting or poem is concerned. Form is defined as the "operation of forces that carry the experience of an event, object, scene, and situation to its own integral fulfillment." [24] Thus everything contained in the art-process must lead on to such fulfillment. For analytic purposes, we can consider a number of levels on which integra-

20. *Art as Experience*, p. 23.
21. *Art as Experience*, p. 55.
22. *Democracy and Education* (New York: Macmillan Co., 1916), p. 49.
23. *Democracy and Education*, p. 60. The reader will do well to consult the whole of Chapter 4, "Education as Growth," pp. 49–62.
24. *Art as Experience*, p. 137.

tion occurs, even though the levels cannot finally be separated from one another. They appear to be the plastic, the psychological, and the cultural.

Borrowing from Albert Barnes's analysis of painting, Dewey regards the elements as line, color, light, and space. As plastic, the elements must be fused in a painting that is successful. Genuine art is produced by those who can master the interrelations of the elements in their work, such as Renoir and Cézanne were able to do. Raphael is said to have fallen short. The test of whether such fusion occurs lies in immediate experience. The psychological level has two aspects, the conscious and the unconscious, but Dewey virtually ignores the latter. The conscious level is intense experience, emotional and motor as opposed to pallid recognition. Characteristic of the live creature, it requires the union of "sense, impulse, and action." Reluctant to admit Freudian notions of the unconscious,[25] he nevertheless acknowledges a version of the unconscious when in speaking of properties of objects defined by lines and movements, he says they are "deeply embedded." Moreover,

> These properties are resonances of a multitude of experiences in which, in our concern with objects, we are not even aware of lines as such. Different lines and different relations of lines have become subconsciously charged with all the values that result from what they have done in our experience in our every contact with the world about us.[26]

Much of the richness of his theory of art derives from the fact that, however converted, nature lends to art a portion of its substance. By this acknowledgment Dewey saves art from sheer formalism. And if art gains from the resonances of nature, it also gains from the ingress of cultural traits, which the artist absorbs from his first breath of life. Art is not propaganda, but it cannot but be weighted with rites and ceremonies and other communal practices which "are the sources out of which all fine arts have developed." [27] Various communal modes have "united the practical, the social, and the educative in an integrated whole having esthetic form." [28] If art is the unified product of

25. Cf. *Art as Experience*, p. 316.
26. *Art as Experience*, p. 101.
27. *Art as Experience*, p. 327.
28. *Art as Experience*, p. 327.

the various levels integrated into a qualitative unique structure, art-criticism takes its clue from the product regarded as experience, clarified, intensified, and vivified.

The extreme virtue of art resides not in any truths that it may reveal but in its embodiment of meaning, for meaning is broader than truth, richer and more poignant.

> Poetic meanings, moral meanings, a large part of the goods of life are matters of richness and freedom of meanings, rather than of truth; a large part of our life is carried on in a realm of meanings to which truth and falsity as such are irrelevant.[29]

Criticism is justified to the extent it aids one to realize meaning in his own experience. Otherwise, it is dogma, sham, or self-indulgence. Steering a course between "judicial criticism" and "impressionistic criticism," Dewey seizes upon "immanent criticism" as that which alone lays bare the course by which æsthetic experience comes to fulfillment. Judicial criticism is dogmatic, authoritarian, partisan; it dulls experience, because it is tight and programmatic. Impressionistic criticism is self-indulgent, irresponsible, voyeuristic. It limits the import of art to the momentary, rather than to developed experience. The core of authentic criticism resides in relating matter to form, and in understanding the medium and the nature of the expressive object. "Stating what a work of art is as an experience, may render particular experiences of particular works of art more pertinent to the object experienced, more aware of its own content and intent. This is all any criterion can do."[30] Criticism supplements creation in that it fosters communication and social participation. Reversing Santayana's assertion that the value of experience is in the ideals which it reveals, Dewey regards the value of ideals as lying in the experiences to which they lead. This reversal calls attention to an aspect of his philosophy that deserves fuller treatment in that consequences need to be emphasized, as well as a more active aspect of the art-process, which often gets shortchanged in his discussion of the fine arts in *Art as Experience*. Dewey has distinguished the art-process from the æsthetic process, and the former has a significance that ought not get merged into the latter.

29. *Experience and Nature*, p. 411.
30. *Art as Experience*, p. 309.

### Art as Making

Whereas the æsthetic process is the appreciator's re-making of art out of an object already formed, the art-process is the artist's original forming of an object capable of being perceived and enjoyed.[31] Having reviewed Dewey's description of the æsthetic process, we note now that an understanding of the art-process introduces new considerations about the fine arts, art-production, and finally artistic fecundity. Much of the discussion involves mostly differences in emphases; some of it, however, involves differences in kind.

A preëminent virtue of Dewey's theory is his refusal to separate the fine arts into a class by themselves. Fine art is continuous with the practical arts, first, in that the latter are never merely practical, but always contain a consummatory aspect; and secondly, in that any object which is experienced as a finality is to be regarded as fine art.[32] This insight is deeply embedded in the character of the æsthetic process, which is instrumental-consummatory. Hence, it is a process both enjoyed and progressively realized as actuality. It has inherent integrity; it is not routinized, nor accidental, nor commercialized. In it means and end are never separated; they include whatever stuff nature may provide and are forged into experience marked by intrinsic fulfillment.[33] The enemy of the æsthetic is not the practical, but monotonous repetition of capricious impulse. Yet, the æsthetic process is capable of a wide range of realization, including such things as rugs, baskets, hunting knives, and other instrumentalities that are capable of being æsthetically enjoyed. Moreover, there is reason to acknowledge consummatory experience as accompanying "the whole orchestration of life" instead of being confined to masterpieces—especially to those found in the galleries. Yet, in the middle sections of *Art as Experience* Dewey does emphasize the fine arts as a kind of distilled essence of consummatory experience. He delights over the intricate balances to be found in painting; sculpture "communicates a sense of movement with extraordinarily delicate

31. Cf. *Art as Experience*, p. 46, and *Experience and Nature*, pp. 357–58.
32. *Experience and Nature*, p. 80.
33. *Experience and Nature*, pp. 361 ff.

energy . . . [as] arrested in a single and enduring poise";[34] in poetry "medium and meaning seem to fuse as by a preëstablished harmony, which is the 'music' and euphony of words."[35] We may applaud Dewey, as apparently Leo Stein did, that he could find a place in his philosophy for the fine arts as well as for the practical. Such recognition, however, does not overcome the fact that there is a difference between rugs and baskets and hunting knives, on the one hand, and poems and novels and sonatas, on the other, since the latter are incapable of providing protection from elements and beasts or of holding grain. Even if there is a relation between the practical arts and the fine arts as traditionally conceived—and Dewey has done as much as any thinker to underscore the relation—this does not erase the distinctions.[36] Much more important, however, is the recognition of a more fundamental connection between the practical and the fine arts, and that connection resides in the *activity* of making. Although Dewey recognizes this too, he often blurs the distinction in an effort to point to the kind of identity that holds between the artistic and the æsthetic process—both involving immediate satisfaction grounded in a satisfactory object. The identity is real, but so is the difference, and the difference lies in activity that is more than perceptual.

The poet is a maker, and the artist is an artisan. No philosopher was ever more aware of this than Dewey. The artist as artisan works with his hands; the gallery goer or music hall listener in any significant way does not. (The listener who taps out a rhythm calls attention to it at the expense of musical subtleties.) However indispensable looking and hearing are to art, they are not a making in the sense that painting a still life or composing a sonata is a making. Looking and hearing no doubt require training; but looking at paintings or listening to symphonies does not make painters or composers.[37] Art is made of sterner stuff. And although the appreciator participates in the creative process, requiring memory, imagination, and reason, together with a background of experience inured to cultural attitudes, he is nevertheless a pale version of the artist as ar-

34. *Art as Experience*, p. 234.
35. *Art as Experience*, p. 242.
36. *Art as Experience*, p. 26.
37. Even the Barnes Foundation, to which Dewey was wedded, does not try to train one to paint. It foregoes this activity in favor of the "activity" of looking.

tisan, and knows neither the hardships nor risks nor failures of the latter. Even more important, he would not know how to carry on from what he had learned. Who could have anticipated the Rasoumowsky quartets from knowing Beethoven in his early Mozart style? Or knowing the Rasoumowsky, who could have anticipated the later quartets? Fecundity of production feeds less on music halls and museums than on "finalities" that produce further "finalities."

Dewey glories in emphasizing the aspect of fecundity in areas other than æsthetics. In æsthetics, he only hints at it. Truth achieves importance because it produces other truths. In other words, science is an unending discipline constantly out-moding itself—just as technology constantly advances by out-moding itself. Or again, growth produces more growth, both biologically and educationally. And in a not too obscure state-ment in *Art and Education*, he applies the same principle to æsthetics. He writes:

> As to the scientist knowledge is a means to more knowledge, so to the artist æsthetic insight is a means to further æsthetic insight, and not merely to enhancement of life in general. The distinction between æsthetic and the artistic, important as it is, is thus, in the last analysis, a matter of degree.[38]

And again,

> Thus we reach a conclusion regarding the relations of instru-mental and fine art which is precisely the opposite of that intended by selective æstheticians; namely, that fine art con-sciously undertaken as such is peculiarly instrumental in qual-ity. It is a device in experimentation carried on for the sake of education. It exists for a specialized use, use being a new training of modes of perception. The creators of such works of art are entitled, when successful, to the gratitude that we give to inventors of microscopes and microphones; in the end, they open new objects to be observed and enjoyed.[39]

The difference in degree between artistic and æsthetic becomes greatly increased when "the peculiarly instrumental" and the "experimentation . . . for the sake of education" are viewed as

38. "Experience, Nature and Art," *Journal of the Barnes Founda-tion*, I (1925), 9.
39. "Experience, Nature and Art," p. 10.

a relation of the artist's prior works to his later ones. The acknowledgment of this relation places in perspective motor man, without detracting from the instrumental-consummatory perceptions that Dewey so eloquently emphasizes.[40] If the gallery is regarded as an instrument of education, rather than an end in itself, then it may lend itself to "recovering the continuity of esthetic experience with normal processes of living."[41] The terms of this continuity, so well articulated in the first and last chapters of *Art as Experience*, often become overshadowed in the middle portions, where the fine arts are too often treated as finalities.

### Art as Culturally Engendered

Finalities in the fine arts appear less than final when attention is drawn to the way art figures in the continuities of life. The origins of art are found in the activities of men, practical and culturally entrenched. And if art is festive and celebrative, which it surely is, it also carries over into formative aspects of culture.

> Esthetic experience is a manifestation, a record and celebration of the life of a civilization, a means of promoting its development, and is also the ultimate judgment upon the quality of a civilization. For while it is produced and enjoyed by individuals, those individuals are what they are in the content of their experience because of the cultures in which they participate.[42]

This pronouncement may overdo the integral connection between æsthetic experience and culture, but it serves in an important way to focus upon art in a meaningful context. Even when the artist is critical of his society, as Sophocles, or Matthew Arnold, or T. S. Eliot each in his own way was, he nevertheless criticizes from a position within his culture and his criticism has relevance to it. Dewey pushes the argument to the point of saying "every culture has its own collective individuality"[43]

40. *Experience and Nature*, pp. 361 ff.
41. *Art as Experience*, p. 10.
42. *Art as Experience*, p. 326.
43. *Art as Experience*, p. 330.

which its art reflects. And he reminds us again that "art is a strain in experience rather than an entity in itself." [44]

Art, good art, haunts us. It haunts us just because in penetrating so deeply, the soul cries out for further expression. The mordant colors of El Greco are sought in the approaching storm, or the magic mountain is seen wherever there is isolation or withdrawal, or Cézannish patterns of solid, colored blocks are seen over and over again as we approach new landscapes. The qualities are there because they have entered experience to form new attitudes to be expressed not just in the *View of Toledo*, etc., but in our own more creative ventures as they civilize life as a result of the vigors derived from antecedent experience. By acknowledging the æsthetic as a "strain," we are obliged to acknowledge it *as æsthetic* — as a disposition needing constantly to express itself in forms appropriate to mood and circumstance.

Dewey reads art into its cultural setting and recognizes that the setting modifies the expression. The popular arts are no less æsthetic for being popular. As popular, the galleries, subtly devoted to nationalistic and militaristic enterprise, are not a match for the arts that are not recognized as arty — the comics, the movies, jazz, and the like. The tempo and mood of life as they get caught in vivid perception are nevertheless sufficiently "moving" to support the æsthetic strain of experience. Where this is interrupted, there is where exists not only æsthetic defeat but the defeat of practical and intellectual life as well; for although constituted as different strains, they are nevertheless of a piece.

Focusing upon contemporary culture, Dewey's consistent appraisal is that our problems have arisen out of the challenge of science and modern technology and that they must also be solved in these terms. In *Freedom and Culture*, he writes:

> Science through its physical technological consequences is now determining the relations which human beings, severally and in groups, sustain to one another. If it is incapable of developing moral techniques which will also determine these relations, the split in modern culture goes so deep that not only democracy but all civilized values are doomed. Such at least is the problem. A culture which permits science to destroy traditional values but which distrusts its power to create new ones is a

44. *Art as Experience*, p. 330.

culture which is destroying itself. War is a symptom as well as a cause of the inner division.[45]

The relevance to art is clear. The artist responds to the generic qualities of his culture; they are embedded in his art. But then the artist is capable of doing this only because he is more acutely sensitive to these qualities than the rest of us. We all respond more or less sensitively to these same qualities; we must respond to them for they are implicit in our enculturations, however dimly or sharply we are capable of reading those qualities out of our actions. Although there exists no preëstablished harmony from which we can read off the sense of a community, there are nevertheless common traits deeply embedded in experience and culturally conditioned so that the æsthetic provides the least arbitrarily constructed mode of communication. Dewey writes:

> Every art communicates because it expresses. It enables us to share vividly and deeply in meanings to which we had been dumb, or for which we had but the ear that permits what is said to pass through in transit to overt action. . . . Communication is the process of creating participation, of making common what had been isolated and singular.
>
> The expressions that constitute art are communication in its pure and undefiled form. Art breaks through barriers that divide human beings, which are impermeable in ordinary association.[46]

Because art is expressive it is communicative, but for the same reason it is also criticism.

The clarity of æsthetic experience is achieved because it is critical experience. Dewey believes that intelligence is at work in every step of art-creation. The artist must be in command of his materials and make them hang together in the final product. Critical judgment is thus of the essence of the creative process. This being so, philosophy is only one step beyond æsthetics. Like literature, philosophic discourse "is a comment on nature and life in the interest of a more intense and just appreciation of the meanings present in experience." [47] Natural philosophy thus has natural goods as its subject-matter and human goods culturally engendered as its distinctive end.

45. *Freedom and Culture* (New York: G. P. Putnam's Sons, 1939), p. 154.
46. *Art as Experience*, p. 244.
47. *Experience and Nature*, p. 407.

## Critical Questions

I suggested at the outset that Dewey's æsthetics raises
questions at every turn. I wish now to locate a few of them,
which I regard as being most fundamental to the argument, and
to indicate how he copes with them. I shall limit myself to the
following three questions:   *1)* How establish continuity between nature and art?   *2)* How establish continuity within the
art object? and   *3)* How establish continuity between art and
society? Common to all these questions is the avoidance of
æstheticism. Dewey wishes both to acknowledge immediacy and
fulfillment as characteristic of æsthetic experience and to read
the experience into the setting in nature and culture.

A naturalistic account of æsthetic experience requires nature as its ground, and yet this ground is never quite experienced as ground. Dewey holds that although art is a continuation of nature and a kind of fulfillment of it, yet it is
noncognitive in import. It is attached to nature, but does not
reveal it. This attachment implies the continuity of art and
nature when he writes,

> If experience actually presents esthetic and moral traits, then
> these traits may also be supposed to reach down into nature,
> and to testify to something that belongs to nature as truly as
> does the mechanical structure attributed to it in physical sci-
> ence.[48]

Dewey told us that art is a "resonance" of nature and that its
rhythms, though not copies, are utilizations of rhythms in
nature.[49] Thus, art is a conversion of nature, not a mirror of it.
But how know this? Here is the catch. Art is not knowledge—
Dewey is emphatic on this point. In fact, art permits a relaxation
of the overbearing demand to know. It invites; it presents; it
releases; and yet it means, for it is not just an internal gush or
overflow. Even though it is not knowledge, it is regarded, in a
sense, superior to science, which is knowledge. And because of
this superiority, it presents a challenge to philosophy.[50] These
complexities of art hold the answer to the question of how it can

48. *Experience and Nature,* p. 2.
49. Cf. *Experience and Nature,* pp. 8–9.
50. *Art as Experience,* pp. 274 ff.

be continuous with nature. The answer takes us afield, but we can at least state its terms.

Experience is not possible without one's encountering qualitative immediacies, the wet of the rain, the heat of the sun, the fragrance of the raspberry, the stench of the decaying squirrel, along with their appropriate emotional fixities. Apart from discernible qualities, experience would be a meaningless flow, possessing neither identity nor habitation. Qualities mark off things from one another. But nature is a space-time continuum, and it does not mark off spaces or tell times. *We* make boundaries and *we* make appointments. Yet nature co-operates, even if shorelines are not as we see them or claps of thunder as we hear them. Recurrences can be seized upon and can be described as relations, cast in mathematical-mechanical terms. Because hydrogen and oxygen over and over again combine to form water, we can ignore the particular occurrence, and state the relation as a universal. As for inanimate things, "their immediate individuality is got around; [individuality] is impertinent for science, concerned as the latter [i.e., science] is with relationships." [51] Consequently, red and green differ in physical science in that they give

> specific meaning to two sets of numbers applied to vibrations, or two different placements of lines in a spectrum. . . . But as far as calculation and prediction are concerned these differences remain designable by non-qualitative indices of number and form. But in an organic creature sensitive to light, these differences of potentiality may be realized as differences in immediate sentiency. [52]

Dewey thus attempts to provide us with a theory of emergence without mystery.

> To see the organism *in* nature, the nervous system in the organism, the brain in the nervous system, the cortex in the brain is the answer to the problems which haunt philosophy. And when thus seen they will be seen to be *in*, not as marbles are in a box but as events are in history, in a moving, growing never finished process. [53]

The methods of science are all that we have with which to gain knowledge, but art can go beyond science, clarifying and inten-

51. *Experience and Nature*, p. 266.
52. *Experience and Nature*, pp. 266–67.
53. *Experience and Nature*, p. 295.

sifying experience and still able "to testify to something that belongs to nature as truly as does the mechanical structure attributed to it in physical science." [54] Here is the beginning of Dewey's Kantianism, purged of "realms" or "domains." Art is not noumenal, but it is value-laden in its immediacies, as science is in its mediacies.

The continuity within the art-object is in a sense more difficult to explain and in another sense simpler. Dewey's explanation is found in his extended discussion from Chapter 4 through Chapter 12 of *Art as Experience*. It is contained in his notion of the structure of the art-product as it organically blends into consummated experience. It is properly analyzable only in terms of the dynamics of the experience, and that means, as we have seen, in terms of process which yields product. In a variety of ways, Dewey has described the process—the expressive coming to expression, emotion achieving fulfillment, perception growing into experience, matter becoming form, rhythm consummated, energies organized. They all say the same thing, and having said it need not be said. They are the "ladders" become expendable—because it is the experience that counts and that contains its own justification. Otherwise one is guilty of an intellectualization of that which cannot be intellectualized, and "whereof one cannot speak, thereof one must be silent." But this is not quite so, Dewey has insisted. There is a sense in which these things need not even be said, for experience is the thing that counts and contains its own justification. In any event, the saying is precarious and may be destructive of experience.

There is a way, however, of analyzing experience which does not fracture it. The process of constructing, of creating or appreciating, can be counted, or recounted, because it is not cognitive. It is purification in the way that King Lear in *Lear* purifies the "darker purpose" that "we shall express," that is to say, in the way that the turbid, dark purpose becomes clarified in the drama. The point may more easily be made if we turn to the arts, like painting, where the physical object can be more obviously denoted. The purpose clarified can be effected only in the art-object, which is the physical become æsthetic, because the object is what it is and the perception what it is; and they are not, in the experience, two, but one. If there occurs separation of

54. *Experience and Nature*, p. 2.

means and its expressiveness, then the result is not art but artifice. Then the seams show, and so does the artificer—at just the point that he should not. Also, this is the point where so many æstheticians go wrong, for they can be guilty of making separations where the artist has been skillful enough to avoid them.

Æstheticians do create needless problems, first, in separating what is as experience inseparable, and second, in employing the fractured pieces to prove that the pieces neither involve one another nor imply a verdict about the quality of the art-object as a whole. From a painter's palette what can we conclude about his art, or from the number of characters in a drama, what about the drama itself? Thus, it may be argued that there are qualities, such as gay, or lithe, or somber, or delicate, or gentle, and the list is endless, which do not derive from normal eyes and ears alone.[55] If Dewey is right, the unpardonable sin is to disrelate the perceptual and the æsthetic and then ask how to relate them again. First, they don't disrelate except for analytic purposes. And secondly, for such purposes, time stands still, the processes of expression are violated, and therefore the end is denied. The method, consequently, is contrary to æsthetic fulfillment, and leaves unsatisfied the demand for unity of experience.

There is today another kind of attitude toward art which, though antiunity, is not antiæsthetic. Emile Capouya in a New York *Times Book Review* writes of a talented author, that in his novel Le Roi Jones has left the "innocent naturalism" of the Joycean stream of consciousness far behind and that

> Mr. Jones rejects the formal logic of exposition; he invites verbal and emotional accidents, willingly or wilfully connecting ideas and impressions that have no common focus outside his own mind. Thus, he puts into practice the essential program of contemporary art—to find esthetic value in chaos, accidental juxtapositions, happenings." [56]

55. "Analytic æsthetics" has plumbed the distinctions to the very depths, though with varying conclusions. The reader can conveniently consult a number of such writers in Joseph Margolis, *Philosophy Looks at the Arts: Contemporary Readings in Æsthetics* (New York: Charles Scribner's Sons, 1962), and also in William Elton, *Æsthetic and Language* (London: Blackwell, 1959). Special attention in this connection might well be paid to essays by Frank Sibley, Arnold Isenberg, Vincent Tomas, and Paul Ziff.

56. 28 Nov. 1965, p. 4.

Dewey's overbearing bias may be regarded as one which insists on organic unity as the essence of consummatory experience. Indeed, he may be overdoing this theme at the expense of both the accidents of life that find their way into art, and the instrumental values of art, especially when the latter are regarded, not as insipid utilities but as part of the rich texture of moving experience. Jazz music, literature and drama of the absurd, pop and op art, and the like may violate the traditional canon of beginning, middle, and end; they may have only a middle, never quite a beginning or an ending. Coincidences, uncertainties, contingencies, half-truths, doubts—these are the stuff of tragedy and art, and, as we have already noted, Dewey does recognize them, even if he often underplays them. Certainly they are embedded deeply in his conception of experience and nature, and exist with a profundity much greater than is contained in ethical meliorism.[57]

The final critical question I wish to consider is, How may there be continuity between art and society? The question arises because, on the one hand, art is said to be unique, each experience has its own identity, and the heart of criticism is to exhibit as well as possible the relation of matter and form.[58] On the other hand, art has generic properties, works endure which have received "objective expression," beneath expression there are "ordered movements" that sustain it, and art contains "generalized representation of the formal sources of ordinary emotional experience." [59] The question is disturbing, since, if art is just unique and unanalyzable, it loses all meaning except for what is contained within the experience, momentary and then not again recoverable as that particular experience. Surely, art is more important than what Ruskin called a mere "tickling and fanning of the soul's sleep." Again, if art is just one of those universals to be come across here and there, it loses its vaunted freshness that marks it off from ordinary experience. Although Dewey insists that duality of individual and universal are overcome in

57. Cf. in this regard Sidney Hook's Presidential Address at the Eastern Divison of the American Philosophical Association, entitled "Pragmatism and the Tragic Sense of Life," *Proceedings*, XXXIII (1959–60), 5–26.

58. *Art as Experience*, pp. 82, 94, 108, 185, 192, 274, 309.

59. Cf. *Art as Experience*, pp. 147, 326, 331, 332; *Experience and Nature*, p. 391.

the work of art and that in it "personal act" and "objective result" are organically connected,[60] yet the resolution remains uneasy.

Criticism may not be able to avoid the question of "the adequacy of form to matter," but it surely cannot be satisfied with leaving the question there, first, because a work of art reaches out to other works and they mutually reinforce one another, and secondly, because such criticism underrates the *aesthetic* significance of art as a social force. If the virility of art consists in stimulating the creation of more art, then effeminacy is surely a narcissistic satisfaction in limiting enjoyment to a single work. He who has read a single book is, to say the least, aesthetically deprived and culturally innocent. Unless one can make comparative judgments of works of art, one surely has no authentic grasp of art.[61] Even though ridiculous comparisons are often made and even though historical judgments are often pedantic and sterile, yet without a lively sense of comparative styles, one has no notion of the range an artist can exploit and the special virtues of his work. For this reason, it is worth repeating that appreciation is not a match for creation. Virile art requires much more than consummations; it also requires experimentation—even when it fails of consummatory experience. Present-day art is testimony to the experimental mood, however much it falls short of attaining finalities.

Secondly, there is an aesthetic role that art can play in the formation of cultural attitudes and in making members of a society aware of the brutalities of life. In coping with such issues, Dewey proved himself to be a master. "This task," he wrote, "is to restore continuity between the refined and intensified forms of experience that are works of art and the everyday events, doings, and sufferings that are universally recognized to constitute experience." [62] In this statement, he recognizes both that art is an institution and that a satisfactory culture must come to terms with it as well as with the institutions of power.[63] With a sure hand, he relates not just the practical and the fine

60. *Art as Experience*, p. 82.
61. I owe a debt to Professor Thomas Munro, who in personal conversation emphasized for me the importance of this point in relation to Dewey's aesthetics.
62. *Art as Experience*, p. 3.
63. On this point, cf. the author's *Philosophical Aspects of Culture* (Yellow Springs, Ohio: Antioch University Press, 1961.)

arts, but also economic and political realities with refined experience. Production and conditions of life—both are to be measured in relation to the institutions of expression, and all are to be subject to philosophical criticism, that is, criticism of criticisms. Art achieves its full power only in a full culture, for then the result is that "every culture has its own collective individuality." [64]


## Conclusion

The French philosopher D. Parodi observes that the main purpose of Dewey's philosophy is "to reintegrate human knowledge and activity in the genuine framework of reality and natural processes." To this observation, Dewey responds, "I doubt if another as brief a sentence can be found to express as well the problem which has most preoccupied me." [65] The response appears just. As early as 1893 in a review of Bosanquet's *A History of Æsthetic*, Dewey took exception to the author's treatment of the distinction between the realm of art and that of commonplace reality. Although he does not deny the distinction, he nevertheless objects to Bosanquet's making something

> positive and rigid of the distinction; he makes it a datum which can be used in marking off regions of experience and deciding questions. I should have thought, on the contrary, that the distinction was a problem lying at the very heart of æsthetic.[66]

Except for some lapses, possibly under Barnes's influence, Dewey's æsthetic does cope with the distinction as a problem, not a solution. In the same review of 1893, he acknowledges "Ruskin's and Morris's insistence upon the place of the individual workman in all art, the necessity that art be a genuine expression of the joy of the worker in his work, and the consequent attention to the minor arts, so-called." [67] He consistently devel-

64. *Art as Experience*, p. 330.
65. "Experience, Knowledge and Value: A Rejoinder," in *The Philosophy of John Dewey* (The Library of Living Philosophers, Vol. I, ed. Paul Arthur Schilpp [Evanston, Chicago: Northwestern University, 1939]), p. 597.
66. Review of *A History of Æsthetic* by Bernard Bosanquet, *Philosophical Review*, II (1893), 68.
67. Review of *A History of Æsthetic*, p. 68.

ops the theme in most of his writings and certainly he gives eloquent expression to it in *Experience and Nature*. For example:

> For all intelligent activities of men, no matter whether expressed in science, fine arts, or social relationships, have for their task the conversion of causal bonds, relations of succession, into a connection of means-consequence, into meanings. When the task is achieved the result is art: and in art everything is common between means and ends.[68]

> For these critics, in proclaiming that esthetic qualities in works of fine art are unique, in asserting their separation from not only every thing that is existential in nature but also from all other forms of good, in proclaiming that such arts as music, poetry, painting have characters unshared with any natural things whatsoever:—in asserting such things the critics carry to its conclusion the isolation of fine art from the useful, of the final from efficacious. They thus prove that the separation of the consummation from the instrumental makes art wholly esoteric.[69]

Borrowing from Ruskin, Dewey advances the theme by acknowledging the intrinsic qualities of art as "keeping alive the sense of purposes that outrun evidence and of meanings that transcend indurated habit."[70] But he achieved solid results only because he placed art in a context of culture, both sophisticated and humanistically tempered. Differences did not become identities in his respect for the seamless web of life, which is physical, biological, and social, and in which art is central to its plenitude.

68. *Experience and Nature*, pp. 369–70.
69. *Experience and Nature*, pp. 388–89.
70. *Art as Experience*, p. 348.

## CHECKLIST

"Poetry and Philosophy," in *The Early Works of John Dewey, 1882–1898*, Vol. III, pp. 110–24. Carbondale: Southern Illinois University Press, 1969. [Reprinted in C–10, pp. 3–17, with the title "Matthew Arnold and Robert Browning."]
Review of *The Story of the Odyssey* by Alfred John Church, in *Early Works*, III, 193–94.
Review of *A History of Æsthetic* by Bernard Bosanquet, *Philosophical Review*, II (Jan. 1893), 63–69.

"The Æsthetic Element in Education," in *Addresses and Proceedings,* National Educational Association, 1897, pp. 329–30, and discussion, p. 346.

"Play and Imagination in Relation to Early Education," *Kindergarten Magazine,* XI (June 1899), 636–37; discussion, 638, 639–40; *School Journal,* LVIII (May 1899), 589.

[Discussion of address by William T. Harris], *Kindergarten Magazine,* XI (May 1899), 608.

"Art in Education," in *A Cyclopedia of Education,* I, ed. Paul Monroe, 223–25. New York: Macmillan Co., 1911.

*Democracy and Education: An Introduction to the Philosophy of Education* (Text-Book Series in Education, ed. Paul Monroe). New York: Macmillan Co., 1916. xii, 434 pp.

*Experience and Nature* (Lectures upon the Paul Carus Foundation, First Series). Chicago, London: Open Court Publishing Co., 1925. xi, 443 pp. [2d ed., with a Preface, New York: W. W. Norton, 1929. ix, 1a–4a, 1–443 pp. 3d ed., LaSalle, Ill.: Open Court Publishing Co., 1958. xviii, 360 pp.]

"Experience, Nature and Art," *Journal of the Barnes Foundation,* I (Oct. 1925), 4–10. [Adapted from *Experience and Nature,* Ch. 9, pp. 354–93.] [Reprinted in *Art and Education* by Dewey et al., pp. 3–12. Merion, Pa.: Barnes Foundation Press, 1929.]

"Individuality and Experience," *Journal of the Barnes Foundation,* II (Jan. 1926), 1–6. [Reprinted in C–11, pp. 619–27, with the title "Individuality and Freedom"; C–16, pp. 149–56; *Art and Education* by Dewey et al., pp. 175–83, Merion, Pa.: Barnes Foundation Press, 1929.]

"Art in Education—and Education in Art," *New Republic,* XLVI (Feb. 1926), 11–13.

"Affective Thought in Logic and Painting," *Journal of the Barnes Foundation,* II (Apr. 1926), 3–9. [Reprinted in C–7, pp. 117–25, with the title "Affective Thought"; C–16, pp. 141–48; *Art and Education* by Dewey et al., pp. 63–72, Merion, Pa.: Barnes Foundation Press, **1929.]**

*The Quest for Certainty.* New York: Minton, Balch and Co., 1929. 318 pp. [Ch. 4 and passim.]

*Construction and Criticism.* New York: [Columbia University Press], 1930. 25 pp.

"Qualitative Thought," *Symposium,* I (Jan. 1930), 5–32. [Reprinted in C–7, pp. 93–116.]

"Appreciation and Cultivation," *Harvard Teachers Record,* I (Apr. 1931), 73–76.

"Shall We Abolish School 'Frills'? No," *Rotarian,* XLII (May 1933), 18–19, 49; *Modern Thinker,* III (June 1933), 149–53. (Reply to: Henry Louis Mencken, "Shall We Abolish School 'Frills'? Yes," *Rotarian,* XLII [May 1933], 16–17, 48.)

*Art as Experience.* New York: Minton, Balch and Co., 1934. viii, 355 pp. [Part of Ch. 1 first published as "Art In a Vacuum," *Saturday Review of Literature,* X (Feb. 1934), 501–3.]

"Foreword," in *The Art of Renoir* by Albert Coombs Barnes and Violette de Mazia, pp. vii–x. New York: Minton, Balch and Co., 1935.

"Subject Matter in Art," *New Republic,* LXXXX (Apr. 1937), 335. [Review of *Representation and Form: A Study of Esthetic Values in Representational Art* by Walter Abell.]

"The Educational Function of a Museum of Decorative Arts," *Chronicle of the Museum for the Arts of Decoration of Cooper Union* (New York), I (Apr. 1937), 93–99.

"The Philosophy of the Arts." Typescript of lecture given before the Washington Dance Association at Phillips Memorial Gallery in Washington, 13 Nov. 1938. 17 pp. [Fletcher Free Library, Burlington, Vt.]

*Freedom and Culture.* New York: G. P. Putnam's Sons, 1939. 176 pp.

"Experience, Knowledge and Value: A Rejoinder," in *The Philosophy of John Dewey* (The Library of Living Philosophers, Vol. I, ed. Paul Arthur Schilpp), pp. 517–608. Evanston, Chicago: Northwestern University, 1939. (Pp. 549–55 are in reply to: Stephen C. Pepper, "Some Questions on Dewey's Esthetics," in *The Philosophy of John Dewey,* pp. 369–89.)

[Address in Honor of American Artists Who Contributed Toward Decorations in Federal Buildings], *Congressional Record,* 76th Congress, 3d Session, 29 Apr. 1940, Appendix, LXXXVI, Pt. 15, 2477–78.

"Introduction," in *The Way Beyond "Art"—The Work of Herbert Bayer* by Alexander Dorner, pp. 9–11. New York: Wittenborn, Schultz, 1947.

"Foreword," in *The Unfolding of Artistic Activity: Its Basis, Processes, and Implications* by Henry Schaefer-Simmern, pp. ix–x. Berkeley: University of California Press, 1948.

"A Comment on the Foregoing Criticisms," *Journal of Æsthetics and Art Criticism,* VI (Mar. 1948), 207–9. (Reply to: Benedetto Croce, "On the Æsthetics of Dewey," *Journal of Æsthetics and Art Criticism,* VI [Mar. 1948], 203–7.)

Patrick Romanell, "A Comment on Croce's and Dewey's Æsthetics," *Journal of Æsthetics and Art Criticism,* VIII (Dec. 1949), 125–28.

Reply by Dewey, "Æsthetic Experience as a Primary Phase and as an Artistic Development," *Journal of Æsthetics and Art Criticism,* IX (Sept. 1950), 56–58.

"Introduction," in *Selected Poems* by Claude McKay, pp. 7–9. New York: Bookman Associates, 1953.

# 7

# Dewey's Theory of Valuation

## S. MORRIS EAMES

JOHN DEWEY'S interest in constructing a general theory of value began with his early reactions to idealism, with the impact which he saw Darwin's theories making on general thought processes, and with his attempt to offer a positive answer to the revolutions which science had brought to modern intellectual life. His awareness of the problems involved in valuational theory appears to have sprung from his early studies in ethical theory and his views gradually matured until he set them forth in *Theory of Valuation* in 1939.[1]

The fullest statement of Dewey's general theory of value came late in his career, and even then he found his ideas on the subject difficult to express. When he was asked to prepare the monograph for the *International Encyclopedia of Unified Science*, he thought that he could not perform this task without "getting into ethics more or less."[2] Even after the publication of this major work, Dewey continued to have questions about some specific aspects of the problem. Subsequently, in an article

1. (International Encyclopedia of Unified Science, Vol. II, No. 4 [Chicago: University of Chicago Press, 1939]).

2. Letter to S. Morris Eames from Charles Morris, 6 Feb. 1965. Morris did the main editorial work on Dewey's manuscript, *Theory of Valuation*. A portion of Morris's letter is quoted here because it throws light on subsequent discussion: "For some time Dewey's monograph was tentatively entitled 'Empirical Axiology,' then 'Empirical Theory of Value,' and was finally published in 1939 under the title of 'Theory of Valuation.' The term 'valuation' appeared suitable since it could be interpreted to cover both 'values' and 'evaluation'."

published in 1944 under the title, "Some Questions about Value," [3] he raised four main categories of problems. Summarized briefly, the questions were: *1)* What is the connection between prizing and enjoyment? *2)* Is something of the nature of appraisal required in prizing? *3)* Are evaluative propositions different from other kinds of propositions? *4)* Is the scientific method of inquiry, taken broadly, applicable to value situations? The article in which these questions appeared became the basis for a study by Dewey and other scholars and was published in 1949 under the title, *Value: A Cooperative Inquiry.* [4] In this book Dewey contributed a very significant essay on "The Field of 'Value'."

The major work, *Theory of Valuation*, and the two articles mentioned above are the sources of the mature statement of Dewey's views on a general theory of value. A strange paradox is encountered, however, in the article on "The Field of 'Value'." Here Dewey says that until the field of value "is reasonably settled, discussion is a good deal like firing bird-shot in the dark at something believed to exist somewhere, the 'where' being of the vaguest sort." [5] Dewey recognized that the general theory of value had specifiable aspects to it in special subject-matters, such as æsthetics, ethics, economics, and even in logical theory for a methodology. But he thought that "reification of aspects into separate types" has been one of the main factors in producing lack of agreement among contemporary thinkers. He goes on to say that "forays into these subjects are so far from being helpful as to add to the present state of confusion in any attempt to arrive at a sound theory of 'value'." [6]

What is to be made of this? Dewey himself wrote voluminously on ethics, social philosophy, æsthetics, and even religion, before his major work on valuational theory appeared. In other words, Dewey's practice during his career seems inconsistent with his later judgment. One answer which might resolve this apparent contradiction on the priority of value studies is that Dewey has a general theory of value, though vaguely conceived

3. *Journal of Philosophy*, XLI (1944), 449–55.
4. "The Field of 'Value'," in *Value: A Cooperative Inquiry*, ed. Ray Lepley (New York: Columbia University Press, 1949), pp. 64–77.
5. "The Field of 'Value'," p. 64.
6. "The Field of 'Value'," p. 73.

and not too often expressed, which underlies all his writings in the specific fields.

In a manner consistent with his general approach to philosophizing, Dewey analyzes the problem of value in two ways: *1)* the confusion which abounds in contemporary value theory; *2)* delimiting the field of value. In *Theory of Valuation*, he starts with a statement of the confusion in theory, a confusion which he thinks arises over "what the facts are to which theory applies, and indeed whether there are any facts to which a theory of value can apply." [7] Thus, we are confronted with various theories which may be termed "emotivism" and "a priori rationalism" (and intermediate theories between these extremes), with "epistemological theories about idealism and realism," and with "metaphysical theories regarding the 'subjective' and the 'objective.'" Historical factors have entered into the problem of present valuational theory as the elimination of final ends has taken place in certain scientific studies. Since "values" were eliminated from science one by one as the latter eliminated final ends from their studies and since value-facts and value-consequences cannot, "by any stretch of the imagination," now be found in any of the fields purporting to be scientific, what happened to the field of value? [8]

According to Dewey's analysis, conflicting positions have evolved in contemporary theory of value. *1)* There are those who hold that there are no genuine value-propositions or judgments. *2)* Others hold that value-propositions are located in a "mentalistic" realm. *3)* And there are others who maintain that value-categories are located in a higher realm than scientific propositions, the latter being only partial. These views, Dewey says, are typical, but not exhaustive. The positions outlined do point up, however, the reaction of some thinkers to the elimination of final ends in scientific subject-matters, and in some instances these views show how crucial is the relation of science to value in the contemporary world, a relation which Dewey claims is the central problem of modern life. [9]

Dewey attempts to put forth his own hypothesis as to where the field of value is located. The field wherein one is to

7. *Theory of Valuation*, p. 1.
8. *Theory of Valuation*, pp. 2–3.
9. *The Quest for Certainty* (New York: Minton, Balch and Co., 1929), p. 255.

look for value-facts is *human behavior*, where this term refers exclusively to "events of the nature of *life-processes* in general and animal life-processes in particular." [10] In some of his earlier writings are found suggestions of his behavioral approach to valuings and evaluations, but it is in his later writings that the behavioral analysis is put forth in more detail. In *Experience and Nature*, he wrote that values "occur whenever any object is welcomed and lingered over; whenever it arouses aversion and protest; even though the lingering be but momentary and the aversion a passing glance toward something else." [11] These behavioral processes are also described as "slight agreeable acceptances" and as "annoyed rejections." In a later analysis, Dewey refers to these processes as "selections" and "rejections" or, as "selection-rejection behavior." In still another work, he refers to these activities as "attractions" and "aversions." In the Lepley volume, Dewey presents a summary statement of his behavioral approach, but one must go to his other works to fill in the gaps of his complete theory.

The connection of value theory with organic activities follows a line of development from the gross movement of the organism called *impulsion* [12] to the strictly defined and mediated value-object constructed in inquiry. Impulsion is the forward movement of the organism which encounters many things which deflect and oppose it. If the organism did not meet these obstacles, it would remain thought-less and emotion-less, and the objects encountered would not become significant. At first, this impulsion is a sort of blind surge; as blind surge it meets obstacles and becomes differentiated into *impulses*. Then this welling-up and over-flowing of the energy of the organism becomes channeled by means of its environment into forms of behavior called *habits*. Impulse and habit, however, do not come ready-made and carrying their own symbolic designations in childhood experience; they are named and described by his adults in terms of the consequences to which these energetic activities lead. It is in a biological, psychological, and sociologi-

10. "The Field of 'Value'," p. 65.
11. *Experience and Nature*, 2d ed. (New York: W. W. Norton, 1929), p. 400.
12. *Art as Experience* (New York: Minton, Balch and Co., 1934), p. 58.

cal context that the activities of a child take on meaning.[13] At this point it should be mentioned that in an early essay Dewey pointed out that moral theory in particular is dependent upon psychological and sociological analyses as conditions of controlling ethical judgments, and he noted at the time the backward states of these two disciplines in the application of scientific method.[14] In 1939 he was of the same opinion; psychology was not yet developed enough, and "without such a science systematic theoretical control of valuation is impossible."[15] There is needed also a science of human relations, and again this field is singled out as "a further condition of the development of a theory of valuation."[16] Given the foregoing conditions of psychology and sociology in their present developments, Dewey's approach to valuational theory can be only exploratory and suggestive.

In his later writings Dewey turns to the task of giving some designations to terms he thinks are found in valuational studies. On his account *vital impulses* play a role in value-behavior, but the more complex activities of value-behavior cannot be reduced to mere impulse. Theories which attempt to designate value-expressions as "ejaculatory" or "emotive" are rejected by Dewey.[17] Some theories of this kind imply or allow the inference that the value statement refers only to an emotional state of the person holding and expressing the value statement. Dewey thinks valuational behavior is more complex than this. Dewey holds to an emergent or developmental view of naturalism in which the more complex forms cannot be reduced to the simpler foreshadowings found in biological processes, and the role of impulse in valuational behavior is a case of this kind. Not all organic activities are valuational, but all valuational activities are rooted in vital impulses. Vital impulses foreshadow the more complex behavior of *desires* and *interests*.

Dewey makes long lists of terms which he thinks belong

13. *Human Nature and Conduct* (New York: Henry Holt and Co., 1922), Pts. I, II.
14. "Logical Conditions of a Scientific Treatment of Morality," in *Investigations Representing the Departments, Part II: Philosophy*, *Education* (University of Chicago, The Decennial Publications, First Series, Vol. III [Chicago: University of Chicago Press, 1903]), Secs. 6, 7.
15. *Theory of Valuation*, p. 62.
16. *Theory of Valuation*, p. 63.
17. *Theory of Valuation*, pp. 6–13.

to valuational behavior, but "prizing," "holding dear," "caring-for," will suffice to demonstrate his point. The behaviors designated by these terms and others of their kind are called *valuings*. The activities to which these terms refer can be taken in either of two aspects of a valuational situation: *1)* they refer to attempts "to bring something into existence which is lacking"; or *2)* they refer to attempts "to conserve in existence something which is menaced by outside conditions." [18] The suggestions which Dewey makes for the meanings of "desire" and "interest" are perhaps more than suggestions; they are meanings which he actually adopted and used in his own theory. He says that "desire" can be taken to be "the behavioral attitude that arises when prizings are temporarily blocked or frustrated," and that "interest" can be taken as standing for "an enduring, or long-time-span, disposition . . . which holds together in system a variety of acts otherwise having diverse directions." [19] The idea of "interest" is given a prominent place in Dewey's behavioral theory. His treatment of interest in relation to the social and moral self, especially as put forth in the *Ethics* of 1932, needs careful study, for it is this concept, perhaps more than any other, which sets him off from the utilitarianism of Bentham and Mill.[20] Dewey goes on to say that the term "enjoyment" can stand for the consummatory phase of prizing. For a more detailed treatment of the consummatory phase of an experience, it is necessary to consult passages in *Art as Experience*.[21]

When valuing is defined in terms of desiring, Dewey claims that desire must be treated "in terms of the existential context in which it arises and functions." [22] For desire is not taken in the large, that is, without a specifiable content and connection with environing conditions. To take desire in the large, without an object for its connection, is to relapse into a mentalistic psychology. The behavioral approach to desire is an example of the attempt to get terms out into the open so that they can be treated by scientific study. Dewey's objection to

18. *Theory of Valuation*, p. 15.
19. "Some Questions About Value," *Journal of Philosophy*, XLI (1944), 450.
20. *Ethics*, rev. ed., with James H. Tufts (New York: Henry Holt and Co., 1932), pp. 315–44.
21. For example, see p. 17.
22. *Theory of Valuation*, p. 16.

some theories which connect desire to valuation is that a psychological theory of "desire and liking is supposed to cover the whole ground of the theory of values; in it, immediate feeling is the counterpart of immediate sensation." [23] Dewey does not object to connecting theory of value with desires and satisfactions, for, as he says, this is the only way he sees that the "pallid remoteness of the rationalistic theory" (Kant's) and the "institutional theory of transcendental values" (supernatural theories) can be escaped.[24] On the other hand, Dewey does not think that connecting value theory with desire is all there is to the complete account; it is but a starting point. The difference between Dewey's view and the traditional and current empirical theories of value will be discussed later. At this juncture, one further point should be made concerning desire and object. Dewey's view of connecting value theory with desire and interest is slightly different from that held by Ralph Barton Perry who maintained that "a value is any object of any interest." For Dewey this statement is too broad; it should be modified to read that a value is some specific object of some specific interest.[25]

It is the connection of desire, behaviorally understood, with value theory which Dewey claims makes his theory naturalistic. Dewey's naturalism is founded upon a *postulate*,[26] the postulate of naturalism which holds that there is a *continuity* between physical processes and the ideational processes of human life. There is no break in this continuity, and there is nothing which exists outside it or above it which can serve a metaphysical or epistemological purpose. The naturalistic postulate is not arbitrary, for its use leads to fruitful results in inquiry.

We must return for a moment to Dewey's contention that his theory of value begins with selection-rejection behavior, animal as well as human, in order to find that the distinctly human type of selection-rejection behavior can have a new dimension, a dimension in which the distinguishing marks are "carings-for" with *foresight*.[27] Anticipation or foresight of the outcome of activities and the recognition of the result as the ground or reason for engaging in them make the selection-

23. *The Quest for Certainty*, p. 258.
24. *The Quest for Certainty*, p. 258.
25. *Theory of Valuation*, pp. 18–19.
26. *Logic: The Theory of Inquiry* (New York: Henry Holt and Co., 1938), p. 23.
27. "The Field of 'Value'," p. 68.

rejection behavior of humans different from that of animals. Here, attention is called to the term *ground or reason*, for Dewey makes a distinction between the *causes* for events and the *ground or reasons* for events. Much of human behavior is explained by causes, or, as he says, "much of human behavior is so direct that no desires and ends intervene and no valuations take place." In these instances, vital impulses and habits operate in a causal manner. Examples given for a description of this kind of behavior are those of a man pushing an obstacle off his foot when it is stepped on, of a man continuing to walk without stopping at each step to ask how that step is related to the object in view. Direct behavior (causal) is found in an animal eating because its organic tensions of hunger drive it to perform certain acts. In none of these cases do desires, ends, and valuations take place. Desire and end-in-view take place in the following way:

> But if and when *desire* and *an end-in-view* intervene between the occurrence of a vital impulse or a habitual tendency and the execution of an activity, then the impulse or tendency is to some degree modified and transformed: a statement which is purely tautological, since the occurrence of a desire related to an end-in-view *is* a transformation of a prior impulse or routine habit. It is only in such cases that valuation occurs.[28]

Attention is drawn to the word *transformation*, for, on Dewey's view of emergent naturalism, vital impulses have the possibility of being transformed into valuations, but it is not always the case that they become so. This is why Dewey's theory of value is nonreductive, for transformed activities which are valuations cannot be reduced to impulses, even though there is a vital connection between them.

On Dewey's view, both stability and instability are characteristic of experience. Stable things become unstable, unsettled; and on the other hand, unstable things become stable, settled. If it were not for the latter condition, life would be one long experience of distress. These "generic traits" of existence, of course, apply to valuational behaviors. Qualitative immediacy of things prized or enjoyed becomes disrupted. The disruption is felt as immediate, and the pulsation of these feeling states may bring about mediation, but there is no guarantee that this will be

28. *Theory of Valuation*, p. 34.

the case. If valued things were plentiful, there would be no occasion for thought or mediation, but this is not the case in the kind of world in which we live. "Values," says Dewey, "are as unstable as the forms of clouds." The objects which possess value are "exposed to all the contingencies of existence, and they are indifferent to our likings and tastes." [29]

What happens when the felt qualities, such as prizings, carings-for, enjoyments, become felt qualities of instability? How is this condition accounted for? The locus of the source of instability may be either within the organism or in the organism's environment, taking these terms, however, as designations within a unified whole. The changes in ourselves are not limited to the exhaustion of our bodily organs; other organic changes may cause enjoyed objects to become unstable. When such organic changes are added to the external vicissitudes to which values are subjected, Dewey thinks "there is no cause to wonder at the evanescence of immediate goods." [30] A thing enjoyed at one time may lead to disturbing consequences, or as Dewey puts it, "some things sweet in the having are bitter in after-taste," thus, "primitive innocence does not last." When disruptions occur, "enjoyment ceases to be a datum and becomes a problem." [31] Enjoyments are qualitatively a part of everyday experience, but experience shows us that something happens to these enjoyments. They become unstable, sources of problems, warnings of consequences which may not be enjoyed. When instability, indeterminacy, perplexity, and doubt occur, there is a possibility for a transition to some other kind of experience.

The manner in which immediately enjoyed objects pass into mediation is not entirely clear in Dewey's theory. Evidence for this statement is found in the cases where he speaks of how immediacy passes *insensibly* over into mediation and in cases where there is a definite shock or felt difficulty. When Dewey defended his position against the attacks of Philip Rice, he restated his view on the relation of immediate valuings to mediation and final judgment by replying that in his theory "situation" is the key word. His description of the "valuational situation" follows what he said about situation in other contexts, that is, that "situation" denotes a condition which is directly and im-

29. *Experience and Nature*, p. 399.
30. *Experience and Nature*, p. 399.
31. *Experience and Nature*, p. 398.

mediately qualitative, and that some situations *may* evoke inquiry.[32] Note the emphasis upon the term *may*, for it is not necessary that indeterminate situations evoke inquiry; some other form of behavior may take place when indeterminacy occurs, such as falling back on some impulse, old habit, or accepting custom, tradition, or authority as the answer. If inquiry is evoked, then it is successful when the final judgment culminating the inquiry, when acted upon, brings about or terminates in "an ordered, unified situation." [33]

Students of Dewey's theory of valuation may find some passages confusing when they try to untangle his views on the problem of the relation of the noncognitive to the cognitive, because he admits that in writings previous to 1949 he had written as though this relationship is sharp and discrete, whereas he had always intended to mean that the relation is one of continuity. This issue is crucial for many aspects of Dewey's theory of valuation.[34] If the relationship of the noncognitive to the cognitive is read as one discretely and sharply divided, then this would place Dewey in the camp of realists in the theory of value who have the problem of maintaining that the value-object is given in experience as a kind of antecedent reality, thus limiting the later thought and mediation to the role of describing what has already been given. On the other hand, if Dewey says he means for this relationship to be one of continuity and one in which from germinal experiences of prizings, carings-for are constructed in inquiry, it is easy to read him as an idealist, an idealist who might claim that ideas formed in the mind exhaust all reality. Dewey spurns both of these positions. He is not a realist in the sense of G. E. Moore and he is not an idealist in the sense of F. H. Bradley. The end-in-view which is constructed in inquiry is operational in that it intervenes between the indeterminate situation which is given and in which a valuing has been doubted and the final outcome in which the existing need or lack has been resolved. It should be noted here that the end-in-view is different from an end or terminus. The end-in-view goes

32. "Further as to Valuation as Judgment," *Journal of Philosophy,* XL (1943), 550.

33. "Valuation Judgments and Immediate Quality," *Journal of Philosophy,* XL (1943), 314.

34. See my article, "The Cognitive and the Noncognitive in Dewey's Theory of Valuation," *Journal of Philosophy,* LVIII (1961), 179–85.

through a process of transformation during inquiry, and when it is acted upon in final judgment of a problematic situation eventuates in an end or terminus which is existential.

The emergence of immediate valuings into inquiry or mediation is a gradual one. Dewey says, "after the first dumb, formless experience of a thing as a good, subsequent perception of the good contains at least a germ of critical reflection." [35] This passage suggests that Dewey's theory might contain levels of immediacy and mediation, levels which pass from vague, formless experience to clearness and distinctness on the higher levels of mediation. Once doubt evokes an inquiry, then a process of discrimination takes place. Even these logical determinations and discriminations are foreshadowed in biological behavior as when an amoeba pushes out into its environment and unconsciously begins to classify its world into friendly and unfriendly. On the human level, the responses of exploration and withdrawal are still there, and out of these more complex mediational processes emerge. With the development of symbolic behavior, logical processes such as definitions, classifications, generalizations, anticipations, and predictions occur. It becomes important to note and distinguish the "kind" of situation which the human encounters, for situations in valuational behavior are of a different kind from those, say, of physics and chemistry. Furthermore, within the broad field of valuational behavior, various kinds of valuational situations occur and recur. It is true that any "this" of a situation, valuational or otherwise, is unique in that it occurs only once in space and time. But it shares generic qualities with other situations of the same kind. If recurrence of kinds of situations did not occur, then we could never develop generic universals or generalizations or construct norms.

Dewey makes a distinction between propositions *about* values, which signify events which are "had," "prized," "desired," and "enjoyed," and valuational propositions in the *distinctive* sense.[36] This issue concerns the *appraisal* of propositions about values, of determining if some acts of prizing are better than others. Propositions about "immediate valuings" are propositions about value-facts, and they stand on the same footing with propositions about potatoes or any other factual proposi-

35. *Experience and Nature*, p. 401.
36. *Theory of Valuation*, p. 20.

tions. The crux of the issue concerns the status and function of appraisal propositions or what Dewey calls *evaluative* propositions. On his theory, valuational inquiries must make a distinction between something as satisfying, which is a proposition of fact, and something as satisfactory, which is "a judgment, an estimate, an appraisal." [37] Physical propositions differ from distinctive valuational propositions in that the latter "inherently involve a means-end relationship." The intervention of a personal act involving foresight and use of cause-effect determinations of science turns these determinations into means-ends relationships. This means that there is a difference between events which will happen (prediction in the physical sciences) and events which "shall" or "should" happen. It is in some such sense that judgments of evaluation "rest upon" judgments of scientific inquiries. This is the manner in which Dewey thinks that "norms" are constructed in human behavior. "Norms" in Dewey's sense are "conditions to be conformed to," and are not imported into the recurring situations from without; they are not transcendental or obtained by some intuitive leap. They grow out of the situations men encounter and then become formed and consolidated as experience verifies their continued usefulness.

The institution of the personal factor in the context of manipulating cause-effect relationships in such ways that they are used as the basis for means-ends relationships in human behavior explains how human behavior is *regulated*. This point of the regulation of valuings through evaluations is at once the basis for the criticism Dewey makes of current empirical theories of value and for his own view. He says,

> The fundamental trouble with the current empirical theory of values is that it merely formulates and justifies the socially prevailing habit of regarding enjoyments as they are actually experienced as values in and of themselves. It completely side-steps the question of regulation of these enjoyments.[38]

Statements of fact, of what objects are or have been enjoyed, are not enough for a complete theory of value. Judgments of appraisal are required to determine if the value-facts have any worth.

It should be noted that the preceding quotation mentions the fact that some contemporary theorists hold the view that

37. *The Quest for Certainty*, p. 261.
38. *The Quest for Certainty*, p. 259.

values *as* experienced are values "in and of themselves." This brings in the problem of "intrinsic values." Dewey thinks that some sentences in the writings of G. E. Moore can be read to mean that Moore holds to a theory of intrinsic values. Dewey objects to Moore's type of theory because it tends to cut off any value-object from its conditions and consequences, thus making the value-object nonrelational. The denial of connections of any value-object with its antecedents and consequences is the basis for views which hold to "absolute" values. Once intrinsic and inherent qualities are admitted in a nonrelational universe, then there arises the metaphysics of Being with its singular beings and orders of Being. The consequences of the postulate of intrinsic values cuts away the possibility for regulation and control of all values. The view of nonrelational value not only is nonnatural in Moore's account of the naturalistic fallacy, thus making his value theory rely upon intuition for its epistemological method, but also it seals off the conditions for the creation of new values by human endeavor. On a theory like that of Moore's, the intuition of each particular value must carry its own credentials in an order of preference, otherwise there is no way of choosing among values or of ranking them in an order of worth and preference.

Critics of Dewey's theory maintain that he has no ground for holding to the "intrinsic worth" of individuals, or that he has any reason for treating other human beings as equals. This criticism is made in spite of Dewey's long history of emphasizing the importance of the individual, of driving home the idea, perhaps more than any other philosopher in the twentieth century, that social arrangements – political, economic, educational – must be judged in terms of the effects upon the individual. Throughout Dewey's writings on all aspects of valuational experience, he is sensitive to what consequences are brought by social arrangements upon the individual's perceptions, memories, imaginations, and thoughts. Children are not born with the notion of the value of another human being or that other human beings should be treated as equals. Nor can the idea of the value of another individual be obtained later in life by revelation, intuition, or by some act of pure reason which grasps the principle from some transcendental realm. Men must learn to value each other, to "care-for," "prize," and "love" each other. To hold otherwise is to convert a social ideal into an antecedent reality, and to blame men for not recognizing a fact when we should be engaged at the task of teaching children and men to actualize the ideal.

One of the most controversial issues arising out of Dewey's theory of valuation has centered around his analysis of the *desired* and the *desirable*. Long before the publication of *Theory of Valuation*, which contains his mature statement of the issue, he engaged in a discussion over the meanings of these terms and the related problems of immediate valuings and judgments of evaluation with various scholars, among them Ralph Barton Perry and D. W. Prall.[39] The history of this controversy is too long to include here. Among the claims which came to the fore in the discussion were that Dewey's valuation-judgments are an unnecessary invention of his own, and that the distinction between desire and desirable is that the latter is simply a desire with some critical reflection attending it. Dewey's treatment of desire and desirable also came under criticism some years later when Morton White tried to show that Dewey's position was untenable.[40] Subsequently, Irving Block has maintained that Dewey's position on these issues "runs as subjective a gauntlet as hedonism or any other modern ethical view." [41] In the course of his inquiry on this problem, Dewey continued to be critical of the kind of statement made by John Stuart Mill on the desired and the desirable, and he never relinquished his position on the earlier distinction he had made concerning the role of critical reflection in the construction of the desirable. In fact, in his later writings he continued his analysis into the distinction to prove his contention that traditional and current empirical theories of value had neglected distinctive judgments of valuation, or what he called judgments of *evaluation*.

The foregoing analysis of Dewey's theory of valuation has shown how he thought the confusion in theory had developed during his lifetime. Dewey sought to push theoretical discussion

39. For a listing of the articles which carry this discussion, see the bibliography below. One article which reviews part of the controversy should be noted: "Valuation and Experimental Knowledge," *Philosophical Review*, XXXI (1922), 325–51. Note that articles which treat of the controversy appear in other sources, both preceding and subsequent to the one mentioned here.

40. Morton White, " 'Value' and 'Obligation' in Dewey and Lewis," *Philosophical Review*, LVIII (1949), 321–29.

41. Irving Block, "The Desired and the Desirable in Dewey's Ethics," *Dialogue*, II (1963), 170–81.

a little further, but he was aware of the many problems yet unsolved. To him the relation of scientific conclusions about the world to beliefs about the regulation of conduct is the most serious problem of our age. He was aware of the confusion, of the ambiguity, of the language of value, and he offered suggestions as to how some value terms might be defined. He saw, too, that the behavioral sciences, psychology and sociology in particular, must become more exact before an adequate theory of value can be developed. He was not always clear on his distinction between the noncognitive and the cognitive, terms which have played such an important role in contemporary discussion. It is understandable that some theorists starting from positions other than the naturalistic find his treatment of intrinsic values unacceptable. His treatment of desire and desirable stirred up a storm of controversy which still continues. Controversy still rages over the function and status of norms in both physical and valuational inquiries.

One of the most crucial problems which Dewey did not solve, and one in which in some ways his own practice confuses the issue, is the relation of the specific fields of value—ethics, æsthetics, economics, social philosophy, and religion—to the general theory of value. There are further difficulties if his view is accepted that the starting place is determination of a general theory of value before the special fields can be determined.

Dewey maintained throughout his writings that his theory of valuation is a special case of his general method of inquiry, that valuation-judgments are not marked off methodologically from other kinds of judgments, and that a unified logical method is needed for the solution of all problematic situations.[42] But he did little to show the exact manner in which specific features of his general method of inquiry are used in determining the solution of valuational problems. What, for instance, are the roles played by singular, particular, generic, and universal propositions in the determination and settlement of a value problem? At times, he uses examples which indicate that abstract conceptions, such as Justice, are needed in a full development of inquiry into valuational matters, but he never developed points of this nature.

John Dewey was aware of the many problems involved in

42. "The Field of 'Value'," p. 77.

developing an adequate theory of value in the context of a scientific age, an age which could not return to the conceptions of nature and of thought which preceded it. He tried to offer some answers to these problems, but in all his writings, he offers conclusions which are tentative. He has helped us see the theoretical problems more clearly and he has indicated a way in which the field of value behavior can be investigated by the use of scientific procedures. He has bequeathed to subsequent generations some suggestions to follow out in the attempt to solve the most crucial problem of our age, the relation of science to value.

## CHECKLIST

"Logical Conditions of a Scientific Treatment of Morality," in *Investigations Representing the Departments: Part II, Philosophy, Education* (University of Chicago, The Decennial Publications, First Series, Vol. III), pp. 113–39. Chicago: University of Chicago Press, 1903. [Reprinted separately, Chicago: University of Chicago Press, 1903, 27 pp.; also reprinted in C–8, pp. 211–49; C–16, pp. 23–60.]

*Ethics*, with James Hayden Tufts (American Science Series). New York: Henry Holt and Co., 1908. xiii, 618 pp.

"Is Nature Good? A Conversation," *Hibbert Journal*, VII (July 1909), 827–43. [Reprinted in C–2, pp. 20–45, with the title "Nature and Its Good: A Conversation."]

Review of *The Eternal Values* by Hugo Münsterberg, *Philosophical Review*, XIX (Mar. 1910), 188–92.

"The Problem of Values," *Journal of Philosophy*, X (May 1913), 268–69.

"The Objects of Valuation," *Journal of Philosophy*, XV (May 1918), 253–58. (Reply to: Ralph Barton Perry, "Dewey and Urban on Value Judgments," *Journal of Philosophy*, XIV [Mar. 1917], 169–81; and Wendell T. Bush, "Value and Causality," *Journal of Philosophy*, XV [Feb. 1918], 85–96.)

*Human Nature and Conduct.* New York: Henry Holt and Co., 1922. vii, 336 pp. [Enl. ed., with Foreword, New York: Modern Library, 1930. ix, vii, 336 pp. Also, Armed Forces ed. (from original plates), 1944.]

"Valuation and Experimental Knowledge," *Philosophical Review*, XXXI (July 1922), 325–51.

Response by David Wight Prall, "In Defense of a *Worthless* Theory of Value," *Journal of Philosophy*, XX (Mar. 1923), 128–37.

Reply by Dewey, "Values, Liking, and Thought," *Journal of Philosophy*, XX (Nov. 1923), 617–22.

Reply by Prall, "Values and Thought-Process," *Journal of Philosophy*, XXI (Feb. 1924), 117–25.

Reply by Dewey, "The Meaning of Value," *Journal of Philosophy*, XXII (Feb. 1925), 126–33.

*Experience and Nature* (Lectures upon the Paul Carus Foundation, First Series). Chicago, London: Open Court Publishing Co., 1925. xi, 443 pp. [2d ed., with a Preface, New York: W. W. Norton, 1929.

ix, 1a–4a, 1–443 pp. 3d ed., LaSalle, Ill.: Open Court Publishing Co., 1958. xviii, 360 pp.]

"Value, Objective Reference and Criticism," *Philosophical Review,* XXXIV (July 1925), 313–32.

*The Quest for Certainty.* New York: Minton, Balch and Co., 1929. 318 pp.

"Foreword," in *Human Nature and Conduct,* pp. v–ix. New York: Modern Library, 1930.

*Ethics,* with James Hayden Tufts. New York: Henry Holt and Co., 1932. xiii, 528 pp. [Rev. ed., with Preface to the 1932 Edition. The 1908 edition has been completely revised, with "about two-thirds of the present edition . . . newly written, and frequent changes in detail . . . in the remainder."]

*Art as Experience.* New York: Minton, Balch and Co., 1934. viii, 355 pp. [Part of Ch. 1 first published as "Art in a Vacuum," *Saturday Review of Literature,* X (Feb. 1934), 501–3.]

*Logic: The Theory of Inquiry.* New York: Henry Holt and Co., 1938. viii, 546 pp.

"The Determination of Ultimate Values or Aims Through Antecedent or *a priori* Speculation or Through Pragmatic or Empirical Inquiry," in *Thirty-seventh Yearbook of the National Society for the Study of Education,* Pt. II, pp. 471–85. Bloomington, Ill.: Public School Publishing Co., 1938.

"Judgment Values," *Daily Princetonian,* 22 Nov. 1938.

*Theory of Valuation* (International Encyclopedia of Unified Science, Vol. II, No. 4). Chicago: University of Chicago Press, 1939. 67 pp.

"Experience, Knowledge and Value: A Rejoinder," in *The Philosophy of John Dewey* (The Library of Living Philosophers, Vol. I, ed. Paul Arthur Schilpp), pp. 517–608. Evanston, Chicago: Northwestern University, 1939.

"The Basic Values and Loyalties of Democracy," *American Teacher,* XXV (May 1941), 8–9.

"The Ambiguity of 'Intrinsic Good'," *Journal of Philosophy,* XXXIX (June 1942), 328–30. [Reprinted in C–8, pp. 282–85.]

"Valuation Judgments and Immediate Quality," *Journal of Philosophy,* XL (June 1943), 309–17. (Reply to: Philip Blair Rice, " 'Objectivity' in Value Judgments," *Journal of Philosophy,* XL [Jan. 1943], 5–14.)

Response by Rice, "Types of Value Judgment," *Journal of Philosophy,* XL (Sept. 1943), 533–43. See also Rice's "Quality and Value," ibid., XL (June 1943), 337–48.

Reply by Dewey, "Further as to Valuation as Judgment," *Journal of Philosophy,* XL (Sept. 1943), 543–52. [Reprinted in C–8, pp. 261–72.]

"Some Questions About Value," *Journal of Philosophy,* XLI (Aug. 1944), 449–55. [Reprinted in C–8, pp. 273–81.] (Reply to: George Raymond Geiger, "Can We Choose Between Values?" *Journal of Philosophy,* XLI [May 1944], 292–98.)

"The Field of 'Value'," in *Value: A Cooperative Inquiry,* ed. Ray Lepley, pp. 64–77. New York: Columbia University Press, 1949.

# 8

# Dewey's Philosophy of Religion

### HORACE L. FRIESS

THE CHARACTER and the movement of John Dewey's published thought on religion can be surveyed by comparing what he said in his late years about "a common faith" with ideas expressed more than forty years earlier in papers and talks at the University of Michigan. Both the consistent direction of his thought and its significant movement invite attention. "There is but one fact," Dewey declared in 1892 in an address at Michigan on "Christianity and Democracy," namely, "the more complete movement of man to his unity with his fellows through realizing the truth of life." [1] This statement can hardly be improved as standing for the unifying and permanently controlling fact in Dewey's own faith and in his thinking about religion.

Yet through the years there occurred also some great changes. That address of 1892 was "delivered before the Students' Christian Association, at the University of Michigan, on Sunday morning, 27 March." [2] In it, as in other papers of the same period, Dewey after the fashion of Hegelian idealism interpreted human progress in truth and freedom as being the essence of what could then and there serve as a liberating version of the Christian gospel. Forty-two years later there is neither Hegelian nor much specifically Christian language left in Dewey's Yale lectures of 1934 on *A Common Faith*. Yet here he is still battling on a broader front for a faith in essence and in

1. "Christianity and Democracy," in *Religious Thought at the University of Michigan* (Ann Arbor: Inland Press, 1893), p. 63.
2. "Christianity and Democracy," p. 60.

many particulars continuous with his earlier convictions. Having gained, in his experience and work of the intervening decades, intellectual methods and cultural relations of new universality and power, Dewey in his 1934 lectures argued that the traditional religions, including Christianity, were no longer viable as liberating and unifying for present and future mankind. Instead of providing a common faith, they divisively enclose religion, he declared, in doctrines and habits which stem from earlier and less informed stages of culture.

*A Common Faith* has by now gone through some twenty printings, and is a statement of ideas on religion with which Dewey will be lastingly identified.[3] The slim little book, comprising three lectures on *1)* "Religion Versus the Religious," *2)* "Faith and Its Object," *3)* "The Human Abode of the Religious Function," offers a compact gathering of long-matured thoughts. The contrast drawn between "religion" and "the religious" has become a familiar and much considered distinction in current discussion of the subject. Dewey explained that he was now using the nouns "religion" and "religions" "to signify a special body of beliefs and practices having some kind of institutional organization, loose or tight." [4] In contrast to this, he would use the adjective "religious" to designate a generic aspect or quality that can accrue to many kinds of experience independently of special doctrines and practices. Stated in his own words:

> The adjective "religious" denotes nothing in the way of a specifiable entity, either institutional or as a system of beliefs. . . . It denotes attitudes that may be taken toward every object and every proposed end or ideal.
>
> It is the polar opposite of some type of experience that can exist by itself.[5]

Dewey added it was his belief "that the present depression in religion is closely connected with the fact that religions now prevent, because of their weight of historic encumbrances, the religious quality of experience from coming to consciousness

3. *A Common Faith* (New Haven: Yale University Press, 1934), 87 pp.

4. *A Common Faith*, p. 9.

5. *A Common Faith*, pp. 9–11.

and finding the expression that is appropriate to present conditions, intellectual and moral." [6]

To set "religion and religions" as institutionalized entities over against "the religious" as a quality of life thus meant for Dewey far more than the making of a formal or semantic distinction. As he developed the contrast between "religion" and "the religious," he gathered into it: his reasons for a naturalistic outlook rejecting "supernaturalism"; his case for "co-operative inquiry" and "idealizing imagination" as reliable methods; his envisioning of a greater freedom as dependent not just on "particular resolve," but on knowledge, imagination, and "the organic plentitude of our being"; [7] his lifelong effort for a more thorough common culture expanding the values of natural human relations in democratic society. Dewey thus associated this opposition of "religion *versus* the religious" with the most pervasive and crucial issues in world-view, in method, in psychological attitude, in society and culture.

In his lectures on *A Common Faith*, Dewey's procedure was largely dialectical and polemic, setting forth those many crucial points on which he saw his own ideas in opposition to other prevalent views. Supporting evidence and explanation in behalf of the positions taken could be but slightly given in the afforded time and space. It must be sought in Dewey's other major works. Dewey indeed took later occasion to say that the Terry lectures were addressed chiefly to those who had already abandoned supernaturalism, and who might mistakenly think of themselves as thereby excluded from sharing in religious qualities of life.[8] While explicit references to religion are brief and scattered in Dewey's major writings (sometimes coming as a kind of flourish or gesture toward a wide horizon near the close of a work), many such passages have an eloquence and a solid support from their context that is hardly equaled in the pages of the Terry lectures.[9]

6. *A Common Faith*, p. 9.
7. *A Common Faith*, p. 17.
8. See "Experience, Knowledge and Value: A Rejoinder," in *The Philosophy of John Dewey* (The Library of Living Philosophers, Vol. I, ed. Paul Arthur Schilpp [Evanston, Chicago: Northwestern University, 1939]), p. 597, where Dewey is replying to criticism.
9. Only a few excerpts from such passages can be cited in this introductory essay, but a discerning reader will come upon many more in the works listed in the accompanying bibliography.

Much of what Dewey said in 1934 in these lectures on *A Common Faith* is fundamentally continuous with earlier ideas already expressed, although in the idiom of Hegel, during his years at Michigan. But some points, slowly gathered it seems in the progress of his reflections, come to relatively new statement in the late work. Dewey's Sunday address in 1892 on "Christianity and Democracy" (for the Michigan Students' Christian Association) did not contrast "religion" and "the religious" in just those words, but it made a partly similar distinction between "cult and creed," on the one hand, and "revelation" as ongoing discovery of the truth of life, on the other. Dewey declared that "looked at from the outside, a religion seems to be a cult and a body of doctrine." And he continued:

> This is the appearance. Research into the origin and development of religion destroys the appearance. It is shown that every religion has its source in the social and intellectual life of a community or race. Every religion is an expression of the social relations of the community; its rites, its cult, are a recognition of the sacred and divine significance of these relationships. The religion is an expression of the mental attitude and habit of a people. . . . Its ideas, its dogmas and mysteries are recognitions, in symbolic form, of the poetic, social and intellectual value of the surroundings. In time this significance, social and intellectual, is lost sight of; it is so thoroughly condensed in the symbols, the rites, the dogmas, that they seem to be the religion. They become an end in themselves. Thus separated from life they begin to decay; it seems as if religion were disintegrating. In reality, the very life, the very complexus of social and intellectual inter-actions which give birth to these forms, is already and continuously at work finding revelation and expression in more adequate relations and truths.[10]

In this same 1892 address, which opens with the views just cited, Dewey proceeds to identify Christianity, "if universal," with ongoing "revelation" rather than with any specific "cult and dogma." "Jesus," he says, "had no cult or rite to impose; no specific forms of worship." [11]

10. "Christianity and Democracy," pp. 60–61.
11. "Christianity and Democracy," pp. 61–62. Dewey quotes John 4:21, 23 to attest Jesus' teaching. And he also cites a Dr. Elisha Mulford, who in his *The Republic of God* holds that Christianity "is not a religion but a revelation."

Christianity, if universal, if revelation, must be the continuously unfolding, never ceasing discovery of the meaning of life. Revelation is the ascertaining of life. It cannot be more than this; it must be all of this.

False also is the doctrine that revelation is the process by which an external God declares to man certain fixed statements about himself and the methods of His working. God is essentially and only the self-revealing, and the revelation is complete only as men come to realize Him.

Revelation means effective discovery, the actual ascertaining or guaranteeing to man of the truth of his life and the reality of the Universe.

Christianity as revelation is not only to, it is *in* man's thought and reason.[12]

Viewed in relation to Dewey's development, these passages are clearly part and parcel of his lifelong commitment to science and to democracy. Viewed for historical affiliation, they stand in the frame of a liberal Hegelianism, with its rejection of dualism and its emphasis on truth developing as the expression of social relations and mentalities. Much later, in autobiographical retrospect, Dewey still recalled with lively feeling that for him "Hegel's synthesis of subject and object, matter and spirit, the divine and the human, was, however, no mere intellectual formula; it operated as an immense release, a liberation. Hegel's treatment of human culture, of institutions and the arts, involved the same dissolution of hard-and-fast dividing walls, and had a special attraction for me." [13]

In yet larger historical perspective, what Dewey said in this 1892 address at Michigan was distinctly in line with prophetic religious teaching, inasmuch as the role of ongoing revelation and criticism was judged to be more determining of

12. "Christianity and Democracy," pp. 62, 64–65.
13. "From Absolutism to Experimentalism," in *Contemporary American Philosophy: Personal Statements*, II, eds. George Plimpton Adams and William Pepperell Montague (New York: Macmillan Co., 1930), 19. Aristotelian influence upon Dewey's nondualism appears in a very early paper on "Soul and Body," in *The Early Works of John Dewey, 1882–1898*, Vol. I (Carbondale: Southern Illinois University Press, 1969), pp. 93–115.

human destiny than was that of cult and creed. Whatever is vitally religious must be more completely life-centered rather than narrowly cult-centered. Dewey's outlook was alive with a prophetic vision of social growth, of bonds loosened and partitions worn away, of democracy developing as freer community and as unifying humanity in "one Commonwealth of truth." [14]

In asserting the claim of "man's thought and reason" to be the organ of true religious revelation, Dewey went a step further than Hegel had gone. According to Hegel, one and the same truth is grasped (albeit with a mounting clarity) in the religious cult, the theological symbol, and the philosophic concept. Dewey's critique of cult, and of theology that is not philosophically reconstructed, is more radical, both being attacked as survivals that harbor superstition and falsehood.[15] The difference signalizes profound changes in the relations of cult and culture as between the 1820s and the 1890s, and also the advance of evolutionary modes of thought. The difference is carried further in Dewey's conception of thought as instrumental, and in his shift from a logic of absolute identity to a logic of experimental reconstruction.[16] When knowledge is no longer viewed as just the finding of an "antecedently real" object, but involves reconstructing both the search and its object, the way is then widened for criticism of doctrines and orders of reality that claim to be above and apart from natural investigation. Much of Dewey's condemnation of supernaturalism was already accomplished in his early Hegelian way of thought, but his development of an "experimental logic" added new leverage for the critique. The view of thought as reconstructive activity gave general intellectual force to the moral judgment that "the demand of righteous-

*14.* "Christianity and Democracy," p. 69.

*15.* A discounting of the truth-value of cult-centered theology, such as Hegel would scarcely have made, appears in a short but trenchant paper of Dewey's in 1893 on "The Relation of Philosophy to Theology," *Monthly Bulletin*, Students' Christian Association, University of Michigan, XVI (1893), 66–68. The most comprehensive and rewarding discussion that I have seen of Dewey's journey in these early papers appears in a chapter by John Blewett, S.J., on "Democracy as Religion: Unity in Human Relations," in *John Dewey: His Thought and Influence*, ed. John Blewett, S.J. (New York: Fordham University Press, 1960), pp. 33–58.

*16.* Cf. the working out of this shift in Dewey's *Studies in Logical Theory* (Chicago: University of Chicago Press, 1903) and in the *Essays in Experimental Logic* (Chicago: University of Chicago Press, 1916).

ness for reverence does not depend upon ability to prove the existence of an antecedent Being who is righteous." [17]

Viewing the whole corpus of Dewey's writings, one can see his thought on religion as hinging upon choice between a faith in natural possibilities still to be realized at risk, and a faith that values are secure in that "antecedent reality" of the world, which rests on the already complete Being of a Supernatural Order. Here lies the problem of "faith and its object." Is it to be faith in a given revelation of powers and directives already established? Or is it to be faith in a process of increasingly voluntary devotion to continuing discovery and ideal vision?

Dewey believed that two cultural revolutions were giving vastly greater promise to the more open experimental road. The first was the intellectual "transformation" in which co-operative scientific inquiry was developing and becoming incomparably the most reliable and productive tool of discovery mankind had ever possessed. Dewey was convinced that this transformation would liberate morals and religious quality of life from dependence upon special, fixed beliefs as to facts of existence. He had faith that moral ideals and religious quality of life could and would "adjust" worthily to "whatever beliefs" become intellectually accredited through the co-operative scientific process. Being so minded, Dewey could summon up no interest in theological controversy as "a leading philosophical problem." [18] From 1894 on he became more and more deeply concerned with issues of education. He looked to the schools and universities as common organs of a freer search for universal truth, and turned away in notable silence from the divisive dogmas of the churches.

Along with this intellectual liberation in beliefs, Dewey pointed to a second cultural revolution, which he held to be even more fundamental in its consequences for religion. This was a change in "the *conditions* under which human beings associate with one another"—a profound shift "in the social center of gravity" toward greater investment in voluntary groups, whereby "idealizing imagination" was much freed from being controlled by and conformed to established ways of nonvolun-

17. *The Quest for Certainty* (New York: Minton, Balch and Co., 1929), p. 304.
18. "From Absolutism to Experimentalism," pp. 19–20. Cf. also *The Quest for Certainty*, pp. 303 ff.

tary Church and State systems.[19] Dewey held that the further interplay of these two revolutions, the scientific and the democratic, held great promise for human freedom, including a productive liberation of religious energies.

Intellectual emancipation from fixed beliefs, however valuable a condition for creative intelligence, does not in itself insure that life will acquire religious quality. But what else is involved? One may begin by noting Dewey's rejection of an answer to this question, which was enjoying considerable fresh favor in his day. This was the identification of religious quality with a special kind or class of experiences—described as "mystical," or by some writers described more broadly as "numinous," or "extraordinary." Dewey observed explicitly that, of course, he did not mean "to throw doubt upon the existence of particular experiences called mystical." But he pointed also to the problematic character of their noetic content, and declared that interpretations of mysticism which "mark off two distinct realms in one of which science has jurisdiction, while in the other, special modes of immediate knowledge of religious objects have authority" do but reinstate "the old dualism between the natural and the supernatural, in terms better adapted to the cultural conditions of the present time." [20]

Conclusions about facts of existence were too dubiously drawn from mystical experiences. But besides, Dewey was not persuaded that religious quality as a generic possibility of human life derives from so special a source. The trend of his thinking, both in philosophy and in psychology, brought him to another view of the nature and the conditions of religious quality of life, which he considered more common and universal. He regarded it as a natural, not a supernatural, condition that can occur in the pursuit of inclusive ideals, when a self thereby finds unification in some general attitude. The thought here is sufficiently complex to require a slightly fuller restatement in Dewey's own words. In an often quoted passage of *A Common Faith*

19. This theme is the principal subject of the third lecture in *A Common Faith*. In a lecture on "Religion and Our Schools," *Hibbert Journal*, VI (1908), 796–809, Dewey discussed for an English audience the American policy of separating state schools and organized religion. See also "Experience, Knowledge and Value," pp. 594–97, where Dewey replies to Edward L. Schaub's view of this lecture in the same volume, pp. 393 ff.

20. *A Common Faith*, p. 38.

Dewey describes "the religious function in experience" and "the faith that is religious" (he uses both expressions on the same page) as "the unification of the self through allegiance to inclusive ideal ends, which imagination presents to us and to which the human will responds as worthy of controlling our desires and choices." [21]

Every term in this statement has roots in and gains distinct meaning from Dewey's years of reflection on human nature and conduct, from his sustained efforts to understand the psychological conditions of ethical values. It has been considered remarkable and even perplexing that this description of what is "religious" in *A Common Faith* was put so overtly in terms of personal self-realization, while Dewey's usually strong focus on social realities is less explicitly developed here. Yet one cannot think that Dewey intends to separate the personal and the social, in view of all that he has repeatedly said on this point. A deeply penetrating clue to his view of their connection, most relevant indeed to understanding his sense of a *common* religious faith, may be found toward the end of his address in 1899 as president of the American Psychological Association. Speaking then on the theme of "Psychology and Social Practice," Dewey declared:

> There is no logical alternative save either to recognize and search for the mechanism of the interplay of personalities that controls the existing distributions of values, or to accept as final a fixed hierarchy of persons in which the leaders assert, on no basis save their own supposed superior personality, certain ends and laws which the mass of men passively receive and imitate. The effort to apply psychology to social affairs means that the determination of ethical values lies not in any set or class, however superior, but in the workings of the social whole; . . . in the complex interactions and interrelations which constitute this whole.
>
> Psychology will never tell us just what to do ethically, nor just how to do it. But it will afford us insight into the conditions which control the formation and execution of aims, and thus enable human effort to expend itself sanely, rationally and with assurance. . . . The psychologist, in his most remote and technical occupation with mechanism, is contributing his bit to

21. *A Common Faith*, p. 33.

that ordered knowledge which alone enables mankind to secure a larger and to direct a more equal flow of values in life.[22]

In these observations one sees clearly the direct connection Dewey is drawing from a possible ordering of social relations to a more equal serving of "personality in all" through better knowledge of the physical and psychological conditions "through which possible values become actual in life." Some thirty years later, in his autobiographical statement and elsewhere, Dewey reflected upon the difficult progress of such better knowledge, and of the patience needed "in wandering in a wilderness like that of the present." He also declared with characteristic candor that "it is futile (and likely to be dishonest) to forecast prematurely just what forms the religious interest will take as a final consequence of the great intellectual transformation that is going on." [23] This openness on Dewey's part toward the future permits one to conclude that he did not intend to equate "a common faith" with uniformity in the particulars of belief, imagination, and self-realization. One may suppose that the common faith espoused means a more universal commitment of mankind to the voluntary variations in ideal and in "self-unification" that become viable with growth of knowledge and freer social structure. Dewey is not completely explicit on this point, yet one cannot doubt that his idea of "a common faith" includes the freeing of religious vitality from conformity to monopolistic institutions.

More problematic is the question whether Dewey's strictures on the way religious institutions harden and become devitalized do enough justice to the actual roles of cult in relation to community. It is surely understandable that, as many ancient heritages became entangled in the common traffic of the modern world, the universality of Christianity as "a religion," or of any other traditional system of religion, became more and more incredible. Dewey's travels in China and Japan, as later on in Soviet Russia and in Turkey, surely served to drive home this point. His reaction was also predictable to the pronounced neo-orthodox trend of much Western theology after World War I,

22. "Psychology and Social Practice," *Psychological Review*, VII (1900), 105–24. [Quoted from *John Dewey: Philosophy, Psychology and Social Practice*, essays selected, edited and with a Foreword by Joseph Ratner (New York: G. P. Putnam's Sons, 1963), pp. 313–15.]

23. "From Absolutism to Experimentalism," pp. 26–27, 20.

its recourse to more or less sophisticated modes of "supernatural" doctrine. From Dewey's viewpoint this presaged nothing less than death and decline. In 1943 he attacked severely the philosophical credit of this trend in an article on "Anti-Naturalism in Extremis." [24] Dewey failed to find that "marriage of emotion with intelligence" which was for him "the only assurance of birth of better ones [institutions]" in current theological thinking; he did not see in it the now needed faith in "passionate intelligence, as ardor in behalf of light shining into the murky places of social existence, and as zeal for its refreshing and purifying effect." [25]

How far such a judgment involved a blind spot in Dewey, besides chronic lassitude and indirection in much theological thought, remains an open question. But it must be noted as a fact that, among the friendly critics and the followers of Dewey in ways of naturalistic philosophy, there were those who found his treatment of "religion" seriously lacking in unprejudiced empirical consideration of the religious arts.[26]

In view of his opposition to supernaturalism, and his explicit advice to abandon "religion" and "the religions" as established entities, it came as something of a surprise that in *A Common Faith* Dewey was still inclined to relate himself positively to using such expressions as "the divine" and even the noun "God." A many-sided controversy arose over this. Dewey himself noted that the tactics of combating supernaturalism were involved, and he took care to explain the sense in which he would use these hallowed terms. He said:

> This idea [of the divine] is . . . one of ideal possibilities unified through imaginative realization and projection. . . . We are in the presence neither of ideals completely embodied

24. "Anti-Naturalism in Extremis," *Partisan Review*, X (1943), 24–39; reprinted in *Naturalism and the Human Spirit*, ed. Y. H. Krikorian (New York: Columbia University Press, 1944), a volume to which many former students of Dewey's contributed.
25. *A Common Faith*, pp. 79–81.
26. See, for example, a review article on *A Common Faith* by J. H. Randall, Jr., entitled "Art and Religion as Education," *Social Frontier*, II (1936). Randall commented: "To free the religious attitude from institutional embodiment in a religion sounds suspiciously like freeing art from any particular work of art." Cf. also the "Critique of Dewey's Anticlerical Religious Philosophy" by a younger philosopher, W. E. Arnett, *Journal of Religion*, XXXIV (1954), and in the same author's book, *Religion and Judgment* (New York: Appleton-Century-Crofts, 1966).

in existence nor yet of ideals that are mere rootless ideals, fantasies, utopias. For there are forces in nature and society that generate and support the ideals. They are further unified by the action that gives them coherence and solidity. It is this *active* relation between ideal and actual to which I would give the name "God." I would not insist that the name *must* be given.[27]

The italics in this passage are Dewey's own. The crucial point thus is that the word "God" is here used to refer to an "active relation between ideal and actual," and not as a name for a uniquely preëxistent and completed Being.

In the course of controversy one important dispute over Dewey's intended meaning was cleared up. In a letter Dewey said that E. E. Aubrey had correctly interpreted him as holding that it required the power of corporate human intelligence to draw the actual given of nature and the projected ideals of the imagination together in a plan of directed activity.[28] He was not using the term "God" for a process whereby ideal and actual might become united without need of human action. H. N. Wieman had found his language open to such an interpretation, but Dewey declined to put a "theist" stress on faith in that possibility.

However one may judge his choice of words as affecting the understanding of his position, it is clear that Dewey maintained his own integrity as a humanist, and did not allow what "God" meant for him to eclipse human freedom and responsibility. He also remained "tough-minded" about "personal immortality"; he displayed no "will-to-believe" in this, stating most briefly in a New York *Times* symposium that for lack of evidence he had "no beliefs" on that subject.[29] Yet Dewey wanted to make very clear that his version of *naturalistic humanism* was not expressing a sense of man's alienation from or defiance

27. *A Common Faith*, pp. 50–51; and cf. pp. 43–57. In 1933 Dewey had joined a group of leaders in signing "A Humanist Manifesto," *New Humanist*, VI (1933), 1–5.

28. The exchanges in this discussion between H. N. Wieman, E. E. Aubrey, and Dewey on "Is John Dewey a Theist?" took place in *Christian Century*, LI (1934). Dewey's statement is on pp. 1551–52.

29. New York *Times*, 8 Apr. 1928, symposium on "Personal Immortality: What I Believe." Cf. also Dewey's review of *The Illusion of Immortality* by Corliss Lamont, *New Republic*, LXXXII (1935), 318; reprinted as an Introduction to the book in its second and third editions (New York: Philosophical Library, 1950, 1959).

toward the universe. On the contrary, it was keyed in a kind of "natural piety"; and Dewey said explicitly: "The essentially unreligious attitude is that which attributes human achievement and purpose to man in isolation from the world of physical nature and his fellows." [30]

As Dewey conceived of religious quality, it is a "generalized attitude" engendered in one's most inclusive "transaction," a pervasive disposition in life in its fullness, which becomes voluntary yet involves much that cannot be forced by particular acts of will. The concern of Dewey in his late years to develop a technical concept of organized "transactions" meant to stress the natural continuity of process in human activities and to avoid polarized accounts of them in such dichotomies as inner and outer, subject and object, etc. In terms of such a concept, it would be unnatural to regard religious quality as given to man apart from his efforts, but just as unnatural to think of it as achieved by men in isolation from a world.

Dewey's intellectual liberation from fixed beliefs of traditional religion is entirely clear. But equally clear is the great continuity in "generalized attitude" that pervaded the "self-unification" he sought. Its application and communication grew steadily broader. It was an attitude that strove to join "creative intelligence" with volition, not alone for particular ends, but with the inclusive ideal of fostering more effective personal and social integration within that critically expanding "imaginative totality we call the Universe." [31] Dewey's statement in 1892 about the one central fact being "the more complete movement of man to his unity with his fellows through realizing the truth of life" harbors this same "generalized attitude" as much as does all he said and did later. And of course, the formation of this attitude went much further back to roots in the personal growth and experience of Dewey in his youth. Religious orthodoxy in the specific Vermont environment in which Dewey grew up, and from which he moved away, was chiefly the practical piety and morality of a conservative Congregationalism. [32]

30. *A Common Faith*, p. 25; also pp. 52–53.
31. *A Common Faith*, p. 19; also p. 85.
32. The present essay stays within the frame of a "Guide" to published writings of Dewey's, and I have not explored the early years where primary materials were not sufficiently available to me. Besides the

Religious energies, shaped by the "general attitude" that developed in John Dewey, were not apt to vegetate in sheer reverie or to turn to fanaticism. There was the likelihood of a more active and critical piety prevailing over submission either to fatalism or to romantic fantasy. Critics of Dewey's "common faith" have pointed to limitations grounded in these same conditions. It has been called the faith of an "incorrigible moralist." [33] It has been regarded as too singly pitched on a note of human assurance. The religious significance of tragic conflict, the longing for redemption of the sinful, for healing of the divided self, receive little illumination. The sublime reaches of contemplation, that may inspire a self little concerned to unify its paltry existence, are not explored. Because of all this, Dewey's "common faith" has been criticized as a provincial expression of recent American Protestant and liberal values, disappointingly heedless of the great range and rich variety of historic and potential religion.[34]

If what is sought for is theoretic oversight of man's religious heritage in its manifold forms and functions, then it must be admitted that what Dewey has written on religion lacks attention to many great themes. But if the point is to develop

---

biographical introduction supplied by Dewey's daughters for *The Philosophy of John Dewey*, the reader can profit by George Dykhuizen's studies of Dewey's Vermont years. See their listing in M. H. Thomas, *John Dewey: A Centennial Bibliography* (Chicago: University of Chicago Press, 1962), p. 190.

In Dewey's emphasis on creative intelligence and well-developed volition, the theologically literate may easily see continuity with the centuries-old view of God in Western traditions as Logos and as Holy Will. One could be tempted further to see some relation between extreme immanential trends in some current Christian theology that talks of "death" of the old cosmic God and Dewey's critique of "antecedent realities." It would seem appropriate, however, to stress the ever-born-anew state of what for Dewey is alive of "the divine," and also that he abandoned any exclusive identification of this with Christ many years ago.

33. See, for example, W. E. Arnett, *Religion and Judgment*, pp. 116 ff., where Dewey's former colleague and friend, Irwin Edman, is cited as so describing him.

34. See J. H. Randall, Jr., "The Religion of Shared Experience," in *The Philosopher of the Common Man, Essays in Honor of John Dewey to Celebrate His Eightieth Birthday* (New York: G. P. Putnam's Sons, 1940), pp. 106–45. Randall makes these and other criticisms drastically, but also extolls Dewey's "unique religious devotion to the possibilities of a community of shared experience."

and to exemplify the religious issues that have evoked insistent concern in one's own situation, one must then be selective. And surely in this light what Dewey has said expresses his authentic and deeply developed concern. There is a passage in *A Common Faith* where George Santayana's connecting of "the religious quality of experience with the imaginative"—with poetry when it intervenes in life—is embraced and interpreted. Says Dewey: "Imagination may play upon life or it may enter profoundly into it." [35] By sharing views and attitudes that had entered so profoundly into his whole life, Dewey genuinely exemplified as well as expounded his own view of "the religious."

In the years of Dewey's blossoming thought at Michigan, to which attention has been drawn, he pondered and occasionally wrote on the relations of poetry, science, and philosophic belief. There is also, we are told, considerable poetry by Dewey himself which has never been published. It is possible that this would reveal variations of mood and feeling less held to the leash of the major themes that Dewey pursued in his philosophical prose. But one is confident that, however great a role he accorded the imagination especially in the projection of values, he would never countenance the setting up of poetry as an alternative to science for knowledge of existence. The comparison Dewey made in 1892 and 1893 of Ernest Renan's faith in *The Future of Science* (1848) and Renan's subsequent "loss of faith in science" gives vital insight into Dewey's lasting convictions on this crucial matter.[36] One judges also that, whatever range of feeling Dewey's poetry might express, the following ideas from the closing pages of *Human Nature and Conduct* would not be dislodged as a central deliverance of their author's thought on religion.

> There is a conceit fostered by perversion of religion which assimilates the universe to our personal desires; but there is also a conceit of carrying the load of the universe from which religion liberates us. Within the flickering inconsequential acts of separate selves dwells a sense of the whole which claims and dignifies them. In its presence we put off mortality and live in

35. *A Common Faith*, pp. 17–18.
36. "Two Phases of Renan's Life: The Faith of 1850 and the Doubt of 1890," in *Early Works*, III, 174–79; and "Renan's Loss of Faith in Science," *Open Court*, VII (1893), 3512–15.

the universal. The life of the community in which we live and have our being is the fit symbol of this relationship. The acts in which we express our perception of the ties which bind us to others are its only rites and ceremonies.[37]

37. *Human Nature and Conduct* (New York: Henry Holt and Co., 1922), pp. 331–32.

## CHECKLIST

"The Obligation to Knowledge of God," in *The Early Works of John Dewey, 1882–1898*, Vol. I, pp. 61–63. Carbondale: Southern Illinois University Press, 1969.

"The Place of Religious Emotion," in *Early Works*, I, 90–92.

"Soul and Body," in *Early Works*, I, 93–115.

Review of *What Is Reality?* by Francis Howe Johnson, in *The Early Works of John Dewey, 1882–1898*, Vol. III, pp. 192–93. Carbondale: Southern Illinois University Press, 1969.

"Two Phases of Renan's Life: The Faith of 1850 and the Doubt of 1890," in *Early Works*, III, 174–79. [Reprinted in C–10, pp. 18–23, with the title "Ernest Renan."]

"Christianity and Democracy," in *Religious Thought at the University of Michigan*, pp. 60–69. Ann Arbor: Inland Press, 1893.

"The Relation of Philosophy to Theology," *Monthly Bulletin*, Students' Christian Association, University of Michigan, XVI (Jan. 1893), 66–68.

"Renan's Loss of Faith in Science," *Open Court*, VII (Jan. 1893), 3512–15. [Reprinted in C–10, pp. 23–30, with the title "Ernest Renan."]

"Psychology and Social Practice," *Psychological Review*, VII (Mar. 1900), 105–24; *Science*, n.s. XI (Mar. 1900), 321–33. [Reprinted separately as University of Chicago Contributions to Education, No. 2. Chicago: University of Chicago Press, 1901. 42 pp.]

"Thought and Its Subject-Matter: The General Problem of Logical Theory," pp. 1–22; "Thought and Its Subject-Matter: The Antecedent Conditions and Cues of the Thought-Function," pp. 23–48; "Thought and Its Subject-Matter: The Datum of Thinking," pp. 49–64; and "Thought and Its Subject-Matter: The Content and Object of Thought," pp. 65–85; in *Studies in Logical Theory* (University of Chicago, The Decennial Publications, Second Series, Vol. XI). Chicago: University of Chicago Press, 1903. [Reprinted in C–3, pp. 75–182, with the titles "The Relationship of Thought and Its Subject-Matter," "The Antecedents and Stimuli of Thinking," "Data and Meanings," and "The Objects of Thought."]

"Religion and Our Schools," *Hibbert Journal*, VI (July 1908), 796–809. [Reprinted in C–10, pp. 504–16; C–11, pp. 702–15, with the title "The Schools and Religions"; C–12, pp. 74–86.]

*Essays in Experimental Logic*. Chicago: University of Chicago Press, 1916. vii, 444 pp. [Chs. 2–5 "represent (with editorial revisions, mostly omissions) the essays taken from the old volume (*Studies in Logical Theory*). . . . The other essays are in part reprinted and in part rewritten, with additions, from various contributions to philosophical periodicals." Preface, p. v.]

*Human Nature and Conduct.* New York: Henry Holt and Co., 1922. [Enl. ed., with Foreword, New York: Modern Library, 1930. ix, vii, 336 pp. Also, Armed Forces ed. (from original plates), 1944.]

"Fundamentals," *New Republic,* XXXVII (Feb. 1924), 275–76. [Reprinted in C–10, pp. 453–58.]

"Personal Immortality: 'What I Believe'," New York *Times,* 8 Apr. 1928.

*The Quest for Certainty.* New York: Minton, Balch and Co., 1929. 318 pp.

"Foreword," in *Human Nature and Conduct,* pp. v–ix. New York: Modern Library, 1930.

"From Absolutism to Experimentalism," in *Contemporary American Philosophy: Personal Statements,* II, eds. George Plimpton Adams and William Pepperell Montague, 13–27. New York: Macmillan Co., 1930.

"What Humanism Means to Me," *Thinker,* II (June 1930), 9–12.

"A Humanist Manifesto," *New Humanist,* VI (May–June 1933), 1–5. [Signed by John Dewey and thirty-three leading United States philosophers, writers, and clergymen.] [Reprinted in *Humanizing Religion,* pp. 6–15. New York: Harper and Bros., 1933.]

"A God or The God?" *Christian Century,* L (Feb. 1933), 193–96. [Review of *Is There a God?—A Conversation by Henry Nelson Wieman, Douglas Clyde Macintosh and Max Carl Otto.*]

Response by Wieman and Macintosh, "Mr. Wieman and Mr. Macintosh 'Converse' with Mr. Dewey," *Christian Century,* L (Mar. 1933), 299–302.

"Dr. Dewey Replies," *Christian Century,* L (Mar. 1933), 394–95.

"The Liberation of Modern Religion," *Yale Review,* XXIII (June 1934), 751–70. [Reprinted in *A Common Faith,* pp. 29–57, with the title "Faith and Its Object."]

*A Common Faith.* New Haven: Yale University Press, 1934. 87 pp.

Review by Henry Nelson Wieman, "John Dewey's Common Faith," *Christian Century,* LI (Nov. 1934), 1450–52.

Response to Wieman by Edwin Ewart Aubrey, "Is John Dewey a Theist?" *Christian Century,* LI (Dec. 1934), 1550.

Reply to Aubrey by Wieman, *Christian Century,* LI (Dec. 1934), 1550–51.

Reply to Aubrey and Wieman by Dewey, *Christian Century,* LI (Dec. 1934), 1551–52.

Review by Norbert Guterman, "John Dewey's Credo," *New Republic,* LXXXII (Feb. 1935), 53.

Reply by Dewey, "Religions and the 'Religious'," *New Republic,* LXXXII (Mar. 1935), 132.

"Intimations of Mortality," *New Republic,* LXXXII (Apr. 1935), 318. [Review of *The Illusion of Immortality* by Corliss Lamont.]

"Mystical Naturalism and Religious Humanism," *New Humanist,* VIII (Apr.–May 1935), 74–75. (Comments on: Bernard Meland, "Mystical Naturalism and Religious Humanism," *New Humanist,* VIII [Apr.–May 1935], 72–74.)

"One Current Religious Problem," *Journal of Philosophy,* XXXIII (June 1936), 324–26. (Reply to: Percy Hughes, "Current Philosophical Problems," *Journal of Philosophy,* XXXIII [Apr. 1936], 212–17.)

"Religion, Science, and Philosophy," *Southern Review,* II (Summer 1936), 53–62. [Review of *Religion and Science* by Bertrand Russell.] [Reprinted in C–8, pp. 169–79.]

"Experience, Knowledge and Value: A Rejoinder," in *The Philosophy of John Dewey* (The Library of Living Philosophers, Vol. I, ed. Paul Arthur Schilpp), pp. 517–608. Evanston, Chicago: Northwestern University, 1939.

Review of *Social Religion* by Douglas Clyde Macintosh, *Review of Religion,* IV (Mar. 1940), 359–61.

"Anti-Naturalism in Extremis," *Partisan Review,* X (Jan.–Feb. 1943), 24–39.

"Religion and the Intellectuals," *Partisan Review,* XVII (Feb. 1950), 129–33.

# 9

# Dewey's Social and Political Commentary

## WILLIAM W. BRICKMAN

A MILESTONE in Dewey's intellectual development was his lecture, "The Ethics of Democracy," delivered in 1888 to the Philosophical Union of the University of Michigan. To Merle Curti, this paper was evidence that Dewey possessed "a thoroughly democratic and even radical social point of view as early as 1888." [1] The philosopher argued that democracy was a broad concept which necessarily embraced not merely politics, but also the economy and industry. He combined "a criticism of quantitative individualistic theory of political democracy with a definitely moral interpretation in terms of 'liberty, equality, fraternity.'" [2] His insistence that no political democracy is possible without economic and industrial democracy was evidently derived from the thought of Henry Carter Adams, a colleague in the field of political economy, who urged "a development in economic life parallel to that which had taken place in politics, from absolutism and oligarchy to popular representation." [3] As interpreted by his daughter, Dewey's political philosophy at this stage in his career was probably not as radical as it sounded. In any event, it was alarming enough to his parents, who came to live with him during the closing years of his tenure at the University of Michigan. "While his father was hurt at his sons'

1. Merle Curti, *The Social Ideas of American Educators* (New York: Charles Scribner's Sons, 1935), pp. 502–3.
2. Jane M. Dewey, ed., "Biography of John Dewey," in *The Philosophy of John Dewey* (The Library of Living Philosophers, Vol. I, ed. Paul Arthur Schilpp [Evanston, Chicago: Northwestern University, 1939]), pp. 12–13.
3. Jane Dewey, "Biography of John Dewey," pp. 12–13.

recreance to the Republican party, associated in his mind with the preservation of the union, and his mother at their defection from the religious teachings of their boyhood, both were sufficiently liberal in their views and had sufficient confidence in their children to keep the family relation a close one." [4]

Externally, to be sure, Dewey maintained a posture of conformity throughout the Michigan period. He "remained the devout Congregationalist, participating in Bible institutes, teaching Bible classes, giving courses on the life of Christ, Paul's Epistles, and Church history, and attending Congregationalist conventions." [5] Yet, either his parents were highly perceptive or else the socialist ideas were penetrating his outward conformist attitude to a degree at the end of his Michigan sojourn. At any rate, Dewey absorbed the spirit of social service, which was manifesting itself in the form of a back-to-the-people movement in literature, sociology, economics, and adult education, both in the United States and abroad. Faculty and students at Michigan became involved in dreaming about and working toward a better society. Dewey, James H. Tufts, George H. Mead, and Alfred Lloyd, philosophers all, and Robert E. Park, a sociologist, "constituted the core of a 'leftist' group," rejecting New England orthodoxy and seeking "liberation in social movements and the new psychology." [6]

Particularly of significance was Dewey's association with the brothers Corydon and Franklin Ford, social reformers of the type of Henry George, Edward Bellamy, and socialists of every description. One outcome was the planning in 1892 of a monthly, "Thought News," under Dewey's editorship, with the objective of discussing political, educational, religious, and scientific issues "as parts of one moving life of man." [7] What Dewey intended to do in this publication was to demonstrate that philosophy was not simply "a matter of lunar politics," but that it had "some use." He disclaimed any notion of a social revolution but stressed instead the role of philosophic ideas "as

---

4. Jane Dewey, "Biography of John Dewey," pp. 12–13.
5. Lewis S. Feuer, "John Dewey and the Back-to-the-People Movement in American Thought," *Journal of the History of Ideas*, XX (1959), 553.
6. Feuer, "John Dewey and the Back-to-the-People Movement," p. 548.
7. Prospectus, quoted in Feuer, "John Dewey and the Back-to-the-People Movement," p. 552.

tools to point out the meaning of phases of social life," thereby having "some life value." [8] Even though this publication was stillborn, the idea underlying it came to life years later in Dewey's political writings in the *New Republic*.

The upshot of Dewey's association with the Ford brothers was the acceleration of his assimilation of socialist thought and action. One example of this was his analysis, in an article published in January 1891, in the *International Journal of Ethics*, on the moral justification of strikes. In a basic work on ethics, *Outlines of a Critical Theory of Ethics*, published in the same year, Dewey again referred, by way of illustration, to the labor problems and summed up his definition of a moral law as "the principle of action, which, acted upon, will meet the needs of the existing situation as respects the wants, powers, and circumstances of the individuals concerned. It is no far-away abstraction, but expresses the *movement* of the ethical world." [9] He ended this discussion by stating that "the consideration of specific institutions, as the family, industrial society, civil society, the nation, etc., with their respective rights and laws, belongs rather to political philosophy than to the general theory of ethics." [10] With these words, Dewey made it clear that moral questions were not to be treated as abstruse philosophic speculation, but rather as issues to be resolved by thought processes leading to action.

It is noteworthy that, in the *Outlines*, his second work on philosophy, Dewey mentioned appreciatively Thomas Hill Green, Francis H. Bradley, Edward Caird, Samuel Alexander —Britons all—as sources of his ideas on ethics. He even was generous enough to pay tribute to Herbert Spencer and Leslie Stephen, with whom he expressed disagreement. To his inspirers Dewey gave credit for the core of his theory: "the conception of the will as the expression of ideas, and of social ideas; the notion of an objective ethical world realized in institutions which afford moral ideals, theatre and impetus to the individual; the notion of the moral life as growth in freedom, as the individual finds and conforms to the law of his social placing." [11] In addi-

8. Interview in Detroit *Tribune*, 13 Apr. 1892.
9. *Outlines of a Critical Theory of Ethics*, in *The Early Works of John Dewey, 1882–1898*, Vol. III (Carbondale: Southern Illinois University Press, 1969), p. 351.
10. *Outlines*, p. 352.
11. *Outlines*, p. 239.

tion, Dewey acknowledged his indebtedness "to my friend, Mr. Franklin Ford," for the point concerning "the treatment of the social bearings of science and art." [12] Interestingly, while he cited the works of the British thinkers, he made no reference to any of the writings by his friend.

Dewey's effort to make philosophy practical in Michigan, in the manner of the Ford brothers, did not turn out to be successful, apparently because their procedures did not suit precisely his character and temperament.[13] However, his talents and ambitions along these lines were furthered to a better degree during the decade, 1894–1904, when he served as chairman of the Department of Philosophy, Psychology, and Pedagogy at the University of Chicago. Here he taught, among others, courses on the History of Political Ethics and Contemporary Theories Regarding Ethical Relations of the Individual and Society.[14] In the field of education, one of his courses was the Evolution of the Curriculum in the Fifteenth to the Seventeenth Centuries "with reference to general social and intellectual conditions." [15] It will be seen that Dewey was stressing the socio-political content in his academic work. Moreover, his initiative in the establishment of a Laboratory School at the University of Chicago involved constant attention to social values and problems.

But Dewey, as might have been expected, was not satisfied to operate within the confines of the campus. America at the turn of the century was seething with political and social unrest related to unemployment, the Populist movement, capital-labor tensions and violence, and revolutionary ideology. Chicago, by the time Dewey arrived, had become "the center of radical thought in the United States," and Jane Addams's Hull House, founded in 1889 to help the impoverished, immigrant laborers, was "its moral spokesman." [16] At Hull House, the philosopher found a fertile field and kindred spirits to encourage him to undertake fresh ventures in the application of his discipline to

12. *Outlines*, p. 239.

13. Feuer, "John Dewey and the Back-to-the-People Movement," p. 555.

14. George Dykhuizen, "John Dewey: The Chicago Years," *Journal of the History of Philosophy*, II (1964), 233.

15. Quoted in Dykhuizen, "John Dewey: The Chicago Years," p. 240.

16. Feuer, "John Dewey and the Back-to-the-People Movement," p. 556.

GUIDE TO THE WORKS OF JOHN DEWEY

the problems of man and society. The persons associated with Hull House, "though filled with idealism, were intensely practical, and had a sense of how to achieve social legislation, and how to make democracy meaningful to persons who had never experienced its workings. They were not single-ideaed, quasi-crackpots such as the brothers Ford but people who combined vision with resourcefulness." [17] Here Dewey met and exchanged ideas with such individuals as Florence Kelley, translator of Friedrich Engels' *The Condition of the Working Class in England in 1884*; and Henry Demarest Lloyd, the muckraker whose *Wealth against Commonwealth* attacked monopolies, especially the Standard Oil Company. "The Hull House circle was the American analogue of the English Fabians, with an admixture of the self-sacrifice of the residents of Toynbee Hall." [18]

During his association with Hull House, John Dewey was able to meet foreign radical and revolutionary thinkers who were guests of the house. Probably the most noted of these was the Russian Prince Peter A. Kropotkin, the theoretical architect of revolutionary anarchism who advocated the substitution of mutual-aid communities for state authority and private property. Among the other socially conscious foreigners met by Dewey was Alexander Zelenko, a Russian engineer who resided during 1903–4 at Hull House and who carried back with him the settlement idea of Jane Addams and most likely Dewey's educational principles as well.[19] Through Zelenko, other Russian educators were influenced to experiment in education along the lines exemplified by Dewey in his Laboratory School. Thus, the celebrated Stanislav T. Shatskii acknowledged his debt to the careful analysis by John Dewey, "especially his 'philosophy of pragmatism' which persistently demanded careful examination of theoretical ideas in their practical application." [20] On another occasion, Shatskii stated: "In 1904 new educational principles coming from American settlements penetrated into Moscow.

17. Feuer, "John Dewey and the Back-to-the-People Movement," p. 556.
18. Feuer, "John Dewey and the Back-to-the-People Movement," p. 557.
19. William W. Brickman, "Soviet Attitudes Toward John Dewey as an Educator," in *John Dewey and the World View*, eds. Douglas E. Lawson and Arthur E. Lean (Carbondale: Southern Illinois University Press, 1964), pp. 68–69.
20. As quoted in Thomas Woody, *New Minds: New Men?* (New York: Macmillan Co., 1932), pp. 47–48.

These principles were based upon the idea of social reform through education."[21] This phrase expressed fully what Dewey was trying to accomplish not only through the Laboratory School, but also through his lectures on social psychology and on the socio-economic philosophy of Henry George at Hull House.[22] This is what he derived from his association with Jane Addams and others in the settlement house.[23]

Since Russia has been mentioned and since it was to occupy at a later date a significant place in Dewey's socio-political thought, it would be appropriate to mention at this point a possible source of his interest in that country. While he must have read about Russia in his undergraduate and graduate periods, he very likely learned even more from his future wife, Alice Chipman, who "was active at the University of Michigan in the Samovar Club which spent its senior year discussing Turgenev, the great novelist of the Russian back-to-the-people movement."[24] No doubt Jane Addams shared with Dewey her impressions of her visit in 1896 with Count Leo Tolstoi at Yasnaya Polyana.[25] Likewise, he may have heard about Tolstoi and his work from President William Rainey Harper of the University of Chicago. These vicarious contacts, plus the awareness of the growing acceptance of his educational doctrines in Russia, must have made Dewey more sensitive to the situation of that country and to the growing momentum toward political and social change.

During his stay in Chicago, there were other important developments in Dewey's thinking. For one thing, he began his gradual divorce from the logic and metaphysics of Hegel.[26] For another, he became more active in psychological circles, to some extent in connection with his educational interests. During 1899–1900, he served as president of the American Psychological Association and emphasized the relation of psychology to

21. S. Shatzky [sic], "The First Experimental Station of Public Education of the People's Commissariat of Education, U.S.S.R.," *New Era*, IX (1928), 13.

22. Jane Addams, *Twenty Years at Hull House* (New York: Macmillan Co., 1920), p. 435; Robert L. McCaul, "Dewey's Chicago," *School Review*, LXVII (1959), 275.

23. Jane Dewey, "Biography of John Dewey," p. 30.

24. Feuer, "John Dewey and the Back-to-the-People Movement," p. 548.

25. Addams, *Twenty Years at Hull House*, pp. 267–73.

26. Dykhuizen, "John Dewey: The Chicago Years," p. 235.

education and social practice in his presidential address in 1899. He indicated that "education is primarily a social affair" and that "educational science is first of all a social science," [27] as is psychology. He deplored "the gap between psychological theory and the existing school practice," [28] as well as the ethically defective teaching method, which, "while giving the child a glibness in the mechanical facility of reading, leaves him at the mercy of suggestion and chance environment to decide whether he reads the 'yellow journal,' the trashy novel, or the literature which inspires and makes more valid his whole life." [29] To him, precept and performance were no less significant in pedagogy than in society.

The teacher "lives in a social sphere—he is a member and an organ of a social life. His aims are social aims; the development of individuals taking ever more responsible positions in a circle of social activities continually increasing in radius and in complexity." [30] Even his methods have to be social and ethical. In short, Dewey was convinced of "the social and teleological nature of the work of the teacher." [31] It is the teacher who must bring about the interrelatedness of pupil, the school, and social life.

The application of psychology to the school constitutes a clear example of the necessity of similar application to other social institutions. Psychology will afford "insight into the conditions which control the formation and execution of aims, and thus enable human effort to expend itself sanely, rationally and with assurance." [32] And the psychologist, even if concerned with technical problems, is a contributor "to that ordered knowledge which alone enables mankind to secure a larger and to direct a more equal flow of values in life." [33] The same, of course, might be said, from Dewey's standpoint, of all the other areas of knowledge.

It would be helpful at this point in the review of the historical high spots in the development of John Dewey's socio-

27. "Psychology and Social Practice," *Science*, n.s. XI (1900), 321.
28. "Psychology and Social Practice," p. 323.
29. "Psychology and Social Practice," p. 328.
30. "Psychology and Social Practice," p. 328.
31. "Psychology and Social Practice," p. 329.
32. "Psychology and Social Practice," p. 333.
33. "Psychology and Social Practice," p. 333.

political involvement to take stock of his published works through 1904. Virtually all of his writings embraced the categories of philosophy, psychology, and education. The social element appears from time to time, but the political is seldom to be seen, except as intertwined with considerations of society. By way of early example, in his address in 1892 to the Students' Christian Association of the University of Michigan, the theme of the relation of Christianity to democracy, Dewey substituted democracy for religion as the road to truth and freedom. "Democracy, as freedom, means the loosening of bonds; the wearing away of restrictions, the breaking down of barriers. . . . Democracy is, as freedom, the freeing of truth." [34] Furthermore, "It is in the community of truth . . . that the brotherhood which is democracy, has its being." [35] Through the medium of democracy the truth based on the social equality of human beings will prevail.

In 1894, Dewey published reviews of works in social psychology and a penetrating review of James Bonar's book on the historical relations of philosophy and political economy.[36] This was perhaps his formal, inchoate initiation into the turbulent world of writing in the arena of applied social sciences.

The social emphasis appeared in such writings on education as "Ethical Principles Underlying Education" and "My Pedagogic Creed," both published in 1897. In the former, he proclaimed that, "apart from the thought of participation in social life the school has no end nor aim," [37] and that "the only way to prepare for social life is to engage in social life." [38]

Before leaving Chicago, Dewey wrote again on socio-political topics of interest to him. The views expressed in his classic, *The School and Society*, found expression once more in an address, "The School as Social Center," which he delivered in 1902 to the National Educational Association. In addition, he

34. "Christianity and Democracy," in *Religious Thought at the University of Michigan* (Ann Arbor: Inland Press, 1893), p. 66.

35. "Christianity and Democracy," p. 67.

36. *The Psychic Factors of Civilization* by Lester Frank Ward, *Social Evolution* by Benjamin Kidd, *Civilization During the Middle Ages* by George Burton Adams, *History of the Philosophy of History* by Robert Flint, and *Philosophy and Political Economy in Some of Their Historical Relations* by James Bonar.

37. "Ethical Principles Underlying Education," in *Third Yearbook* (Chicago: National Herbart Society, 1897), p. 12.

38. "Ethical Principles Underlying Education," p. 14.

published the first of his numerous statements on the nature and significance of academic freedom, a subject which was to occupy his mind and energies for many years.

The period from 1904 to 1930, when Dewey served as professor of philosophy at Columbia University in New York City, was undoubtedly the most fruitful one in his life, especially from the standpoint of socio-political thought and activity. New York, even more than Chicago, was a cosmopolitan center of liberal politics, social welfare, and labor organization. During this quarter-century, the philosopher published more than a score of books and a large number of articles and book reviews. In 1915, he helped to found and served as the first president of the American Association of University Professors, an organization devoted to the preservation of academic freedom. The following year he became a charter member of the Teachers Union in New York City and was one of the few educational leaders to write and work for this type of organization.[39]

Some students of the life and work of Dewey have called attention to the fact that, during the decade of 1904–14, he was chiefly absorbed by technical philosophical problems. His writings were not concentrated on socio-political questions as such. However, "It was the war that precipitated his production for political publics *per se*. And his political public was possibly already recruited to some extent by his educational work."[40] Along with other liberals, Dewey found himself catapulted into the socio-political struggle of ideas and public policy.

In *Ethics*, of which he was coauthor with his former colleague, Professor James H. Tufts, Dewey inveighs against corruption in politics, especially as practiced by the large public utility companies. As he saw it, the proposals for reform involve, at bottom, "questions of the right and wrong use of political power and authority."[41] In other words, Dewey was applying the principles of ethics to the controversies and conflicts engulfing industry, labor, commerce, and government. He summed up his moral criterion to judge social institutions and

39. "Professional Organization of Teachers," *American Teacher*, V (1916), 99–101.
40. C. Wright Mills, *Sociology and Pragmatism: The Higher Learning in America*, ed. Irving Louis Horowitz (New York: Paine-Whitman, 1964), p. 316.
41. *Ethics*, with James H. Tufts (New York: Henry Holt and Co., 1908), p. 481.

political acts in the following formula: "The test is whether a given custom or law sets free individual capacities in such a way as to make them available for the development of the general happiness or the common good." [42] Stated from the standpoint of society, "The test is whether the general, the public, organization and order are promoted in such a way as to equalize opportunity for all." [43] Dewey did not merely play around with words; his actions correlated highly with his statements.

The philosopher rejected both the subordination of the individual to the group and that of the majority to the minority. "A true public or social good will . . . not subordinate individual variations, but will encourage individual experimentation in new ideas and new projects, endeavoring only to see that they are put into execution under conditions which make for securing responsibility for their consequences." [44] A "just social order," in his view, was one in which there existed a balance of the individual and the group. This balance was constituted by the promotion of criticism and the reorganization toward the better distribution of goods. "Not order, but orderly progress, represents the social ideal." [45]

One thought in the *Ethics* deserves special attention. Dewey noted with appreciation the development of national states during recent decades but was also aware of the dangers of unrestrained nationalism. He criticized the notion of *si vis pacem para bellum* and urged instead the consideration of "an international State of federated humanity, with its own laws and its own courts and its own rules for adjudicating disputes." [46] He warned against the dangers of the armament race on the ground that "the possession of irresponsible power is always a direct temptation to its irresponsible use." [47] It was "unmitigated nonsense" to argue for the necessity of war as a preventive measure against "moral degeneration." Dewey thus aligned himself with the historic and contemporary ideas and programs which strove for peace and international political co-operation. What he said did not represent anything novel; long before Kant's essay on "Perpetual Peace" of more than a century prior

42. *Ethics*, pp. 482–83.
43. *Ethics*, p. 483.
44. *Ethics*, p. 485.
45. *Ethics*, p. 485.
46. *Ethics*, p. 482.
47. *Ethics*, p. 482.

to Dewey's book, there were projects by thinkers of various countries to bring about lasting peace and harmony among nations. No doubt, Dewey's voice helped in the formulation of intellectual opinion in behalf of a League of Nations.

The advent of World War I provided John Dewey with much upon which to reflect. His major contribution toward the understanding of some of the issues at stake was *German Philosophy and Politics* (1915). This volume contained the text of three lectures delivered in February 1915 at the University of North Carolina. The air in the United States had not been charged as yet with suspicion against Germany. Dewey acknowledged that Germans had "philosophy in their blood" and that Germany was "the modern state which provides the greatest facilities for general ideas to take effect through social inculcation." [48] While he appreciated that there was "freedom of academic instruction" in Germany, he was also keenly aware that the state played a crucial role in the selection of professors and teachers, especially in fields closely related to political policy. Dewey's sensitivity to academic freedom was evident in his writings [49] and in the fact that in January 1915 he had become one of the founders and the first president of the American Association of University Professors. Moreover, in his capacity as president of this organization, he wrote a letter protesting an editorial in the New York *Times* supporting the dismissal of Scott Nearing, assistant professor of economics, from the University of Pennsylvania.[50]

The "educational and administrative agencies of Germany provide ready-made channels through which philosophic ideas may flow on their way to practical affairs." [51] Such ideas may be those of Kant, Schleiermacher, and Hegel. Yet, Germany lacked, in Dewey's view, a political public opinion such as found in France, Britain, or the United States. It was the university, rather than the newspaper, that gave public opinion its "articulate expression." And this, to Dewey, was a mixed blessing. In point of fact, he saw serious dangers in the indoctrination of the

48. *German Philosophy and Politics* (New York: Henry Holt and Co., 1915), p. 14.
49. "Academic Freedom," *Educational Review*, XXIII (1902), 1–14; and "Freedom, Academic," in *A Cyclopedia of Education*, II, ed. Paul Monroe (New York: Macmillan Co., 1911), 700–701.
50. New York *Times*, 22 Oct. 1915.
51. *German Philosophy and Politics*, p. 16.

public in *a priori* truth by German philosophers, either directly or through the intermediacy of war planners and generals.

Apart from the justification of war by German philosophers, Dewey was also aware of their contribution to the development of a racial ideology in Germany. "A purely artificial cult of race has so flourished in Germany that many social movements—like anti-Semitism—and some of Germany's political ambitions cannot be understood apart from the mystic identification of Race, Culture and the State." [52] To an extent, such ideas were seen by him as stemming from the teachings of Fichte and Hegel.

When the United States entered the war in April 1917, the entire nation was mobilized. The government, in co-operation with the schools and colleges, made an organized attempt to channel the energies of all children, teachers, and administrators to aid the war effort. In 1917, Columbia University, where Dewey was professor of philosophy, issued a series of Columbia War Papers. The first of these pamphlets was Dewey's "Enlistment for the Farm." Here the philosopher, rejecting the idea of military drill for adolescent boys, proposed "training drills with the spade and the hoe," [53] so that the pupils and teachers might help in increasing the nation's food supply. He urged "educators and teachers to develop Constructive Patriotism . . . to help evolve in the growing generation the idea of universal service in the great battle of man against nature, which is something American, something great; and which is not a military idea transplanted from Europe." [54] In this way, the educators will not only contribute toward the conclusion of the war, but they will also have "a chance to link the school with life. It is a chance to develop for the first time in the history of the world in time of war a constructive and industrial instead of a destructive and militaristic patriotism. All can join without distinction of race and creed, or even of previous sympathy. It is service not only for our own country and for the countries on whose side we are fighting, but a service to the whole world when peace shall again dawn." [55]

52. *German Philosophy and Politics*, p. 100.
53. *Enlistment for the Farm* (Columbia War Papers, Series I, No. 1 [New York: Division of Intelligence and Publicity of Columbia University, 1917]), p. 5.
54. *Enlistment for the Farm*, p. 5.
55. *Enlistment for the Farm*, p. 10.

Dewey spoke like a true patriot. He recognized the reality of the war and wished to do what he could to terminate it. His contribution lay in participation on as educational a level as possible, with an eye toward the realization of democratic values and of the values of the peace to come.

In World War I, Dewey proved that he was not a professional pacifist. He did not advocate or practice opposition to or sabotage of the war effort. While not giving up his devotion to peace, he was convinced that peaceful activity, such as agriculture, would in time help bring a more lasting peace than that achieved by force of arms. In any event, this seems to have been the rationale by which he was able to remain at peace with himself.

All through the war, Dewey focused his attention on the peace ahead. In June 1918, for example, he commented on President Wilson's doctrine of a world safe for democracy and insisted that democracy could be safely anchored in the world only if there would be a development toward "a federated world government and a variety of freely coöperating self-governing local, cultural and industrial groups." [56] Autocracy involves uniformity and the straining of human nature to the breaking point. Democracy, the great hope of the future, signifies diversification. It releases and relieves the stresses and strains of human nature—and this, to Dewey, "is the ultimate sanction of democracy, for which we are fighting." [57]

When the possibility of the League of Nations came under increasing discussion and debate in the closing months of the war, Dewey offered his views. His position in November 1918 was in favor of a League, but one which was more than a legal and political organization. As he saw it, the dominant idea of a League which would be engaged in arbitration, conciliation, and military enforcement of its decisions "is negative not constructive, and doomed to fail at some critical moment. . . . The real problem is one of organization for more effective human association and intercourse." [58] This was the lesson drawn by Dewey from the war and he may have had a premonition of the debacle

---

56. "What Are We Fighting For?" *Independent*, XCIV (1918), 483.
57. "What Are We Fighting For?" p. 483.
58. "The Approach to a League of Nations," *Dial*, XVII (1918), 341.

that the League of Nations was to suffer from about 1935 to the beginning of World War II. He made this point repeatedly in speeches and articles, but again he had to suffer neglect and opposition. When the pressure for the United States' joining the League was stepped up in liberal circles with the passing 1920s, Dewey felt it necessary to take a definitive stand. In March 1923, he addressed himself in the *New Republic* to the question, "Shall We Join the League?" [59] Dewey stressed that, among other reasons, the League was weak and "its international character is a farce" so long as Germany and Russia were not permitted to join. Moreover, "Europe does not want and will not tolerate our coöperation except on its own terms, and it is divided against itself as to those terms." [60] The people of the United States, in Dewey's view, were also "ignorant, inexperienced, governed by emotion rather than by information and insight" and, accordingly, "the notion that we have only to offer ourselves as universal arbiter—and paymaster—and all will be well is childish in the extreme." [61] The very fact, he concluded, that "only appeal to emotion can possibly be successful in engaging us to enter the League of Nations is the most conclusive reason possible for our staying out of it." [62] Dewey continued to uphold this position even after criticism in the periodicals. In his reply to a critic, he added another point: "The League is *not* honestly named. It is a League of governments pure and simple." [63]

Dewey was no isolationist. He was in favor of genuine international co-operation on *all* fronts and in relation to *all* peoples. The League of Nations was weighed in his scale of values and was found wanting. Hence, his opposition.

Before leaving the war period, it will be appropriate to refer to an unpublicized inquiry conducted under the direction of Dewey, at the request of Albert C. Barnes, in the spring and summer of 1918, among the Polish immigrants in Philadelphia. The aim of the inquiry, as stated by Mr. Barnes, was to discover the barriers to democratic living among the Poles, so that a

59. "Shall We Join the League?" *New Republic*, XXXIV (1923), 36–37.
    60. "Shall We Join the League?" p. 37.
    61. "Shall We Join the League?" p. 37.
    62. "Shall We Join the League?" p. 37.
    63. *New Republic*, XXXIV (1923), 139–40, in answer to Arthur Oncken Lovejoy's letter, ibid., XXXIV (1923), 138–39.

practical plan might be devised "to eliminate forces alien to democratic internationalism and to promote American ideals in accordance with the principles announced by President Wilson in his various public communications." [64] Dewey's team, which included two young philosophers, Brand Blanshard and Irwin Edman, gathered the data on the life of the Polish immigrants, especially with reference to the conflict between the conservatives and radicals and to its relation to events in Europe. That this information had bearing on the war was evident from the fact that Dewey presented his confidential report in August 1918 to the Military Intelligence Bureau of the Army in Washington. It is possible that recommendations of this eighty-page report may have had some impact on the development of postwar United States policy with regard to the reconstitution of Poland. Probably few philosophers have had the opportunity that Dewey had to participate directly in the process leading to the formation of international policy.

The postwar period was a time of international intellectual exposure for Dewey. During February and March 1919, he lectured at the Imperial University in Tokyo and these lectures resulted the following year in the publication of *Reconstruction in Philosophy*. From 1919 to 1921, he lectured at the National Universities of Peking and Nanking in China. In 1924, he studied the education in Turkey; in 1926, in Mexico; and in 1928, in Soviet Russia.

His *Letters from China and Japan*, written informally in collaboration with his wife, showed considerable insight into the international dynamics of politics, economics, education, and culture.[65] In a more formal way, he presented in *China, Japan and the U.S.A.* (1921) a series of seven articles published originally in the *New Republic*. Here Dewey discussed international political problems and tried to draw some inferences for United States foreign policy in the Far East. His conclusion, typically enough, was that there was a need for China and the Orient to have "freer and fuller communications with the rest of the world"—not merely an open door to commerce, but even

64. *Confidential Report: Conditions Among the Poles in the United States* ([Washington?], 1918), p. 2.
65. See, for example, *Letters from China and Japan*, with Alice C. Dewey, ed. Evelyn Dewey (New York: E. P. Dutton and Co., 1920), pp. 74–76, 179–80, 190, 209, 243–47, and 305–11.

more "to light, to knowledge and understanding." [66] He called upon liberals to "work for the opened door of open diplomacy, of continuous and intelligent inquiry, of discussion free from propaganda." [67] Dewey thus extrapolated his doctrine of interaction in a democratic society on an international scale.

John Dewey's experiences with thinking on international problems during the war and his sojourn abroad after World War I no doubt sensitized him more than ever before to political and social issues involving various nations in different parts of the globe. His writings, whether in book or article form, touched on these problems to a greater or lesser extent. His firsthand exposures to the social and educational systems of Turkey (1924), Mexico (1926), and Soviet Russia (1928) were too brief to permit him to attain any degree of depth. Furthermore, Dewey had no more knowledge of Russian, Spanish, and Turkish than he had of Chinese and Japanese. Since he did quote from original writings, he evidently had to depend upon interpreters, foreigners who were well acquainted with the English language, and any available translations. Consequently, even though he was able to gain insight into social, educational, and political problems in these countries, it is likely that he would have had a clearer understanding had he had the necessary linguistic skills and had his residence there been of longer duration. In any event, this period in Dewey's life, which culminated in his retirement in 1930 from his professorship at Columbia University, was characterized by frequent participation in international cultural and educational activities.

This is not to imply that Dewey did not give due attention to domestic problems in American society. In 1929 alone, he became president of the People's Lobby and national chairman of the League for Independent Political Action. All through the 1920s he was critical of the materialistic values underlying the era of prosperity. Not that he failed to appreciate the importance of economic advances in a democratic society, but he insisted that genuine cultural values be kept free from exploitation by the wealthy. Although Dewey was aware of the existence of a struggle among classes in the United States, he rejected the doctrine of utilizing the class struggle in the achievement of

66. "A Parting of the Ways for America," II., *New Republic*, XXVIII (1921), 317.
67. "A Parting of the Ways for America," II., p. 317.

social change. Unlike other educators, he possessed a "more realistic economic interpretation of institutions and culture"; [68] yet, with many of them, he maintained that education was the major means by which to bring about the improvement of society and of man.

The year 1929 saw the publication of numerous articles and four books: *Characters and Events* (2 vols.), *Impressions of Soviet Russia*, *The Quest for Certainty*, and *The Sources of a Science of Education*. The first of these, subtitled "Popular Essays in Social and Political Philosophy," was a timely collection of articles on recent and current issues at home and abroad originally published in the *New Republic* and in a multitude of other magazines. The first volume includes the material published separately as *Impressions of Soviet Russia*. In the words of the editor, Joseph Ratner, who was Dewey's disciple, this compilation reveals the application of the philosophy of instrumentalism to the criticism of current issues. Instrumentalism states that the home of intelligence is in this world, where it acts "as critic and regulator of the forces operative within it. This doctrine, which is the philosophic *raison d'être* of these essays, is also one of their fundamental unifying principles." [69] A reading of the chapters of both volumes will disclose the correctness of this observation. Dewey was consistent in relating his abstract principles of socio-economic thought to the specific problems of everyday life.

In *Impressions of Soviet Russia*, Dewey brought together fifteen articles which had appeared from 1920 to 1928 in the *New Republic*. Here is a record of his observations and analyses of education, society, culture, and other aspects of life in the USSR, Mexico, China, and Turkey, countries which he had visited. He endeavored to be as objective as possible, and he made certain to express his appreciation, wherever he thought it advisable, of ways of life other than his own. On the other hand, his effort at being fair did not blind him to the dangers of dictatorship. Thus, he referred to the existence of "secret police, inquisitions, arrests and deportations," but went on to balance this by observing that "life for the masses goes on with regular-

68. Curti, *Social Ideas of American Educators*, p. 514.
69. Joseph Ratner, "Preface," in *Characters and Events*, I (New York: Henry Holt and Co., 1929), vi.

ity, safety and decorum." [70] It is debatable as to what extent Dewey attained depth during his visits to Soviet Russia and the other countries. Nevertheless, it is well, especially in the light of later controversies involving Dewey and the Soviet Union, to take note of the fact that the American philosopher did not see Soviet Russia as all black or all white or even all red.

Another work made up of articles reprinted from the *New Republic* is *Individualism, Old and New* (1930). In this little book, Dewey discussed critically various problems of the day and upheld the role and status of the individual in a world where he seemed to be submerged. He urged once more that due attention be paid to the values of the scientific method of thought. "The general adoption of the scientific attitude in human affairs would mean nothing less than a revolutionary change in morals, religion, politics and industry." [71] Possibly one instance of Dewey's use of this type of thinking may be the following statement: "I cannot obtain intellectual, moral or esthetic satisfaction from the professed philosophy which animates Bolshevik Russia. But I am sure that the future historian of our times will combine admiration of those who had the imagination first to see that the resources of technology might be directed by organized planning to serve chosen ends with astonishment at the intellectual and moral hebetude of other peoples who were technically so much further advanced." [72] Let it be noted that these were written three to four years before the coming of the New Deal.

John Dewey, aged seventy when he retired from his professorship at Columbia University, was named professor emeritus of philosophy in residence and he continued in this capacity until 1939. During this decade, he lived through the worldwide economic depression; the New Deal; the emergence and consolidation of dictatorships in Germany, Italy, the USSR, Japan, and Spain; the crises of the Spanish Civil War, the Italo-Ethiopian War, and the Munich Pact; and the onset of World War II. From 1939 to 1952, the year of his death, he experienced the

70. "Impressions of Soviet Russia," II. A Country in a State of Flux, *New Republic*, LVII (1928), 12.

71. *Individualism, Old and New* (New York: Minton, Balch and Co., 1930), p. 155. [Published originally as "Individualism, Old and New," VI. Individuality in Our Day, *New Republic*, LXII (1930).]

72. *Individualism, Old and New*, p. 95.

devastating World War II and the early stages of the cold war. In the socio-political realm, he published *Liberalism and Social Action* (1935), *Freedom and Culture* (1939), and the revision of *German Philosophy and Politics* (1942). Of special interest were the reports issued under his direction: *The Case of Leon Trotsky* (1937) and *Not Guilty* (1938), containing data on the allegations by Stalin against Trotsky; and *The Bertrand Russell Case* (1941), a critique of the ban upon the appointment of the British philosopher at the City College of New York. In addition, he wrote countless articles and reviews in the *New Republic*, the *Social Frontier*, the *Journal of Philosophy*, and other journals, as well as numerous small publications. His productivity went on, seemingly undiminished by advancing age. He was intensely interested, as always, in everything pertaining to man and he gave expression to this interest in his multifarious writings. He followed closely the course of educational development in the United States, participated assiduously in the debate over Progressive Education, and contributed a vigorous volume, *Experience and Education* (1938), in defense of his concept of education and in opposition to the distortions of his doctrine.

One example of Dewey's doctrine of freedom is his advocacy of the objective appraisal of social planning as a method of stabilizing society in a period of turmoil. He stated his conviction that all forms of knowledge and skill should be applied to a social problem without regard necessarily to the fact that a particular procedure is in operation in an antidemocratic milieu. Society should be free to experiment with the technique of organized planning even if it is associated with the Soviet Union. "To hold that such organized planning is possible only in a communistic society is to surrender the case to communism." [73] Instead, the Soviet Russian effort should spur those of a diverse political faith to expend their effort to use all possible knowledge to improve their own social organization and institutions. As Dewey saw it, the situation did not call for a choice between capitalism and communism, but rather "between chaos and order, chance and control: the haphazard use and the planned use of scientific techniques." [74] It will be seen that

73. *Philosophy and Civilization* (New York: Minton, Balch and Co., 1931), p. 328.
74. *Philosophy and Civilization*, p. 328.

Dewey anticipated the thought and activity of those who undertook to set society and its economy aright after the dislocation of the Depression.

The socio-economic crisis of the Depression in the early 1930s led Dewey and other educators to interrelate the situation of society and the school even more closely than ever before. One product of such an effort was a collaborative volume, *The Educational Frontier* (1933), edited by William H. Kilpatrick. Two chapters, "a joint product" of the thought of Dewey and John L. Childs, were "written out" by the former. Here was expressed the conviction that an educational philosophy which is to be meaningful for the United States "must be the expression of a social philosophy and . . . the social and educational theories and conceptions must be developed with definite reference to the needs and issues which mark and divide our domestic, economic, and political life in the generation of which we are a part." [75] The "moral and human import" of the democratic tradition is at the foundation of the social organization. Planning is necessary for a sound society, but not in the way already in practice in Russia and Italy. What is needed is not a planned society, but rather a *planning* society, and herein lies the crucial difference "between autocracy and democracy, between dogma and intelligence in operation, between suppression of individuality and that release and utilization of individuality which will bring it to full maturity." [76]

As a conclusion to the entire volume, Dewey stresses that "life based on experimental intelligence provides the only possible opportunity for *all* to develop rich and diversified experience, while also securing continuous coöperative give and take and intercommunication." [77] The experimental method, as "the only one compatible with the democratic way of life," makes possible an enlarged area of human understanding and consensus. This is not to say that there must be full agreement. The experimental method extends "intelligence as the method of action," so that, in cases of differences, "it will conduce to agreement to differ, to mutual tolerance and sympathy, pending the time

75. "The Social-Economic Situation and Education," in *The Educational Frontier*, ed. William Heard Kilpatrick (New York, London: Century Co., 1933), pp. 35–36.

76. "The Social-Economic Situation in Education," p. 72.

77. "The Underlying Philosophy of Education," in *The Educational Frontier*, p. 317.

when more adequate knowledge and better methods of judging are at hand." [78] The processes of desirable social change and of education are "correlative and interactive. No social modification, slight or revolutionary, can endure except as it enters into the action of a people through their desires and purposes. This introduction and perpetuation are effected by education. But every improvement in the social structure and its operations releases the educative resources of mankind and gives them a better opportunity to enter into normal social processes so that the latter become themselves more truly educative." [79]

The growth of interest in communism and in the USSR in various circles in the early 1930s was a great factor in increasing Dewey's writings, speeches, and activities along socio-political lines. As Communists became more outspoken and activistic in American life, Dewey felt called upon to restate the principles of democracy. In a symposium of philosophers on Marxism, he made clear five reasons why he was not a Communist: The United States is "profoundly different [from the USSR] in its economic, political, and cultural history"; communism uses a "monistic and one-way philosophy of history"; the class war is not "*the* means by which such [class] conflicts can be eliminated and genuine social advance made"; "the emotional tone and methods of discussion and dispute . . . are extremely repugnant"; and "a revolution effected solely or chiefly by violence can in a modernized society like our own result only in chaos." [80] Dewey did not beat around the rhetorical bush; he called a hammer and sickle a hammer and sickle: "official Communism has made the practical traits of the dictatorship *of* the proletariat and *over* the proletariat, the suppression of the civil liberties of all non-proletarian elements as well as of dissenting proletarian minorities, integral parts of the standard Communist faith and dogma." [81] He accused the Communists of responsibility for the growth of fascism. "As an unalterable opponent of Fascism in every form, I cannot be a Communist." [82]

The danger of the Communist and Fascist dictatorships for a democratic society also occupied Dewey's mind in *Liberalism*

78. "Underlying Philosophy of Education," p. 317.
79. "Underlying Philosophy of Education," p. 318.
80. "Why I Am Not a Communist," *Modern Monthly*, VII (1934), 135–37.
81. "Why I Am Not a Communist," p. 135.
82. "Why I Am Not a Communist," p. 137.

*and Social Action* (1935). On the very first page he called attention to the attacks upon liberalism by "those who want drastic social changes effected in a twinkling of an eye, and who believe that violent overthrow of existing institutions is the right method of effecting the required changes." [83] He pointed out that in "three of the great nations of Europe" liberalism ceased to flourish with the suppression of civil liberties. Classical liberalism, in his view, was characterized by the three values of "liberty; the development of the inherent capacities of individuals made possible through liberty, and the central role of free intelligence in inquiry, discussion and expression." [84] One should "look with considerable suspicion upon those who assert that suppression of democracy is the road to the adequate establishment of genuine democracy." [85] Dewey recognized that an apparent exception "to dependence upon organized intelligence as the method for directing social change is found when society through an authorized majority has entered upon the path of social experimentation leading to great social change, and a minority refuses by force to permit the method of intelligent action to go into effect. Then force may be intelligently employed to subdue and disarm the recalcitrant minority." [86] The trouble with the historical liberals was they did not apply organized effort to attain their social objectives. "Earlier liberalism regarded the separate and competing economic action of individuals as the means to social well-being as the end. We must reverse the perspective and see that socialized economy is the means of free individual development as the end." [87]

In *Liberalism and Social Action*, Dewey threw out a direct challenge to his fellow liberals and to the antiliberals. It is not at all surprising that Sidney Hook predicted that this little work "may well be to the twentieth century what Marx and Engels' *Communist Manifesto* was to the nineteenth." [88] Dewey later characterized the views he expressed in *Liberalism and Social Action* and in *Individualism, Old and New* as those of a "demo-

83. *Liberalism and Social Action* (New York: G. P. Putnam's Sons, 1935), p. 1.
84. *Liberalism and Social Action*, p. 32.
85. *Liberalism and Social Action*, p. 87.
86. *Liberalism and Social Action*, p. 87.
87. *Liberalism and Social Action*, p. 90.
88. Sidney Hook, *John Dewey: An Intellectual Portrait* (New York: John Day, 1939), p. 165.

cratic socialist." Such a position, it might well be understood, would invite criticism and censure from both right and left.

Dewey's activities in relation to communism and Soviet Russia were stepped up in the following years. An investigation of the charges made against Leon Trotsky in the Moscow Trials of 1936 was made by a commission under the chairmanship of John Dewey. After hearings in Mexico, Dewey and his colleagues published two volumes in which Trotsky was exonerated from Stalin's charges.[89] In various writings,[90] as well as in these two reports, Dewey reaffirmed his opposition to dictatorship of any kind and his commitment to democracy. The second report, *Not Guilty*, was described by James T. Farrell as "an example of democratic thinking, reasoning, procedure and of Dewey's own conceptions of free inquiry." [91]

Dewey returned to criticize specifically the Marxist theory in his *Freedom and Culture* (1939). While he contrasted democracy with all forms of totalitarian ideologies throughout the book, he devoted an entire chapter to a critique of Marxism, especially as practiced in Soviet Russia. To begin with, Dewey deplored the neglect by many democrats of the relation of culture to democracy. He stated his conviction that "works of art once brought into existence are the most compelling of the means of communication by which emotions are stirred and opinions formed" and that "emotions and imagination are more potent in shaping public sentiment and opinion than information and reason." [92] Totalitarian countries have recognized this principle and have taken full advantage of it in controlling their people. Democracy cannot be taken for granted, insisted Dewey, and democratic conditions cannot be expected to maintain themselves automatically. Constant caution, eternal vigilance, and the maximum use of culture and education will enable a society to retain its democratic integrity in the face of the totalitarian threat.

89. *The Case of Leon Trotsky* (New York: Harper and Bros., 1937); *Not Guilty* (New York: Harper and Bros., 1938).

90. E.g., *"Truth Is on the March,"* Report on the Trotsky Hearings in Mexico (New York: American Committee for the Defense of Leon Trotsky, 1937).

91. James T. Farrell, "Dewey in Mexico," in *John Dewey: Philosopher of Science and Freedom*, ed. Sidney Hook (New York: Dial Press, 1950), p. 375.

92. *Freedom and Culture* (New York: G. P. Putnam's Sons, 1939), p. 10.

The critique of Marxism and of the Soviet Union appears as Chapter 4, "Totalitarian Economics and Democracy," in *Freedom and Culture*. Marxism, states Dewey, isolates a single factor, economics, which cannot be isolated from the other forces of society. The view of the Marxist, as summed up by Dewey, is that "the state of the forces of economic productivity at a given time ultimately determines all forms of social activities and relations, political, legal, scientific, artistic, religious, moral." [93] Economic determinism did not appeal to Dewey, who was convinced that causation is derived from a broader base. He insisted that effects could be traced to causes by concrete investigation only. The adoption of this method of study would result in the abandonment of the single economic cause. "It would put us in the relativistic and pluralistic position of considering a number of interacting factors—of which a very important one is undoubtedly the economic." [94]

Dewey was not simply a critic of Marxism and totalitarianism; he was a devotee of democracy, not just in name but in fact. His standards for society were his own. His faith in man did not permit him to give weight to some of the forces of tradition, the biblical for instance, which taught the equality of man in a context other than the natural. Such a force also proved a potent weapon in the struggle against totalitarianism. Be that as it may, Dewey's *Freedom and Culture* was apparently as severe an indictment of the totalitarian nature of Stalinist communism and of its parent theory, Marxism, as had been written up to his time and, to a very large extent, for some time afterward. At the same time, it should also be regarded as a blueprint for democratic thought and action. [95]

During the World War II years, he continued to uphold the cause of democracy and to denounce dictatorship, whether of

93. *Freedom and Culture*, p. 77.
94. *Freedom and Culture*, p. 77.
95. For other contemporary reaffirmations of democracy, see "Experience, Knowledge and Value: A Rejoinder," in *The Philosophy of John Dewey*, pp. 607–8; ["I Believe"] in *I Believe*, ed. Clifton Fadiman (New York: Simon and Schuster, 1939), pp. 347–54; and "Creative Democracy —The Task Before Us," in *The Philosopher of the Common Man: Essays in Honor of John Dewey to Celebrate His Eightieth Birthday*, ed. Sidney Ratner (New York: G. P. Putnam's Sons, 1940), pp. 220–28. For an interesting interpretation of Dewey as a political philosopher, see Hu Shih, "The Political Philosophy of Instrumentalism," pp. 205–19, in the 80th anniversary *Festschrift*.

the right or the left. He refused to go along with other intellectuals in climbing the bandwagon of conformity at any particular time. Nor did he bow to the pressures which sought to impose views upon the public at large. When he was convinced that a fellow philosopher, Bertrand Russell, with whom he was often in intellectual disagreement, was deprived of his academic freedom, he did not hesitate to speak up orally and in writing. In *The Bertrand Russell Case* (1941), coedited by Dewey and Horace M. Kallen, he assembled statements and documents to illustrate the inequity of the judicial decision preventing the British philosopher from assuming his post at the City College of New York. To this symposium, Dewey contributed an introduction and a chapter, "Social Realities *versus* Police Court Fictions." In his Introduction, Dewey stressed the consensus by the authors of the book with regard to the "belief in the social importance of public discussion of moral problems, when it is conducted upon the plane of scientific method and with a sense of public responsibility." [96] The alternative to a serious discussion by competent individuals disciplined by the scientific method is the adoption of totalitarian methods. Dewey expressed the hope that the book may contribute to "the freedom of the human spirit and the democratic way of life." [97]

In his chapter, Dewey deplored the hypocrisy whereby public opinion delighted in "the mass of cheap sexuality presented on the stage and in public prints," but "is easily rallied to oppose serious intellectual discussion of sex and to revile those who act upon a belief that such discussion is a precondition of a better social ethic." [98] This is a situation of darkness where it becomes "easier for evil customs to endure and to flourish." [99] However, there is hope for the dispelling of such darkness through the co-operation of learned men, educators, and public-minded citizens to defend the academic and scientific freedom of men like Bertrand Russell.

During World War II, Dewey found himself in a relatively lonely position among America's intellectual circles. It had become fashionable, inasmuch as the United States and the

96. "Introduction," in *The Bertrand Russell Case*, eds. John Dewey and Horace M. Kallen (New York: Viking Press, 1941), p. 9.
97. "Introduction," in *Bertrand Russell Case*, p. 9.
98. "Social Realities *versus* Police Court Fictions," in *Bertrand Russell Case*, p. 73.
99. "Social Realities *versus* Police Court Fictions," p. 73.

USSR were now allies in a common struggle against Nazi totalitarianism, to regard the Soviet Communist society as an equal to the free society in a democracy. Dewey was firmly convinced of the falsity and danger of this doctrine. As one who had realized the nature of communism as far back as 1932, when members of the party tried to take over the New York Teachers Union, he lost little time in emphasizing that Soviet Russia had not changed its stripes.

During World War II, Dewey did not permit himself to be blinded by the great pressure in behalf of Soviet-American amity to the extent that he was able to minimize the realities of Stalin and the Communist dictatorship. He called public attention to the need for evaluating Stalin's actions in historical perspective. In addition, he warned against "the fatuous one-sided love feast now going on in this country," whereby Communist sympathizers demanded full consideration for the Soviet Union while giving little or nothing in return.[100] This attitude did not endear Dewey to the Communists, whether in the USSR, the United States, or any other country. The cold war between Dewey and the Communists continued to the year of his death —and beyond.

On the other hand, Dewey contributed to the war effort by writing, in behalf of the United States government, an open letter to the Chinese people. He identified the common goal of the Chinese and the Americans—"to preserve our independence and freedom. We both want to see a world in which nations can devote themselves to the constructive tasks of industry, education, science and art without fear of molestation by nations that think they can build themselves up by destroying the lives and the work of the men, women and children of other peoples." [101] Together with the Chinese, Dewey looked forward to a new and better postwar world, in which good will, kindness, and humaneness would prevail.

At the end of World War II, the philosopher, now beyond the age of eighty-five, continued his interest in the problems of men. In 1946, he joined nineteen Americans, including John Haynes Holmes, Sidney Hook, Robert MacIver, and Norman Thomas, in protesting the deportation of Sudeten Germans and

100. Letter to the New York *Times*, 11 Jan. 1942.
101. "Message to the Chinese People," in National Archives, Washington, D.C., 2 pp.

Hungarians from Czechoslovakia.[102] His writings embraced philosophy and education for the most part. His socio-political statements appeared at rather rare intervals, in part possibly due to the fact that age made his active participation in human affairs less likely.

On the occasion of his ninetieth birthday, Dewey summed up his socio-political viewpoint in a type of swan song. Again, as on countless earlier occasions, he restated his firm conviction that democracy was the way of life, the basis of education, and the foundation of human society. He was thankful for the widespread recognition given him on his ninetieth milestone and interpreted it "as a sign that faith in the will to realize the American dream through continued faith in democracy as a moral and human ideal remains firm and true even in a time when some people in their despair are tending to put their faith in force instead of in the cooperation that is the fruit of reciprocal good will and shared understanding:—and of nothing else." [103]

John Dewey passed away on 1 June 1952 after a long life of putting these principles into practice to the utmost of his power. He made use of the word—spoken and written—but he also resorted to action in relating his socio-political theory to life. He was a thinker and a doer.[104] If he was repetitive, it was because of many demands upon his time and talent, as well as of his recognition that his basic points required restatement in order to attain effectiveness: respect for human nature and dignity, faith in democracy and social intelligence, and progress through co-operation—toward the attainment of the ideal society.

It would be appropriate to conclude with a statement by Paul Arthur Schilpp: "[Dewey] lived what he taught and preached, without regard to the applause of either his professional colleagues or of the masses. Dewey thus showed by action as well as by doctrine his faith in man's intelligent capacities to cope with any situation, with any problem—*provided* man be

102. *Tragedy of a People: Racialism in Czecho-Slovakia* (New York: American Friends of Democratic Sudetens, 1946), pp. 3–6.
103. "John Dewey Responds," in *John Dewey at Ninety*, ed. Harry W. Laidler (New York: League for Industrial Democracy, 1950), p. 35.
104. George R. Geiger, "Dewey's Social and Political Philosophy," in *The Philosophy of John Dewey*.

willing to pay the price in patient, vigorous, continued cooperative inquiry." [105]

105. Paul A. Schilpp, "The Faith of John Dewey," in *Horizons of a
Philosopher: Essays in Honor of David Baumgardt*, eds. Joseph Frank et
al. (Leiden: Brill, 1963), p. 373.


## CHECKLIST

*Outlines of a Critical Theory of Ethics*, in *The Early Works of John Dewey,
1882–1898*, Vol. III, pp. 239–388. Carbondale: Southern Illinois University Press, 1969.

"Thought·News," Detroit *Tribune*, 10 Apr. 1892.

"News for Thought," Detroit *Tribune*, 11 Apr. 1892.

"He's Planned No Revolution," Detroit *Tribune*, 13 Apr. 1892. [Interview.]

"Christianity and Democracy," in *Religious Thought at the University of
Michigan*, pp. 60–69. Ann Arbor: Inland Press, 1893.

Review of *The Psychic Factors of Civilization* by Lester Frank Ward, *Social Evolution* by Benjamin Kidd, *Civilization During the Middle Ages*
by George Burton Adams, and *History of the Philosophy of History*
by Robert Flint, *Psychological Review*, I (July 1894), 400–411.

Review of *Philosophy and Political Economy in Some of Their Historical
Relations* by James Bonar, *Political Science Quarterly*, IX (Dec.
1894), 741–44.

"Ethics and Politics," *University Record*, III (Feb. 1894), 101–2. [Report
of an address to the Philosophical Society in Dec. 1893.]

"Ethical Principles Underlying Education," in *Third Yearbook*, pp. 7–33.
Chicago: National Herbart Society, 1897. [Reprinted separately by
University of Chicago Press, 1908, 34 pp.; also reprinted in C–16, pp.
108–38.]

"Psychology and Social Practice," *Psychological Review*, VII (Mar. 1900),
105–24; *Science*, n.s. XI (Mar. 1900), 321–33. [Reprinted separately
as University of Chicago Contributions to Education, No. 2. Chicago:
University of Chicago Press, 1901. 42 pp.]

"Academic Freedom," *Educational Review*, XXIII (Jan. 1902), 1–14.

*Ethics*, with James Hayden Tufts (American Science Series). New York:
Henry Holt and Co., 1908. xiii, 618 pp.

[Statement] in "Symposium on Woman's Suffrage," *The International*, III
(May 1911), 93–94.

"Freedom, Academic," in *A Cyclopedia of Education*, II, ed. Paul Monroe,
700–701. New York: Macmillan Co., 1911.

*German Philosophy and Politics*. New York: Henry Holt and Co., 1915. 134
pp. [Reset and reprinted with "verbal corrections," a Foreword and
new Introduction, New York: G. P. Putnam's Sons, 1942.]

Comments by William Ernest Hocking, "Political Philosophy in Germany," *New Republic*, IV (Oct. 1915), 234–36.

Dewey's "In Reply," letter in *New Republic*, IV (Oct. 1915), 236.

"Professorial Freedom," letter in New York *Times*, 22 Oct. 1915. [Re-
printed as "The Control of Universities," *School and Society*, II (Nov.
1915), 673.]

"Universal Service as Education," I, *New Republic*, VI (Apr. 1916), 309–10;

II, ibid., VI (Apr. 1916), 334–35. [Reprinted in C–10, pp. 465–73; C–12, pp. 92–100.]

"The Schools and Social Preparedness," *New Republic,* VII (May 1916), 15–16. [Reprinted in C–10, pp. 474–78; C–12, pp. 101–5.]

"Professional Organization of Teachers," *American Teacher,* V (Sept. 1916), 99–101.

"The Hughes Campaign," *New Republic,* VIII (Oct. 1916), 319–21.

"Ill Advised," letter in *American Teacher,* VI (Feb. 1917), 31.

*Enlistment for the Farm* (Columbia War Papers, Series I, No. 1). New York: Division of Intelligence and Publicity of Columbia University, 1917. 10 pp.

"In a Time of National Hesitation," *Seven Arts,* II (May 1917), 3–7. [Reprinted in C–10, pp. 443–46, with the title "The Emergence of a New World."]

"Professor Dewey of Columbia on War's Social Results," New York *World,* 29 July 1917. [Interview with Charles W. Wood.]

"What America Will Fight For," *New Republic,* XII (Aug. 1917), 68–69. [Reprinted in C–10, pp. 561–65, with the title "America and War."]

"Conscription of Thought," *New Republic,* XII (Sept. 1917), 128–30. [Reprinted in C–10, pp. 566–70.]

"War Activities for Civilians," *New Republic,* XII (Sept. 1917), 139–40. [Review of *National Service Handbook.*]

[Statement], New York *Times,* 9 Oct. 1917.

"In Explanation of Our Lapse," *New Republic,* XIII (Nov. 1917), 17–18. [Reprinted in C–10, pp. 571–75.]

"The Case of the Professor and the Public Interest," *Dial,* LXII (Nov. 1917), 435–37.

"Democracy and Loyalty in the Schools," New York *Evening Post,* 19 Dec. 1917; *American Teacher,* VII (Jan. 1918), 8–10.

"Public Education on Trial," *New Republic,* XIII (Dec. 1917), 245–47. [Reprinted in C–12, pp. 133–38.]

*Confidential Report: Conditions Among the Poles in the United States.* [Washington?], 1918. 80 pp.

"Vocational Education in the Light of the World War," Vocational Education Association of the Middle West, *Bulletin No. 4,* Jan. 1918. [Chicago, 1918]. 9 pp.

"America in the World," *Nation,* CVI (Mar. 1918), 287. [Reprinted in C–10, pp. 642–44, with the title "America and the World."]

"Internal Social Reorganization After the War," *Journal of Race Development,* VIII (Apr. 1918), 385–400. [Reprinted in C–10, pp. 745–59, with the title "Elements of Social Reorganization."]

"What Are We Fighting For?" *Independent,* XCIV (June 1918), 474, 480–83. [Reprinted in C–10, pp. 551–60, with the title "The Social Possibilities of War."]

"Autocracy Under Cover," *New Republic,* XVI (Aug. 1918), 103–6.

"The Approach to a League of Nations," *Dial,* LXV (Nov. 1918), 341–42. [Reprinted in C–10, pp. 602–5.]

"The Cult of Irrationality," *New Republic,* XVII (Nov. 1918), 34–35. [Reprinted in C–10, pp. 587–91.]

"The League of Nations and the New Diplomacy," *Dial,* LXV (Nov. 1918), 401–3. [Reprinted in C–10, pp. 606–9.]

"The Fourteen Points and the League of Nations," *Dial,* LXV (Nov. 1918), 463–64.

"The Post-War Mind," *New Republic,* XVII (Dec. 1918), 157–59. [Reprinted in C–10, pp. 596–601.]

"A League of Nations and Economic Freedom," *Dial,* LXV (Dec. 1918), 537–39. [Reprinted in C–10, pp. 610–14.]

"The New Paternalism," *New Republic,* XVII (Dec. 1918), 216–17. [Reprinted in C–10, pp. 517–21, with the title "Propaganda."]

"Japan and America," *Dial,* LXVI (May 1919), 501–3.

"The Student Revolt in China," *New Republic,* XX (Aug. 1919), 16–18.

"The International Duel in China," *New Republic,* XX (Aug. 1919), 110–12.

"Militarism in China," *New Republic,* XX (Sept. 1919), 167–69.

"Liberalism in Japan," I. The Intellectual Preparation, *Dial,* LXVII (Oct. 1919), 283–85; II. The Economic Factor, ibid., LXVII (Oct. 1919), 333–37; III. The Chief Foe, ibid., LXVII (Nov. 1919), 369–71. [Reprinted in C–10, pp. 149–69.]

"Transforming the Mind of China," *Asia,* XIX (Nov. 1919), 1103–8. [Reprinted in C–10, pp. 285–95.]

"Chinese National Sentiment," *Asia,* XIX (Dec. 1919), 1237–42. [Reprinted in C–10, pp. 222–36, with the title "The Growth of Chinese National Sentiment."]

"The American Opportunity in China," *New Republic,* XXI (Dec. 1919), 14–17. [Reprinted in C–10, pp. 296–303, with the title "America and China."]

"Our Share in Drugging China," *New Republic,* XXI (Dec. 1919), 114–17.

*Letters from China and Japan,* with Alice Chipman Dewey. Ed. Evelyn Dewey. New York: E. P. Dutton and Co., 1920. vi, 311 pp.

"The Sequel of the Student Revolt," *New Republic,* XXI (Feb. 1920), 380–82.

"Shantung, as Seen from Within," *New Republic,* XXII (Mar. 1920), 12–17. [Reprinted in C–4, pp. 9–21.]

"Our National Dilemma," *New Republic,* XXII (Mar. 1920), 117–18. [Reprinted in C–10, pp. 615–19.]

"The New Leaven in Chinese Politics," *Asia,* XX (Apr. 1920), 267–72. [Reprinted in C–10, pp. 244–54, with the title "Justice and Law in China."]

"What Holds China Back," *Asia,* XX (May 1920), 373–77. [Reprinted in C–10, pp. 211–21, with the title "Chinese Social Habits."]

"Americanism and Localism," *Dial,* LXVIII (June 1920), 684–88. [Reprinted in C–10, pp. 537–41.]

"China's Nightmare," *New Republic,* XXIII (June 1920), 145–47. [Reprinted in C–10, pp. 193–98.]

"How Reaction Helps," *New Republic,* XXIV (Sept. 1920), 21–22. [Reprinted in C–10, pp. 815–19.]

"A Political Upheaval in China," *New Republic,* XXIV (Oct. 1920), 142–44. [Reprinted in C–4, pp. 27–32.]

"Industrial China," *New Republic,* XXV (Dec. 1920), 39–41. [Reprinted in C–5, pp. 237–51.]

"Is China a Nation?" *New Republic,* XXV (Jan. 1921), 187–90. [Reprinted in C–10, pp. 237–43, with the title "Conditions for China's Nationhood"; C–5, pp. 252–70. (Reply to: J. W. Helburn, letter in *New Republic,* XXV [Jan. 1921], 187.)

"The Siberian Republic," *New Republic,* XXV (Jan. 1921), 220–23. [Reprinted in C–10, pp. 185–92.]

"The Far Eastern Deadlock," *New Republic,* XXVI (Mar. 1921), 71–74.

"The Consortium in China," *New Republic,* XXVI (Apr. 1921), 178–80.

"Old China and New," *Asia,* XXI (May 1921), 445–50, 454, 456. [Reprinted in C–10, pp. 255–69, with the title "Young China and Old."]

"New Culture in China," *Asia*, XXI (July 1921), 581–86, 642. [Reprinted in C–10, pp. 270–84.]

"Hinterlands in China," *New Republic*, XXVII (July 1921), 162–65. [Reprinted in C–4, pp. 21–27.]

Response by Dora Winifred Black, "American Policy in China," *New Republic*, XXVIII (Nov. 1921), 297.

Rejoinder by Dewey, *New Republic*, XXVIII (Nov. 1921), 297.

"Divided China," I., *New Republic*, XXVII (July 1921), 212–15; II., ibid., XXVII (July 1921), 235–37. [Reprinted in C–4, pp. 33–44.]

"Shantung Again," *New Republic*, XXVIII (Sept. 1921), 123–26.

"Tenth Anniversary of the Republic of China: A Message," *China Review*, I (Oct. 1921), 171.

"Federalism in China," *New Republic*, XXVIII (Oct. 1921), 176–78. [Reprinted in C–4, pp. 44–50.]

"China and Disarmament," *Chinese Students' Monthly*, XVII (Nov. 1921), 16–17.

"A Parting of the Ways for America," I., *New Republic*, XXVIII (Nov. 1921), 283–86; II., ibid., XXVIII (Nov. 1921), 315–17. [Reprinted in C–4, pp. 51–64.]

"The Issues at Washington," I. Causes of International Friction, Baltimore *Sun*, 14 Nov. 1921; II. The Anglo-Japanese Alliance and the United States, ibid., 15 Nov. 1921; III. China's Interest, ibid., 16 Nov. 1921; IV. Suggested Measures, ibid., 17 Nov. 1921.

"Public Opinion in Japan," *New Republic*, XXVIII (Nov. 1921), Sup. to No. 363, 15–18. [Reprinted in C–10, pp. 177–84, with the title "Japan Revisited: Two Years Later."]

"Shrewd Tactics Are Shown in Chinese Plea," Baltimore *Sun*, 18 Nov. 1921.

"Four Principals [*sic*] for China Regarded as but Framework," Baltimore *Sun*, 23 Nov. 1921.

"Underground Burrows Must Be Dug Open," Baltimore *Sun*, 29 Nov. 1921.

"Angles of Shantung Question," Baltimore *Sun*, 5 Dec. 1921.

"The Conference and a Happy Ending," *New Republic*, XXIX (Dec. 1921), 37–39.

"Chinese Resignations," Baltimore *Sun*, 9 Dec. 1921.

"Three Results of Treaty," Baltimore *Sun*, 11 Dec. 1921.

"A Few Second Thoughts on Four-Power Pact," Baltimore *Sun*, 17 Dec. 1921.

"Education by Henry Adams," *New Republic*, XXIX (Dec. 1921), 102–3.

"As the Chinese Think," *Asia*, XXII (Jan. 1922), 7–10, 78–79. [Reprinted in C–10, pp. 199–210, with the title "The Chinese Philosophy of Life."]

"America and Chinese Education," *New Republic*, XXX (Mar. 1922), 15–17. [Reprinted in C–10, pp. 303–9, with the title "America and China."]

"The American Intellectual Frontier," *New Republic*, XXX (May 1922), 303–5. [Reprinted in C–10, pp. 447–52.]

"Mind in the Making," letter in *New Republic*, XXXI (June 1922), 48. (Reply to: "Liberalism and Irrationalism," editorial on *The Mind in the Making* by James Harvey Robinson, *New Republic*, XXX [May 1922], 333–34.)

"Future Trends in the Development of Social Programs Through the Schools," in *Proceedings of the National Conference of Social Work, Washington, May 16–23, 1923*, pp. 449–53. Chicago, 1923. Also in *Journal of Social Forces*, I (Sept. 1923), 513–17.

"A Sick World," *New Republic,* XXXIII (Jan. 1923), 217–18. [Reprinted in C–10, pp. 760–64.]

"China and the West," *Dial,* LXXIV (Feb. 1923), 193–96. [Review of *The Problem of China* by Bertrand Russell.]

"Shall We Join the League?" *New Republic,* XXXIV (Mar. 1923), 36–37. [Reprinted in C–10, pp. 620–24; C–11, pp. 499–502, with the title "On International Coöperation."]

Response by Arthur Oncken Lovejoy, "Shall We Join the League of Nations?" letter in *New Republic,* XXXIV (Mar. 1923), 138–39.

Reply by Dewey, *New Republic,* XXXIV (Mar. 1923), 139–40. [Reprinted in C–10, pp. 625–28; C–11, pp. 502–3, with the title "On International Coöperation."]

"If War Were Outlawed," *New Republic,* XXXIV (Apr. 1923), 234–35. [Reprinted in C–10, pp. 672–76.]

"What Outlawry of War Is Not," *New Republic,* XXXVI (Oct. 1923), 149–52.

"War and a Code of Law," *New Republic,* XXXVI (Oct. 1923), 224–26. [Reprinted with "What Outlawry of War Is Not," as *Outlawry of War: What It Is and Is Not,* Chicago: American Committee for the Outlawry of War, 1923, 16 pp.; also reprinted in C–10, pp. 677–84, 685–90.] (The two articles are in answer to: Walter Lippmann, "The Outlawry of War," *Atlantic Monthly,* CXXXII [Aug. 1923], 245–53.)

"Shall the United States Join the World Court?" Pt. II, *Christian Century,* XL (Oct. 1923), 1329–34. [Reprinted in C–10, pp. 650–65, with the title "Which World Court Shall We Join?" C–11, pp. 511–25, with the title "International Law and the War-System."] (See: Manley Ottmer Hudson, "Shall the United States Join the World Court?" Pt. I, *Christian Century,* XL [Oct. 1923], 1292–97; and "Shall the United States Join the World Court?" Pt. III, *Christian Century,* XL [Oct. 1923], 1367–70. [This installment includes statements by Dewey and Hudson and exchanges between them.])

"Science, Belief and the Public," *New Republic,* XXXVIII (Apr. 1924), 143–45. [Reprinted in C–10, pp. 459–64.]

"Secularizing a Theocracy: Young Turkey and the Caliphate," *New Republic,* XL (Sept. 1924), 69–71. [Reprinted in C–10, pp. 324–29, with the title "Young Turkey and the Caliphate"; C–5, pp. 220–34.]

"Angora, the New," *New Republic,* XL (Oct. 1924), 169–70. [Reprinted in C–10, pp. 330–34; C–5, pp. 208–19.]

"Dewey Aids La Follette," New York *Times,* 23 Oct. 1924.

"The Turkish Tragedy," *New Republic,* XL (Nov. 1924), 268–69. [Reprinted in C–10, pp. 335–39; C–5, pp. 197–207.]

"The Problem of Turkey," *New Republic,* XLI (Jan. 1925), 162–63. [Reprinted in C–10, pp. 340–45.]

"Highly-Colored White Lies," *New Republic,* XLII (Apr. 1925), 229–30. [Reprinted in C–10, pp. 312–16, with the title "The White Peril."]

"Is China a Nation or a Market?" *New Republic,* XLIV (Nov. 1925), 298–99. [Reprinted in C–10, pp. 316–21, with the title "The White Peril."]

"We Should Deal with China as Nation to Nation," *Chinese Students' Monthly,* XXI (May 1926), 52–54.

"America and the Far East," *Survey,* LVI (May 1926), 188. [Reprinted in C–10, pp. 309–11, with the title "America and China."]

"A Key to the New World," *New Republic,* XLVI (May 1926), 410–11. [Review of *Education and the Good Life* by Bertrand Russell.]

"Church and State in Mexico," *New Republic,* XLVIII (Aug. 1926), 9–10. [Reprinted in C–10, pp. 352–57; C–5, pp. 137–49.]

"From a Mexican Notebook," *New Republic,* XLVIII (Oct. 1926), 239–41.

[Reprinted in C–10, pp. 358–63, with the title "The New and Old in Mexico"; C–5, pp. 168–80.]

"Bishop Brown: A Fundamental Modernist," *New Republic*, XLVIII (Nov. 1926), 371–72. [Comments on *My Heresy* by William Montgomery Brown.] [Reprinted in C–10, pp. 83–86, with the title "William Montgomery Brown."]

"America's Responsibility," *Christian Century*, XLIII (Dec. 1926), 1583–84. [Reprinted in C–10, pp. 691–96; C–11, pp. 503–8.]

"Introduction," in *Militarizing Our Youth: The Significance of the Reserve Officers' Training Corps in Our Schools and Colleges* by Roswell P. Barnes, pp. 3–4. New York: Committee on Militarism in Education, 1927.

"Imperialism Is Easy," *New Republic*, L (Mar. 1927), 133–34. [Reprinted in C–10, pp. 372–77, with the title "Mexico and the Monroe Doctrine"; C–5, pp. 181–94.]

"The Real Chinese Crisis," *New Republic*, L (Apr. 1927), 269–70.

"Psychology and Justice," *New Republic*, LIII (Nov. 1927), 9–12. [Reprinted in C–10, pp. 526–36.]

"A Critique of American Civilization," *World Tomorrow*, XI (Oct. 1928), 391–95.

"To the Chinese Friends in the United States," *Chinese Students' Bulletin*, I (Mar. 1928), 4.

" 'As an Example to Other Nations,' " *New Republic*, LIV (Mar. 1928), 88–89. [Reprinted in C–10, pp. 697–702.]

Response by James Thomson Shotwell, "Divergent Paths to Peace," *New Republic*, LIV (Mar. 1928), 194.

Rejoinder by Dewey, *New Republic*, LIV (Mar. 1928), 194–96.

"China and the Powers: II. Intervention a Challenge to Nationalism," *Current History*, XXVIII (May 1928), 212–13. [Reprinted in C–10, pp. 321–23, with the title "The White Peril."] (Reply to: Major General William Crozier, U.S.A. [Ret.], "China and the Powers: I. What Hope for China?" *Current History*, XXVIII [May 1928], 205–12.)

"Outlawing Peace by Discussing War," *New Republic*, LIV (May 1928), 370–71. [Reprinted in C–10, pp. 703–6.]

"Why I Am for Smith," *New Republic*, LVI (Nov. 1928), 320–21.

"Impressions of Soviet Russia," I. Leningrad Gives the Clue, *New Republic*, LVI (Nov. 1928), 343–44; II. A Country in a State of Flux, ibid., LVII (Nov. 1928), 11–14; III. A New World in the Making, ibid., LVII (Nov. 1928), 38–42; IV. What Are the Russian Schools Doing? ibid., LVII (Dec. 1928), 64–67; V. New Schools for a New Era, ibid., LVII (Dec. 1928), 91–94; VI. The Great Experiment and the Future, ibid., LVII (Dec. 1928), 134–37. [Reprinted in C–10, pp. 378–431; C–5, pp. 3–133.]

"Introduction," in *Humanity Uprooted* by Maurice Hindus, pp. xv–xix. New York: Jonathan Cape and Harrison Smith, 1929.

"Labor Politics and Labor Education," *New Republic*, LVII (Jan. 1929), 211–14.

Response by Matthew Woll, *New Republic*, LVIII (Feb. 1929), 19–20.

Reply by Dewey, *New Republic*, LVIII (Feb. 1929), 20.

Further reply by Dewey, "Mr. Woll as a Communist Catcher," *New Republic*, LVIII (Mar. 1929), 99.

"What Do Liberals Want?" editorial in *Outlook and Independent*, CLIII (Oct. 1929), 261.

[Statement on Censorship], *Laughing Horse*, No. 17 (Feb. 1930), p. [5].

"What I Believe," *Forum,* LXXXIII (Mar. 1930), 176–82. [Revised statement in *I Believe,* ed. Clifton Fadiman, pp. 347–54. New York: Simon and Schuster, 1939.]

"In Response," in *John Dewey, the Man and His Philosophy: Addresses Delivered in New York in Celebration of His Seventieth Birthday,* pp. 173–81. Cambridge: Harvard University Press, 1930.

"Religion in the Soviet Union: An Interpretation of the Conflict," *Current History,* XXXII (Apr. 1930), 31–36.

"Individualism, Old and New," I. The United States, Incorporated, *New Republic,* LXI (Jan. 1930), 239–41; II. The Lost Individual, ibid., LXI (Feb. 1930), 294–96; III. Toward a New Individualism, ibid., LXII (Feb. 1930), 13–16; IV. Capitalistic or Public Socialism? ibid., LXII (Mar. 1930), 64–67; V. The Crisis in Culture, ibid., LXII (Mar. 1930), 123–26; and VI. Individuality in Our Day, ibid., LXII (Apr. 1930), 184–88. [Reprinted in C–6, pp. 35–171.]

*Individualism, Old and New.* New York: Minton, Balch and Co., 1930. 171 pp. [". . . material that originally appeared in the columns of (the *New Republic*) . . . now incorporated in connection with considerable new matter, in this volume." Prefatory Note.]

"Our Illiteracy Problem," *Pictorial Review,* XXXI (Aug. 1930), 28, 65, 73.

[Letter to Senator George William Norris], New York *Times,* 26 Dec. 1930.

*Philosophy and Civilization.* New York: Minton, Balch and Co., 1931. vii, 334 pp. [Reprints, with revisions, of previously published articles.]

"The Need for a New Party," I. The Present Crisis, *New Republic,* LXVI (Mar. 1931), 115–17; II. The Breakdown of the Old Order, ibid., LXVI (Mar. 1931), 150–52; III. Who Might Make a New Party? ibid., LXVI (Apr. 1931), 177–79; IV. Policies for a New Party, ibid., LXVI (Apr. 1931), 202–5.

" 'Surpassing America,' " *New Republic,* LXVI (Apr. 1931), 241–43. [Review of *The Challenge of Russia* by Sherwood Eddy, *The Soviet Challenge to America* by George Sylvester Counts, and *These Russians* by William Chapman White.]

"Is There Hope for Politics?" *Scribner's Magazine,* LXXXIX (May 1931), 483–87.

"Full Warehouses and Empty Stomachs," *People's Lobby Bulletin,* I (May 1931), 1–3.

"The President and the Special Session," *People's Lobby Bulletin,* I (June 1931), 1.

"Secretary Klein Asked Basis of Optimism," *People's Lobby Bulletin,* I (June 1931), 3–4.

Response by Klein, *People's Lobby Bulletin,* I (Aug. 1931), 3–4.

Reply by Dewey, *People's Lobby Bulletin,* I (Aug. 1931), 4–5.

"Challenge to Progressive Senators to Act for Relief," *People's Lobby Bulletin,* I (June 1931), 5.

"The Key to Hoover's Keynote Speech," *People's Lobby Bulletin,* I (July 1931), 3–6.

"Lobby Challenges Senator Borah's Opposition to Reconsideration of Interallied Debts," *People's Lobby Bulletin,* I (July 1931), 7–8; "Contradicts Borah on Debt Revisions," New York *Times,* 15 July 1931.

"Should America Adopt a System of Compulsory Unemployment Insurance?" *Congressional Digest,* X (Aug. 1931), 212.

"The People's Lobby," *New Republic,* LXVIII (Aug. 1931), 48.

"President Dewey Opposes Blanket Freight Increase," *People's Lobby Bulletin,* I (Aug. 1931), 6–8.

"President Dewey Calls on Hoover to Recognize Government Responsibility for Unemployment," *People's Lobby Bulletin*, I (Sept. 1931), 1.

"President Dewey Opposes Community Chest Drives for Unemployed," *People's Lobby Bulletin*, I (Sept. 1931), 1–2.

"Setting New Goals at Seventy," New York *World-Telegram*, 4 Nov. 1931. [Interview with William Engle.]

"The Federal Government and Unemployment," *People's Lobby Bulletin*, I (Dec. 1931), 5.

*Ethics*, with James Hayden Tufts. New York: Henry Holt and Co., 1932. xiii, 528 pp. [Rev. ed., with Preface to the 1932 Edition. The 1908 edition has been completely revised, with "about two-thirds of the present edition . . . newly written, and frequent changes in detail . . . in the remainder."]

*The Place of Minor Parties in the American Scene* (Government Series Lecture No. 13). [Chicago]: University of Chicago Press, 1932. ii, 9 pp.

"Foreword," in *The Coming of a New Party* by Paul Howard Douglas, pp. vii–viii. New York: Whittlesey House, 1932.

"Education and Birth Control," *Nation*, CXXXIV (Jan. 1932), 112.

"A Third Party Program," *New Republic*, LXX (Feb. 1932), 48–49.

"The Only Way to Stop Hoarding," *People's Lobby Bulletin*, I (Mar. 1932), 1.

"To Replace Judge Cardozo," *New Republic*, LXX (Mar. 1932), 102.

"Instrument or Frankenstein?" *Saturday Review of Literature*, VIII (Mar. 1932), 581–82. [Review of *Man and Technics* by Oswald Spengler.]

"Peace—by Pact or Covenant?" *New Republic*, LXX (Mar. 1932), 145–47.

"Church Leaders Ask Church to Act on Unemployment," John Dewey et al., *People's Lobby Bulletin*, I (Mar. 1932), 2.

"Prosperity Dependent on Building From Bottom Up," *People's Lobby Bulletin*, I (Apr. 1932), 1.

"You Must Act to Get Congress to Act," *People's Lobby Bulletin*, II (May 1932), 1.

"The Senate Birth Control Bill," *People's Lobby Bulletin*, II (May 1932), 1–2.

"Joint Committee on Unemployment Demands Congress Act; Speeches at Morning Session," *People's Lobby Bulletin*, II (May 1932), 3–4.

*Are Sanctions Necessary to International Organization?* Yes [by] Raymond Leslie Buell; No [by] John Dewey. (Foreign Policy Association Pamphlet No. 82–83, Series 1931–32, June 1932.) New York: Foreign Policy Association, 1932. 39 pp. [Reprinted in C–11, pp. 566–602, with the title "Sanctions and the Security of Nations."]

"Voters Must Demand Congress Tax Wealth Instead of Want," *People's Lobby Bulletin*, II (June 1932), 1.

"Making Soviet Citizens," *New Republic*, LXXI (June 1932), 104. [Review of *New Minds: New Men?* by Thomas Woody and *History of Russian Educational Policy* by Nicholas Hans.]

"President Dewey Asks Senators to Stay on Guard," *People's Lobby Bulletin*, II (June 1932), 2–3.

*Democracy Joins the Unemployed*. New York: League for Independent Political Action, 1932. 4 pp.

"Prospects for a Third Party," *New Republic*, LXXI (July 1932), 278–80.

"John Dewey Surveys the Nation's Ills," New York *Times*, 10 July 1932. [Interview with S. J. Woolf.]

"Get Mayor and Governor to Demand Relief," *People's Lobby Bulletin*, II (Nov. 1932), 1.

"The Social-Economic Situation and Education" and "The Underlying Philosophy of Education," with John Lawrence Childs, in *The Educational Frontier*, ed. William Heard Kilpatrick, pp. 32–72, 287–319. New York, London: Century Co., 1933.

"Outlawry of War," in *Encyclopaedia of the Social Sciences*, XI, 508–10. New York: Macmillan Co., 1933.

"Preface" [to the English edition], *Terror in Cuba* (Paris: Courbevoie, la Cootypographie, 1933), pp. 9–10, trans. Jo Ann Boydston, in "Terror in Cuba in 1933," *School and Society*, XCVI (Nov. 1968), 444–46.

*Steps to Economic Recovery* (Pamphlets on the Economic Crisis of 1929, Vol. IX, No. 9). New York: Robert Schalkenbach Foundation, [1933?]. 15 pp.

"Unemployed and Underpaid Consumers Should Not Pay Billion Dollar Subsidy to Speculators," *People's Lobby Bulletin*, II (Jan. 1933), 1–2.

"The Future of Radical Political Action," *Nation*, CXXXVI (Jan. 1933), 8–9.

Review of *Mr. Justice Brandeis*, ed. Felix Frankfurter, *Columbia Law Review*, XXXIII (Jan. 1933), 175–76.

"Relief Is Vital," *People's Lobby Bulletin*, II (Feb. 1933), 1–2.

"The Banking Crisis," *People's Lobby Bulletin*, II (Mar. 1933), 1–2.

"The Drive against Hunger," *New Republic*, LXXIV (Mar. 1933), 190.

"Social Stresses and Strains," *International Journal of Ethics*, XLIII (Apr. 1933), 339–45. [Review of *Recent Social Trends in the United States. Report of the President's Research Committee on Social Trends*.]

"Congress Faces Its Test on Taxation," *People's Lobby Bulletin*, II (Apr. 1933), 1–2.

"The Real Test of the 'New Deal'," *People's Lobby Bulletin*, III (May 1933), 1.

"Superficial Treatment Must Fail," *People's Lobby Bulletin*, III (June 1933), 1–3.

"Inflationary Measures Injure the Masses," *People's Lobby Bulletin*, III (July 1933), 1–2.

"Plenty *vs.* Scarcity," *Commerce and Finance*, XXII (Aug. 1933), 751–52.

"The Imperative Need for A New Radical Party," *Common Sense*, II (Sept. 1933), 6–7.

"Wild Inflation Would Paralyze Nation," *People's Lobby Bulletin*, III (Sept. 1933), 1–2.

"Lobby Asks Special Session on Debts," *People's Lobby Bulletin*, III (Oct. 1933), 1.

"Unemployment Committee Asks Adequate Relief," *People's Lobby Bulletin*, III (Oct. 1933), 5–6.

"Farm Processing and Other Consumption Taxes Must Be Repealed," *People's Lobby Bulletin*, III (Nov. 1933), 1.

"The Next Session [of Congress] and the People's Lobby," *People's Lobby Bulletin*, III (Dec. 1933), 1.

"Introduction," in *Challenge to the New Deal*, eds. Alfred Mitchell Bingham and Selden Rodman, pp. v–vii. New York: Falcon Press, 1934.

"President's Policies Help Property Owners Chiefly," *People's Lobby Bulletin*, III (Jan. 1934), 1–2.

"New Deal Program Must Be Appraised," *People's Lobby Bulletin*, III (Jan. 1934), 5.

"A Real Test of the Administration," *People's Lobby Bulletin*, III (Feb. 1934), 1–2.

"America's Public Ownership Program," *People's Lobby Bulletin*, III (Mar. 1934), 1.

"Facing the Era of Realities," *People's Lobby Bulletin*, III (Apr. 1934), 1–2.
"Why I Am Not a Communist," *Modern Monthly*, VII (Apr. 1934), 135–37.
"What Keeps Funds Away from Purchasers?" *People's Lobby Bulletin*, IV (May 1934), 1–2.
"Acquiescence and Activity in Communism," *New Humanist*, VII (May–June 1934), 22. [Review of *A Philosophic Approach to Communism* by Theodore B. Brameld.]
"No Half Way House for America," *People's Lobby Bulletin*, IV (Nov. 1934), 1.
*Liberalism and Social Action*. New York: G. P. Putnam's Sons, 1935. viii, 93 pp.
"Needed—A New Politics," in *World Fellowship* by Charles Frederick Weller, pp. 119–25. New York: Liveright Publishing Corp., 1935.
"Socialization of Ground Rent," *People's Lobby Bulletin*, IV (Jan. 1935), 1.
"International Cooperation or International Chaos," *People's Lobby Bulletin*, IV (Feb. 1935), 6–7.
"Toward Administrative Statesmanship," *Social Frontier*, I (Mar. 1935), 9–10. [Reprinted in C–8, pp. 66–69, with the title "Democracy and Educational Administration."]
"Taxation as a Step to Socialization," *People's Lobby Bulletin*, IV (Mar. 1935), 1–2.
"United, We Shall Stand," *Social Frontier*, I (Apr. 1935), 11–12; *School and Community*, XXI (Apr. 1935), 143–45. [Reprinted in C–8, pp. 72–76, with the title "The Teacher and His World."]
"When America Goes to War," *Modern Monthly*, IX (June 1935), 200.
"Our Un-Free Press," *Common Sense*, IV (Nov. 1935), 6–7.
[Letter to the editor], *New Republic*, LXXXVIII (Oct. 1936), 249.
*The Case of Leon Trotsky*. New York, London: Harper and Bros., 1937. xix, 617 pp. [Stenographic report of hearings in Mexico City.]
*"Truth Is On the March."* Reports and Remarks on the Trotsky Hearings in Mexico. New York: American Committee for the Defense of Leon Trotsky, 1937. 15 pp.
Report of radio broadcast by Dewey and rejoinder by Corliss Lamont, New York *Times*, 14 Dec. 1937.
Response by Sidney Hook, "Corliss Lamont: 'Friend of the G.P.U.',"
*Modern Monthly*, X (Mar. 1938), 5–8, including telegram from Dewey, p. 8.
"Pravda on Trotsky," *New Republic*, LXXXX (Mar. 1937), 212–13.
"Righting an Academic Wrong," *New Republic*, LXXXX (Mar. 1937), 242.
"The Future of Democracy," *New Republic*, LXXXX (Apr. 1937), 351.
"John Dewey, Great American Liberal, Denounces Russian Dictatorship," Washington *Post*, 17 Dec. 1937. [Interview with Agnes Ernst Meyer (Mrs. Eugene Meyer).]
"In Defense of the Mexican Hearings," in "Violence, For and Against: A Symposium on Marx, Stalin and Trotsky," *Common Sense*, VII (Jan. 1938), 20–21.
"Introduction," in *Looking Forward: Discussion Outlines*, p. 3. New York: League for Industrial Democracy, 1938.
*Freedom and Culture*. New York: G. P. Putnam's Sons, 1939. 176 pp.
"Experience, Knowledge and Value: A Rejoinder," in *The Philosophy of John Dewey* (The Library of Living Philosophers, Vol. I, ed. Paul Arthur Schilpp), pp. 517–608. Evanston, Chicago: Northwestern University, 1939.
"No Matter What Happens—Stay Out," *Common Sense*, VIII (Mar. 1939), 11.

"The Basis for Hope," *Common Sense*, VIII (Dec. 1939), 9–10.

"The Case for Bertrand Russell," *Nation*, CL (June 1940), 732–33.

"Introduction" and "Social Realities *versus* Police Court Fictions," in *The Bertrand Russell Case*, eds. John Dewey and Horace M. Kallen, pp. 7–10, 55–74. New York: Viking Press, 1941.

"Creative Democracy—The Task Before Us," in *The Philosopher of the Common Man: Essays in Honor of John Dewey to Celebrate His Eightieth Birthday*, ed. Sidney Ratner, pp. 220–28. New York: G. P. Putnam's Sons, 1940.

"Address of Welcome," in *Thirty-five Years of Educational Pioneering* (L.I.D. Pamphlet Series), pp. 3–6. New York: League for Industrial Democracy, 1941.

"Foreword to Revised Edition" and "The One-World of Hitler's National Socialism," in *German Philosophy and Politics*, 2d ed., pp. 5–7, 13–49. New York: G. P. Putnam's Sons, 1942. [New Foreword and Introduction to 1915 edition, which was "reprinted without change, save for a few verbal corrections."]

"Foreword," in *S. O. Levinson and the Pact of Paris: A Study in the Techniques of Influence* by John E. Stoner, pp. vii–viii. Chicago: University of Chicago Press, 1942.

"Message to the Chinese People," 2 pp., typewritten. [Original English version in National Archives, Washington, D.C.]

"Russia's Position: Mr. [Joseph Edward] Davies's Book [*Mission to Moscow*] Regarded as Incorrect Picture," letter to New York *Times*, 11 Jan. 1942; reprinted as "Can We Work with Russia?" *Frontiers of Democracy*, VIII (Mar. 1942), 179–80.

Comments by John Lawrence Childs, *Frontiers of Democracy*, VIII (Mar. 1942), 181–82.

Reply by Dewey, "Dr. Dewey on Our Relations with Russia," *Frontiers of Democracy*, VIII (Apr. 1942), 194.

["Several Faults Are Found in 'Mission to Moscow' Film"], letter of John Dewey and Suzanne La Follette to the editor, New York *Times*, 9 May 1943.

Response by Arthur Upham Pope, New York *Times*, 16 May 1943.

Reply by Dewey and Miss La Follette, New York *Times*, 24 May 1943.

Reply by Pope, New York *Times*, 12 June 1943.

Reply by Dewey and Miss La Follette, New York *Times*, 19 June 1943.

"Hitler's Spirit Still Lives: Introduction," John Dewey et al., in *Tragedy of a People: Racialism in Czecho-Slovakia*, pp. 3–6. New York: American Friends of Democratic Sudetens, June 1946.

"Behind the Iron Bars," *New Leader Literary Section*, 13 Sept. 1947. [Review of *Forced Labor in Soviet Russia* by David J. Dallin and Boris I. Nicolaevsky.]

"American Youth, Beware of Wallace Bearing Gifts," *Liberal* (Organ of the New York State Liberal Party), II (Oct. 1948), 3–4; *New Leader*, XXXI (Oct. 1948), xliv, 1, 14, with the title "Wallace vs. a New Party."

"How to Anchor Liberalism," *Labor and Nation*, IV (Nov.–Dec. 1948), 14–15.

"Communists as Teachers," New York *Times*, 21 June 1949.

"John Dewey at 90, Finds Tension of World May Result in Good," New York *Herald Tribune*, 15 Oct. 1949. [Interview with Lester Grant.]

"John Dewey, at 90, Reiterates His Belief that Good Schools Are Essential in a Democracy," New York *Times*, 16 Oct. 1949. [Interview with Benjamin Fine.]

"John Dewey Responds," in *John Dewey at Ninety*, ed. Harry Wellington

Laidler, pp. 32–35. New York: League for Industrial Democracy, 1950.

"Mr. Acheson's Critics: Their Attacks Feared Damaging to Our World Prestige," letter to the New York *Times,* 19 Nov. 1950.

"Modern Labor Leader" and "Master Craftsman of Labor," in *David Dubinsky: A Pictorial Biography,* pp. 13–19, 21–28. New York: Inter-Allied Publications, 1951.

[Contribution to a Symposium], in *Democracy in a World of Tensions: A Symposium Prepared by UNESCO,* eds. Richard McKeon and Stein Rokkan, pp. 62–68. Chicago: University of Chicago Press, 1951.

# 10
## Dewey on Education and Schooling

GEORGE E. AXTELLE
AND
JOE R. BURNETT

FOR DEWEY, education is the most important testing ground for philosophic theory, "the laboratory in which philosophic distinctions become concrete and are tested." [1] Indeed, he remarks: "The most penetrating definition of philosophy which can be given . . . is that it is the theory of education in its most general phases." [2] Because Dewey is a systematic thinker, it follows that his view of education furnishes the philosopher with some of the most concrete illustrations and suggestions of what his basic philosophic ideas mean. By a similar token, one must understand Dewey's basic philosophical concepts to understand adequately Dewey's view of education.

In this essay we concentrate almost exclusively upon Dewey's views on education and schooling. We depend upon the accompanying essays in this volume and upon other readily available accounts [3] to give the reader insight into the philosoph-

1. *Democracy and Education* (New York: Macmillan Co., 1916), p. 384.

2. *Democracy and Education*, p. 386.

3. In addition to the essays in this volume, the reader may wish to refer to two excellent volumes of essays: Sidney Hook, ed., *John Dewey: Philosopher of Science and Freedom* (New York: Dial Press, 1950); and Paul Arthur Schilpp, ed., *The Philosophy of John Dewey* (The Library of Living Philosophers, Vol. I [Evanston, Chicago: Northwestern University, 1939]). Perhaps the finest general exposition of Dewey's philosophy and its educational significance for Dewey and his followers is found in John L. Childs, *American Pragmatism and Education* (New York: Henry Holt and Co., 1956).

A number of works deal admirably with the criticism (and counter-criticism) which occurred as Dewey's thought came to have a major impact on education. The following are especially recommended: John S.

ical concepts which often we can only mention in explicating Dewey's educational thought.

## Education and Schooling

Dewey often used the term "education" in a normative sense. For Dewey, not every modification of experience or behavior is to be considered educative; much that is ordinarily referred to as educative may, in fact, be miseducative. For him, an educative experience should be considered as one which is a "reconstruction or reorganization of experience which adds to the meaning of experience, and which increases ability to direct the course of subsequent experience." [4] In one important sense, education can be said to be coextensive with anything reconstructive and progressively liberating in human experience. Dewey meant exactly this when he said that education is the "laboratory" wherein philosophic distinctions attain concreteness and test.

This very broad conception of education and of testing cannot be forgotten by the professional educator even if, on first glance, it seems so broad as to be nonfunctional. To forget the broad conception is to fail to see from Dewey's perspective the more specialized or formal educative processes in their relation to general life and societal goals. But it is equally true that the professional educator must attend to what Dewey says about specific educational endeavors, the endeavors of formal schooling, if philosophy is to have a "laboratory" in any strict and distinct sense. Even though education can take place in practically any social institution—the family, the church, the factory, the military, or whatever—the school has what Dewey terms a special function which distinguishes it from other social institutions in serving the educative process.

---

Brubacher, "Ten Misunderstandings of Dewey's Educational Philosophy," *Bulletin of the School of Education, Indiana University*, XXXVI (1960), 27–42; Sidney Hook, "John Dewey: His Philosophy of Education and Its Critics," in *Dewey on Education: Appraisals*, ed. Reginald D. Archambault (New York: Random House, 1966), pp. 127–60.

4. *Democracy and Education*, pp. 89–90. Cf. *Experience and Education* (New York: Macmillan Co., 1938), pp. 13–14; also, *Interest and Effort in Education* (Boston: Houghton Mifflin Co., 1913), pp. 54–55.

In his most often reprinted article, "My Pedagogic Creed" (1897), Dewey lays down one of several educational "axioms" which he does not change in his later writings. The school, he says, "is primarily a social institution. Education being a social process, the school is simply that form of community life in which all those agencies are concentrated that will be most effective in bringing the child to share in the inherited resources of the race [of man] and to use his own powers for social ends." [5] This, again, is a normative statement; Dewey is saying that the school *should be* such an institution. He is manifestly aware that most schools in America are not such. In *Democracy and Education* he briefly describes the school as having a special educative "office" or function consisting of at least four duties. [6]

First, he says, formal schooling provides a "simplified environment." That is, the tyros' entry into cultural understanding does not consist in their being presented the culture in its entirety. Instead, there is an attempt to introduce those elements which are judged to be basic and essential for understanding the culture's most important characteristics.

Second, the school is a "purified medium of action." Formal schooling gives the child instruction in those aspects of the culture which the initiated members by and large regard as decent, just, beautiful, and honorable.

Third, Dewey maintains that it is the "office of the school environment to balance the various elements in the social environment." Precisely what Dewey means by this is not altogether clear. But he means, at the very least, that the school has the task of helping children gain an understanding and appreciation of the patterns of life which different individuals and groups within their community exhibit.

Fourth, Dewey says that the school has the function of "coördinating within the disposition of each individual the diverse influences of the various social environments into which he enters." In one sense, this is but a restatement of the third point. In another sense it can be taken to require that the individual acquire a balanced but critical understanding of and sensitivity to the social environment. This seems to require that schooling help develop a positive understanding and appreciation of the various modes of thinking, feeling, and acting possessed by

5. "My Pedagogic Creed," *School Journal*, LIV (1897), 78.
6. *Democracy and Education*, pp. 24–27.

groups other than those to which the individual belongs. The language of the account seems to emphasize the student's acquiring a balanced *psychological* disposition, *an integrity of character*, not merely an intellectual understanding and acceptance of the variety in the cultural scene.

Two points require special note in dealing with Dewey's conception of the main functions of the school. First, in each of the functions, schooling is a deliberately contrived and structured affair designed to reduce the waste and confusion of random experience and the general socialization process. One of the most frequent and patently false charges which Dewey's critics make against him is that he proposed that schooling be tolerant of random and casual experience and that schooling should indeed maximize such experience. Lack of deliberate structure and adult guidance, he remarks, "is really stupid. For it attempts the impossible, which is always stupid; and it misconceives the conditions of independent thinking." [7] He specifically rejects that "so-called idealizing of childhood which in effect is nothing but lazy indulgence. . . . Even though it is not always easy to tell whether what appears to be mere surface fooling is a sign of some nascent as yet untrained power, we must remember that manifestations are not to be accepted as ends in themselves. . . . They are to be turned into means of development, of carrying power forward, not indulged or cultivated for their own sake." [8] Dewey especially emphasizes these points in *Experience and Education*, making the principle of continuity the criterion for judging a truly educative experience: Where does the experience lead? What are its potentialities for physical, intellectual, moral growth? Is there increase of meaning and ability to direct subsequent experience into richer channels? [9] Likewise, in *How We Think* he stresses the idea that the aim of schooling, insofar as cognition is concerned, is not idle musing but systematic reflection or inquiry. [10]

The second point of note is that this particular listing of the special functions of schooling is not specific enough for the practical educator. Obviously, not just any simplification of the

7. "Individuality and Experience," *Journal of the Barnes Foundation*, II (1926), 4.

8. *Democracy and Education*, p. 61.

9. *Experience and Education*, pp. 29 ff.

10. *How We Think*, 2d ed. (New York: D. C. Heath and Co., 1933), Ch. 1.

environment is to be recommended; not just any notion of what constitutes purification is to be countenanced; not just any view of what makes a harmony of either curriculum items or student disposition is acceptable. The question is, what criteria provide defensible conceptions of "simplicity," "purification," the "balanced" curriculum, and "balanced" student disposition? There are two main sources in Dewey's writings for the answer to this question. One lies in his criticism of and proposals for the administration of schools. The other lies in his conception of the aims of education, a conception which is itself rooted in his view of the nature of man and culture. Let us begin with a discussion of the latter.

## The Aims and Functions of Education

Man is a creature of nature like any other animal; he differs from other animals in that many of his behavior patterns are developed socially rather than genetically. Instead of highly specific response in novel situations, man is characterized by dispositions, drives, "plastic" tendencies which take definite shape as a result of experience and, especially, of reflective activity. Of equal significance, man invents progressively sophisticated modes of communication which allow him to teach his fellows and his youth ways of adjustment to, and subjugation of, environmental forces. Communication is thus one foundation of social life, one signal achievement which allows man to make and remake himself and his environment. Of all human affairs, Dewey says, communication "is the most wonderful," indeed "a wonder by the side of which transubstantiation pales." [11]

The "wonder" of communication is itself founded on an aspect of human nature. Man strives, on the average at least, for greater and greater value, reason, and control over his experience. It is the "common purpose of men," Dewey remarks, to seek "nothing but the best, the richest and fullest experience possible." [12]

A modest theory of progress is involved in this conception of human nature and in the conception of what the societal

11. *Experience and Nature*, 2d ed. (New York: W. W. Norton, 1929), p. 166.
12. *Experience and Nature* (1929), p. 412.

process of communication allows human nature to become. This amounts to saying that "Here is what has worked; let us study it, improve upon it where possible, and see if it will work even better." There is no guarantee of success; but there is a faith based upon evidence that what has worked well before can, if improved upon, work better now and in the future.

The evidence, however, is ambiguous. Communication and social processes have on occasion destroyed life and they have not always advanced the quality of life even when they have helped maintain it. The task for man is to find what types of communication and social life seem to have functioned most effectively in history, subject these to scrutiny, and project what appear to be the desirable elements of these types as ideals for deliberate pursuit and evaluation. It bears repeating that mistakes and failures can occur in all phases of the analysis. History is the cemetery not only of individuals but also of societies. The task is to find what seems *most likely* to work best, given the possibility that anything at all can work.

Dewey's answer to the question of which type of social life functions best is democracy. What he means by the term is somewhat unusual. He means style of social interaction or communication in which  A) the consciously shared interests of participants are numerous and varied, and  B) the participants have full and free interplay with other groups and their interests.[13] Thus, "a democracy is more than a form of government; it is primarily a mode of associated living, of conjoint communicated experience." [14] Dewey gives us, in these criteria, a way of evaluating all types of societal interactions and communication. It is not the form of a socio-political system, be it composed of two people or many millions, that is important, but the sharing of numerous and diverse interests, and critical openness to other perspectives.

Dewey says much the same thing in his discussion of growth. "Growth" is the criterion for judging individual behavior in much the same sense that democracy is the criterion for judging social relationships. Growth requires much more than fulfillment of hereditary capacities in a given social and physical environment. It requires that the individual actively judge and

13. *Democracy and Education*, p. 100.
14. *Democracy and Education*, p. 101.

choose those alternatives which promise to expand the opportunity for the greatest long-range value.[15] Growth is not neutral or amoral development. It is life guided with an eye to the enrichment of present and future development. Further, it is a process which must function within the channel of what is possible on the basis of individual capacities and within the provisions of the physical and social environment. One can "grow"—in a non-Deweyan sense—as a criminal; but it is doubtful if it can be said with assurance that in any culture criminality is a customary and opportune route to a life which is long, full, free, and vivid. It is true that some criminals reach an old age, relatively untouched by social demands, and die rich. For all the seeming glamour of their life of luxury, the secrecy required to exploit others leads to stultification.

Dewey's critics and some of his followers have written of growth as though Dewey thought it to be an ideal end. It is not an ideal end, but rather a criterion for judging aspects of ongoing, developing character. As long as there is life, there is no final, ideal end; there are interruptions and recoveries (or "flights and perchings" as William James said). It is important to judge progress during interruptions and recoveries rather than judge progress by purported "ultimate" ends. "Growth" represents a criterion for judging qualitative change in a process whose ultimate outcome is not known.

What are the characteristics of growth? As one of the authors has remarked elsewhere, they are "flexibility, openness to new insights, new possibilities, hospitality to novelty, to the imaginative and to the creative." Growth involves, at the same time, "integrity, balance, proportion, dynamic equilibrium, a unified wholeness of character. It involves the integral expression of all the resources and powers of the self." [16]

The school is for Dewey one of the main engines of progress, democracy, and growth. More than any other institution in America, it aims to effect a refinement and elevation of the power of the individual to attain something ever closer to "nothing but the best." The school must help the individual in a multitude of ways—by developing intellectual power, moral re-

15. *Democracy and Education*, Ch. 4, and p. 63.
16. George Axtelle, "John Dewey's Conception of the Religious," *Religious Humanism*, I (1967), 66–67.

sponsibility, æsthetic sensitivity, æsthetic expression, practical day-to-day competence in ordinary affairs, and a ruling integrity of character.

Dewey means for the school to seek these ends in a most concrete fashion, reminding us that it is not education or schooling which has aims but individuals—students, teachers, administrators, parents—who have aims. For an "educational aim" to be concrete it must meet a number of criteria. First, it must be relevant to the individual's particular experience; that is to say, it must be an aim *in* the individual's experience and education. Second, the aim must be flexible, able to guide activity but also able to be modified by activity. Third, the aim must function to liberate or free action in a planned sequence.[17]

Dewey warns educators against ends of education which are purportedly "general and ultimate." They may be general and ultimate in the sense that they are cut off from any specific context, and thus make the teaching-learning process a "mere means of getting ready for an end disconnected from the means." A *defensible* general aim is one which leads the individual to see a great number of possible and probable consequences, as well as the means to their attainments, which can flow from action. Defensible general aims function for the educator as hypotheses do for the scientist. To the extent that they emerge from situational problems, and give guidance to help resolve those problems, then to that extent the educator needs a vast number of general aims just as the scientist needs a vast number of hypotheses. To the extent that general aims are unrelated to situational problems, are "dogmatically ultimate," or are merely platitudinous, then to that extent they create additional problems.[18]

### Teaching-Learning and the Curriculum

The education which is its own reward for the learner is education which is interesting to him. In one of his most systematic and lucid discussions of interest,[19] Dewey notes that *genuine* interest refers to an identification of the self with an object or

17. *Democracy and Education*, pp. 118–29.
18. *Democracy and Education*, pp. 128–29.
19. *Interest and Effort*, Ch. 4.

objects—"material, subject-matter, conditions upon which to operate" [20]—in such a way that one's well-being is tied intrinsically to bringing about a specific state of affairs which will most likely produce satisfaction. The identification of self with an ongoing, developing nature calls forth energy, enthusiasm, and thought. Genuine interest is not passing excitation or titillation. Such a relation of object and self "is not only *not* educative, but it is worse than nothing." [21]

One of the finest outcomes of genuine interest is reflective thought, the function of which is *"to transform a situation in which there is experienced obscurity, doubt, conflict, disturbance of some sort, into a situation that is clear, coherent, settled, harmonious."* [22]

Reflective thinking can be summarized as having the following "key" characteristics:   A) a situation in which one's habitual modes of activity are challenged, thus producing confusion, doubt, concern;   B) an impulsive, anticipatory assessment of what the situation seems to forebode;   C) a critical consideration of the relevant data which will help one specify with exactitude the nature of the problematic situation;   D) the formation of hypotheses which, while tentative, are consistent with all known facts;   E) commitment to the hypotheses in the order that they seem most warranted, until one leads to action which removes the problem; and   F) reflection on whether any other hypothesis and action could have resolved the situation more effectively.[23]

The conception of human nature involved here is fairly obvious. The organism seeks to have its desires or interests rewarded; when they are blocked, it seeks to remove the blockage; because it has the ability to reflect, it can delay and perfect plans of action; because it has a societal storehouse of knowledge, it can increase chances of success.

If we conceive of nature, as Dewey does, as being precarious or problematic, of "life as a series of interruptions and

20. *Interest and Effort*, p. 65.
21. *Interest and Effort*, p. 91.
22. *How We Think* (1933), pp. 100–101.
23. There is no definite number of "key" characteristics which can be insisted upon. Dewey himself varied the number which he used. In the educational writings, two of Dewey's most succinct accounts are: *Democracy and Education*, pp. 176–77; and *How We Think* (1933), pp. 107–17.

recoveries," it follows that the individual often is being challenged and thus is often thinking at least in some crude sense. This means that formal schooling can assume a good deal on the part of the student. The school does not have to *force* the student to be interested, to learn, to be motivated—for the student *is* interested, *is* learning, *is* motivated. These are responses which the school must encourage rather than frustrate by mistakenly thinking that they must be brought into being *de novo*. The school's initial questions are: What is the student interested in that is *significant*? How *well* is he learning? For what is he motivated that is *excellent*?

It is easy to think that the student represents a "void," his mind a *tabula rasa*. This often occurs because, "to the one who is learned, subject matter is extensive, accurately defined, and logically interrelated. To the one who is learning, it is fluid, partial, and connected through his personal occupations. The problem of teaching is to keep the experience of the student moving in the direction of what the expert already knows. Hence the need that the teacher know both subject matter and the characteristic needs and capacities of the student." [24]

Although Dewey often has been charged with relegating subject-matter to a secondary or tertiary role, he in fact does not. The teacher has, in this outlook, if anything, more need for competence in subject-matter than in almost any other. In his discussion of the method of intelligence Dewey singles out the gathering and proper use of warranted evidence as the features that most distinguish the method from sheer trial and error thinking.[25] Since cultural problems involve for their solution many of the disciplines known to man, the teacher certainly needs breadth of perspective and grounding in a number of disciplines. As the child grows into adolescence and his interests focus in specialized problem-subject areas, the teacher needs depth of understanding in those areas. If anything, Dewey might be accused of making excessive subject-matter demands on teachers. The demands might seem most excessive with regard to range (if not depth) on the part of elementary teachers, since they must cope with the widest range of childhood problems.

The extraordinary abilities which Dewey expected of the

24. *Democracy and Education*, p. 216.
25. *Democracy and Education*, pp. 176–77.

elementary teacher are suggested most fully in the two volumes, *The Child and the Curriculum* and *The School and Society*. These two volumes provide the fullest view of how the elementary school teacher and the student should approach subject-matter. In the former volume it becomes clear that there are three key dimensions of every study or subject.[26] There is one dimension which is properly the concern of experts, those who are concerned with research or innovations in a subject field. The elementary teacher has a different interest in the subject as *"representing a given stage and phase of the development of experience.* His problem is that of inducing a vital and personal experiencing."[27] The child is interested in still another dimension, the subject as it can be brought to bear upon his interests, problems, and progress.

Pedagogically, then, the teacher of the very young should *not* stress an academic subject in its abstract, systematic, and technical character. Rather, he should use subject-matter to enliven the interest and activity of the student. Presentation of subject-matter in its abstract, systematic, and technical character results in three evils: the child sees the subject as *merely* abstract, without relevance to his experience or interest; the child's motivation drops off because there is no obvious relevance; and when most of the sophisticated subjects are directly taught to the very young, the subjects have to be so simplified or distorted that their logical character is obscured.[28]

The way to have the learner grasp a subject in its abstract, systematic, and technical nature is to begin with it as the child can make immediate and personal use of it. How long should this pedagogical mode of proceeding be continued? One of Dewey's accounts of stages of child growth would indicate that it is most relevant for the child until about eight years of age. From eight or nine years of age, until eleven or twelve, the emphasis should shift. During this time most children will have come to recognize "distinct and enduring ends which stand out and demand attention on their own account, [and] the previous

26. *The Child and the Curriculum* (Chicago: University of Chicago Press, 1902), pp. 22, 29 ff. Dewey mentions only the two dimensions explicitly (and his main emphasis is on science). But the context makes it evident that his concern is with the dimensions of expert, teacher, *and* student.

27. *The Child and the Curriculum*, p. 30.

28. *The Child and the Curriculum*, pp. 31–33.

vague and fluid unity of life is broken up." [29] Subject-matter can now be approached in its systematic character. The child seeks regular patterns of nature and experience which will help him understand the reliable modes of thought and action which have enabled man to achieve his ideals. He now has come to "recognize the necessity of a similar development within himself—the need of securing for himself practical and intellectual control of such methods of work and inquiry as will enable him to realize results for himself." [30] At the end of this period, when the child is roughly eleven or twelve years of age, he will be ready to undertake "distinctive studies and arts for technical and intellectual aims." [31]

The teacher's function is to shift subject-matter emphasis with the educational level of the student. The teacher's emphasis is heavily sociological and psychological in the early years, with subject-matter ( *qua* subject-matter) emphasis being minimal in what is explicitly presented to children. By the time of late elementary school or early secondary school, the student is ready to pursue subject-matter in something approaching a systematic and technical sense.

This is Dewey's answer to the antagonism which many feel to exist between established subject-matters of great sophistication, on the one hand, and activities such as drawing, performing music, taking nature excursions, and engaging in manual training, on the other hand. The latter activities draw upon the established subject-matters to enable the child to gain control over his experience in a way which is direct and personal. As the child comes to understand and appreciate the power which theoretical ideas have in his experience, he becomes progressively interested in them. Theoretical ideas themselves gradually become personal, immediate concerns and the youth desires to study them in their abstract, systematic, and technical characters.[32]

29. "The Psychology of the Elementary Curriculum," *Elementary School Record*, Monograph No. 9 (Chicago: University of Chicago Press, 1900), p. 227.
30. "Psychology of the Elementary Curriculum," p. 228.
31. "Psychology of the Elementary Curriculum," p. 232.
32. "The Situation as Regards the Course of Study," in *Addresses and Proceedings*, National Educational Association, 1901, pp. 337 ff. (Cf. Dewey's discussion of "experience," "data," "ideas," and "theories" in *Democracy and Education*, Ch. 12; also, cf. the truncated account, pp. 216–23.)

The arts and sciences play an enormously important role in man's history; but one errs in trying to teach them to young children in a way which    A) is unrelated to the interests of the children, and    B) simplifies the logical and sophisticated nature of the subjects themselves. An equally grievous error lies in so proliferating activities of immediate import, thereby so trivializing the subjects, that the child gets little or no appreciation of the theory necessary to lure him to mastery of the great arts and sciences.[33]

Thus Dewey resolves the apparent conflict between the psychological demands of the young learner and the formal demands of the established disciplines. In the process, he also resolves another conflict, the pedagogical conflict between those who stress "how to think" and those who stress "what to think." Dewey's resolution of this problem amounts to saying (paraphrasing Kant) that "method without data is empty; data without method are blind." [34]

Reflective thinking should be one of the most significant outcomes of the curriculum and the teaching-learning process. Two things, especially, are essential to its attainment. One of these, interest, has already been discussed. The other is a social framework in which interest can be cultivated or heightened for both the individual and society. What we need, says Dewey, is "the improvement of the methods and conditions of debate, discussion and persuasion. That is *the* problem of the public." [35] There is only one way by which this improvement can occur: "The problem of securing diffused and seminal intelligence can be solved only in the degree in which local communal life becomes a reality. . . . Logic in its fulfillment recurs to the primitive sense of the word: dialogue." [36]

Dewey obviously thought that the school was one of the few remaining institutions in American society which could provide children with a rich sense of dialogue and community. The older bases for community, in the extended family and the communal neighborhood, were fast being destroyed by industrialization, urbanization, specialization of jobs, and increasing

33. "Course of Study," pp. 337 ff.
34. *The School and Society* (Chicago: University of Chicago Press, 1899), p. 66.
35. *The Public and Its Problems* (New York: Henry Holt and Co., 1927), p. 208.
36. *Public and Its Problems*, pp. 217–18.

mobility. As one of the most astute students of Dewey's social thought puts it, reflective thinking or "scientific inquiry is not enough; in Dewey's opinion, the roots of a vital democracy can be securely planted only in the intimate, face-to-face associations of the local community." [37] This idea, perhaps more than any other, must be understood if Dewey's specific recommendations concerning childhood education are to be grasped. Democratic community life in the schools is the basis of individual intelligence and a viable social order under modern conditions of social life. Dewey put it most succinctly in *The School and Society* (1899):

> The introduction of active occupations, of nature study, of elementary science, of art, of history; the relegation of the merely symbolic and formal to a secondary position; the change in the moral school atmosphere, in the relation of pupils and teachers—of discipline; the introduction of more active, expressive, and self-directing factors—all these are not mere accidents, they are necessities of the larger social evolution. It remains but to organize all these factors, to appreciate them in their fullness of meaning, and to put the ideas and ideals involved into complete, uncompromising possession of our school system. *To do this means to make each one of our schools an embryonic community life*, active with types of occupations that reflect the life of the larger society, and permeated throughout with the spirit of art, history, and science. When the school introduces and trains each child of society into membership within such a little community, saturating him with the spirit of service, and providing him with the instruments of effective self-direction, we shall have the deepest and best guarantee of a larger society which is worthy, lovely, and harmonious [italics added].[38]

### Some Specialized Aspects of Teaching-Learning and the Curriculum

Between 1894 and 1904 Dewey had the opportunity to put his curriculum theory into practice. As head of the Department of Philosophy, Psychology, and Pedagogy at the University of

37. William O. Stanley, *Education and Social Integration* (New York: Teachers College Bureau of Publications, 1953), pp. 231–32.
38. *School and Society* (1899), pp. 39–40.

Chicago, he elaborated and systematized his educational views at considerable length; but, unfortunately, largely as concerned only elementary education. The reason for the limitation lies in the fact that Dewey established the Laboratory School at Chicago (in 1896) for elementary students, and was to leave Chicago (in 1904) just as secondary education was to be incorporated into the program.

ACTIVE OCCUPATIONS. Dewey's writings during the period show that he thinks that "active occupations," the endeavors in the community and the tasks at home, with which the children are familiar and in which they have come to have a natural interest, furnish one important basis for organizing the curriculum in childhood education. This much Froebel and Pestalozzi had argued, but Dewey looks beyond hearth and provincial community to deal with occupations as they were coming to be shaped by the scientific and industrial revolutions. He argues that in the study of occupations there is the possibility of introduction to the life and history of modern civilization. In the study of occupations and their interrelatedness there is to be found the communication, the shared activity, and mutual interdependence which unify people as they strive to meet their individual and collective problems. In the study of modern occupations, given declining family and community life, there is the chance to raise questions about how leisure and æsthetic potential can be utilized, and about how craftsmanship and intellectual virtues can be sustained in a highly organized industrial system.[39]

Dewey is aware that young children's interests are not sustained, and that often they represent little more than "a desire to 'mess around,' perhaps to imitate the activities of older people." Rather than humor such flighty interests, the school should help the child see progressively how such interests are frustrated by the "actual world of hard conditions," how interests must adapt themselves to hard conditions, and how important to this are "the factors of discipline and knowledge."[40]

Dewey claims that four interests are obvious as children

39. *The School and Society*, 2d ed. (Chicago: University of Chicago Press, 1915), pp. 132–37.

40. *School and Society* (1915), p. 39. Cf. *Democracy and Education*, pp. 231–32.

actively study occupations: interest in conversation or communication, interest in discovering things, interest in constructing
things, and interest in artistic creation. These he calls the "natural resources, the uninvested capital" upon which schooling
should depend in giving the child wider and deeper mastery of
his environment.[41]

Each of these interests should be built upon in order to
facilitate community, inquiry, and self-development. Conversation and æsthetic expression are modes for communicating one's
thoughts and feelings. The older form of the recitation in which
the child was examined upon his mastery of material largely
alien to his interests is transformed and becomes a way of
reporting upon what is of interest to the child, what "he has
found out," what he has done with his interest. It enables him to
enlist the thought and activities of his fellows in further inquiry.
The older form of the recitation, indeed, passes out of existence.
Community participation in the classroom enters.[42] "The recitation becomes the social clearing-house, where experiences and
ideas are exchanged and subjected to criticism, where misconceptions are corrected, and new lines of thought and inquiry are
set up." [43]

Providing for the child's interests in discovery and in
construction makes demands upon the physical structure of the
school. It requires, as the saying goes, "moveable furniture," a
school in which there are laboratories, workshop space, the
instruments for everything from plumbing to art, classrooms in
which children can, as need dictates, work in groups or individ-
ually engage in active research. It requires everything, indeed,
which Dewey says "the educational authorities who write edi-
torials in the daily papers generally term 'fads' and 'frills.' " [44]

TYPES OF INTEREST AND THE DISCIPLINES IN CHILDHOOD
EDUCATION. As is indicated, it is not activity, as such, that is
important. Rather, activity is the means whereby the young
child comes to form the vital identification of his self and interests with the objects or subject-matter in his environment. The
first and earliest type of relevant activity is physical. But, there

41. *School and Society* (1915), p. 45.
42. *School and Society* (1915), pp. 48–50.
43. *School and Society* (1915), p. 49.
44. *School and Society* (1915), p. 33.

is an intellectual or mental element involved even in these. Further, the mental element will be curtailed to the extent that activity is arbitrarily restricted or, on the other hand, left without the direction which the child naturally seeks.[45]

If free activity is well provided and directed in preschool education, the school can concentrate on developing another type of educative interest. The child will be ready, desirous of mastering the use of extraorganic tools to deal with his environment. In the first type of educative interest, free play is dominant, with the child often imagining or pretending modification of objects or environment. In the second type, which develops prior to school years, physical and conceptual tools are sought. Free *play* begins to yield to *games* and *work*, in both of which there is an emphasis upon techniques and rules which are involved in the overt and purposeful planning of sequences of action for obtaining desired, concrete outcomes. Games and work overtly introduce intellectual qualities into activity. Here the teacher must be careful that fatigue does not cause games and work to become toil; or, that activity does not lead to ends which are irrelevant to the interests of the learner, in which case games and work become *drudgery*.[46]

During this phase, in late preschool and early schooling, the emphasis will be on "all forms of expression and construction with tools and materials, all forms of artistic and manual activity so far as they involve the conscious or thoughtful endeavor to achieve an end." Specifically recommended by Dewey for this purpose are painting; drawing; clay modeling; cooking; gardening; sewing; manual training with such materials as wood, metal, textiles; and the manual activities of scientific inquiry, covering "the collection of materials for study, the management of apparatus, the sequence of acts in carrying on and in recording experiments." [47]

Dewey thinks that history and geography (including nature study in the latter) are the "information studies *par excellence* of the schools." [48] These studies provide, respectively, the social and material matrices in which direct experience can be

---

45. *Interest and Effort*, pp. 67 ff.
46. *Interest and Effort*, pp. 76–79. Cf. *Democracy and Education*, Ch. 15.
47. *Interest and Effort*, p. 81.
48. *Democracy and Education*, p. 246.

understood, its connections and possibilities unveiled and enriched. Properly dealt with, each starts with the world which the child knows in his local environment. Geography is broadly conceived as mathematical, astronomical, physiographic, topographic, political, and commercial. It serves to help children to find relations which obtain in ordinary physical events. History is used to illustrate the "activities and sufferings" of people whose affairs are connected to the child's own situation or whose affairs are different enough to offer striking contrasts.[49]

The activities and studies relevant to the first two types of interests introduce materials which gradually come to appeal to a third type of educative interest, one which is distinctively intellectual: "When any one becomes interested in a problem as a problem and in inquiry and learning for the sake of solving the problem, interest is distinctively intellectual." [50]

Science education apparently begins through active occupations of an ordinary sort, becomes more sophisticated through dealing with studies in geography (broadly conceived, as noted above), and reaches a specialized focus as problems themselves become highly specialized.[51] Mathematics as a subject of interest and study emerges in the same way as any specialized scientific interest or study. Games and work, and to a limited extent play, early lead the child to be interested in questions of quantity and magnitude. As Dewey remarks, when "the child is sufficiently mature, he passes without mental friction to conscious recognition [of number as used to value quantity]." This, he continues, "rests upon continuous experimenting and observation in a school where the child's number sense is developed strictly in connection with construction operation in manual training, cooking, sewing, and science work, where number relations are introduced as instrumental to practical valuations." [52]

There is a fourth type of educative interest which, like the third, is found in embryonic form almost from the outset of the child's life; namely, social interest in persons. Indeed, the early interest in *things* can be seen to be almost as one with the social

49. *Democracy and Education*, pp. 246–65.
50. *Interest and Effort*, pp. 83–84.
51. Cf. *Democracy and Education*, Ch. 17.
52. "Some Remarks on the Psychology of Number," *Pedagogical Seminary*, V (1898), 434.

interest since the child animistically infuses the nonsocial world with social or personal qualities.[53]

Dewey thinks history is the subject which capitalizes on this interest, and its highest achievement is the moral one of "cultivating a socialized intelligence." [54] Primitive, industrial, economic, art, and scientific history all point to the conditions for tragedy and triumph in the life of both individual and society: "Surely no better way could be devised of instilling a genuine sense of the part which mind has to play in life than a study of history which makes plain how the entire advance of humanity from savagery to civilization has been dependent upon intellectual discoveries and inventions, and the extent to which the things which ordinarily figure most largely in historical writings have been side issues, or even obstructions for intelligence to overcome." [55]

VOCATIONAL EDUCATION. The need for concentration on "active occupations" in childhood education requires, in particular, expanded resources in vocational education, resources which allow the school to help children move with ease and ever-growing competence into careers in industrial society. Elementary education, Dewey comments, arose in large part as a substitute for apprenticeship training, a substitute demanded by the introduction of new modes of production and distribution. Apprenticeship training seldom was particularly educative, in a genuine sense, since it neglected the theoretical for the practical. But elementary education also is not educative in a genuine sense because it typically does not pay close enough attention to the practical conditions for a career of rewarding, intelligent work.[56] The same is true of secondary education, since it does not fuse the theoretical and practical to lead students into careers of intelligent work in a workaday world ever more dependent upon sophisticated scientific and technological thought and devices.[57]

The changing demands of industry present a new need requiring educational reform. Dewey says that the need can be

53. *Interest and Effort*, pp. 84–89.
54. *Democracy and Education*, p. 254.
55. *Democracy and Education*, p. 254.
56. *Schools of To-morrow*, with Evelyn Dewey (New York: E. P. Dutton and Co., 1915), p. 237.
57. *Schools of To-morrow*, pp. 236–37.

indicated by calling attention to three moral principles. First, "never before was it as important as it is now that each individual should be capable of self-respecting, self-supporting, *intelligent* work." Second, in a highly interdependent society, social endeavors produce effects which extend throughout society. Under such a condition, "acquisition of modes of skill apart from realization of the social uses to which they may be put is fairly criminal." Third, science and technology race ahead to alter the conditions of both social and industrial life, threatening to make workers "blind cogs and pinions in the apparatus they employ," unless somehow the schools can help children fuse intelligence, work, and social responsibility.[58] Vocational education should lead to sophisticated social understanding and participation, as well as providing career training which enables the individual to retrain himself continuously.

MORAL EDUCATION. Just as active occupations can lay the groundwork for entry into a rich vocational and social life, so can they provide the basis for development of morality if there is a constant concern for the social import of the occupation undertaken and studied. The child, says Dewey, "is born with a natural desire to give out, to do, to serve."[59]

The emphasis, then, should be upon providing a social matrix in which this natural desire can be most fully fulfilled. In early education the child should work and study co-operatively with others in order to learn how community life is sustained and how it progresses through the joint efforts of men. To accomplish this, the school must function as a miniature community, and study and play are to be concerned with typical, important modes of the larger social life.[60] In active occupations, as opposed to bookish and isolated study, the child involves himself in give and take with others. The moral forces in the larger society, in the school community, and in the child himself, lead as a matter of course into the development of what Dewey considers the only viable type of morality—one rooted in habit and impulse. Occupations, or studies,

58. *Schools of To-morrow*, pp. 244–46. Cf. *Democracy and Education*, pp. 224–27.
59. *Moral Principles in Education* (Boston: Houghton Mifflin Co., 1909), p. 22. Cf. "Chaos in Moral Training," *Popular Science Monthly*, XLV (1894), 440–41.
60. *Democracy and Education*, p. 418.

are of moral value in the degree in which they enable the pupil sympathetically and imaginatively to appreciate the social scene in which he is a partaker; to realize his own indebtedness to the great stream of human activities which flow thru and about him; the community of purpose with the large world of nature and society and his consequent obligation to be loyal to his inheritance and sincere in his devotion to the interests which have made him what he is and given him the opportunities he possesses.[61]

In moral education, Dewey does *not* want occupations or studies used as a pretext for moralizing.[62] Moralizing may lead to the child's being conscious of moral lessons or precepts, but it is no guarantee of moral behavior. Indeed, it may produce moral outcomes which are "insecure and accidental." [63] Subjects which are used as the basis for moralizing, moreover, often have their very educative significance destroyed.[64]

Dewey is in favor of a *formal* study of ethics during or just before high school. The emphasis in the study of ethics is upon the common features of human interaction, with the students expected to formulate decisions concerning the ethical issue involved, the type of moral action required, and the type of concrete action which would appear most likely to accomplish

61. "The Moral Significance of the Common School Studies," *Topics for General Sessions: Moral and Religious Training in the Public Schools, November 5th and 6th, 1909, Elgin, Illinois*, Northern Illinois Teachers' Association, p. 27. Dewey concludes his statement: "If such moral training seems slow and roundabout, we may yet encourage ourselves with the reflection that virtue is not a miracle but a conquest, and character not an accident but the efficacious growth of organic powers" (p. 27).

62. *Moral Principles*, pp. 2, 40.

63. "Moral Significance of Common School Studies," pp. 21–22. Cf. "Teaching Ethics in the High School," *Educational Review*, VI (1893), 313–15.

64. For instance, speaking of the use of a piece of literature for such a purpose, Dewey comments: "Nothing is more absurd in theory or harmful in practice than first insisting upon the intrinsic ethical value of literature, and then impressing by suggestion, question, and discourse, the moral point or lesson to be derived from the piece of literature. What this really means is that the teacher has no faith in the moral force of the scene and ideas presented, but has great faith in his own conversation and personal influence. . . . The result is the destruction of the piece in question as a work of art; and whatever accidental moral influence accrues being due to the teacher's personality and method, it could have been got as well from the multiplication table by the exercise of a little ingenuity" ("Moral Significance of Common School Studies," pp. 22–23).

the moral aim. The aim of such a course, he says, is *"the formation of a sympathetic imagination for human relations in action*; this is the ideal which is substituted for training in moral rules."[65]

Dewey likewise rejects religious education which is a mere training in rules. We must assume that, unless somehow the universe is "out of gear," the child can and will find his religious way and power in a manner appropriate to his needs and interests. If children do not have such an ability and such potential power, then it is very hard to explain how adults ever attained it! Once again, moralizing or sermonizing is regarded by Dewey as a great danger: the problem is that of "bringing the child to appreciate the truly religious aspects of his own growing life, not one of inoculating him externally with beliefs and emotions which adults happen to have found serviceable to themselves." The religious qualities of life, like the moral ones, can themselves be destroyed by such a process.[66]

Genuine morality emerges naturally in average or above-average teaching-learning situations and is rooted in habit and impulse. But, when habit and impulse are thwarted by problematic moral situations, moral action in a sophisticated or reflective fashion is necessary. If one has entered fully into a genuinely democratic community, reflective moral thought will occur in a way which represents the highest form of moral integrity; and, in a society in which such thought is common in men, it represents one of the finest accomplishments of civilization.[67] Dewey's account of what constitutes reflective thinking about ethical or moral matters is not greatly different from the account of reflective thinking generally. The individual encounters  A) a situation in which his habits or low-level organic prizings are frustrated;  B) the frustration or blockage is responded to by an impulsive, anticipatory response with respect to what seems possible and desirable;  c) there is criticism and evaluation

65. "Teaching Ethics in the High School," p. 316.
66. "Religious Education as Conditioned by Modern Psychology and Pedagogy," *Proceedings of the Religious Education Association* (1903), pp. 61, 63–64. Cf. "Religion and Our Schools," *Hibbert Journal*, VI (1908), 808–9.
67. Probably the best account of the reflective moral act, and its relation to civilization, is found in *Ethics*, rev. ed., with James H. Tufts (New York: Henry Holt and Co., 1932). Pt. I (by Tufts) gives an historic view of the rise of civilization and reflective morality; Pt. II (by Dewey), Ch. 1, details the nature of the reflective moral act.

based upon a more detailed study of the situation;   D) there arises commitment to—"unified desire" for—that value which seems to be most obviously desirable in removing the blockage; and   E) there is action in which the individual chooses concretely and then judges the aptness of his choice, his previous habits, and accordingly will change (or rest content with) his previous beliefs, habits, values, and character.[68] Individuals or groups in conflict can, when they have a proper sense of community, be described as most effectively reaching agreement in this or a closely similar manner.[69]

ÆSTHETIC EDUCATION.     Æsthetic endeavor has a particularly important place in the education of the child, largely because it early and naturally flows from the child's desire to express himself. Drawing, music, dance, and storytelling are modes for channeling this desire. The central problems with æsthetic education are the same as with moral and religious education. On the one hand, some teachers tend to force on the very young standards which are abstract and remote. Thus æsthetic sensitivity is threatened, motivation is stifled, and the true quality of products in the heritage of art is lost or distorted for the child. On the other hand, other teachers tend to identify art education with unbridled or random freedom of expression. Because this approach violates the child's craving for developing structure and organization, it ultimately produces much the same effect as the first approach. Again, there is the need for freedom *and* discipline, both at a level pertinent to the child's capacities, interests, and situation.[70]

For Dewey the central fact is that art and science are at bottom rooted in the same principles and serve the same needs.[71] The principles are those constituted by intelligent insights into the technical, specialized ways of relating things; the fundamental needs are those of man's nature, especially his need for progressively harmonizing and enriching his experience. As

68. *Theory of Valuation* (International Encyclopedia of Unified Science, Vol. II, No. 4 [Chicago: University of Chicago Press, 1939]).

69. Dewey's views on this matter are summarized in Stanley, *Education and Social Integration*, pp. 208–17, 230–32. Also see Ch. 6 of *Public and Its Problems*.

70. "Individuality and Experience," pp. 1–2.

71. "Affective Thought in Logic and Painting," *Journal of the Barnes Foundation*, II (1926), 6.

Dewey says of paintings, "to make of paintings an educational means is to assert that the genuine intelligent realization of pictures is not only an integration of the specialized factors found in the paintings as such, but is such a deep and abiding experience of the nature of fully harmonized experience as sets a standard or forms a habit for all other experiences." [72]

We cannot expect the child to be interested in art and science as highly developed systems; but the child can make use of particular generalizations and techniques that make art and science vital. (Also, becoming *an* artist or *a* scientist is not the desire, or perhaps within the capacity, of every child.) Initial aims of schooling must include helping *every* child learn to think reflectively about key occupations in society and to find ways of obtaining æsthetic satisfaction—both in creation and appreciation.

Dewey does not think that the schools can do the job alone. Social conditions are such that drudgery is a commonplace; face-to-face community is much less common than previously. New modes of production and distribution constantly require redirection of individual talents. He argues that the schools should help children learn how to express effectively their natural propensities for intelligence, morality, religiosity, and æsthetic creation and appreciation. But the problem is not merely one of helping the child attain such individual power; it is one of community. Particularly it is one of making the school the type of community in which such individual-social qualities can and will come to fruition.

Earlier in this essay the question was raised as to where one shall look for the criteria which will give a defensible notion of the special functions of the school. One source of the answer has been provided and elaborated upon. It rests upon Dewey's conception of the aims of education and the nature of man and culture. A second source for the answer is found in Dewey's conception of, and proposals for, the administration of schools.

72. "Affective Thought," p. 9.

### The Administration of Schools

People acting together always employ some form of governmental or administrative mode of control. Dewey notes that, in a democracy, there are questions about how extensive that control should be in a political sense; [73] but, he leaves no doubt that it should be as extensive as possible in the social or moral sense. As he puts it,

> political democracy is not the whole of democracy. . . . It can be effectively maintained only where democracy is social—where, if you please, it is moral. . . . Since democracies forbid, by their very nature, highly centralized governments working by coercion, they depend upon shared interests and experiences for their unity and upon personal appreciation of the value of institutions for stability and defense.[74]

In the case of the governance or administration of schooling, Dewey thinks that the social-moral quality is sorely lacking. He thinks that children are taught by teachers who display little inclination to share vital experiences in such a way as to vivify the learning experience. The inclination is lacking because teachers are so governed by school administrators that they have no freedom to vivify either their students' or their own schooling experiences. He thinks that school administrators are so selected and governed by school boards that the administrators are incapable of extending freedom in any important way to teachers or students. Finally, he regards the school boards as reflecting the wishes of vested interest groups which stress an archaic, individualistic philosophy which stands in active opposition to ideals of social democracy. He does not go so far as Mark Twain, who remarks that God first created fools, something He did for practice before creating school boards. But Dewey does put the blame for the lack of social-moral qualities in schooling squarely and heavily on vested interest groups in society. In one unusually strong statement he remarks:

> There is little genuine relation between the existing social control of the school system and its educative work. In fact, the

73. "Democracy and Educational Administration," *School and Society*, XLV (1937), 459–60.
74. "Need for an Industrial Education in an Industrial Democracy," *Manual Training*, XVII (1916), 410.

connection that exists is detrimental to the truly educative work of the schools. School boards at present [1935], taking the country as a whole, are representative of a special class or group in the community, not of community interests. They regard themselves after the analogy of private employers of labor and the teaching staff as their hired men and women.

This situation is reflected in the administrative organization of the schools. On the one hand, there is little real co-operation between administrative officers and classroom teachers. The former make out courses of study, prepare syllabuses for instruction, and lay down methods of instruction. The latter take orders, and, in the degree in which they do so, their professional initiative is blunted, and their own work rendered routine and mechanical. On the other hand, the administrators are dependent for their jobs upon undue conformity to the desires of the economic class that is dominant in school boards as the agents of social control.[75]

In a word, Dewey sees great room for improvement throughout the system, and the basic administrative change he desires would grant a fair measure of administrative control to everyone, including teachers and students, within the educational system.

SCHOOL ADMINISTRATORS. It would be difficult to say just how important Dewey regards school administrators—superintendents, principals, etc.—in effecting democracy in education. In principle, they can be very important and, on occasion, Dewey does appeal to them. But it seems somewhat strange that he and they sought each other out so seldom especially since Dewey's experience as an administrator at the University of Chicago Laboratory School must have given him the basis for a continuing interest in the problems of school administration.[76] Also, he had been an admirer and friend of several gifted administrators, among whom was Colonel Francis Wayland

75. "The Need for Orientation," *Forum*, XCIII (1935), 334–35.
76. For three very good accounts, each from a different perspective, of Dewey's work at the Laboratory School, see: Melvin Charles Baker, *Foundations of John Dewey's Educational Theory* (New York: Teachers College Bureau of Publications, 1955), Ch. 7; Robert L. McCaul, "Dewey, Harper, and the University of Chicago," in *John Dewey: Master Educator*, 2d ed., eds. W. W. Brickman and Stanley Lehrer (New York: Society for the Advancement of Education, 1961), Chs. 4, 5, and 6; Arthur Wirth, *John Dewey as Educator: His Design for Work in Education (1894–1904)* (New York: John Wiley and Sons, 1966), Pt. I.

Parker, whose work in the Quincy (Massachusetts) school system and in Chicago wrought great change in American education.[77] One must also note that he did not often praise educational administrators. His later, urgent appeals to them on
behalf of the democratization of public education [78] were much
like his early appeals; [79] and, when he did note that some limited
progress had been made toward democratization, he did not
indicate that he thought that school administrators, as a group,
were primarily responsible.

On one occasion Dewey describes (in three brief paragraphs) what he takes to be "at least three phases" of the
function of administrators. The first of these is the "intellec-
tual-professional" one of determining how minds and character
are to be formed within the school and the social order. Part of
the responsibility of the administrator in this phase consists in
seeing that his own intellectual leadership is not so extensive as
to deny it to others in the school. Basically, his description of
intellectual leadership amounts to a veiled criticism of those
administrators who devise and enforce "teacher proof" (as they
are today called) curricula and teaching methods. Even when
administrator preplanning is not so complete, this brief statement concludes, "there are too few cases in which the teaching
corps takes an active and cooperative share in developing the
plan of education." [80]

The second phase of the administrative function consists of
personal-relations problems. The administrator must deal with a
large number of teachers who are dissimilar in training and
outlook, with politicians and ordinary citizens, and with his
school board. The superintendent, for instance, "is an interme-
diary between the teaching staff and the members of the public.
He is compelled to face two ways, and is fortunate if he can
escape the tendency towards a divided personality." [81]

The third phase of the administrative function involves "a

77. Cf. Merle Curti, *The Social Ideas of American Educators*
(Paterson, N.J.: Littlefield, Adams and Co., 1959), Ch. 11.

78. "Democracy and Educational Administration," p. 63.

79. "Democracy in Education," *Elementary School Teacher*, IV
(1903), 194–95. But cf. pp. 196–97, wherein Dewey does credit some
school administrators to a considerable degree.

80. "Toward Administrative Statesmanship," *Social Frontier*, I
(1935), 9.

81. "Toward Administrative Statesmanship," p. 9.

large amount of detail and routine." As school systems grow larger the administrator, if he is not careful, will become a tool of routine work. This trend, says Dewey, "is increased because the powerful influence of business standards and methods in the community affects the members of an educational system, and then teachers are regarded after the model of employees in a factory." [82]

Dewey thinks that the three phases require such divergent activities that good work in any one area will be negated by poor work in the others unless the school administrator has a clear, comprehensive, and defensible point of view—a philosophy of education. There is no mistaking what Dewey would have the philosophy of education be, although he describes it only briefly in his writings on school administration. It would be to transform society rather than merely perpetuate it. It would be to search for ways whereby coworkers could be given opportunity for significant measures of intellectual and moral control over the educational system. It would be to conceive public education as "essentially education of the public," all of the public affected by a school system, in such a way that the administrator communicates to his community "his own ideals and standards, inspiring others with the enthusiasm of himself *and his staff* for the function of intelligence and character in the transformation of society." [83]

The requirements stated and suggested by Dewey's discussion of the three phases of democratic administration demand almost the same incredible effort, intellectuality, and sensitivity of administrators as Dewey's conception of teaching-learning imposes upon teachers.

TEACHERS. Dewey gave numerous speeches and wrote numerous articles encouraging classroom teachers to become agents of educational and social transformation. There seems little doubt that Dewey saw teachers as the best and noblest hope for democratizing education. This is indicated not only in the number of addresses and articles which he prepared for audiences of teachers, but also by his active involvement in teacher unionization activities, by his work helping found the American Associa-

82. "Toward Administrative Statesmanship," p. 9. Dewey saw this same problem affecting higher education also. Cf. "Academic Freedom," *Educational Review*, XXIII (1902), 12.

83. "Toward Administrative Statesmanship," p. 10.

tion of University Professors, and by his appeals to school administrators to democratize schooling.

Dewey uses several arguments to defend the thesis that teachers' environments should be made more democratic. The first argument is the general but vital one that every institution should encourage all the social democracy possible for those conducting and those centrally affected by its work. The schools have a special obligation for operating as institutions in which social democracy is a *modus vivendi*; for, says Dewey,

> it is the main business of the family and the school to influence directly the formation and growth of attitudes and disposi- tions, emotional, intellectual and moral. Whether this educa- tive process is carried on in a predominantly democratic or non-democratic way becomes, therefore, a question of tran- scendent importance not only for education itself but for its final effect upon all the interests and activities of a society that is committed to the democratic way of life.[84]

Second, the teacher is in direct contact with the child. Nondemocratic control in all institutions directly or indirectly stifles the qualities of democratic citizenship. If the teacher is authoritarian, or the passive agent of an authoritarian system, then "there is bound to be an unfavorable reaction back into the habits of feeling, thought and action" of the student and thus, eventually, of the society.[85]

Primarily for the above reasons, Dewey maintains that each teacher should "have some regular and organic way in which he can, directly or through representatives democratically chosen, participate in the formation of the controlling aims, methods and materials of the school of which he is a part." [86]

However, Dewey thinks that teachers are partially at fault for their failure to gain a fair share of control in school adminis- tration. Particularly, teachers are charged with having an image of themselves which results in their being easy prey for nondem- ocratic control: they disdain considering themselves with the only other group, the workers on farms and in industry, who

84. "Democracy and Educational Administration," p. 460.
85. "Democracy and Educational Administration," p. 460. Also see "Democracy in Education," pp. 197–99; "Education as Politics," *New Republic*, XXXII (1922), 140; and "The Duties and Responsibilities of the Teaching Profession," *School and Society*, XXXII (1930), 188–89.
86. "Democracy and Educational Administration," p. 460.

face the same lack of control over their productive lives and the conduct of social affairs generally.

Dewey argues that teachers are engaged in the very same process of productive labor as are industrial wage earners.[87] To err by thinking otherwise leads to a second error, that of becoming isolated in sentiment and political action from those with whom one should join in common cause. Teachers are called upon to alter their image of themselves, and to avail themselves of the same unionization procedures which their fellow workers employ with promise of success. What is meant by "success" is the democratization of society, the equitable spreading of political and moral control to people who have been without it and who cannot be left without it if our society is to advance democratically. It is not to the private gain of teachers that Dewey appeals, of course, but to the ideal of a better education for each child and, thus, of a better and more just society. These are the ideals which will unite teachers in common task with kindred workers who seek the same goals in their own ways.

Dewey apparently had an unwavering belief that the unionization of teachers, and their co-operative work with other workers, would be the best way to attain more perfect political and moral democracy. His principle was simply that every teacher "should have some regular and organic way" of exercising a proper share of control over school affairs. Without question, Dewey knew the alternatives to unionization for teachers during his time, and he chose unionization as the only viable solution for effective democracy in education.

Before leaving the role of the teacher in the administration of schooling, it is necessary to note Dewey's response to an old argument for not giving teachers more freedom in determining the conduct of schools. It is the argument "that the average teacher is incompetent to take any part in laying out the course of study or in initiating methods of instruction or discipline." [88] Dewey notes that this is an argument which often has been used to check the progress of democracy. Democracy requires that individuals *have* a say about the conduct and goals of their

87. "Democracy in Education," p. 197.
88. "Why I Am a Member of the Teachers Union," *American Teacher*, XII (1928), 3–6; also: "The Teacher and the Public," *Vital Speeches*, I (1935), 278–79.

tasks. Democracy is in part justified or warranted because trust and involvement of practitioners *have* lifted the level of individual and social life more than planning and regimentation by the few, no matter how benevolent or sage the few might have been historically. How, asks he, "can we justify our belief in the democratic principle elsewhere, and then go back entirely upon it when we come to education?" [89]

Three clinching arguments are added. If teachers are so inept, as the argument claims, then surely they are too inept to carry out even preformulated dictates well; and, if they are so inept, it would seem to be that they need be given some chance to share in devising their duties and goals in order that they become proficient. Finally, if teachers are inept, it is because their situation is so bad that the best minds and talents are not drawn to the teaching profession. There is, says Dewey metaphorically, "a natural law of spiritual gravitation," and his meaning is simply that the nondemocratic schooling situations often drive good teachers out of teaching and many potentially good teaching recruits away. [90] Thus, by Dewey's logic, it cannot altogether be the teachers who are at fault.

STUDENTS.   Dewey obviously thinks that teachers should be very influential in the governance of schooling. The student also should be influential. The student's growth—emotionally, morally, intellectually, socially—is contingent upon his receiving progressively greater control and responsibility as successes and promise warrant. Every argument which Dewey used to challenge those who severely limit teacher participation can also be used to challenge those who would severely limit student participation.

But here one must again note that Dewey does not sanction the kind of absurd permissiveness which came to be associated with progressive education generally. It is true that children's interests are of vital importance when those interests are channeled in a way which will produce beneficial outcomes for both child and society. Yet, excessive permissiveness in classroom or school control is no more warranted than it is in the conduct of the teaching-learning process. A very important point regard-

89. "Democracy in Education," pp. 197–98.
90. "Democracy in Education," pp. 197–98.

ing administrative control is that young children are not fully developed moral agents. Their characters are not stable or formed. Their ability to foresee either personal or social consequences of action is limited.

There is an equally important point, however. How do the characters of children become formed and stable? How do children learn to foresee personal and social consequences of their actions? How do children become both free and responsible? In a word, how do children become the type of citizen which Dewey envisions as most desirable? Students become this type of citizen by progressively engaging in citizenship in a social structure which is concerned to see that their tendency toward sociality, self-discipline, co-operative inquiry, and control over their destinies are maximized.

### School and Society

Dewey has a faith that a lot of things are "right" with education and schooling, particularly American education and schooling. His theory of human nature, and of the democratic process which has begun to emerge, has optimistic connotations even though he certainly does not believe that there is any guarantee of inevitable progress.

But the possibility for progress, however modest, is there. The young child strives, however blindly and with however much frustration, for self-realization and control. So do adults strive, often blindly and often in a self-defeating fashion, to provide their offspring the conditions for self-realization and control. Why do adults strive in this manner? Perhaps it is because they have, as adults, goals which are comparable to those they had as children. There certainly are many things wrong with education; but, in education, says Dewey,

> meet the three most powerful motives of human activity. Here are found sympathy and affection, the going out of the emotions to the most appealing and the most rewarding object of love—a little child. Here is found also the flowering of the social and institutional motive, interest in the welfare of society and in its progress and reform by the surest and shortest means. Here, too, is found the intellectual and scientific motive, the interest in knowledge, in scholarship, in truth for its

own sake, unhampered and unmixed with any alien ideal. Copartnership of these three motives—of affection, of social growth, and of scientific inquiry—must prove as nearly irresistible as anything human when they are once united. And, above all else, recognition of the spiritual basis of democracy, the efficacy and responsibility of freed intelligence, is necessary to secure this union.[91]

91. "Democracy in Education," pp. 203–4.

## CHECKLIST

"Education and the Health of Women," in *The Early Works of John Dewey, 1882–1898,* Vol. I, pp. 64–68. Carbondale: Southern Illinois University Press, 1969.

"Psychology in High-Schools from the Standpoint of the College," in *Early Works,* I, 81–89.

"Health and Sex in Higher Education," in *Early Works,* I, 69–80.

"Inventory of Philosophy Taught in American Colleges," in *Early Works,* I, 116–21.

"Ethics in the University of Michigan," in *The Early Works of John Dewey, 1882–1898,* Vol. III, pp. 48–50. Carbondale: Southern Illinois University Press, 1969.

"A College Course: What Should I Expect from It?" in *Early Works,* III, 51–55.

"Philosophy in American Universities: The University of Michigan," in *Early Works,* III, 90–92.

"Lectures *vs.* Recitations: A Symposium," in *Early Works,* III, 147.

"The Scholastic and the Speculator," in *Early Works,* III, 148–54.

Review of *Elementary Psychology* by James Hutchins Baker, in *Early Works,* III, 190–92.

"How Do Concepts Arise from Percepts?" in *Early Works,* III, 142–46.

"Teaching Ethics in the High School," *Educational Review,* VI (Nov. 1893), 313–21.

"Why Study Philosophy?" *Inlander* (University of Michigan), IV (Dec. 1893), 106–9.

[Comments on Cheating], *Monthly Bulletin,* Students' Christian Association, XV (Dec. 1893), 38.

"The Chaos in Moral Training," *Popular Science Monthly,* XLV (Aug. 1894), 433–43.

*The Psychology of Number and Its Applications to Methods of Teaching Arithmetic,* with James Alexander McLellan (International Education Series, Vol. XXXIII, ed. William Torrey Harris). New York: D. Appleton and Co., 1895. xv, 309 pp.

Review by Henry Burchard Fine, *Science,* n.s. III (Jan. 1896), 134–36. Reply by Dewey, "Psychology of Number," *Science,* n.s. III (Feb. 1896), 286–89.

*Plan of Organization of the University Primary School.* [Caption-title; n.p., n.d., (Chicago 1895?)]. 25 pp.

"The Results of Child-Study Applied to Education," *Transactions of the Illinois Society for Child-Study,* I (Jan. 1895), 18–19.

["Letter to the Editor"], Chicago *Evening Post,* 19 Dec. 1895.

*Educational Ethics: Syllabus of a Course of Six Lecture-Studies.* Chicago: University of Chicago Press, 1895. 12 pp.

"Interest as Related to [Training of the] Will," in *Second Supplement to the Herbart Year Book for 1895,* pp. 209–46. Bloomington, Ill.: National Herbart Society, 1896. [Rev. ed., Chicago: The Society, 1899.] [Reprinted in C–16, pp. 260–85, with the title "Interest in Relation to Training of the Will."]

"Interpretation of the Culture-Epoch Theory," *Public-School Journal,* XV (Jan. 1896), 233–36.

"The Influence of the High School upon Educational Methods," *School Review,* IV (Jan. 1896), 1–12.

Review of *The Number Concept: Its Origin and Development* by Levi Leonard Conant, *Psychological Review,* III (May 1896), 326–29.

[Remarks on the Study of History in Schools], *School Review,* IV (May 1896), 272.

"A Pedagogical Experiment," *Kindergarten Magazine,* VIII (June 1896), 739–41.

"The Imagination in Education," Chautauqua *Assembly Herald,* 24 July 1896. [Summary of address (lecture) delivered by John Dewey at Chautauqua, New York, Thursday, 23 July 1896.]

"Comments on the Work in Pedagogy at the University of Chicago," Chautauqua *Assembly Herald,* 23 July 1896.

"Imagination and Expression," *Kindergarten Magazine,* IX (Sept. 1896), 61–69. [Revised by Dewey for use in the Chicago public schools study course.]

"Pedagogy as a University Discipline," I, *University [of Chicago] Record,* I (Sept. 1896), 353–55; II, ibid., I (Sept. 1896), 361–63.

Review of *Studies of Childhood* by James Sully, *Science,* n.s. IV (Oct. 1896), 500–502.

"The University School," *University [of Chicago] Record,* I (Nov. 1896), 417–19.

"Philosophy of Education." Stenographic report of class lectures, University of Chicago, 1896. 101 pp. (?). [Private collection of Frederick W. Eby.]

*Educational Psychology: Syllabus of a Course of Twelve Lecture-Studies.* Chicago: University of Chicago Press, 1896. 24 pp.

"Ethical Principles Underlying Education," in *Third Yearbook,* pp. 7–33. Chicago: National Herbart Society, 1897. [Reprinted separately by University of Chicago Press, 1903, 34 pp.; also reprinted in C–16, pp. 108–38.]

"Plan for Organization of Work in a Fully Equipped Department of Pedagogy," typewritten enclosure in letter to William R. Harper, Chicago, 8 Jan. 1897. 7 pp. [With marked reprint of "Pedagogy as a University Discipline." Published as Appendix in *American Educational Theory* by Charles J. Brauner. Englewood Cliffs, N.J.: Prentice-Hall, 1964.]

"My Pedagogic Creed," *School Journal,* LIV (Jan. 1897), 77–80. [Reprinted in C–12, pp. 3–17; C–15, pp. 19–32; C–16, pp. 427–39.]

"The Æsthetic Element in Education," in *Addresses and Proceedings,* pp. 329–30, and discussion, p. 346. National Educational Association, 1897.

"The Kindergarten and Child Study," in *Addresses and Proceedings,* pp. 585–86. National Educational Association, 1897.

"Criticisms Wise and Otherwise on Modern Child Study," in *Addresses and Proceedings,* pp. 867–68. National Educational Association, 1897.

"The Psychological Aspect of the School Curriculum," *Educational Review,* XIII (Apr. 1897), 356–69.

"The Interpretation Side of Child-Study," *Transactions of the Illinois Society for Child-Study,* II (July 1897), 17–27.

"Pedagogy I B 19: Philosophy of Education" [Syllabus], 1898–1899— Winter Quarter. [Chicago]: University of Chicago, [1898]. 11 pp.

"Report of the Committee on a Detailed Plan for a Report on Elementary Education," in *Addresses and Proceedings,* pp. 335–43. National Educational Association, 1898.

"Some Remarks on the Psychology of Number," *Pedagogical Seminary,* V (Jan. 1898), 426–34. (Reply to: Daniel Edward Phillips, "Number and Its Application Psychologically Considered," *Pedagogical Seminary,* V [Oct. 1897], 221–81.)

"The Primary-Education Fetich," *Forum,* XXV (May 1898), 315–28. [Reprinted in C–12, pp. 18–35.]

"[William Torrey] Harris's *Psychologic Foundations of Education,*" *Educational Review,* XVI (June 1898), 1–14.

"The Method of the Recitation," A Partial Report of a Course of Lectures Given at the University of Chicago. Privately Printed for the Use of Classes at the Oshkosh [Wisconsin] Normal School, 1899. 52 pp.

*The School and Society.* Chicago: University of Chicago Press, 1899. 125 pp. [All subsequent printings of the first edition have 129 pp., with an Author's Note on pp. 13–14; 2d ed., Chicago: University of Chicago Press, 1915, 164 pp.]

"Play and Imagination in Relation to Early Education," *Kindergarten Magazine,* XI (June 1899), 636–37; discussion, 638, 639–40; *School Journal,* LVIII (May 1899), 589.

"Principles of Mental Development as Illustrated in Early Infancy," *Transactions of the Illinois Society for Child-Study,* IV (Oct. 1899), 65–83.

"Theory of Logic." Stenographic report of class lectures, [H. Heath Bawden], University of Chicago, 1899–1900. 302 pp. [St. Louis University.]

[Discussion of address by William T. Harris], *Kindergarten Magazine,* XI (May 1899), 608.

"General Principles of Work, Educationally Considered" [Introduction to Group III], *Elementary School Record,* Monograph No. 1, pp. 12–15. Chicago: University of Chicago Press, Feb. 1900.

"Historical Development of Inventions and Occupations, General Principles" [Introduction to Group IV], *Elementary School Record,* Monograph No. 1, pp. 21–23. Chicago: University of Chicago Press, Feb. 1900.

"General Introduction to Groups V and VI," *Elementary School Record,* Monograph No. 2, pp. 49–52. Chicago: University of Chicago Press, Mar. 1900.

"Psychology of Occupations," *Elementary School Record,* Monograph No. 3, pp. 82–85. Chicago: University of Chicago Press, Apr. 1900.

"Reflective Attention," *Elementary School Record,* Monograph No. 4, pp. 111–13. Chicago: University of Chicago Press, May 1900.

"Froebel's Educational Principles," *Elementary School Record,* Monograph No. 5, pp. 143–51. Chicago: University of Chicago Press, June 1900.

"The Aim of History in Elementary Education," *Elementary School Record,* Monograph No. 8, pp. 199–203. Chicago: University of Chicago Press, Nov. 1900.

"The Psychology of the Elementary Curriculum," *Elementary School Record*, Monograph No. 9, pp. 221–32. Chicago: University of Chicago Press, Dec. 1900.

*Mental Development.* [Chicago], 1900. 21 pp., mimeographed.

"Psychology and Social Practice," *Psychological Review*, VII (Mar. 1900), 105–24; *Science*, n.s. XI (Mar. 1900), 321–33. [Reprinted separately as University of Chicago Contributions to Education, No. 2. Chicago: University of Chicago Press, 1901. 42 pp.]

"The Situation as Regards the Course of Study," in *Addresses and Proceedings*, pp. 332–48. National Educational Association, 1901. Also in *Educational Review*, XXII (June 1901), 26–49; *School Journal*, LXII (Apr., May 1901), 421–23, 445–46, 454, 469–71. [Reprinted in C–1, pp. 9–49, with the title "The Educational Situation: As Concerns the Elementary School."]

"Are the Schools Doing What the People Want Them to Do?" *Educational Review*, XXI (May 1901), 459–74; *Review of Education*, VII (June 1901), 10–11. [Reprinted in C–12, pp. 36–52, with the title "The People and the Schools."]

"Educational Lectures," June 1901. Ten lectures delivered "before the Brigham Young Academy Summer School." Reports made by Alice Young and edited by N. L. Nelson. 241 pp.

"The Place of Manual Training in the Elementary Course of Study," *Manual Training Magazine*, II (July 1901), 193–99. [Reprinted in C–12, pp. 53–61.]

*The Child and the Curriculum* (University of Chicago Contributions to Education, No. 5). Chicago: University of Chicago Press, 1902. 40 pp. [Reprinted in C–15, pp. 91–111; C–16, pp. 339–58.]

*The Educational Situation* (University of Chicago Contributions to Education, No. 3). Chicago: University of Chicago Press, 1902. 104 pp. [". . . revised papers originally prepared for three different bodies." The "Prefatory Word" and "III. As Concerns the College," pp. 7–8, 80–104, were published here for the first time.]

"Discussion," in *Addresses and Proceedings*, pp. 719–20. National Educational Association, 1902.

"The School as Social Center," in *Addresses and Proceedings*, pp. 373–83. National Educational Association, 1902. Also in *Elementary School Teacher*, III (Oct. 1902), 73–86.

"Academic Freedom," *Educational Review*, XXIII (Jan. 1902), 1–14.

"Current Problems in Secondary Education," *School Review*, X (Jan. 1902), 13–28. [Reprinted with the title "The Educational Situation: As Concerns Secondary Education," in C–1, pp. 50–79; C–16, pp. 404–21.]

"In Remembrance: Francis W. Parker," *Journal of Education*, LV (Mar. 1902), 199.

["In Memoriam: Colonel Francis Wayland Parker"], *Elementary School Teacher*, II (June 1902), 704–8. [Reprinted in C–10, pp. 95–99, with the title "Francis W. Parker."]

"The Battle for Progress," *Journal of Education*, LVI (Oct. 1902), 249.

"The University of Chicago School of Education," *Elementary School Teacher*, III (Nov. 1902), 200–203.

"Principles of Education." Stenographic report of class lectures, University of Chicago, 1902. 121 pp. [Northern Illinois University.]

"Religious Education as Conditioned by Modern Psychology and Pedagogy," *Proceedings of the Religious Education Association*, pp. 60–66. 1903.

"Introduction," in *The Psychology of Child Development* by Irving Walter King, pp. xi–xx. Chicago: University of Chicago Press, 1903.

"Discussion," *School Review,* XI (Jan. 1903), 17–20. (Remarks on: Frank Louis Soldan, "Shortening the Years of Elementary Schooling," *School Review,* XI [Jan. 1903], 4–17.)

"The Psychological and the Logical in Teaching Geometry," *Educational Review,* XXV (Apr. 1903), 387–99.

"The Organization and Curricula of the [University of Chicago] College of Education," *Elementary School Teacher,* III (May 1903), 553–62.

"Method of the Recitation," *Elementary School Teacher,* III (May 1903), 563.

Review of *The Place of Industries in Elementary Education* by Katharine Elizabeth Dopp, *Elementary School Teacher,* III (June 1903), 727–28.

"Democracy in Education," *Elementary School Teacher,* IV (Dec. 1903), 193–204. [Reprinted in C–12, pp. 62–73.]

"Total Isolation," *Journal of Education,* LVIII (Dec. 1903), 433.

*Education, Direct and Indirect.* [Chicago], 1904. 10 pp.

"The Relation of Theory to Practice in Education," in *Third Yearbook,* National Society for the Scientific Study of Education, Pt. 1, pp. 9–30. Bloomington, Ill.: Public School Publishing Co., 1904. [Reprinted in C–16, pp. 313–38.]

"Significance of the School of Education," *Elementary School Teacher,* IV (Mar. 1904), 441–53.

"Culture and Industry in Education," *Proceedings of the Joint Convention of the Eastern Art Teachers Association and the Eastern Manual Training Association* (1906), pp. 21–30.

"Education as a University Study," *Columbia University Quarterly,* IX (June 1907), 284–90.

*Ethics,* with James Hayden Tufts (American Science Series). New York: Henry Holt and Co., 1908. xiii, 618 pp.

"Religion and Our Schools," *Hibbert Journal,* VI (July 1908), 796–809. [Reprinted in C–10, pp. 504–16; C–11, pp. 702–15, with the title "The Schools and Religions"; C–12, pp. 74–86.]

"The Bearings of Pragmatism upon Education," First Paper, *Progressive Journal of Education,* I (Dec. 1908), 1–3; Second Paper, ibid., I (Jan. 1909), 5–8; Concluding Paper, ibid., I (Feb. 1909), 6–7.

*Moral Principles in Education* (Riverside Educational Monographs, ed. Henry Suzzallo). Boston: Houghton Mifflin Co., 1909. xii, 61 pp.

"History for the Educator," *Progressive Journal of Education,* I (Mar. 1909), 1–4.

"Symposium on the Purpose and Organization of Physics Teaching in Secondary Schools, XIII," *School Science and Mathematics,* IX (Mar. 1909), 291–92. [Closing paper in a series.]

"Teaching That Does Not Educate," *Progressive Journal of Education,* I (June 1909), 1–3.

"The Moral Significance of the Common School Studies," *Topics for General Sessions: Moral and Religious Training in the Public Schools, November 5th and 6th, 1909, Elgin, Illinois,* Northern Illinois Teachers' Association, pp. 21–27.

*How We Think.* Boston: D. C. Heath and Co., 1910. vi, 224 pp.

"Science as Subject-Matter and as Method," *Science,* n.s. XXXI (Jan. 1910), 121–27; *Journal of Education,* LXXI (Apr. 1910), 395–96, 427–28, 454. [Reprinted in C–10, pp. 765–75, with the title "Science and the Education of Man"; C–16, pp. 182–92.]

"Abstraction," 14; "Accommodation," 24–25; "Activity; Logical Theory

and Educational Implication of," 33–34; "Adaptation," 35; "Adjustment," 38–39; "Altruism and Egoism," 105–6; "Analogy—Logic of," 116; "Analysis and Synthesis," 117–19; "Art in Education," 223–25; "Causation," 553–54; "Character," 569–72; in *A Cyclopedia of Education*, I, ed. Paul Monroe. New York: Macmillan Co., 1911.
"Comparison," 163; "Conception," 171–72; "Concrete and Abstract," 173; "Conduct," 175; "Conflict," 175; "Control," 196; "Course of Study, Theory of," 218–22; "Culture and Culture Values," 238–40; "Culture Epoch Theory," 240–42; "Custom," 243–44; "Deduction," 275; "Definition," 280–81; "Democracy and Education," 293–94; "Demonstration," 294; "Determinism," 318; "Development," 319–20; "Dialectic," 321–22; "Didactics," 327; "Discipline," 336; "Dualism," 374; "Dynamic," 380; "Education," 398–401; "Education and Instruction," 414; "Effort," 421–22; "End in Education," 451; "Environment and Organism," 486–87; "Epistemology," 491; "Evidence," 528; "Evolution.—The Philosophical Concepts," 528–29; "Experience and the Empirical," 546–49; "Experiment in Education," 550–51; "Experimentation, Logic of," 554–55; "Explanation," 555; "External Object," 559; "Fact," 567–68; "Form and Content," 641–42; "Freedom, Academic," 700–701; "Freedom of Will," 705–6; "Function," 723–24; in *A Cyclopedia of Education*, II, ed. Paul Monroe. New York: Macmillan Co., 1911.
"The Problem of Truth," I. Why Is Truth a Problem? *Old Penn, Weekly Review of the University of Pennsylvania*, IX (Feb. 1911), 522–28; II. Truth and Consequences, ibid., IX (Feb. 1911), 556–63; III. Objective Truths, ibid., IX (Mar. 1911), 620–25.
"Is Co-education Injurious to Girls?" *Ladies Home Journal*, XXVIII (June 1911), 22, 60–61.
"The Study of Philosophy," *Columbia Monthly*, VIII (Aug. 1911), 367–68.
"Present Tendencies in College Education," in *College Requirements and the Secondary Curriculum; Addresses Presented at the Educational Conference Held at the University of Vermont in Connection with the Inauguration of Guy Potter Benton as President of the University, October 5, 1911*, p. 5. Burlington: University of Vermont, 1911.
"Generalization," 15; "Harmony, Harmonious Development," 217; "Hedonism," 242–43; "Humanism and Naturalism," 338–40; "Humanities, The," 340; "Hypothesis," 363–64; "Idea and Ideation," 370–71; "Idealism," 371–73; "Idealism and Realism in Education," 373–75; "Imitation in Education," 389–90; "Individuality," 421–22; "Induction and Deduction," 422–24; "Infancy, Theory of, in Education," 445–46; "Inference," 455; "Information," 455–56; "Initiative," 457; "Innate Idea," 458–59; "Interest," 472–75; "Intuition," 480; "Isolation," 499; "Judgment," 571–72; "Knowledge," 611–13; "Law," 655–56; in *A Cyclopedia of Education*, III, ed. Paul Monroe. New York: Macmillan Co., 1912.
"Education from a Social Viewpoint," trans. Jo Ann Boydston, *Educational Theory*, XV (Apr. 1965), 73–82, 104. [First published as "L'éducation au point de vue social," *L'année pédagogique*, III (1913), 32–48.]
*Interest and Effort in Education* (Riverside Educational Monographs, ed. Henry Suzzallo). Boston: Houghton Mifflin Co., 1913. x, 102 pp.
"Should Michigan Have Vocational Education Under 'Unit' or 'Dual' Control?" in *Bulletin 18*, pp. 27–34. Peoria, Ill.: National Society for the Promotion of Industrial Education, 1913.
"Introduction," in *Directory of the Trades and Occupations Taught at the Day and Evening Schools in Greater New York* by Henry Street

Settlement, Committee on Vocational Scholarships, pp. 2–3. New York, 1913.

"Liberal Education," 4–6; "Many-Sided Interest," 129; "Materialism," 158; "Metaphysics," 202; "Method," 202–5; "Monism," 296; "Morality and Moral Sense," 314; "Nativism," 386–87; "Nature," 387–89; "Neo-Humanism," 408; "Object and Subject," 523; "Opinion," 552; "Optimism," 552–53; "Pantheism," 598; "Pedantry," 622–23; "Personality," 649–50; "Pessimism," 654–55; "Phenomenalism," 666; "Philosophy of Education," 697–703; "Plato," 722–25; "Play," 725–27; "Pluralism," 730; in A Cyclopedia of Education, IV, ed. Paul Monroe. New York: Macmillan Co., 1913.

"Positivism," 18–19; "Pragmatism," 22–24; "Problem," 47; "Process," 49; "Progress," 51–52; "Proposition," 54; "Rationalism," 109; "Scientific Method," 292–93; "Self," 317–19; "Self-Consciousness," 319–20; "Sensationalism," 324–25; "Stimulus and Response," 422; "Subject," 446–47; "Syllogism," 492–93; "System," 496; "Term," 566; "Theism," 581; "Theory and Practice," 606–7; "Tradition," 621; "Transcendentalism," 622–23; "Truth," 632–33; "Universal," 651; "Utilitarianism," 700; "Validity," 703; "Values, Educational," 704–5; in A Cyclopedia of Education, V, ed. Paul Monroe. New York: Macmillan Co., 1913.

"An Undemocratic Proposal," American Teacher, II (Jan. 1913), 2–4; Vocational Education, II (May 1913), 374–77. [Revised and reprinted in Child Labor Bulletin, I (Feb. 1913), 69–74, with the title "Some Dangers in the Present Movement for Industrial Education"; revised version also printed separately as Pamphlet No. 190 of the National Child Labor Committee, New York, 1913.]

"Industrial Education and Democracy [Pt. 1]," Survey, XXIX (Mar. 1913), 870–71, 893. (Answer to: H. E. Miles, "Work and Citizenship: The Wisconsin Experiment in Industrial Education," Survey, XXIX [Feb. 1913], 682–85.)

"Cut-and-Try School Methods," Survey, XXX (Sept. 1913), 691–92.

"Professional Spirit Among Teachers," American Teacher, II (Oct. 1913), 114–16.

"Reasoning in Early Childhood," Teachers College Record, XV (Jan. 1914), 9–15. [Stenographic report of a paper.]

"Report on the Fairhope [Alabama] Experiment in Organic Education," Survey, XXXII (May 1914), 199.

"On Rousseau, Pestalozzi, Froebel and Montessori," Kindergarten-Primary Magazine, XXVI (Mar. 1914), 186; "On Social Motives in School Life," ibid., XXVI (Apr. 1914), 215; "On Pestalozzi," ibid., XXVI (May 1914), 251; "Comparison of Herbart and Froebel," ibid., XXVI (May 1914), 255–56. [Report by Jenny B. Merrill of lectures Dewey presented to the Federation of Child Study.]

"Psychological Doctrine and Philosophical Teaching," Journal of Philosophy, XI (Sept. 1914), 505–11.

"A Policy of Industrial Education," New Republic, I (Dec. 1914), 11–12; Manual Training and Vocational Education, XVI (Mar. 1915), 393–97.

Schools of To-morrow, with Evelyn Dewey. New York: E. P. Dutton and Co., 1915. 316 pp.

"The American Association of University Professors: Introductory Address," Science, n.s. XLI (Jan. 1915), 147–51.

"Industrial Education—A Wrong Kind," New Republic, II (Feb. 1915), 71–73.

"State or City Control of Schools?" New Republic, II (Mar. 1915), 178–80.

# GUIDE TO THE WORKS OF JOHN DEWEY

"Splitting Up the School System," *New Republic*, II (Apr. 1915), 283–84.

"Conditions at the University of Utah," letter in *Nation*, C (May 1915), 491–92; *Science*, n.s. XLI (May 1915), 685. [Signed by Dewey, as President of the American Association of University Professors, and by the Secretary and Committee Chairman.]

"Education *vs.* Trade-Training—Dr. Dewey's Reply," letter in *New Republic*, III (May 1915), 42–43. (Reply to: David Snedden, "Vocational Education," *New Republic*, III [May 1915], 40–42.)

"Dr. Dewey Replies," letter in *New Republic*, III (May 1915), 72. (Reply to: Charles P. Megan, "Parochial School Education," *New Republic*, III [May 1915], 72.)

["Letter to William Bagley and His Editorial Staff"], *School and Home Education*, XXV (Oct. 1915), 35–36.

"Professorial Freedom," letter in New York *Times*, 22 Oct. 1915. [Reprinted as "The Control of Universities," *School and Society*, II (Nov. 1915), 673.]

"Annual Address of the President," *Bulletin of the American Association of University Professors*, I (Dec. 1915), 9–13.

"Faculty Share in University Control," *Journal of Proceedings, Association of American Universities*, 17th (1915), 27–32.

*Democracy and Education: An Introduction to the Philosophy of Education* (Text-Book Series in Education, ed. Paul Monroe). New York: Macmillan Co., 1916. xii, 434 pp.

"Our Educational Ideal in Wartime," *New Republic*, VI (Apr. 1916), 283–84. [Reprinted in C–10, pp. 493–97, with the title "Our Educational Ideal"; C–12, pp. 87–91.]

"Nationalizing Education," in *Addresses and Proceedings*, pp. 183–89. National Education Association, 1916. Also in *Journal of the National Education Association*, I (Sept. 1916–June 1917), 183–89; *Journal of Education*, LXXXIV (Nov. 1916), 425–28. [Reprinted in C–12, pp. 112–21.]

"Method in Science-Teaching," in *Addresses and Proceedings*, pp. 729–34. National Education Association, 1916. Also in *General Science Quarterly*, I (Nov. 1916), 3–9; *Journal of the National Education Association*, I (Mar. 1917), 725–30.

"The Need of an Industrial Education in an Industrial Democracy," *Manual Training and Vocational Education*, XVII (Feb. 1916), 409–14.

"Organization in American Education," *Teachers College Record*, XVII (Mar. 1916), 127–41.

"Vocational Education," *New Republic*, VI (Mar. 1916), 159. [Review of *Learning to Earn* by John Augustus Lapp and Carl Henry Mote.]

"American Association of University Professors," letter in *Nation*, CII (Mar. 1916), 357. (Reply to: Letter of "A Looker-On in Babylon," *Educational Review*, LI [Mar. 1916], 310–13.)

"Universal Service as Education," I, *New Republic*, VI (Apr. 1916), 309–10; II, ibid., VI (Apr. 1916), 334–35. [Reprinted in C–10, pp. 465–73; C–12, pp. 92–100.]

"The Schools and Social Preparedness," *New Republic*, VII (May 1916), 15–16. [Reprinted in C–10, pp. 474–78; C–12, pp. 101–5.]

"American Education and Culture," *New Republic*, VII (July 1916), 215–17. [Reprinted in C–10, pp. 498–503; C–11, pp. 725–28, with the title "Education and American Culture"; C–12, pp. 106–11; C–16, pp. 289–94.]

"Professional Organization of Teachers," *American Teacher*, V (Sept. 1916), 99–101.

"Ill Advised," letter in *American Teacher*, VI (Feb. 1917), 31.

"Experiment in Education," *New Republic*, X (Feb. 1917), 15–16. [Reprinted in C–12, pp. 122–25.]

"Learning to Earn: The Place of Vocational Education in a Comprehensive Scheme of Public Education," *School and Society*, V (Mar. 1917), 331–35. [Reprinted in C–12, pp. 126–32, with the title "Learning to Earn."]

"Current Tendencies in Education," *Dial*, LXII (Apr. 1917), 287–89.

"Federal Aid to Elementary Education," *Child Labor Bulletin*, VI (May 1917), 61–66.

"The Modern Trend toward Vocational Education in Its Effect upon the Professional and Non-Professional Studies of the University," in *Association of American Universities Journal of Proceedings and Addresses of the Nineteenth Annual Conference* (1917), pp. 27–32. [Chicago]: The Association, 1917.

"The Case of the Professor and the Public Interest," *Dial*, LXII (Nov. 1917), 435–37.

"Democracy and Loyalty in the Schools," New York *Evening Post*, 19 Dec. 1917; *American Teacher*, VII (Jan. 1918), 8–10.

"Public Education on Trial," *New Republic*, XIII (Dec. 1917), 245–47. [Reprinted in C–12, pp. 133–38.]

*Education for Democracy*. [n.p., n.d.] 2 pp.

"Vocational Education in the Light of the World War," Vocational Education Association of the Middle West, *Bulletin No. 4*, Jan. 1918. [Chicago, 1918]. 9 pp.

"Introductory Word," in *Man's Supreme Inheritance* by Frederick Matthias Alexander, pp. xiii–xvii. New York: E. P. Dutton and Co., 1918.

"Reply to a Reviewer," letter in *New Republic*, XV (May 1918), 55. (Reply to: Randolph Bourne, Review of *Man's Supreme Inheritance* by Frederick Matthias Alexander, *New Republic*, XV [May 1918], 28–29.)

"Education and Social Direction," *Dial*, LXIV (Apr. 1918), 333–35. [Reprinted in C–12, pp. 139–43.]

"The Psychology of Drawing," *Teachers College Bulletin* (Series 10, No. 10, 1 Mar. 1919), pp. 3–5. New York: Teachers College, Columbia University, 1919. [First general publication of this article; it appears here with reprints of "Imagination and Expression" and "Culture and Industry in Education."]

"Aims and Ideals of Education," in *Encyclopaedia and Dictionary of Education*, I, ed. Foster Watson, 32–34. London: Sir Isaac Pitman and Sons, 1921.

"Some Factors in Mutual National Understanding," *Kaizō* [Reconstruction], III (Mar. 1921), 17–28.

"Education by Henry Adams," *New Republic*, XXIX (Dec. 1921), 102–3.

"America and Chinese Education," *New Republic*, XXX (Mar. 1922), 15–17. [Reprinted in C–10, pp. 303–9, with the title "America and China."]

"The American Intellectual Frontier," *New Republic*, XXX (May 1922), 303–5. [Reprinted in C–10, pp. 447–52.]

"Prof. John Dewey on the Hysteria Which Holds Teaching in Check," New York *World*, 27 Aug. 1922. [Interview with Charles W. Wood.]

"Education as a Religion," *New Republic*, XXXII (Sept. 1922), 63–65. [Reprinted in C–12, pp. 144–49, with the title "Education as Religion."]

"Education as Engineering," *New Republic*, XXXII (Sept. 1922), 89–91. [Reprinted in C–12, pp. 150–56.]

"Education as Politics," *New Republic,* XXXII (Oct. 1922), 139–41. [Reprinted in C–10, pp. 776–81; C–12, pp. 157–63.]

"Industry and Motives," *World Tomorrow,* V (Dec. 1922), 357–58. [Reprinted in C–10, pp. 739–44.]

"Mediocrity and Individuality," *New Republic,* XXXIII (Dec. 1922), 35–37. [Reprinted in C–10, pp. 479–85; C–12, pp. 164–70.]

"Individuality, Equality and Superiority," *New Republic,* XXXIII (Dec. 1922), 61–63. [Reprinted in C–10, pp. 486–92; C–12, pp. 171–77.]

"Culture and Professionalism in Education," *Columbia Alumni News,* XV (Oct. 1923), 31–32; *School and Society,* XVIII (Oct. 1923), 421–24. [Reprinted in C–12, pp. 178–83.]

"Future Trends in the Development of Social Programs Through the Schools," in *Proceedings of the National Conference of Social Work, Washington, May 16–23, 1923,* pp. 449–53. Chicago, 1923. Also in *Journal of Social Forces,* I (Sept. 1923), 513–17.

"Introduction," in *Constructive Conscious Control of the Individual* by Frederick Matthias Alexander, pp. xxi–xxxiii. New York: E. P. Dutton and Co., 1923.

"Social Purposes in Education," *General Science Quarterly,* VII (Jan. 1923), 79–91.

"Individuality in Education," *General Science Quarterly,* VII (Mar. 1923), 157–66.

" 'What Is a School For?' " New York *Times,* 18 Mar. 1923.

*Report and Recommendation upon Turkish Education.* 1924[?]. 27 pp. [Issued in English by Research and Measurement Bureau of the Ministry of Education, Dec. 1960; published in 1939 in Turkish, reprinted in 1952.]

"The Class Room Teacher," *General Science Quarterly,* VIII (Mar. 1924), 463–72.

"Science, Belief and the Public," *New Republic,* XXXVIII (Apr. 1924), 143–45. [Reprinted in C–10, pp. 459–64.]

"The Prospects of the Liberal College," *Independent,* CXII (Apr. 1924), 226–27. [Reprinted in C–12, pp. 184–89.]

"The Liberal College and Its Enemies," *Independent,* CXII (May 1924), 280–82. [Reprinted in C–12, pp. 190–97.]

"Foreign Schools in Turkey," *New Republic,* XLI (Dec. 1924), 40–42. [Reprinted in C–10, pp. 346–51, with the title "America and Turkey."]

*Experience and Nature* (Lectures upon the Paul Carus Foundation, First Series). Chicago, London: Open Court Publishing Co., 1925. xi, 443 pp. [2d ed., with a Preface, New York: W. W. Norton, 1929. ix, 1a–4a, 1–443 pp. 3d ed., LaSalle, Ill.: Open Court Publishing Co., 1958. xviii, 360 pp.]

"Dedication Address," *Journal of the Barnes Foundation,* I (May 1925), 3–6.

"Literature or Mathematics?" *School and Society,* XXI (June 1925), 786. [Comments on *Boy's Own Arithmetic* by Raymond Weeks.]

"What Is the Matter with Teaching?" *Delineator,* CVII (Oct. 1925), 5–6, 78.

"Individuality and Experience," *Journal of the Barnes Foundation,* II (Jan. 1926), 1–6. [Reprinted in C–11, pp. 619–27, with the title "Individuality and Freedom"; C–16, pp. 149–56; *Art and Education* by Dewey et al., pp. 175–83, Merion, Pa.: Barnes Foundation Press, 1929.]

"Art in Education—and Education in Art," *New Republic,* XLVI (Feb. 1926), 11–13.

"Affective Thought in Logic and Painting," *Journal of the Barnes Founda-*

*tion,* II (Apr. 1926), 3–9. [Reprinted in C–7, pp. 117–25, with the title "Affective Thought"; C–16, pp. 141–48; *Art and Education* by Dewey et al., pp. 63–72, Merion, Pa.: Barnes Foundation Press, 1929.]

"Foreword," in *The Story of Philosophy* by William James Durant, p. v. New York: Simon and Schuster, 1926. [First printing only.]

"Mexico's Educational Renaissance," *New Republic,* XLVIII (Sept. 1926), 116–18. [Reprinted in C–10, pp. 364–71; C–5, pp. 150–67.]

"Introduction," in *Militarizing Our Youth: The Significance of the Reserve Officers' Training Corps in Our Schools and Colleges* by Roswell P. Barnes, pp. 3–4. New York: Committee on Militarism in Education, 1927.

"Bankruptcy of Modern Education," *Modern Quarterly,* IV (June–Sept. 1927), 102–4. [Review of *The American College and Its Rulers* by John Ervin Kirkpatrick.]

"Progressive Education and the Science of Education," *Progressive Education,* V (July–Sept. 1928), 197–204. [Reprinted separately, Washington: Progressive Education Association, 1928, 14 pp.; also reprinted in C–15, pp. 113–26; C–16, pp. 169–81.]

[Address], in *A Tribute to Professor Morris Raphael Cohen, Teacher and Philosopher,* pp. 17–20. New York, 1928.

"Why I Am a Member of the Teachers Union," *American Teacher,* XII (Jan. 1928), 3–6.

"The Manufacturers' Association and the Public Schools," *Journal of the National Education Association,* XVII (Feb. 1928), 61–62.

"The Direction of Education," *School and Society,* XXVII (Apr. 1928), 493–97; *Teachers College Record,* XXX (Oct. 1928), 7–12. [Reprinted in C–12, pp. 198–202.]

"Brave Gospel," *Saturday Review of Literature,* IV (July 1928), 1016. [Review of *An Adventure with Children* by Mary Hammett Lewis.]

*The Sources of a Science of Education.* New York: Horace Liveright, 1929. 77 pp.

"Foreword," in *First Yearbook,* pp. xiii–xiv. New York: Eastern Commercial Teachers Association, 1929.

"Introduction: Group Action and Group Learning," in *Training for Group Experience: A Syllabus of Materials from a Laboratory Course for Group Leaders Given at Columbia University in 1927,* ed. Alfred Dwight Sheffield, pp. ix–xv. New York: The Inquiry, 1929.

"Freedom in Workers Education," *American Teacher,* XIII (Jan. 1929), 1–4.

"Labor Politics and Labor Education," *New Republic,* LVII (Jan. 1929), 211–14.

Response by Matthew Woll, *New Republic,* LVIII (Feb. 1929), 19–20.

Reply by Dewey, *New Republic,* LVIII (Feb. 1929), 20.

Further reply by Dewey, "Mr. Woll as a Communist Catcher," *New Republic,* LVIII (Mar. 1929), 99.

"General Principles of Educational Articulation," *School and Society,* XXIX (Mar. 1929), 399–406. [Reprinted in C–12, pp. 203–15.]

Review of *School and Society in Chicago* by George Sylvester Counts, *New Republic,* LVIII (Apr. 1929), 231–32.

["Juvenile Reading."], *Saturday Review of Literature,* VI (Nov. 1929), 398.

"Philosophy and Education," in *Addresses Delivered at the Dedication of the New Campus and New Buildings of the University of California at Los Angeles,* pp. 46–56. Berkeley: University of California Press, 1930.

"How Much Freedom in New Schools?" *New Republic*, LXIII (July 1930), 204–6. [Reprinted in C–12, pp. 216–23.]

"Our Illiteracy Problem," *Pictorial Review*, XXXI (Aug. 1930), 28, 65, 73.

"The Duties and Responsibilities of the Teaching Profession," *School and Society*, XXXII (Aug. 1930), 188–91. [Reprinted in C–12, pp. 224–29.]

*The Way Out of Educational Confusion*. Cambridge: Harvard University Press, 1931. 41 pp.

*American Education Past and Future*. [Chicago]: University of Chicago Press, 1931. 14 pp. Also in *School and Society*, XXXIV (Oct. 1931), 579–84, with the title "Some Aspects of Modern Education."

[Remarks], in *The Curriculum for the Liberal Arts College*, p. 7. Winter Park, Fla.: Rollins College, 1931. [Report of the Curriculum Conference held at Rollins College, 19–24 Jan. 1931; John Dewey, Chairman.]

"College Sons—and Parents," *New Republic*, LXV (Feb. 1931), 332–33. [Review of *Life in College* by Christian Gauss.]

"Teachers as Citizens," *American Teacher*, XVI (Oct. 1931), 7. [Report by Anna L. P. Collins of an address by Dewey before Local 195 of the American Federation of Teachers at Cambridge, Mass., 9 Apr. 1931.]

*Ethics*, with James Hayden Tufts. New York: Henry Holt and Co., 1932. xiii, 528 pp. [Rev. ed., with Preface to the 1932 Edition. The 1908 edition has been completely revised, with "about two-thirds of the present edition . . . newly written, and frequent changes in detail . . . in the remainder."]

"Introduction," in *The Use of the Self: Its Conscious Direction in Relation to Diagnosis, Functioning and the Control of Reaction* by Frederick Matthias Alexander, pp. xiii–xix. New York: E. P. Dutton and Co., 1932.

"Education and Birth Control," *Nation*, CXXXIV (Jan. 1932), 112.

"Monastery, Bargain Counter, or Laboratory in Education?" *Barnwell Bulletin* (Central High School, Philadelphia), IX (Feb. 1932), 51–62. [Reprinted in C–12, pp. 230–43.]

"Political Interference in Higher Education and Research," *School and Society*, XXXV (Feb. 1932), 243–46. [Reprinted in C–12, pp. 244–49.]

"The Schools and the White House Conference," *American Teacher*, XVI (Feb.–Mar. 1932), 3–4.

"Dewey Describes Child's New World," New York *Times*, 10 Apr. 1932.

"Bending the Twig," *New Republic*, LXX (Apr. 1932), 242–44. [Review of *The Theory of Education in the United States* by Albert Jay Nock.]

"The Economic Situation: A Challenge to Education," *Journal of Home Economics*, XXIV (June 1932), 495–501. [Reprinted in C–12, pp. 260–68.]

"The Meiklejohn Experiment," *New Republic*, LXXII (Aug. 1932), 23–24. [Review of *The Experimental College* by Alexander Meiklejohn.]

"Making Soviet Citizens," *New Republic*, LXXI (June 1932), 104. [Review of *New Minds: New Men?* by Thomas Woody and *History of Russian Educational Policy* by Nicholas Hans.]

*How We Think*. Boston: D. C. Heath and Co., 1933. x, 301 pp. [Expanded, revised, and rewritten edition of the 1910 *How We Think*.]

"The Social-Economic Situation and Education" and "The Underlying Philosophy of Education," with John Lawrence Childs, in *The Educa-*

*tional Frontier,* ed. William Heard Kilpatrick, pp. 32–72, 287–319. New York, London: Century Co., 1933.

"The Crisis in Education," *American Teacher,* XVII (Apr. 1933), 5–9. [Reprinted separately, n.p., n.d., 16 pp.]

"Education and Our Present Social Problems," *School and Society,* XXXVII (Apr. 1933), 473–78; *Educational Method,* XII (Apr. 1933), 385–90. [Reprinted in C–12, pp. 250–59.]

"Dewey Outlines Utopian Schools," New York *Times,* 23 Apr. 1933.

"On the Grievance Committee's Report," *Union Teacher* (Teachers Union of the City of New York), X (May 1933), 2–4.

"Shall We Abolish School 'Frills'? No," *Rotarian,* XLII (May 1933), 18–19, 49; *Modern Thinker,* III (June 1933), 149–53. (Reply to: Henry Louis Mencken, "Shall We Abolish School 'Frills'? Yes," *Rotarian,* XLII (May 1933), 16–17, 48.)

"Why Have Progressive Schools?" *Current History,* XXXVIII (July 1933), 441–48. [Reprinted in C–12, pp. 269–81.]

"To Save the Rand School," *Nation,* CXXXVII (July 1933), 47.

"Education for a Changing Social Order," in *Addresses and Proceedings,* pp. 744–52. National Education Association, 1934. [Reprinted separately, New York: League for Industrial Democracy, 1934, 1949, 14 pp., with the title "Education and the Social Order."]

"Democracy and Education" (Comment and Criticism by Some Educational Leaders in Our Universities, III), *The Activity Movement,* National Society for the Study of Education, Thirty-third Yearbook, pp. 81–86. Bloomington, Ill.: The Society, 1934.

"The Supreme Intellectual Obligation," *Science Education,* XVIII (Feb. 1934), 1–4; *Science,* n.s. LXXIX (Mar. 1934), 240–43. [Reprinted in C–12, pp. 282–87.]

"Tomorrow May Be Too Late: Save the Schools Now," *Good Housekeeping,* XCVIII (Mar. 1934), 20–21, 222, 225–27. [Interview with Katherine Glover.]

"Individual Psychology and Education," *Philosopher* (London), XII (Apr. 1934), 56–62.

"Character Training for Youth," *Rotarian,* XLV (Sept. 1934), 6–8, 58–59.

"The Need for a Philosophy of Education," *New Era in Home and School* (London), XV (Nov. 1934), 211–17. [Reprinted in C–12, pp. 288–99; C–16, pp. 3–14.]

"Can Education Share in Social Reconstruction?" *Social Frontier,* I (Oct. 1934), 11–12.

"Radio's Influence on the Mind," *School and Society,* XL (Dec. 1934), 805. [Summary of a radio address.]

"Foreword," in *Education in the Soviet Union,* ed. William Allan Neilson, p. 3. New York: American Russian Institute, 1935.

"Introduction," in *Growth: A Study of Johnny and Jimmy* by Myrtle Byram McGraw, pp. ix–xiii. New York: D. Appleton-Century Co., 1935.

"The Teacher and His World," *Social Frontier,* I (Jan. 1935), 7. [Reprinted in C–12, pp. 300–302; C–8, pp. 70–72.]

"The Crucial Role of Intelligence," *Social Frontier,* I (Feb. 1935), 9–10. [Reprinted in C–8, pp. 80–82, with the title "The Teacher and His World."]

"Toward Administrative Statesmanship," *Social Frontier,* I (Mar. 1935), 9–10. [Reprinted in C–8, pp. 66–69, with the title "Democracy and Educational Administration."]

"The Teacher and the Public," *Vital Speeches,* I (Jan. 1935), 278–79;

*American Teacher,* XIX (Mar.–Apr. 1935), 3–4. [Reprinted in C–12, pp. 303–7.]

"United, We Shall Stand," *Social Frontier,* I (Apr. 1935), 11–12; *School and Community,* XXI (Apr. 1935), 143–45. [Reprinted in C–8, pp. 72–76, with the title "The Teacher and His World."]

"Youth in a Confused World," *Social Frontier,* I (May 1935), 9–10. [Reprinted in C–12, pp. 308–10.]

"Government and Children," *American Teacher,* XIX (May–June 1935), 20.

"The Need for Orientation," *Forum,* XCIII (June 1935), 333–35. [First article in "Education and Our Society, A Debate."] [Reprinted in C–8, pp. 88–92.] (See second article: Tyler Dennett, "Education Cannot Lead," *Forum,* XCIII [June 1935], 335–37.)

"Toward a National System of Education," *Social Frontier,* I (June 1935), 9–10. [Reprinted in C–12, pp. 311–15.]

"Introduction" and Appendix II: "The Theory of the Chicago Experiment," in *The Dewey School: The Laboratory School of the University of Chicago 1896–1903* by Katherine Camp Mayhew and Anna Camp Edwards, pp. xv–xvi, 463–77; new matter by Dewey also on pp. 361–62, 365–72, 414–15, 417, 431–32. New York: D. Appleton-Century Co., 1936.

"Introduction," in *Self Government and Politics in School* by Richard Ward Greene Welling. (Binder's title; bound collection of articles and reprints.)

"Education and New Social Ideals," *Vital Speeches,* II (Feb. 1936), 327–28.

"The Social Significance of Academic Freedom," *Social Frontier,* II (Mar. 1936), 165–66. [Reprinted in C–12, pp. 320–24; C–8, pp. 76–80, with the title "The Teacher and His World."]

"Class Struggle and the Democratic Way," *Social Frontier,* II (May 1936), 241–42. [Reprinted in C–11, pp. 696–702, with the title "Educators and the Class Struggle"; C–12, pp. 325–30.]

"Anniversary Address," *Journal of the Michigan Schoolmasters' Club 1936* (University of Michigan Official Publication), XXXVIII (July 1936), 5–13.

"Authority and Resistance to Social Change," *School and Society,* XLIV (Oct. 1936), 457–66. [Reprinted in C–8, pp. 93–110.]

"Horace Mann Today," *Social Frontier,* III (Nov. 1936), 41–42.

"Rationality in Education," *Social Frontier,* III (Dec. 1936), 71–73. [Discussion of *The Retreat from Reason* by Lancelot Hogben and *The Higher Learning in America* by Robert Maynard Hutchins.] [Reprinted in C–12, pp. 331–36.]

"Education, the Foundation for Social Organization," in *Educating for Democracy, a Symposium,* pp. 37–54. Yellow Springs, Ohio: Antioch Press, 1937.

"Freedom," in *Implications of Social-Economic Goals for Education: A Report,* National Education Association, Committee on Social-Economic Goals, pp. 99–105. Washington: The Association, 1937.

"The Forward View: A Free Teacher in a Free Society," with Goodwin Watson, in *The Teacher and Society* (First Yearbook of the John Dewey Society), pp. 330–45. New York: D. Appleton-Century Co., 1937.

"President Hutchins' Proposals to Remake Higher Education," *Social Frontier,* III (Jan. 1937), 103–4.

Response by Robert Maynard Hutchins, "Grammar, Rhetoric, and Mr. Dewey," *Social Frontier,* III (Feb. 1937), 137–39.

Reply by Dewey, " 'The Higher Learning in America,' " *Social Frontier,* III (Mar. 1937), 167–69.

"The Challenge of Democracy to Education," *Progressive Education,* XIV (Feb. 1937), 79–85. [Reprinted in C–8, pp. 46–56.]

"Righting an Academic Wrong," *New Republic,* LXXXX (Mar. 1937), 242.

"The Educational Function of a Museum of Decorative Arts," *Chronicle of the Museum for the Arts of Decoration of Cooper Union* (New York), I (Apr. 1937), 93–99.

"Democracy and Educational Administration," *School and Society,* XLV (Apr. 1937), 457–62. [Reprinted in C–11, pp. 400–404 and 716–21, with the titles, "The Democratic Form" and "Democracy in the Schools"; C–12, pp. 337–47; C–8, pp. 57–66.]

" 'Either—Or,' " *Nation,* CXLIV (Apr. 1937), 412–13. [Review of *Education and the Class Struggle: A Critical Examination of the Liberal Educator's Program for Social Reconstruction* by Zalmen Slesinger.]

"Education and Social Change," *Social Frontier,* III (May 1937), 235–38. [Reprinted in C–11, pp. 691–96; C–12, pp. 348–58.]

"Educational Philosophy." Stenographic typescript of eighteen hours of lectures, Summer, 1937, University of Cincinnati. 237 pp.

*Experience and Education.* New York: Macmillan Co., 1938. xii, 116 pp.

"To Those Who Aspire to the Profession of Teaching," in *My Vocation . . . or What Eminent Americans Think of Their Calling,* comp. Earl Granger Lockhart, pp. 325–34. New York: H. W. Wilson Co., 1938.

*Democracy and Education in the World of Today.* New York: Society for Ethical Culture, 1938. 15 pp. [Reprinted in C–12, pp. 359–70; C–8, pp. 34–45.]

"The Relation of Science and Philosophy as the Basis of Education," *School and Society,* XLVII (Apr. 1938), 470–73. [Reprinted in C–8, pp. 164–68; C–16, pp. 15–19.]

"What Is Social Study?" *Progressive Education,* XV (May 1938), 367–69. [Reprinted in C–8, pp. 180–83.]

"Education, Democracy, and Socialized Economy," *Social Frontier,* V (Dec. 1938), 71–72.

*Theory of Valuation* (International Encyclopedia of Unified Science, Vol. II, No. 4). Chicago: University of Chicago Press, 1939. 67 pp.

"Introduction," with William Heard Kilpatrick, in *Talks to Teachers on Psychology* by William James, pp. iii–viii. New ed. New York: Henry Holt and Co., 1939.

"Education: 1800–1939," *Vermont Alumnus,* XVIII (May 1939), 169–70, 188–89.

"College Youth Better Mannered," *Vermont Alumnus,* XVIII (June 1939), 196–97. [Interview with Mary Spargo Wardwell.]

"A Philosopher's Philosophy," *New York Times,* 15 Oct. 1939. [Interview with Samuel Johnson Woolf.]

"A Foreword to This Issue," *Educational Trends,* VII (Nov.–Dec. 1939), 5.

"Higher Learning and War," *Bulletin of the American Association of University Professors,* XXV (Dec. 1939), 613–14.

[Quotation from a Letter to Nelson Prentiss Mead, Acting President of City College, Defending the Appointment of Bertrand Russell], New York *Times,* 12 Mar. 1940.

"Investigating Education," New York *Times,* 6 May 1940.

Response by Merwin Kimball Hart, "Dr. Dewey's Stand Disputed," New York *Times*, 9 May 1940.

Reply by Dewey, "Censorship Not Wanted," New York *Times*, 14 May 1940.

"The Case for Bertrand Russell," *Nation*, CL (June 1940), 732–33.

[Statement on Academic Freedom], New York *Times*, 5 Oct. 1940.

"Introduction" and "Social Realities *versus* Police Court Fictions," in *The Bertrand Russell Case*, eds. John Dewey and Horace M. Kallen, pp. 7–10, 55–74. New York: Viking Press, 1941.

"Address of Welcome," in *Thirty-five Years of Educational Pioneering* (L.I.D. Pamphlet Series), pp. 3–6. New York: League for Industrial Democracy, 1941.

"The Basic Values and Loyalties of Democracy," *American Teacher*, XXV (May 1941), 8–9.

"For a New Education," *New Era in Home and School* (London), XXII (June 1941), 134–35.

[Statement on Released Time Bill], New York *Times*, 14 Nov. 1940.

"Introduction," in *The Little Red Schoolhouse* (New York City) by Agnes De Lima and the Staff of the Little Red Schoolhouse, pp. ix–x. New York: Macmillan Co., 1942.

"The Democratic Faith and Education," *Antioch Review*, IV (June 1944), 274–83. [Reprinted in C–8, pp. 23–33.]

"Challenge to Liberal Thought," *Fortune*, XXX (Aug. 1944), 155–57, 180, 182, 184, 186, 188, 190. [Reprinted in C–8, pp. 143–59.]

Response by Alexander Meiklejohn, *Fortune*, XXXI (Jan. 1945), 207–8, 210, 212, 214, 217, 219.

Rejoinder by Dewey, *Fortune*, XXXI (Mar. 1945), 10, 14.

Further reply by Meiklejohn, *Fortune*, XXXI (Mar. 1945), 14.

Letter from Dewey, *Fortune*, XXXI (Mar. 1945), 14.

"The Problem of the Liberal Arts College," *American Scholar*, XIII (Oct. 1944), 391–93. [Reprinted in C–8, pp. 83–87.]

"John Dewey, at 85, Defends Doctrines," New York *Times*, 20 Oct. 1944. [Interview.]

"Introduction," in "Method in Science Teaching," *Science Education*, XXIX (Apr.–May 1945), 119–20. [Written by Dewey, 1 Mar. 1945, to accompany reprint of article first published in *Addresses and Proceedings*, National Education Association, 1916.]

"Foreword," in *Education in the British West Indies* by Eric Williams, pp. vii–viii. Port-of-Spain, Trinidad, B.W.I.: Guardian Commercial Printery, 1946.

"Foreword," in *Education for What Is Real* by Earl C. Kelley, pp. v–vi. New York: Harper and Bros., 1947.

"S.2499: Its Antidemocratic Implications," *Nation's Schools*, XXXIX (Mar. 1947), 20–21; *Progressive Education*, XXIV (Apr. 1947), 206–7.

"Boyd H. Bode: An Appreciation," *Teachers College Record*, XLIX (Jan. 1948), 266–67.

"Communists as Teachers," New York *Times*, 21 June 1949.

"John Dewey, at 90, Reiterates His Belief that Good Schools Are Essential in a Democracy," New York *Times*, 16 Oct. 1949. [Interview with Benjamin Fine.]

[Message to the American Federation of Teachers], *American Teacher*, XXXIV (Oct. 1949), 16.

"A Statement to the Society," in *A History of the National Society of College Teachers of Education, (1902–1950)*, pp. 2–3. [N.p., n.d.; written 11 Nov. 1950.]

"Introduction," in *William Heard Kilpatrick: Trail Blazer in Education* by Samuel Tenenbaum, pp. vii–x. New York: Harper and Bros., 1951.

"Introduction," in *The Use of Resources in Education* by Elsie Ripley Clapp, pp. vii–xi. New York: Harper and Bros., 1952. [Reprinted in C–15, pp. 127–34.]

*Lectures in the Philosophy of Education, 1899.* Ed. Reginald Archambault. New York: Random House, 1966. 366 pp. [Stenographic report of class lectures.]

# 11

# Dewey's Critical and Historical Studies

## MAX H. FISCH

UNDER THIS head are grouped book reviews and review articles; essays in interpretation and criticism of classical texts and of philosophers and movements in the history of philosophy; contributions to dictionaries and encyclopedias; and Dewey's one anthology (*The Living Thoughts of Thomas Jefferson*). Reviews listed under previous heads are not repeated here, but I shall refer to a few of them, and also to chapters of historical interpretation and criticism in major works already discussed.

Since interpretation and criticism are integral to the greater part of Dewey's work, and history also to much of it, some degree of arbitrariness attaches to the present list. It was arrived at less by selection than by nonselection. If an item could be readily placed under one of the previous heads by reason of topic or subject-matter, it was placed there. Even so, the list is so long that not everything in it can be mentioned in this essay, and very little of it can be discussed. Since Dewey's interpretation of Greek philosophy has been most studied,[1] and since he took little account of medieval philosophy, I shall emphasize modern philosophy, and I shall draw my illustrations more particularly from American philosophy.

But first I must give some preliminary indications of the

1. John Herman Randall, Jr., "Dewey's Interpretation of the History of Philosophy," in *The Philosophy of John Dewey* (Library of Living Philosophers, Vol. I, ed. Paul Arthur Schilpp [Evanston, Chicago: Northwestern University, 1939]), pp. 77–102; John P. Anton, "John Dewey and Ancient Philosophies," *Philosophy and Phenomenological Research*, XXV (1965), 477–99; Frederick M. Anderson, "Dewey's Experiment with Greek Philosophy," *International Philosophical Quarterly*, VII (1967), 86–100.

range, the general characteristics, the occasions, and the media of publication of Dewey's critical and historical studies.

To begin with, "history and criticism" is an accurate brief description of Dewey's training in philosophy, as well as of his early teaching and writing. Scottish and Kantian intuitionalism was the critical standpoint of his teacher Torrey at Vermont, and of Dewey's first two published essays.[2] Hegelian idealism was the critical standpoint of his teacher Morris at The Johns Hopkins, of Dewey's early teaching, and of the rest of his early writing.

Morris had translated Ueberweg's *History of Philosophy*, and had inserted long passages on two of his own teachers in Germany, Ulrici and Trendelenburg. That on Ulrici he took from Erdmann, but that on Trendelenburg he composed himself. He thereby gave even greater prominence than Ueberweg had given to the "Ideal Realism" that Ulrici and Trendelenburg shared with Schleiermacher; the attempt, that is, "to effect the harmonious union" of the idealistic (or subjective) and the realistic (or objective) elements in Kant's philosophy, which Kant had left "without mediation, side by side."[3] It was by way of an Aristotelianized Hegelianism that Trendelenburg's synthesis was effected, and it was his form of Ideal Realism that Morris and Dewey adopted. Their Hegelian idealism, therefore, was, more exactly, the Aristotelianized Hegelianism of Trendelenburg. For Dewey, though not for Morris, it was a solvent powerful enough to assimilate "the new psychology," physiological and experimental, that was brought from Germany by another of Dewey's Hopkins teachers, G. Stanley Hall. Even for Dewey, however, it was not powerful enough to assimilate the logic of his third Hopkins teacher, C. S. Peirce, though Peirce, like his father before him, was also an Ideal Realist, and also, like Dewey, engaged in assimilating the new psychology.[4]

2. "The Metaphysical Assumptions of Materialism," *Journal of Speculative Philosophy*, XVI (1882), 208–13; "The Pantheism of Spinoza," ibid., XVI (1882), 249–57. Reprinted in *The Early Works of John Dewey, 1882–1898*, Vol. I (Carbondale: Southern Illinois University Press, 1969), pp. 3–8, 9–18. See Lewis E. Hahn's Introduction, pp. xxiii–xxv.

3. Frederick Ueberweg, *History of Philosophy*, II, trans. George S. Morris (New York: Charles Scribner and Co., 1873), 136. Passage on Ulrici, pp. 299–305; on Trendelenburg, pp. 325–30.

4. Peirce and his father were closer to Ulrici; see Peirce's definition of ideal-realism in the *Century Dictionary* (1889–91), p. 2974.

In each of Dewey's two years at The Johns Hopkins (1882–84), Morris taught only the first half-year there and the second at Michigan. In the first half of 1882–83, Dewey took Morris's lecture courses on British philosophy and on Hegel's philosophy of history, and his seminar on Plato's *Theaetetus* and Aristotle's *De anima*; in the first half of 1883–84, his lecture course on German philosophy from Leibniz to Hegel, and his seminar on Spinoza's *Ethics*. The course in British philosophy prompted Dewey's third published paper, a criticism of Spencer, which was presented to the Metaphysical Club at Hopkins in December 1882.[5] Dewey himself taught a continuation of that course in the second half-year, using Morris's translation of Ueberweg as text. In April 1883 he presented a paper to the Metaphysical Club on "Hegel and the Theory of Categories," which he did not publish. A companion piece, "Kant and Philosophic Method," written about the same time, accompanied his application for a fellowship for the following year.[6]

In his second year, Dewey wrote a thesis on "The Psychology of Kant," as opposed to his logic. No copy survives, but its bearings may be guessed from the fellowship essay, from letters, and from subsequent publications.[7] He also presented three papers to the Metaphysical Club.[8] Only the third of these, on "The New Psychology," was published. The new psychology includes physiological psychology, which for the first time has put psychology on an experimental footing; but it finds both

5. "Knowledge and the Relativity of Feeling," *Journal of Speculative Philosophy*, XVII (1883), 56–70; *Early Works*, I, 19–33; cf. Hahn's Introduction, p. xxvi.

6. *Journal of Speculative Philosophy*, XVIII (1884), 162–74; *Early Works*, I, 34–47. This was the fourth and last of Dewey's contributions to his first medium of publication. Like many another magazine, it was always behind schedule. This issue appeared nearly ten months late; those referred to in notes 2 and 5 above, from five and a half to seven and a half months late. Articles were sometimes written after their nominal dates of publication. This seems not to have been the case with any of Dewey's four.

7. George Dykhuizen, "John Dewey at Johns Hopkins (1882–1884)," *Journal of the History of Ideas*, XXII (1961), 103–16, at pp. 112 f. *Early Works*, I, 153: "By Kant's logical method we mean the inquiry into the *necessary conditions* of experience; by his psychological method the inquiry into the *actual nature* of experience."

8. "The Psychology of Consciousness," 13 November 1883; "Delboeuf on Living and Dead Matter," 11 December 1883; "The New Psychology," 11 March 1884. *Johns Hopkins University Circulars*, III (1883–84), 46, 96.

materials and problems in all the social and historical sciences. Cradle and asylum, prison and penitentiary, are among its laboratories. It draws on biology for conceptions of organism and environment, continuity and process, function and teleology. It rejects both Hume's nominalism and the "formalistic intuitionalism" of the Kantian and Scottish reactions to Hume. "The chief characteristic distinguishing it from the old psychology is undoubtedly the rejection of a formal logic as its model and test." [9]

During the next four years (1884–88), at Michigan under Morris's chairmanship, Dewey gave courses in Formal Logic, Greek Science and Philosophy, Kant's *Critique of Pure Reason*, Spencer's *First Principles*, and seminars in Plato's *Republic* and Kant's Ethics; but chiefly he taught psychology (six different courses!), wrote his *Psychology*, and contributed to *Mind* a series of articles in which he argued that the mistakes of British Empiricism from Locke through the Mills and Spencer, and likewise the partial failure of Kant, were due not to adopting the psychological standpoint but to lapsing from it into ontology or formal logic. Hegel supplies the necessary corrective, but only if we understand his logic and philosophy of nature as abstractions from his philosophy of mind; that is, from his psychology. From the standpoint of psychology, the distinctions of subject and object, ideal and real, universal and individual, fall within consciousness or experience; psychology both makes the distinctions and transcends them. "Psychology, and not Logic, is the method of Philosophy"; and if we not only adopt the psychological standpoint but adhere to it, the result is Absolute Idealism.[10]

As if that were not enough for a man in his twenties, Dewey wrote a second book, *Leibniz's New Essays Concerning the Human Understanding*, his chief single work devoted en-

9. "The New Psychology," *Andover Review*, II (1884), 278–89; *Early Works*, I, 48–60, at pp. 58 f.

10. For the courses: George Dykhuizen, "John Dewey and the University of Michigan," *Journal of the History of Ideas*, XXIII (1962), 513–44, at pp. 515 f. For the *Psychology*: *Early Works*, II. The *Mind* series: "The Psychological Standpoint," XI (1886), 1–19; "Psychology as Philosophic Method," XI (1886), 153–73; " 'Illusory Psychology,' " XII (1887), 83–88; "Knowledge as Idealisation," XII (1887), 382–96; "On Some Current Conceptions of the Term 'Self'," XV (1890), 58–74; the first four reprinted in *Early Works*, I, 122–93, where see p. 149 for the quotation and p. 135 for the Absolute Idealism; the fifth reprinted in *Early Works*, III, 56–74.

tirely to history and criticism. He wrote it at Morris's request, for a series of "German Philosophical Classics for English Readers and Students," of which Morris was editor, and which Morris had launched in 1882 with a "critical exposition" of Kant's *Critique of Pure Reason*. In that programmatic volume, after sketching "the universal nature and historic results of philosophical inquiry," Morris had treated of "*1)* the starting-point of Kant's *Kritik*, *2)* the goal of demonstration actually reached in the *Kritik*, and *3)* the further goal, not reached in the *Kritik*, but to which the latter both positively and negatively points." [11] Other volumes by other authors were being devoted to Kant's ethics, his *Critique of Judgment*, Schelling's *Transcendental Idealism*, Fichte's *Science of Knowledge*, Hegel's *Logic, Philosophy of Religion*, and *Philosophy of Art*; and Morris had already begun the concluding volume of the series, *Hegel's Philosophy of the State and of History*.

The only pre-Kantian work included was Leibniz's *New Essays*. Morris's first choice for this was G. H. Howison, an able Leibnizian and mature philosopher. Howison had been working on it at Michigan in the year before Dewey came, but withdrew from the undertaking at the end of his second year at Berkeley, in July 1886. Morris turned to Dewey as his second choice, and slightly less than two years later, in June 1888, when Dewey was not yet twenty-nine, the volume was in print. [12]

There is no scholarly apparatus whatever—no index, no bibliography, no notes, no references for quotations. Dewey nowhere tells us what edition of Leibniz or of Locke he is using. Slowly, however, we come to sense the philosophic and scholarly care, on Morris's part as well as Dewey's, that has gone into the book. Criticism is postponed to the twelfth and last chapter. Until then Dewey endeavors to identify his thought with that of Leibniz, "to assume his standpoint and method," to keep his relations to Locke in view, "and to show the *Nouveaux Essais* as typical of the distinction between characteristic British and Ger-

11. *Johns Hopkins University Circulars*, II (1882–83), 81. See quotation over note 21 below.

12. *Leibniz's New Essays Concerning the Human Understanding: A Critical Exposition* (Chicago: S. C. Griggs and Co., 1888); *Early Works*, I, 251–435. Morris's letters to Howison are in the Howison Papers in the Bancroft Library at the University of California in Berkeley.

man thought." [13] Leibniz's criticisms of Locke are acknowledged to be external throughout. Dewey briefly states Locke's
views from time to time, without exposition or defense, and
solely to identify Leibniz's targets. The "English Reader" to
whom the series is addressed is presumed to know Locke by
inheritance or osmosis if not by study. As we expect from the
design of the series, it is Leibniz as forerunner of Kant and
Hegel that is brought into bold relief for us; Leibniz's criticism
of Locke is to prepare us for Kant's of Hume, and to justify
Kant's claim that " 'The Critique of Pure Reason' may be
regarded as the real apology for Leibniz, even against his professed followers." [14] We are not surprised when Dewey concludes that Leibniz's failures, like Kant's are "results of his
assuming, without examination, the validity of formal logic as a
method of truth." [15] The last sentence of the volume, if read
with the emphasis my italics invite, is a perfect statement of its
place in Morris's series: "And in a broad sense, the work of
Kant *and of his successors* was the discovery of a method which
should justify the objective idealism of Leibniz, and which in its
history has more than fulfilled this task." [16]

After four years at Michigan, Dewey moved to the chair of
philosophy at Minnesota; but Morris died untimely in the spring
of 1889, and Dewey was called back to take his place. Morris's
death had cut the umbilical cord, and, with no loss of affection or
esteem, the slow sea-change from absolute idealism toward instrumentalism, pragmatism, and naturalism began. Dewey
turned the psychology courses over first to J. H. Tufts and later
to G. H. Mead. He revised his *Psychology* for a second edition
in 1889 and a third in 1891, and then ceased. Although he had
called Leibniz "the greatest intellectual genius since Aristotle,"
he never revised the book he had written for Morris on the *New
Essays*, and it is even doubtful that he ever looked into Leibniz
again. He took over the courses in ethics and social philosophy
that Morris had taught. Besides these, he taught Kant's *Critique*, Hegel's *Logic*, Hegel's Philosophy of Spirit, and "Advanced Logic: The Theory of Scientific Method." In connection
with the last of these, he worked on a volume to be called

13. *Early Works*, I, 253 f.
14. *Early Works*, I, 429.
15. *Early Works*, I, 415.
16. *Early Works*, I, 435.

*Principles of Instrumental Logic*, which was announced at least as early as 1893 as "in preparation" for Muirhead's Library of Philosophy, but which never came out.

Morris had been responsible not only for Dewey's interpretation of the movement from Leibniz through Kant to Hegel and beyond, but also for his affair with British idealism. Morris had spent part of the summer of 1885 in Scotland and England visiting leaders of the Movement. In Dewey's ensuing *Mind* series (1886–90),[17] "The Psychological Standpoint" had taken off from Green[18] and had criticized Bain and Spencer. "Psychology as Philosophic Method" had regretted that Green, "(of whom the writer would not speak without expressing his deep, almost reverential gratitude), when following out Kant's work from its logical side, hardly escaped Kant's negative results";[19] had quoted Caird, Adamson, and Seth with approval; and had appealed to the authority of Bradley's *Principles of Logic*. " 'Illusory Psychology' " had made a weak reply to a strong criticism by Shadworth Hodgson of the two preceding articles. "Knowledge as Idealization" had criticized Spencer and Lewes in the spirit of Green, and bowed again toward Bradley. And now "On Some Current Conceptions of the Term 'Self' " took off from Seth's *Hegelianism and Personality* and came up to a problem in Green, all in relation to Kant and Hegel.

In a nearly parallel series of articles and reviews in the *Andover Review*, in which "The New Psychology" had appeared, the slow liberation from Morris's influence is more apparent.[20] "Ethics and Physical Science" had criticized Spen-

17. See note 10 above.
18. Charles H. Ames in his unpublished Harrisiana (copies of which are in The Houghton Library at Harvard University and in the Hoose Library of Philosophy at the University of Southern California) reports that W. T. Harris said of this on 17 February 1886, that "Dewey had a good deal of ability. He seemed, however, to be much colored by the men he read. Had evidently been reading Green of England. A good thing to read the Oxford men, but not good to be chameleon-like. He (H.) found that he got colored but slowly by another man's style." Dewey said of himself in 1930 that he seemed to be "chameleon-like, yielding one after another to many diverse and even incompatible influences; struggling to assimilate something from each and yet striving to carry it forward in a way that is logically consistent with what has been learned from its predecessors" (*Contemporary American Philosophy*, II, eds. George Plimpton Adams and William Pepperell Montague [New York: Macmillan Co., 1930], 13–27, at p. 22).
19. *Early Works*, I, 153.
20. *Andover Review* series: "The New Psychology," II (1884),

cer and Lewes. "The Philosophy of Thomas Hill Green," coming out just after Morris's death, reviewed with complete sympathy Green's criticisms of Hume and of Spencer and Lewes, and the constructive doctrine of his *Prolegomena to Ethics*. A year later came the most unreservedly eulogistic review that Dewey ever wrote, that of Edward Caird's *Critical Philosophy of Kant*, "the richest and wisest outcome yet published of the philosophic Renascence now in progress in Great Britain"—not only "the best English account of the Kantian philosophy" but "the best account of philosophy itself in the English language." Caird "has absorbed all the results of such criticism as that of Thomas Hill Green, but . . . has a positive, constructive touch which in finals seems to have been denied Green," who "seems never to have quite freed himself from the negative element in Kant." Caird's criticism is wholly immanent.

> We are shown whence Kant started; we are shown the nature and requirements of Kant's own method in dealing with the subject-matter; we are shown how far Kant goes in the reconstruction of the views from which he sets out; and we are shown how much further he should have gone in order to be true to his own principle. . . . In this way the book becomes, in effect, a summary of the entire Kanto-Hegelian movement, and, in addition, a statement of constructive philosophic results.[21]

This is, Caird has proved for Dewey an abler teacher than Morris, but of the same lesson.[22]

A month later, in reviewing Erdmann's *History of Philosophy* (in the English translation edited by Hough), Dewey compared it with Ueberweg's, which Morris had translated.

---

278–89 (see note 9 above); "Ethics and Physical Science," VII (1887), 573–91; "The Philosophy of Thomas Hill Green," XI (1889), 337–55; review of *The Critical Philosophy of Immanuel Kant* by Edward Caird, XIII (1890), 325–27; review of *Kant's Critical Philosophy for English Readers* by John Pentland Mahaffy and John Henry Bernard, ibid., 328; review of *A History of Philosophy* by Johann Eduard Erdmann (English trans. by Williston Samuel Hough), XIII (1890), 453–54; review of *Studies in Hegel's Philosophy of Religion* by James MacBride Sterrett, XIII (1890), 684–85. Reprinted in *Early Works*, I, 48–60, 205–26; III, 14–35, 180–84, 184–85, 185–87, 187–90. See the Introduction to *Early Works*, III (xxi–xxxviii) by S. Morris Eames.

   21. *Early Works*, III, 181, 182.
   22. See quotation over note 11 above.

Industry, accuracy, and a fair degree of philosophic understanding may give us a work like Ueberweg's, but Erdmann's
history, while in no way superseding Ueberweg's as a handbook for general use, yet occupies a different position. Erdmann wrote his book, not as a reference-book, to give in brief
compass a digest of the writings of various authors, but as a
genuine history of philosophy, tracing, in a genetic way, the
development of thought in its treatment of philosophic problems. Its purpose is to develop a philosophic intelligence rather
than to furnish information.[23]

Unfortunately, in the third volume, "Since Hegel," the translation (by a hand other than Hough's), left much to be desired.
By a reference to pages 72–77 as particularly bad, Dewey be-
trayed his having read with special interest the account of
Feuerbach and Bauer, Hegelians of the left. Having become
with Morris an Hegelian of the center, and having moved with
Morris and the British idealists toward Hegelianism of the right,
had Dewey not begun to swing to the left?

The liberating effect of Morris's death was due in large
part to its coming at a fortunate juncture. Dewey's apprenticeship had lasted just long enough. His attention was being turned
by Franklin Ford to some of the great social issues of the day.
The rapid expansion of education at all levels was opening the
way to changes in methods, and inviting experimentation with a
view to the guidance of change; and Dewey's marriage and
children were pulling him in that direction. But, above all,
American philosophy was itself coming of age. Laymen were
succeeding clergymen as professors of philosophy. The *Journal
of Speculative Philosophy*, too closely identified with the German idealism of sixty to eighty years earlier, was about to
expire. Journals of a more independent, professional, and secular character, more open to new movements and to original
work, were multiplying. To name but half a dozen, the *Monist*
and *Ethics* began in 1890, the *Educational Review* in 1891, the
*Philosophical Review* in 1892, the *Psychological Review* in 1894,
and the *Journal of Philosophy* in 1904. Dewey contributed articles or reviews or both to one or more of these six journals in
each but seven of the sixty years 1890–1949. In his first two
articles in the *Philosophical Review*, to be sure, he was still
taking leave of Green, whom he now called Neo-Fichtean, and

23. *Early Works*, III, 186.

his first review was of Bosanquet's *History of Æsthetic*.[24] After that, however, the books that he reviewed and the works that he criticized in his articles in these and other journals were for the most part, and in increasing proportion, by American philosophers.

The shift of perspective may be traced to two works of evident independence, originality, and power by American philosophers that appeared shortly after Morris's death: James's *Principles of Psychology* in 1890 and Peirce's six articles in the *Monist* from 1891 to 1893 developing a scientific metaphysics. Dewey's response was immediate. In 1891, revising his own *Psychology* for the third and last time, he reworked his theory of sensation and emotion in the light of James's; and he began using the *Principles* as text in an advanced course in psychology. After Tufts left Michigan, Dewey appointed first G. H. Mead and then A. H. Lloyd, both trained at Harvard by James and Royce. Peirce's second article, "The Doctrine of Necessity Examined," prompted Dewey to write for the *Monist* an article on "The Superstition of Necessity." In two footnotes in his 1894 article, "The Ego as Cause," Dewey made trenchant criticisms of James's theory of the will.[25] The advent of James's *Principles* was the great literary event of Dewey's life, and he had begun the long process of sorting out its strengths and weaknesses. He and Bentley were still at it fifty years later.[26] Of Peirce there will be more to say shortly.

Dewey became head of the Department of Philosophy at the University of Chicago in 1894. A year later, he also became head of its new Department of Pedagogy, which soon afterward started its experimental elementary school. He was a member of the board of trustees of Hull House, took part in many of its activities, and became a devoted admirer of Jane Addams. He still taught Hegel's *Logic*, along with such other courses as

24. "Green's Theory of the Moral Motive," *Philosophical Review*, I (1892), 593–612 [*Early Works*, III, 155–73]; review of *A History of Æsthetic* by Bernard Bosanquet, II (1893), 63–69; "Self-Realization as the Moral Ideal," II (1893), 652–64, at p. 663. (James is quoted with approval at p. 657.)

25. *Philosophical Review*, III (1894), 337–41, at pp. 339, 340–41.

26. *John Dewey and Arthur F. Bentley: A Philosophical Correspondence, 1932–1951*, selected and edited by Sidney Ratner and Jules Altman (New Brunswick, N.J.: Rutgers University Press, 1964), passim.

Contemporary Idealism (Green, Bradley, Royce), History of Political Ethics, and Development of English Utilitarianism.[27] At Chicago, and from 1905 at Columbia, he was drawn increasingly into civic, national, and international affairs. When the *New Republic* began appearing in 1914, it became his chief single medium of publication on the issues of the day. From 1922 to 1937 he was listed as Contributing Editor. Among the more philosophical books he reviewed for it were Santayana's *Egotism in German Philosophy*, *Scepticism and Animal Faith*, *The Realm of Essence*, and *Some Turns of Thought in Modern Philosophy*; Lippmann's *Public Opinion* and *The Phantom Public*; Ogden and Richards, *The Meaning of Meaning*; Russell's *Education and the Good Life*; Peirce's *Chance, Love and Logic*, the first volume of his *Collected Papers*, then the fifth, and then I–VI; Whitehead's *Science and the Modern World* and *Adventures of Ideas*; Hocking's *Man and the State*; Cohen's *Reason and Nature*; Bergson's *Two Sources of Morality and Religion*; and Perry's *Thought and Character of William James*. If to his reviews in the professional journals we add those in the *New Republic* and other nonprofessional ones, we are ready to risk the guess that there was never a philosopher of his eminence who reviewed the best work of his contemporaries so promptly and with so near an approach to completeness.[28]

Nearly as remarkable among philosophers was Dewey the encyclopedist. To *Johnson's Universal Cyclopædia* in 1894 he contributed long historical articles on "Intuitionalism" and "Moral Philosophy." To the first volume of Baldwin's *Dictionary of Philosophy and Psychology* in 1901 he made no contribution except to add his approving initials to Royce's article, "History of Philosophy"; but to the second in 1902 he contributed well over a hundred articles, many of them historical; for examples, those on Neo-Platonism, Scepticism, Scholasticism, Scotism, and Summists.[29] To the *Encyclopedia Americana* in

27. George Dykhuizen, "John Dewey: The Chicago Years," *Journal of the History of Philosophy*, II (1964), 227–53, at p. 233.

28. On the slighted Europeans, see Gérard Deledalle, *L'idée d'expérience dans la philosophie de John Dewey* (Paris: Presses Universitaires de France, 1967), pp. 498 f. The slighted *field* was formal logic.

29. Dewey was both a consulting and a contributing editor. As a contributor, he "procrastinated . . . to such an extent that the titles of his articles had to be changed again and again in such a way as to shift the matter to synonymous terms lower down in the alphabet." James

1903, the article "Ethics." To the *Century Dictionary Supplement* in 1909, the article "Pragmatism." To Monroe's *Cyclopedia of Education* in 1911–13, well over a hundred articles. (Many of these sketch the history of philosophic treatment of their several topics, often starting from Plato and Aristotle and concluding with "the present tendency." The historical sketches have little or no fresh research behind them, but the summaries of "current tendencies" are convenient sources for Dewey's own opinions on a wide range of topics. It is perhaps worth noting that "Democracy and Education" occurs first as a brief article in Monroe's *Cyclopedia* in 1911, then as the concluding chapter of *Schools of To-morrow* in 1915, then as Dewey's most influential single work in 1916, and finally as a section of *Problems of Men* in 1946.) To Foster Watson's *Encyclopedia and Dictionary of Education* in 1921, the article "Aims and Ideals of Education." To the *Encyclopaedia of the Social Sciences* in the early 1930s, four articles: "Human Nature," "Logic," "Outlawry of War," and "Philosophy," and finally to the *International Encyclopedia of Unified Science* in the late 1930s, two articles, "Unity of Science as a Social Problem," and what must count as one of his major works, "Theory of Valuation."

That he contributed to the last of these encyclopedias needs explaining, since it had something of a party line and Dewey was not a member of the party. In a letter to Bentley in 1944, he said he wrote the first article "at the express wish of Neurath and also followed rather closely suggestions which he made. . . . I think now he wanted something as an offset to the Carnap influence." And of the second: "Although my piece was in the rather miscalled *Unity of Science* series, my main object was to criticize the point of view of the 'logical positivists' regarding value, to point out its sources, and to point out the dualistic consequences." [30]

"Theory of Valuation" is Dewey's most exasperating work, because it is the extreme case of his worst fault as a critic. Not only are there no references for his numerous quotations,

Mark Baldwin, *Between Two Wars, 1861–1921*, 2 vols. (Boston: Stratford Co., 1926), I, 72; cf. p. 74.

30. *Dewey and Bentley: Correspondence*, pp. 343, 74. On the relation between Neurath and Dewey see also Corliss Lamont, ed., *Dialogue on John Dewey* (New York: Horizon Press, 1959), pp. 11–13 (reminiscences of Ernest Nagel and J. T. Farrell).

but not a single author is so much as named. The reader is
baffled until, from clues in the "Selected Bibliography," he finds
by searching that the object of attack in Part II is A. J. Ayer's
*Language, Truth and Logic*; in Part III, R. B. Perry's *General
Theory of Value*. Perry's book had also been the nameless butt
of criticism in Dewey's previous essay in value theory, Chapter
10 of *The Quest for Certainty*, on "The Construction of Good."
The reader's exasperation does not, however, cease when he has
located Dewey's targets; for, if he remembers Perry's book or
has it open before him, he soon realizes that Dewey's criticisms
are grossly unfair, considered as criticisms of Perry's book or of
his general theory. (The scolder of philosophers for suppression
and neglect of context is himself, when it comes to quotations,
the worst offender.) Yet his criticisms do not seem malicious;
and the reader comes eventually to the charitable conclusion
that, as so often elsewhere, Dewey leaves the sources of his
quotations unidentified because he wishes to criticize not the
philosopher, still less the man, nor even a theory as actually
held, but a *possible* theory by contrast with which to bring his
own into sharper relief; and that he gathers suitable quotations
to breathe a show of life into it, lest he seem to be shooting at
targets of straw. He is more dialectician than critic. Naturalist
though he now is, the *movement* of his thinking is still Hegelian.

Between the two world wars, Columbia University became
the chief center in the United States for the study of the history
of philosophy. To the three volumes of its *Studies in the History
of Ideas* (1918, 1925, 1935), Dewey contributed essays which
were not only among the best in their respective volumes, but
among the best historical essays he ever wrote: "The Motivation of Hobbes's Political Philosophy" in Volume I, "The 'Socratic Dialogues' of Plato" and "The Development of American
Pragmatism" in Volume II, and "An Empirical Survey of Empiricisms" in Volume III. To this period also belongs another of
his best historical essays, "Substance, Power and Quality in
Locke," in the *Philosophical Review* for January 1926. In each of
these essays, Dewey argues for relatively novel or at least non-
standard interpretations. The early dialogues should be interpreted not as Socratic but as "dialectic refutations of thinkers
claiming to be Socratic" among Plato's own contemporaries,
such as the Cynics and Cyrenaics, and as "the critical prepara-

tory try-outs" for the *Republic*.[31] What Hobbes wanted was not absolute sovereignty but unified sovereignty, not divided between state and church; he wanted to put morals and politics on a secular and scientific basis; he is best understood as a social utilitarian, a forerunner of Bentham.[32] Locke's secondary qualities are not states of consciousness; the distinction between primary and secondary is not metaphysical but functional; primary qualities are more reliable as signs; the key to the understanding of Locke is not the epistemological problem but the insight that scientific objects are relational; that "Things however absolute and entire they seem in themselves, are but retainers to other parts of nature for that [for] which they are most taken notice of by us." [33] Pragmatism, Instrumentalism, Experimentalism, are best defined, and misunderstandings of them obviated, by tracing their development on the one hand from Kant and the post-Kantians (in the case of Peirce and in that of Dewey and his associates) and on the other from British Empiricism (in the case of James), and showing how "American thought merely continues European thought." [34] Instrumentalism owes more to James's *Psychology* than to his later writings; more particularly, to its biological teleology, not to its stream-of-consciousness theme.[35] Our still developing empiricism may be enlightened and guided by a review of the growth of the concept of experience, from the Greeks through Locke and his followers to that most recent stage in which, by coming to include hypothesis-and-experiment scientific experience, it has acquired an emphatic forward reference.[36]

Dewey's greatest historical essay, however, was not any of these but a much earlier one. In the winter and spring of 1909,

31. "The 'Socratic Dialogues' of Plato," in *Studies in the History of Ideas* by the Department of Philosophy of Columbia University, Vol. II (New York: Columbia University Press, 1925), pp. 1–23, at pp. 6, 12, 17.

32. "The Motivation of Hobbes's Political Philosophy," in *Studies*, I (1918), 88–115, at pp. 98, 107, 109, 114.

33. "Substance, Power and Quality in Locke," *Philosophical Review*, XXXV (1926), 22–38, at pp. 22, 27, 32, 33, 36, 38.

34. "The Development of American Pragmatism," in *Studies*, II (1925), Supplement, 353–77, at pp. 353, 368, 373. (First published in French translation in 1922; retranslated from French into English by Herbert W. Schneider.)

35. "Development of American Pragmatism," pp. 369–71.

36. "An Empirical Survey of Empiricisms," in *Studies*, III (1935), 3–22.

in the fiftieth year after the publication of the *Origin of Species*, there was a course of public lectures at Columbia University on "Charles Darwin and His Influence on Science" in which Dewey gave a lecture on "Darwin's Influence upon Philosophy." The other lectures there and elsewhere have been forgotten, and so have those of the centennial year, 1959, but Dewey's continues to be read as the most penetrating assessment of "the scientific revolution that found its climax in the 'Origin of Species.'" It is perhaps a sufficient explanation that no abler philosopher, no abler student of the history of philosophy, has addressed himself to the theme. But Dewey had a personal stake in it that no other philosopher has had. He was born in 1859. The *Origin of Species* was his birthright, but it had taken him half a century to enter into it and become the spokesman of "the Darwinian genetic and experimental logic." [37] There is nothing more remarkable about Dewey's development than his slowness in rising from the details of Darwin's works, such as his theory of emotion, to their larger logical and philosophical bearings, which Chauncey Wright and Peirce had seen in the 1870s.

After the Leibniz volume, Dewey's only book devoted exclusively to history and criticism was *German Philosophy and Politics*. It consisted of three lectures delivered at the University of North Carolina in February 1915, over two years before our entry into World War I. As if answering the idealists who thought that Germany had now proved false to the spirit of her great philosophers, Dewey the ex-idealist traced Prussian militarism to Kant, Fichte, and Hegel, and above all to Kant's doctrine of the two worlds. Of Hegel he said: "It is customary to call him an Idealist. In one sense . . . he is the greatest realist known to philosophy. He might be called a Brutalist." [38] Except perhaps for this remark, Dewey's language is temperate throughout. Among the wartime writings of the philosophers of Germany, France, Great Britain, and the United States, his book even stands out as a paragon of sanity. In 1942, before our entry into World War II, he reissued the book with minor corrections and a new introduction, "The One-World of Hitler's

37. "Darwin's Influence upon Philosophy," *Popular Science Monthly*, LXXV (1909), 90–98; reprinted in *The Influence of Darwin on Philosophy and Other Essays in Contemporary Thought* (New York: Henry Holt and Co., 1910), pp. 1–19, at pp. 19, 18.

38. *German Philosophy and Politics* (New York: Henry Holt and Co., 1915), p. 107.

National Socialism."[39] One, that is, in place of Kant's Two. (The philosophy of war is a subject for a book which is much to be desired, which should begin with, or devote a long appendix to, a review of what eminent philosophers have written about war in general and about particular wars.)

I come now to some of the more striking passages of history and criticism in the major works of Dewey's maturity.

Of the four essays with which *Studies in Logical Theory* began, the second, third, and fourth are explicitly criticisms of Lotze's *Logic*,[40] and the first implicitly so. The first exposition of Dewey's instrumentalism thus appears in the guise of the resolution of the contradictions in Lotze's theory of the validity of thought. These four essays reappear as essays II–V in *Essays in Experimental Logic*. Not until 1938, in his *Logic: The Theory of Inquiry*, when he was nearly eighty, did Dewey offer access to his logical theory otherwise than through the thickets of his criticism of Lotze.[41]

In the *Ethics* of Dewey and Tufts (1908), Part II, "Theory of the Moral Life," by Dewey, is cluttered with quotations and with references to and criticisms of authors who would better have been ignored. One of the merits of the rewritten second edition (1932) is that most of this baggage has been jettisoned, and the relations between the major classical theories and Dewey's become clearer. Even Green is dropped from the text, though his *Prolegomena* is retained in the bibliographies, the last of which refers us "for criticism of Green" to Dewey's article of thirty-nine years earlier.[42]

In *Democracy and Education* (1916), which defines philosophy as *"the general theory of education,"*[43] there is much criticism of the Greeks, especially of the Sophists, Socrates,

39. *German Philosophy and Politics* (New York: G. P. Putnam's Sons, 1942), pp. 13–49.

40. In Bosanquet's translation. Bosanquet's own *Logic* is criticized by one of Dewey's students in the fifth essay. There is criticism of Mill, and further criticism of Bosanquet, in subsequent essays.

41. *Studies in Logical Theory* (Chicago: University of Chicago Press, 1903); *Essays in Experimental Logic* (Chicago: University of Chicago Press, 1916); *Logic: The Theory of Inquiry* (New York: Henry Holt and Co., 1938).

42. *Ethics*, with James H. Tufts (New York: Henry Holt and Co., 1908); revised edition (1932), p. 344. The reference is to "Self-Realization as the Moral Ideal," for which see note 24 above.

43. *Democracy and Education* (New York: Macmillan Co., 1916), p. 383.

Plato, and Aristotle; and there are thumbnail sketches of the views of several modern theorists. The "see also" list under Dualism in the index is a convenient list of the dualisms Dewey attacked throughout his long life.

*Reconstruction in Philosophy* (1920) and *The Quest for Certainty* (1929) are critical interpretations of the whole tradition of Western philosophy. They also contain striking passages on particular philosophers, notably that on Bacon in the earlier book and that on Spinoza in the later. Bacon, in spite of some absurdities and a quite imperfect grasp of the nature of induction, was "the real founder of modern thought," "the prophet of a pragmatic conception of knowledge," of "a logic of discovery," and of "the organization of co-operative research." [44] Spinoza, on the other hand, "exemplifies with extraordinary completeness the nature of the problem of all modern philosophies which have not deserted the classic tradition, and yet have made the conclusions of modern science their own," though without foreseeing the eventual subordination of its mathematical to its experimental phases.[45]

Understanding by philosophy the "organon of criticism," *Experience and Nature* (1925) draws "a ground-map of the province of criticism." Its key third chapter, "Nature, Ends and Histories," uses the class structure of Greek society to explain and criticize Aristotle's natural teleology, and reviews the steps by which the doctrine of final causes as "the proper objects of science . . . met its doom in the scientific revolution of the seventeenth century," only to go on and ask, "is there an ingredient of truth in ancient metaphysics which may be extracted and re-affirmed?" [46] Dewey's answer is affirmative, and the rest of the chapter and book supports it. This is his greatest work, chiefly because in it he achieves his most nearly perfect balance and interplay of history, interpretation, criticism, and reconstruction.

*The Public and Its Problems* (1927) is a response to, and in part a criticism of, Walter Lippmann's *The Phantom Public*

44. *Reconstruction in Philosophy* (New York: Henry Holt and Co., 1920), pp. 28–38, at pp. 28, 38, 31 (cf. p. 33), 37.

45. *The Quest for Certainty* (New York: Minton, Balch and Co., 1929), pp. 53–57, at p. 56. (Contrast the wholly polemical treatment of Spinoza in Dewey's essay of 1882, for which see note 2 above.)

46. *Experience and Nature* (Chicago, London: Open Court Publishing Co., 1925), pp. 94, 96.

and his earlier *Public Opinion*, both of which Dewey had reviewed. It is regrettable that he did not come to grips with more substantial works of social theory, such as Elijah Jordan's *Forms of Individuality* (1927) and *Theory of Legislation* (1930).[47]

In *Art as Experience* (1934), criticism follows construction. After developing in eleven chapters the æsthetic theory he had already announced in his essay on "Qualitative Thought" (1930) [48]—that of fusion by underlying, dominant, regulative, pervasive quality—he considers in the twelfth "The Challenge to Philosophy" posed by æsthetic experience as so understood. He states and criticizes the major æsthetic theories—including those of Plato, Aristotle, Plotinus, Kant, Schiller, Schopenhauer, Croce, Santayana—as each exaggerating some one "element" or "strand" of æsthetic experience—illusion, play, imitation, essence, intuition, expression—and neglecting others.

And finally, in *Logic: The Theory of Inquiry* (1938), criticism again follows construction. Though there is incidental criticism in earlier chapters, like that of Aristotelian logic in Chapter 5 and that of theories of immediate knowledge in Chapter 8, Chapters 1–34 develop Dewey's theory of the continuum of inquiry and of its recurring pattern, and argue for his "fundamental thesis," that "Logical forms accrue to subject-matter when the latter is subjected to controlled inquiry." [49] The final chapter (35), "The Logic of Inquiry and Philosophies of Knowledge," then reviews systematically "some of the main types of epistemological theory which mark the course of philosophy," and shows that "each type represents a selective extraction of some conditions and some factors out of the actual pattern of controlled inquiry." [50] Since the strength of each theory lies in the way the elements it arbitrarily isolates from the continuum of inquiry do actually function there, and its weakness lies in ignoring, or failing to do justice to, other elements of equal or greater functional value, this critical review, like that in *Art as*

47. *New Republic*, XXX (1922), 286–88; XLV (1925), 52–54. Bentley tried to interest Dewey in Jordan: *Dewey and Bentley: Correspondence*, p. 58 (cf. p. 60 for Dewey's reply), pp. 571–72 (referring to Jordan's *The Aesthetic Object*).

48. *Symposium*, I (1930), 5–32; reprinted in *Philosophy and Civilization* (New York: Minton, Balch and Co., 1931), pp. 93–116.

49. *Logic: The Theory of Inquiry* (New York: Henry Holt and Co., 1938), p. 101.

50. *Logic*, p. 514.

*Experience*, affords "indirect confirmation of conclusions already set forth." [51]

The *Logic* completed *Experience and Nature* in one direction, as *Art as Experience* had in another. The assimilation of the theory of science to that of art, however, and of both to that of nature, is such as to make of the three books one great work, Dewey's *opus majus*, rich in history and criticism as well as strong in construction.

In the Preface to the *Logic* (1938), Dewey says that his "point of view and method of approach" remain the same as in *Studies in Logical Theory* (1903) and *Essays in Experimental Logic* (1916), but that "the statement of them has been maturing for over forty years." [52] The most obvious change in the definitive statement is one that Dewey does not mention, the complete sloughing off of the critique of Lotze. The change to which he invites our attention is the application throughout the book of "the principle of the continuum of inquiry, a principle whose importance, as far as I am aware, only Peirce had previously noted." [53] He says further, concerning "logical treatises and their authors," that he has learned most from those with whose positions he has in the end been compelled to disagree, "with the outstanding exception of Peirce." [54]

We must now examine more closely a few of Dewey's reviews and essays in criticism. Perhaps the least arbitrary and most illuminating selection would be that of his reviews and essays dealing with some one philosopher to whom he had frequent occasion to return over a long period of time. On that assumption, James would be the obvious first choice, and Santayana the second. But since what he made of them is familiar or accessible, and since the most striking things in Dewey's culminating work, the *Logic*, are those he credits Peirce for, whereas the most striking thing about his training at The Johns Hopkins nearly sixty years earlier was his inability to learn from Peirce, I make the obvious third choice, that of his reviews of Peirce's writings, and his criticisms of Peirce's interpreters and critics. I begin by sketching in the background.

In his first year at The Johns Hopkins, Dewey avoided

51. *Logic*, p. 515.
52. *Logic*, p. v.
53. *Logic*, p. iii.
54. *Logic*, p. iv.

Peirce's logic course as being too mathematical—a scientific rather than a philosophical course. In his second year he took it but was of the same opinion still.[55] He also took Peirce's course in Philosophical Terminology and a graduate course of seventeen "Educational Lectures" organized by Hall in which Peirce gave the eighth and ninth: "The Observational Element in Mathematics" and "The *a priori* Element in Physics." [56]

In 1891–93 Peirce had a series of essays in the *Monist* on the evolution of the laws of nature. Two things struck Dewey: the critique of "The Doctrine of Necessity" in the second essay, and the theory of continuity in the third, on "The Law of Mind." To the former Dewey responded immediately with an essay of his own on "The Superstition of Necessity." [57] His response to the latter was delayed. In 1902 he wrote for Baldwin's *Dictionary* a short article on Tychism based on Peirce's series. In a letter to James in March 1903 he expressed reservations about the "hypostatizing of chance." "I must say, however, that I can see how far I have moved along when I find how much I get out of Peirce this year, and how easily I understand him, when a few years ago he was mostly a sealed book to me, aside from occasional inspirations." [58] What he valued most was the synechism of "The Law of Mind." In his "Logical Conditions of a Scientific Treatment of Morality" (1903) he said that "the postulate of moral science is the continuity of scientific judgment" and that, so far as he knew, Peirce was "the first to call attention to this principle, and to insist upon its fundamental logical import." [59]

Meanwhile *The Psychology of Number* by McLellan and Dewey (1895) had been reviewed at length by Peirce in the *Nation*. "As long as nothing but psychology is called for, what

55. Dykhuizen, "John Dewey at Johns Hopkins," p. 106.

56. Max H. Fisch and Jackson I. Cope, "Peirce at The Johns Hopkins University," in *Studies in the Philosophy of Charles Sanders Peirce*, eds. Wiener and Young (Cambridge: Harvard University Press, 1952), pp. 277–311, at p. 306; cf. pp. 369–70, notes 18 and 19, and pp. 373–74.

57. *Monist*, IV (1893), 362–79.

58. R. B. Perry, *The Thought and Character of William James*, II (Boston: Little, Brown and Co., 1935), 523.

59. In *Investigations Representing the Departments, Part II: Philosophy, Education* (University of Chicago, the Decennial Publications, First Series, Vol. III [Chicago: University of Chicago Press, 1903]), pp. 113–39; reprinted in *Problems of Men* (New York: Philosophical Library, 1946), pp. 211–49, at pp. 244 and 228n.

they say is admirable. . . . When we come down to details, depending upon the nature of mathematical thought, they are more often wrong than right." [60] Though Dewey had taken note of Peirce's 1898 article, "The Logic of Mathematics in Relation to Education," he seems to have made nothing of it.[61] But he had supported Peirce's unsuccessful application to the Carnegie Institution in 1902–3 for aid in preparing his researches for publication. "So far as the interests of general philosophy and logic are concerned, I do not see any way in which the Institution could better further them." [62]

When Dewey in 1903, at the age of forty-four, published *Studies in Logical Theory* by himself and seven of his pupils, the only precedent was that in 1883, in Dewey's first year at Hopkins, Peirce, also at the age of forty-four, had published *Studies in Logic by Members of The Johns Hopkins University*, that is, by four of his pupils and himself. A comparative study of the two books would be instructive. Neither Peirce's book nor Peirce himself is mentioned in Dewey's. Peirce reviewed it for the *Nation*, favorably as work toward "a natural history of thought," unfavorably as a substitute for the normative science of logic.[63] In a letter to Dewey, Peirce regretted "your making everything turn on Lotze, as if he were a Hume." [64]

Though Peirce had defined philosophical terms for the *Century Dictionary* (1889–91) and might have included his own "pragmatism," he did not. When the two supplementary volumes of 1909 were being prepared, pragmatism was the movement of the day and could no longer be omitted. James, Schiller, and Dewey had made it move, and Peirce had restated his own theory, now called "pragmaticism," in a new series of *Monist* essays. With some help from materials supplied by Peirce,[65] Dewey constructed the article on "pragmatism" for the supplement. In an effort to represent fairly the views and priorities of

60. *Nation*, LXI (1895), 395.
61. *Lectures in the Philosophy of Education: 1899*, ed. R. D. Archambault (New York: Random House, 1966), pp. 8, 344.
62. Letter to H. H. D. Peirce, 19 Jan. 1903, Charles S. Peirce Papers, The Houghton Library, Harvard University, Ms. L 75.
63. *Nation*, LXXIX (1904), 219–20; reprinted in *Collected Papers of Charles Sanders Peirce*, eds. Hartshorne, Weiss, and Burks, 8 vols. (Cambridge: Harvard University Press, 1931–58), VIII, ¶188–¶190. (Later references will be in the form: CP 8.188–90.)
64. CP 8.244.
65. CP 5.13n1.

Peirce, James, Schiller, and himself, he arranged the meanings of the term "in the order of descending generality."

After Peirce's death in 1914 it was suggested to the editors of the *Journal of Philosophy* that an issue be devoted to him. It appeared in December 1916. The essay by Dewey was the best account so far of the relations between the earlier and later forms of "The Pragmatism of Peirce," between his pragmatism and his synechism, and between his pragmatism and James's. It was much to be desired that his *Popular Science Monthly* papers should be reprinted in book form. "Discussion since 1878 has caught up with Peirce, and his views would awaken much more response now than when published." It might even be asked "whether recourse to Peirce would not have a most beneficial influence in contemporary discussion." [66]

Among other contributions to the Peirce issue was a bibliography of his writings by Morris R. Cohen. As if pursuing Dewey's suggestion, Cohen edited in 1923 a volume entitled *Chance, Love and Logic*, reprinting both the pragmatism series of 1877–78 and the cosmology series of 1891–93, and, as a "supplementary essay," the article in which Dewey had made the suggestion. Dewey reviewed the book in the *New Republic*. For the first time in print he permitted himself to judge the man as well as the philosopher. "He was a wayward worker"; he did not readily "fit in"; he lacked "the inner impetus to controlled sustained endeavor." (That is, he was not Dewey.) But he "was probably the most original philosophic mind this country has produced; certainly one of the seminal minds of this generation. . . . He was ahead of his time; he belonged to no school and while his contemporaries were developing older theories, making them over to suit the temper of the day, he was breaking new ground." The cosmology series contained "his boldest speculations. But they are certainly much easier reading than they were thirty years ago, and his idea of chance . . . as characteristic of nature . . . now has many adherents." "If the day of Mr. Peirce has not arrived, his night has passed. Harvard University has in preparation an edition of Peirce's works, including those still in manuscript." [67]

Six volumes of *Collected Papers* appeared in 1931–35.

66. *Journal of Philosophy*, XIII (1916), 709–15, at pp. 712n. and 715.
67. *New Republic*, XXIX (1924), 136–37.

Dewey in the *New Republic* reviewed the first and fifth separately and then all six together.[68] In the first review he took Peirce's "fallibilism" as "central in his thinking." Its intent was not sceptical but constructive, to keep the road of inquiry open, for example toward continuity and evolution. As Dewey quoted with approval, "The principle of continuity is the principle of fallibilism objectified." [69] Peirce (like Dewey) was steeped in the history of philosophy. "Like all independent minds, however, he took great liberties in interpreting historic views, and often gave their authors the benefit of his own greater insight." Aristotle and the scholastics would surely shrink from the turn he gives their realism, for he "understands by the reality of a 'general' the reality of a way, habit, disposition, of behavior . . . acquired and modifiable."

Volume V, he said, contained "the most independent and thoroughgoing analysis that I know of the nature of common-sense perception, from which all natural science proceeds and to which it must go back." "To have grasped in its totality the significance of scientific experimental method and to have applied it to a restatement of traditional logic is, I am convinced, an achievement whose importance will stand out more and more as the years go by." What distinguishes Peirce's pragmatism from all forms of positivism is that it locates the meaning of a conception in practical consequences, that is, in "habits of ever increasing generality, of what he terms 'concrete reasonableness'—a reasonableness that is concrete because it does not consist in reasoning merely, but in *ways of acting*—that have an ever widening scope and ever deepening richness of meaning."

In the last review, of Volumes I–VI together, Dewey takes a route I am unable to follow from Peirce's Critical Commonsensism through his Phenomenology and back to his Fallibilism, this time under the unauthorized name of Probabilism. More illuminating is the considered estimate, based on the *Collected Papers*, of the man and philosopher who had been Dewey's teacher fifty-four years earlier. He was far ahead of his time; he was just now coming into his own; his influence would grow

68. "Charles Sanders Peirce," *New Republic*, LXVIII (1932), 220–21; "The Founder of Pragmatism," ibid., LXXXI (1935), 338–39; "Charles Sanders Peirce," ibid., LXXXIX (1937), 415–16. Vols. II–IV, containing Peirce's more technical work in logic, were reviewed by Ernest Nagel, *New Republic*, LXXX (1934), 315–16.

69. CP 1.171.

greatly in the future. It might perhaps have begun earlier but for the admixture of the arbitrary and fantastic, even in his most prophetic "anticipations of the direction in which science would move and the consequences which would ensue." There were so many "perplexing contradictions"; so many bright starts; so few sober finishes. "He united, one might say, a disciplined mind and an undisciplined personality." (The tragic flaw.) He would always remain "a philosopher's philosopher."

"Perplexing contradictions" had been alleged by Thomas A. Goudge a year and a half earlier in "The Views of Charles Peirce on the Given in Experience," [70] more exactly on the phenomenological category of Firstness. Coming at Peirce through C. I. Lewis, Goudge thought he found "at least three mutually incompatible views." [71] In one of these, moreover, Peirce's metaphysical panpsychism was smuggled into his phenomenology under cover of the description of Firstness as "quality of feeling." [72] Dewey defended "Peirce's Theory of Quality" [73] by pointing out "fundamental misconceptions" in Goudge's account, the correction of which should dissolve the alleged inconsistencies. He deprecated the panpsychism even more than Goudge did, but argued that the phenomenology in no way assumed it.[74] (In defending Peirce, Dewey was defending the theory of quality he had himself stated in "Qualitative Thought" and developed in *Art as Experience*.[75] This appears from his frequent use to interpret Peirce of such non-Peircian phrases as "permeating total quality," "totalizing unifying quality," "pervasive unifying quality." He was also defending the more general position of *Experience and Nature*, as appears from this tribute to Peirce in his last paragraph: "I am quite sure that he, above all modern philosophers, has opened the road which permits a truly experiential philosophy to be developed which does not, like traditional empirical philosophies, cut experience off from nature.") Goudge, in "Further Reflections on Peirce's Doctrine of the Given," [76] acknowledged that several of Dewey's strictures were just, and amended his account accord-

70. *Journal of Philosophy*, XXXII (1935), 533–44.
71. "Views of Peirce," pp. 538, 544.
72. "Views of Peirce," p. 543.
73. *Journal of Philosophy*, XXXII (1935), 701–8.
74. "Peirce's Theory of Quality," pp. 701, 704n., 707, 708.
75. See text over note 48 above.
76. *Journal of Philosophy*, XXXIII (1936), 289–95.

ingly, but could not see that the inconsistencies were thereby removed. Moreover, he convicted Dewey of error on Firstness as "possibility." [77] Dewey did not resume the argument, though in my judgment he might greatly have advanced the understanding of Peirce, as well as of his own philosophy, by doing so.

In 1939 Paul A. Schilpp inaugurated The Library of Living Philosophers with *The Philosophy of John Dewey*. Hans Reichenbach and Bertrand Russell criticized views of Peirce subscribed to by Dewey; Reichenbach criticizing sympathetically his theory of induction, and Russell unsympathetically his definitions of "truth." Dewey's rejoinder to Russell on this score is the most devastating passage in the volume, but I pass it over because it is also the best known of all Dewey's discussions of Peirce.

Arriving now at Dewey's last recourse to Peirce, we are taken behind the scenes by his correspondence with Bentley. [78] In the *Logic* he acknowledged secondary debts to Bentley and Mead along with the primary debt to Peirce. [79] While the first six volumes of Peirce's *Collected Papers* had been appearing in Cambridge (1931–35), Bentley's *Linguistic Analysis of Mathematics* and his *Behavior, Knowledge, Fact* had come out in Bloomington, and Mead's works were being edited in Chicago by Charles W. Morris and others. In the same year with the *Logic* and the last of the Mead volumes (1938), Morris's own *Foundations of the Theory of Signs* was published. To Bentley and Dewey it seemed that Morris did violence to Peirce and Mead in a misguided effort to synthesize and systematize their work with that of Carnap. Bentley was at first more sensitive on this score than Dewey because, of the "four great insights" of Peirce that Dewey, Mead, and he, in their several ways, had been developing, the one that had specially struck him was that "all thought is in signs." [80] From intensive study of the *Logic*, he turned to intensive study of the *Collected Papers* — all six volumes — and to planning a book on "the basic Peirce." [81]

77. "Further Reflections," pp. 290–91.
78. See note 26 above.
79. *Logic* (see note 49 above), pp. iv–v. In the index under Peirce add the following page references: iii, iv, 40, 345n6, 437, 469, 490. Preparatory studies contain material on Peirce not fully incorporated in the *Logic*; for example, "What Are Universals?" *Journal of Philosophy*, XXXIII (1936), 281–88, at pp. 283–84.
80. *Dewey and Bentley: Correspondence*, p. 71.
81. *Dewey and Bentley: Correspondence*, pp. 72, 100.

Dewey encouraged Bentley's further explorations and, after four years, suggested the collaboration that eventuated in *Knowing and the Known*.[82] Dewey's own return to Peirce, however, was prompted in 1945 by Charles Stevenson's *Ethics and Language*.[83] That was "a curious mixture of good and very bad things"; and since it claimed to be based on an "analysis of how means and ends are related" that was "not dissimilar, in its broad outlines," to Dewey's,[84] a critique of the bad things was in order. One of these was the identification of the "pragmatic" with the psychological aspects of meaning, for which Stevenson "relies upon the authority of Morris's extraordinary interpretation of Peirce's theory of signs and meanings." [85] At this point, Dewey wrote Bentley, "I was led to go back to Peirce." "I hadn't realized before either quite what a falsification Morris's account of Peirce's theory of signs and meanings is, nor yet how close Peirce's theory is to yours—ours." [86] The result, in Dewey's eighty-seventh year, was one of his most vigorous essays, on "Peirce's Theory of Linguistic Signs, Thought, and Meaning." [87]

Of the three "dimensions" of semiosis distinguished by Morris—the semantic, syntactic, and pragmatic—the pragmatic was "the relation of signs to interpreters." Dewey objected to the label as misrepresenting pragmatism, but that was a secondary matter; the root error was bringing interpreters into the analysis at all. "To Peirce, 'interpreter,' if he used the word, would mean *that which interprets*," and that which interprets is not a person, nor on the other hand a thing, but always another sign, the interpret*ant*.[88] Morris replied that he had not claimed that his analysis represented Peirce's views; that he had cautioned against confusing pragmatism as a philosophy with pragmatics as a division of semiotic; but that Peirce *does* use the term "interpreter"; and he adduced in evidence a passage in which Peirce inquires into "the nature . . . of the essential

82. *Dewey and Bentley: Correspondence*, pp. 137–38. *Knowing and the Known*, with Arthur F. Bentley (Boston: Beacon Press, 1949).

83. *Dewey and Bentley: Correspondence*, pp. 456–57.

84. Charles L. Stevenson, *Ethics and Language* (New Haven: Yale University Press, 1944), p. 12.

85. "Ethical Subject-Matter and Language," *Journal of Philosophy*, XLII (1945), 701–12, at p. 708n.

86. *Dewey and Bentley: Correspondence*, p. 457.

87. *Journal of Philosophy*, XLIII (1946), 85–95.

88. "Peirce's Theory," p. 87.

effect upon the interpreter, brought about by the semiosis of the sign, which constitutes the logical interpretant." [89] Morris might have adduced many such occurrences of "interpreter" in the *Collected Papers* of Peirce, from his earliest to his latest expositions of his theory of signs, though only one (not that one) is indexed. Nevertheless, even more than in the case of his controversy with Goudge, it is regrettable that Dewey did not continue the argument, for he was on the right track. He might have replied that "interpreter" was one of the vestiges of Peirce's early mentalistic philosophy from which he never wholly freed himself. He might better have replied that it belonged not to the technical language of Peirce's semiotic but to the ordinary language he used to explain the technical term "interpretant." But the best reply he could have made would have been to quote from the excerpts of Peirce's letters to Lady Welby in a book that Dewey had reviewed twenty-two years earlier, and to which he and Bentley were making reference: *The Meaning of Meaning*, by Ogden and Richards.[90] Peirce had written: "I define a sign as anything which is so determined by something else, called its Object, and so determines an effect upon a person, which effect I call its Interpretant, that the latter is thereby mediately determined by the former. My insertion of 'upon a person' is a sop to Cerberus, because I despair of making my own broader conception understood." [91] Of that broader conception Dewey, in spite of clerical inaccuracies, had a better grasp than Morris.

Closer study of Dewey's dealings with Peirce, his works, and his interpreters and critics, would, I believe, confirm what this very imperfect sketch suggests: that in his judgments of Peirce the man and philosopher he was explaining to himself his own early and protracted blindness, and the slowness with which the various aspects of Peirce's thought came within his slowly growing range of interest and comprehension; that for the most part what he came to see in Peirce was what he had

89. *Journal of Philosophy*, XLIII (1946), 196, 363–64; "Signs about Signs about Signs," *Philosophy and Phenomenological Research*, IX (1948), 115–33, at p. 125.

90. *New Republic*, XXXIX (1924), 77–78. *Dewey and Bentley: Correspondence*, pp. 52, 152, 324. *Knowing and the Known*, pp. 4, 263n.

91. C. K. Ogden and I. A. Richards, *The Meaning of Meaning* (New York: Harcourt, Brace and Co., 1923), pp. 442–43.

already made out for himself in other ways; that in defending Peirce against his critics he was defending his own philosophy; that his study of Peirce was never sufficiently detailed to protect him against oversights and misstatements; and yet that he had a great philosopher's understanding of a great philosopher, such as perhaps only Royce before him had had.

In their nineteen-years-long correspondence, Dewey and Bentley frequently exchanged comments about their respective methods of working, their critical styles, their views of the relevance and importance of the history of philosophy, and their particular critical and historical essays—each about the other's as well as his own. This is the chief single source of insight into Dewey's critical and historical studies. The present essay has made too little use of it. It remains nearly unexplored.

## CHECKLIST

"The Pantheism of Spinoza," in *The Early Works of John Dewey, 1882–1898*, Vol. I, pp. 9–18. Carbondale: Southern Illinois University Press, 1969.

"Kant and Philosophic Method," in *Early Works*, I, 34–47.

*Leibniz's New Essays Concerning the Human Understanding*, in *Early Works*, I, 250–435.

"The Late Professor Morris," in *The Early Works of John Dewey, 1882–1898*, Vol. III, pp. 3–13. Carbondale: Southern Illinois University Press, 1969.

"The Philosophy of Thomas Hill Green," in *Early Works*, III, 14–35.

"The Lesson of Contemporary French Literature," in *Early Works*, III, 36–42.

Review of *The Critical Philosophy of Immanuel Kant* by Edward Caird, in *Early Works*, III, 180–84.

Review of *Kant's Critical Philosophy for English Readers* by John Pentland Mahaffy and John Henry Bernard, in *Early Works*, III, 184–85.

Review of *A History of Philosophy* by Johann Eduard Erdmann (English trans. by Williston Samuel Hough), in *Early Works*, III, 185–87.

Review of *Studies in Hegel's Philosophy of Religion* by James MacBride Sterrett, in *Early Works*, III, 187–90.

"Poetry and Philosophy," in *Early Works*, III, 110–24. [Reprinted in C–10, pp. 3–17, with the title "Matthew Arnold and Robert Browning."]

"[Thomas Hill] Green's Theory of the Moral Motive," in *Early Works*, III, 155–73.

"English Transcendentalism." Class lecture notes typewritten by Edwin Peck, University of Michigan, 1892. 23 pp. [Michigan Historical Collections.]

"Intuitionalism," in *Johnson's Universal Cyclopædia*, IV, 657–59. New York: D. Appleton and Co., 1894.

"Moral Philosophy," in *Johnson's Universal Cyclopædia*, V, 880–85. New York: D. Appleton and Co., 1894.

"Commentary on Logic of Hegel." Class lecture notes, handwritten and typewritten, [H. Heath Bawden], University of Chicago, 1894(?). 75 pp. [St. Louis University.]

"The Philosophic Renascence in America," *Dial*, XVIII (Feb. 1895), 80–82. [Review of *The Elements of Metaphysics* by Paul Deussen, *Three Lectures on the Vedanta Philosophy* by F. Max Müller, *Genetic Philosophy* by David Jayne Hill, *Philosophy of Mind* by Georg Wilhelm Friedrich Hegel (trans. William Wallace), *Our Notions of Number and Space* by Herbert Nichols and William E. Parsons, *Diseases of the Will* by Théodule Ribot, *The Psychic Factor* by Charles Van Norden, *Basal Concepts in Philosophy* by Alexander Thomas Ormond, and *A Primer of Philosophy* by Paul Carus.]

Review of *Studies in Character* by Sophie Willock Bryant and *Hedonistic Theories from Aristippus to Spencer* by John Watson, *Psychological Review*, III (Mar. 1896), 218–22.

"Hegel's Philosophy of Spirit." Stenographic report of lectures by John Dewey, [H. Heath Bawden], University of Chicago, 1897. 103 pp. [St. Louis University.]

"Mind (in philosophy)" [J. M. B., J. D.], 81–82; "Natural," 133; "Natural Realism," 134; "Naturalism (1)," 137–38; "Naturalism (in art)" [J. H. T.–J. D.], 138; "Nature," 138–41; "Nature (philosophy of)," 142; "Necessity," 143–45; Neo-criticism," 149; "Neo-Platonism," 150; "Neo-Pythagoreanism," 150; "Nescience," 167; "Nexus," 176; "Nihilism," 177–78; "Nisus," 178; "Noetic," 178–79; "Nominalism," 180; "Non-being," 180–81; "Non-ego," 181; "Noology," 181–82; "Norm and Normative (in the moral sciences)," 182; "Noumenon, and -al," 184–85; "Nous," 185–86; "Nullibrists," 186; "Number (in metaphysics)," 189; "Object (-ive; general and philosophical)," 191–92; "Objectivism," 194; "Occamism," 199; "Occasionalism," 199; "One (the)," 201; "Ontological Argument," 202–3; "Ontologism (2)," 203; "Ontology," 203–4; "Opinion (in philosophy)," 205; "Optimism and Pessimism," 210–12; "Organic," 213; "Organism," 218–19; "Outness," 251; "Oversoul," 252; "Palingenesis," 254; "Panentheism," 255; "Panlogism," 255; "Panpneumatism," 256; "Panpsychism," 256; "Pantheism," 256–57; "Panthelism," 257–58; "Parousia," 263; "Passion and Passive," 266–67; "Peripatetics," 280; "Permanence," 280; "Perseity (1)," 281; "Phase," 288; "Phenomenalism," 288; "Phenomenology," 288–89; "Phenomenon," 289; "Philosophy," 290–96; "Phoronomy," 297; "Plenum," 305; "Pleroma," 305; "Plexus," 305–6; "Pluralism," 306; "Plurality," 306; "Pneuma," 307–8; "Pneumatology," 308; "Posit," 310–11; "Positive," 311; "Positivism," 312–13; "Possibility, Impossibility, and Possible," 313–14; "Pre-established Harmony," 329–30; "Presentationism (2)," 333; "Primary, Primitive, Primordial," 340; "Primum mobile," 341; "Principle," 341–42; "Property," 359–60; "Psychologism," 382; "Pure (in philosophy)," 401; "Quietism," 412; "Rationalism," 415–16; "Realism," 421–24; "Reals," 424; "Reify (-fication)," 439; "Relation," 439–42, 443; "Same (the) and (the) Other," 484–85; "Scepticism," 489–90; "Schema," 490; "Schematism," 490–91; "Scholasticism (the Schoolmen)," 491–95; "Schopenhauerism (or -eanism)," 499; "Scotism," 503; "Seminal Reasons," 514; "Sensationalism," 515–17; "Sensualism (in ethics)," 520; "Singularism," 533; "Speculation (1)" [J. D.–K. G.], 568; "Speculation (2) and (3)," 568; "Statue of Condillac," 601, [last paragraph, J. M. B., J. D.], 601; "Subject (-ive)," 607–8; "Subjectivism," 611; "Substance," 612; "Substantiality Theory or Substantialism," 614;

"Sui Generis," 620; "Summists," 620–21; "Syncretism (1)," 655; "System," 659; "Tabula Rasa," 661; "Thomism," 696; "Transcendent (-al)," 710–11; "Transcendentalism," 711; "Transient," 712; "Tychism," 721; "Ubication," 723; "Understanding and Reason," 725–26; "Unification of Knowledge," 726; "Unitarianism (1)," 734; "Unity (and Plurality)," 734, 736; "Universal (and Universality) (4) and (5)," 739; "Universal Postulate," 741; "Universe," 742; "Unknowable" [J. D.– J. M. B.], 742; "Unknowable," 743; "Unthinkable," 743; "Vacuum," 747–48; "World," 821, in *Dictionary of Philosophy and Psychology*, II, ed. James Mark Baldwin. New York: Macmillan Co., 1902.

"Emerson—The Philosopher of Democracy," *International Journal of Ethics*, XIII (July 1903), 405–13. [Reprinted in C–10, pp. 69–77, with the title "Ralph Waldo Emerson."]

"The Philosophical Work of Herbert Spencer," *Philosophical Review*, XIII (Mar. 1904), 159–75. [Reprinted in C–10, pp. 45–62, with the title "Herbert Spencer."]

Review of *Henry Sidgwick, A Memoir* by Arthur Sidgwick and Eleanor Mildred Balfour Sidgwick, *Political Science Quarterly*, XXII (Mar. 1907), 133–35.

Review of *Studies in Philosophy and Psychology* by the Former Students of Charles Edward Garman, *Philosophical Review*, XVI (May 1907), 312–21.

"Darwin's Influence upon Philosophy," *Popular Science Monthly*, LXXV (July 1909), 90–98. [Reprinted in C–2, pp. 1–19, with the title "The Influence of Darwinism on Philosophy."]

"William James," *Independent*, LXIX (Sept. 1910), 533–36. [Reprinted in C–10, pp. 111–17.]

"William James," *Journal of Philosophy*, VII (Sept. 1910), 505–8. [Reprinted in C–10, pp. 107–11.]

"Maeterlinck's Philosophy of Life," *Hibbert Journal*, IX (July 1911), 765–78. [Reprinted in C–10, pp. 31–44, with the title "Maurice Maeterlinck."]

Review of *Modern Science and the Illusions of Professor Bergson* by Hugh Samuel Roger Elliot, *Philosophical Review*, XXI (Nov. 1912), 705–7.

"Introduction," in *A Contribution to a Bibliography of Henri Bergson* by Isadore Gilbert Mudge, pp. ix–xii. New York: Columbia University Press, 1913.

"On Rousseau, Pestalozzi, Froebel and Montessori," *Kindergarten-Primary Magazine*, XXVI (Mar. 1914), 186; "On Social Motives in School Life," ibid., XXVI (Apr. 1914), 215; "On Pestalozzi," ibid., XXVI (May 1914), 251; "Comparison of Herbart and Froebel," ibid., XXVI (May 1914), 255–56. [Report by Jenny B. Merrill of lectures Dewey presented to the Federation of Child Study.]

*German Philosophy and Politics.* New York: Henry Holt and Co., 1915. 134 pp. [Reset and reprinted with "verbal corrections," a Foreword and new Introduction, New York: G. P. Putnam's Sons, 1942.]

Comments by William Ernest Hocking, "Political Philosophy in Germany," *New Republic*, IV (Oct. 1915), 234–36.

Dewey's "In Reply," letter in *New Republic*, IV (Oct. 1915), 236.

"On Understanding the Mind of Germany," *Atlantic Monthly*, CXVII (Feb. 1916), 251–62. [Reprinted in C–10, pp. 130–48, with the title "The Mind of Germany."]

"Voluntarism in the Roycean Philosophy," *Philosophical Review*, XXV (May 1916), 245–54.

"The Tragedy of the German Soul," *New Republic,* IX (Dec. 1916), 155–56. [Review of *Egotism in German Philosophy* by George Santayana.]

"The Pragmatism of Peirce," *Journal of Philosophy,* XIII (Dec. 1916), 709–15.

"Spencer and Bergson," ed. Gérard Deledalle, *Revue de métaphysique et de morale,* LXX (juillet–septembre 1965), 327–30. [Preceded by an introduction and followed by a French translation of the previously unpublished manuscript written 1916–17(?).]

["George Sylvester Morris: An Estimate"], in *The Life and Work of George Sylvester Morris* by Robert Mark Wenley, pp. 313–21. New York: Macmillan Co., 1917.

"H. G. Wells, Theological Assembler," *Seven Arts,* II (July 1917), 334–39. [Comments on *God, the Invisible King.*] [Reprinted in C–10, pp. 78–82, with the title "H. G. Wells."]

"The Motivation of Hobbes's Political Philosophy," in *Studies in the History of Ideas* by the Department of Philosophy of Columbia University, Vol. I, pp. 88–115. New York: Columbia University Press, 1918.

"Theodore Roosevelt," *Dial,* LXVI (Feb. 1919), 115–17. [Reprinted in C–10, pp. 87–94.]

Review of *The Life and Work of George Sylvester Morris* by Robert Mark Wenley, *Philosophical Review,* XXVIII (Mar. 1919), 212–13.

"Kant After Two Hundred Years," *New Republic,* XXXVIII (Apr. 1924), 254–56. [Reprinted in C–10, pp. 63–68, with the title "Immanuel Kant."]

"The 'Socratic Dialogues' of Plato," in *Studies in the History of Ideas* by the Department of Philosophy of Columbia University, Vol. II, pp. 1–23. New York: Columbia University Press, 1925.

"The Development of American Pragmatism," in *Studies in the History of Ideas* by the Department of Philosophy of Columbia University, Vol. II, pp. 353–77. New York: Columbia University Press, 1925. [Retranslated (by Herbert Schneider) from the French, "Le développement du pragmatisme américain," *Revue de métaphysique et de morale,* XXIX (octobre 1922), 411–30.] [Reprinted in C–7, pp. 13–35.]

"Substance, Power and Quality in Locke," *Philosophical Review,* XXXV (Jan. 1926), 22–38.

"William James in Nineteen Twenty-Six," *New Republic,* LXVII (June 1926), 163–65. [Review of *The Philosophy of William James,* ed. Horace Meyer Kallen.] [Reprinted in C–10, pp. 117–22, with the title "William James."]

[Address], in *A Tribute to Professor Morris Raphael Cohen, Teacher and Philosopher,* pp. 17–20. New York, 1928.

"George Herbert Mead as I Knew Him," *University of Chicago Record,* XVII (1931), 173–77; also published separately in *George Herbert Mead,* [1931?], pp. 10–23; also published in part, "George Herbert Mead," *Journal of Philosophy,* XXVIII (June 1931), 309–14.

Review of *The Autobiography of a Philosopher* by George Herbert Palmer, *A Defence of Philosophy* by Ralph Barton Perry and *The Genteel Tradition at Bay* by George Santayana, *New England Quarterly,* IV (July 1931), 529–31.

"Charles Sanders Peirce," *New Republic,* LXIX (Jan. 1932), 220–21. [Review of *Principles of Philosophy,* Vol. I of Collected Papers of Charles Sanders Peirce, eds. Charles Hartshorne and Paul Weiss.]

"Foreword," in *The Philosophy of Henry George* by George Raymond Geiger, pp. ix–xiii. New York: Macmillan Co., 1933.

"A Challenge to Criticism," *New Republic,* LXXVI (Aug. 1933), 24–25. [Review of *Academic Illusions in the Field of Letters and the Arts* by Martin Schütze.]

"Santayana's Orthodoxy," *New Republic,* LXXVIII (Feb. 1934), 79–80. [Review of *Some Turns of Thought in Modern Philosophy: Five Essays* by George Santayana.]

"A Great American Prophet," *Common Sense,* III (Apr. 1934), 6–7.

"An Empirical Survey of Empiricisms," in *Studies in the History of Ideas* by the Department of Philosophy of Columbia University, Vol. III, pp. 3–22. New York: Columbia University Press, 1935.

"The Founder of Pragmatism," *New Republic,* LXXXI (Jan. 1935), 338–39. [Review of *Pragmatism and Pragmaticism,* Vol. V of Collected Papers of Charles Sanders Peirce, eds. Charles Hartshorne and Paul Weiss.]

"Bergson on Instinct," *New Republic,* LXXXIII (June 1935), 200–201. [Review of *The Two Sources of Morality and Religion* by Henri Bergson, trans. R. Ashley Audra and Cloudesley Brereton.]

"The Jameses," *New Republic,* LXXXVI (Feb. 1936), 24–25. [Review of *The Thought and Character of William James* by Ralph Barton Perry.]

"Santayana's Novel," *Columbia Review,* XVII (Commencement 1936), 49–51. [Review of *The Last Puritan* by George Santayana.]

"The Work of George Mead," *New Republic,* LXXXVII (July 1936), 329–30. [Review of *Mind, Self and Society* and *Movements of Thought in the Nineteenth Century* by George Herbert Mead.]

"The Philosophy of William James," *Southern Review,* II (Winter 1937), 447–61. [Review of *The Thought and Character of William James* by Ralph Barton Perry.] [Reprinted in C–8, pp. 379–95.]

"Charles Sanders Peirce," *New Republic,* LXXXIX (Feb. 1937), 415–16. [Review of *Collected Papers of Charles Sanders Peirce,* Vols. I–VI, eds. Charles Hartshorne and Paul Weiss.]

["F. C. S. Schiller: A Memorial"], *Transactions of the Charles S. Peirce Society,* III (Fall 1967), 52–54. [Read at New School for Social Research, 28 Nov. 1937.]

"Education: 1800–1939," *Vermont Alumnus,* XVIII (May 1939), 169–70, 188–89.

"Presenting Thomas Jefferson," in *The Living Thoughts of Thomas Jefferson,* ed. Alfred O. Mendel, pp. 1–30. New York: Longmans, Green and Co., 1940. [Jefferson readings, pp. 31–173, selected by Dewey.]

"The Vanishing Subject in the Psychology of James," *Journal of Philosophy,* XXXVII (Oct. 1940), 589–99. [Reprinted in C–8, pp. 396–409.]

"James Marsh and American Philosophy," *Journal of the History of Ideas,* II (Apr. 1941), 131–50. [Lecture delivered at the University of Vermont, 26 Nov. 1929.] [Reprinted in C–8, pp. 357–78.]

Review of *The Philosophy of George Santayana,* ed. Paul Arthur Schilpp, *Mind,* L (Oct. 1941), 374–85.

"Foreword to Revised Edition" and "The One-World of Hitler's National Socialism," in *German Philosophy and Politics,* 2d ed., pp. 5–7, 13–49. New York: G. P. Putnam's Sons, 1942. [New Foreword and Introduction to 1915 edition, which was "reprinted without change, save for a few verbal corrections."]

"William James and the World Today," in *William James, the Man and the Thinker,* pp. 91–97. Madison: University of Wisconsin Press, 1942.

"William James as Empiricist," in *In Commemoration of William James 1842–1942,* pp. 48–57. New York: Columbia University Press, 1942.

"The *Principles,*" *Psychological Review,* L (Jan. 1943), 121. [Comments on *The Principles of Psychology* by William James.]

"Boyd H. Bode: An Appreciation," *Teachers College Record,* XLIX (Jan. 1948), 266–67.

"Foreword," in *Evolution and the Founders of Pragmatism* by Philip Paul Wiener, pp. xiii–xiv. Cambridge: Harvard University Press, 1949.

"Modern Philosophy," in *The Cleavage in Our Culture: Studies in Scientific Humanism in Honor of Max Otto,* ed. Frederick Burkhardt, pp. 15–29. Boston: Beacon Press, 1952.

## 12

# Dewey's Lectures and Influence in China

### OU TSUIN-CHEN

WHILE LECTURING at the Imperial University in Tokyo in 1919, Dewey received a joint invitation from five Chinese academic institutions to lecture in Peking, Nanking, and other cities in China. This invitation was prompted by three of Dewey's former students: Hu Shih, professor at the National Peking University; P. W. Kuo, the president of the National Nanking Teachers College; and Chiang Monlin, the editor of *New Education* magazine. Dewey accepted the invitation, arriving in Shanghai 1 May 1919, accompanied by his wife, Alice Chipman Dewey. This was just three days before the outbreak of the May Fourth Movement. Immediately after his arrival, he addressed the Kiangsu Education Association on "The Relation Between Democracy and Education." After visiting Hangchow and Nanking, Dewey settled in Peking, devoting most of his first year in China to a series of public lectures delivered in Peking and in other cities. As a result of his experiences, Dewey became so interested in China that he let himself be persuaded by his Chinese friends to prolong his stay for another year. During his second year he taught regular courses at National Peking University, National Peking Teachers College, and National Nanking Teachers College. He also lectured in most of the coastal cities and visited eleven different provinces.[1]

Everywhere Dewey was warmly received by teachers, stu-

1. Fongtien, Chili, Shansi, Shantung, Kiangsu, Chekiang, Kiangsi, Hunan, Hupeh, Fukien, and Kwangtung. In one of his speeches, Dewey noted he had visited twelve cities. The number of the cities he actually visited needs to be ascertained by further investigation.

dents, intellectuals, government and social leaders, and the general public. He loved mingling with the people, and once was photographed holding a small boy in his arms. During his visit, Dewey's name was constantly associated with that of Bertrand Russell, who was lecturing in Peking in 1920. They were so widely known that no educated person in any large city was unacquainted with their names.

In 1920, the National Peking University conferred a doctor's degree *honoris causa* on Dewey. He and his wife wrote many letters to their daughter, Evelyn, about their experiences in China which she published in book form as *Letters from China and Japan.* Dewey also wrote several articles on China for the *New Republic* and *Asia.* These have since been reprinted in his collected essays, *Characters and Events.*

Dewey left China on 11 July 1921 and returned to the United States to reassume his teaching duties at Columbia University. All in all, he had spent two years, two months, and ten days in China.

### The Lectures [2]

Dewey delivered two different kinds of lectures which were translated and recorded in Chinese, viz.,   1) major lectures delivered serially, and   2) short speeches. The topics of his major lectures were as follows:

1. 16 lectures on Social and Political Philosophy
2. 16 lectures on Philosophy of Education
3. 15 lectures on Ethics
4.  8 lectures on Types of Thinking
5.  3 lectures on Three Philosophers of the Modern Period (William James, Henri Bergson, and Bertrand Russell)
6.  3 lectures on Trends in Modern Education
7.  3 lectures on Democratic Development in America

Dewey also gave three series of lectures in Nanking on:
1. Philosophy of Education

2. A complete listing of the Chinese Lectures appears in *John Dewey: A Checklist of Translations,* *1900–1967,* ed. Jo Ann Boydston (Carbondale: Southern Illinois University Press, 1969), pp. 71–90.

2. History of Philosophy (limited to a consideration of Socrates, Plato, and Aristotle)
3. Experimental Logic [3]

Dewey gave short talks in various Chinese cities on the following topics:
1. The Relationship between Democracy and Education
2. The Cultivation of Character as the Highest Aim of Education
3. An Address at the Anniversary Commemoration of National Peking University
4. The Concept of Right in Western Thought
5. Student Government Organization
6. A Discussion of Chinese Art
7. Primary Education and the State
8. Farewell Address
9. Spontaneity in Learning
10. Foundations of Democracy
11. National Environment, Social Environment, and Human Life
12. Existing Opportunities for the Teaching Profession
13. Educational Principles for Training Youth
14. The Meaning of Government by the People
15. Impressions of a Journey to Southern China
16. The Organization of the American Educational Association and Its Influence
17. Habits and Thought
18. School Subjects and Society
19. Psychological Elements of Education
20. The Relation of School Organization and Administration to the Society

All of Dewey's lectures and speeches were delivered through an interpreter and recorded in Chinese. Later they were published in Chinese newspapers and periodicals. The first five series of Peking lectures were reprinted as a book by the Peking *Morning Post* under the title *Dewey's Five Major Series of*

3. Hu Shih gave the number of lectures of each of these three series in his speech "Dewey in China." But in their reprints in the *Bulletin of the Ministry of Education*, the number of lectures of each series differs from that mentioned by Hu Shih. Here the number of lectures of each series is omitted, pending further research.

*Lectures.*[4] This book went through fourteen printings of ten thousand copies in two years.

In addition to the *Post*'s reprint of the five major lectures series, the Ministry of Education reprinted all the lectures and speeches which Dewey delivered in Shanghai, Peking, Nanking, and other cities, in its *Bulletins* for the years 1919–21.

The Nanking lectures series on the Philosophy of Education differed in content from an identically named series which Dewey gave in Peking. The former, being addressed to students of the National Nanking University, was more technical and somewhat similar in content to his book *Democracy and Education*. Each of the Nanking lectures was recorded by several different persons. As a consequence, there exist other versions differing from that of the Ministry of Education *Bulletin*.

Besides the above-mentioned publications of the Peking and Nanking lectures, Dewey's lectures on the Philosophy of Education, which he delivered as a regular course at the National Peking Teachers College, were published separately as *Democracy and Education*. The Chinese translation was done by Ch'ang Tao-chih.[5]

Hu Shih has described the process by which Dewey's lectures were translated and recorded: "A number of Dewey's students were asked to interpret his lectures in the Chinese language. For example, I was his translator and interpreter for all his lectures in Peking and in the provinces of Shantung and Shansi. For his several major series of lectures, we also selected competent recorders for reporting every lecture in full for the daily newspapers and periodicals. . . . Typing on his own typewriter, Dewey always wrote out his brief notes for every lecture, a copy of which would be given to his interpreter so that

4. Hu Shih mistakenly included Dewey's three lectures on "Trends in Modern Education" in the *Five Major Series*. Instead of these three lectures, another three lectures on "Three Philosophers of the Modern Period" were included in the *Five Major Series*. The lectures on "Trends in Modern Education" first appeared in the *Weekly Critic* and later were reprinted in *New Education*, I (1919).

5. This book was published by the Commercial Press, Shanghai. Ch'ang Tao-chih was the translator. In the Preface Mr. Ch'ang states that in 1920–21 Dewey taught Philosophy of Education in the postgraduate class of National Peking Teachers College, using his *Democracy and Education* as a textbook. Mr. Ch'ang took class notes in English, this book being the result of the translation of his notes in the light of Dewey's original text, *Democracy and Education* (New York: Macmillan Co., 1916).

he could study them and think out the suitable Chinese words and phrases before the lecture and its translation. After each lecture in Peking, the Dewey notes were given to the selected recorders, so that they could check their reports before publication. I have recently re-read most of his lectures in Chinese translation after a lapse of 40 years, and I could still feel the freshness and earnestness of the great thinker and teacher who always measured every word and every sentence in the classroom or before a large lecture audience." [6] What was true of the procedures followed in Peking, Shanghai, and Shansi was also true of the lectures in Nanking. All the Nanking lectures were interpreted by Liu Pei-ming (Ph.D., Northwestern University), a professor of philosophy, the vice-president of Nanking Teachers College, and a cofounder of the *Academic Critic Review*. They were recorded by eminent students of the college.

Dewey's lectures and speeches in other cities were subjected more or less to the same process of delivery, interpretation, and recording. His Shanghai lecture, for example, on "The Relation Between Democracy and Education" was interpreted by Chiang Monlin, whose translation was as reliable as those of Hu Shih and Liu Pei-ming. The authenticity and accuracy of the Chinese translations of Dewey's lectures, therefore, leave little to be desired.

To present, in limited space, synopses of Dewey's lectures delivered in China is an almost impossible task. What I propose to do here is confined to the following points. First, only his main lectures will be dealt with. Secondly, only the significant features in his main lectures will be stressed. What is significant will be determined according to its relevancy to the then Chinese situation, or according to the light it may throw on the understanding of the subsequent development of Dewey's ideas in related fields.

   *1.*   Philosophy of Education—To begin with I shall take up his two series of lectures on Philosophy of Education. As mentioned before, one of the two series of lectures was given in Peking and the other in Nanking. The contents of both are similar in main lines, but their presentations are different to

   6. Hu Shih, "Dewey in China," in *Philosophy and Culture: East and West*, ed. Charles A. Moore (Honolulu: University of Hawaii Press, 1962), pp. 764–65.

avoid duplication in form and to fit the audiences. The Peking lectures are more popular and easier to grasp for the general audience, while the Nanking lectures are more technical, more philosophical, and specially designed for students of education, mostly of the National Teachers College of Nanking. Compared with the epoch-making book *Democracy and Education* published in 1916, three years before his visit to China, both series of lectures may be considered as adaptations of *Democracy and Education* to the Chinese situation, the Nanking series having more similarity to the original text both in substance and in presentation.

The Peking series of lectures are divided into two main parts. Part One deals with the general elements of education, and Part Two the school system, vocational education, and moral education, which are discussed one by one in the light of general elements analyzed in Part One and in reference to the Chinese situation. In Part One Dewey defines the three fundamental elements of education, i.e., the child, the curriculum, and the society. He holds that the innate drives and interests of the child should be the basis of education, and that the social life should furnish the aims of education, while the curriculum or the subject-matter serving as a bridge should introduce the child into his society. The scheme of education has never been, it seems to me, so distinctly defined and outlined before or even after as in these lectures. The social aspect of education is more stressed than elsewhere, too. To illustrate the point, we may quote what he advances in his third lecture: "As we have already said, fruitful and creative participation in society is the end at which we aim in education; the child as he is when he comes to us is the point from which we start; and the school is the bridge linking the child and his society. The business of education is to help the child walk across this bridge and become a useful, contributing member of his society."

Regarding the school system, Dewey discusses three levels of education from elementary up through secondary to higher education. For each he defines its object and its proper ways of operation, always with special reference to China's circumstances and actual needs.

In elementary education he puts more emphasis on the child's experience to begin with. He thinks the main purpose of elementary education is not so much the inculcation of knowledge as it is the cultivation of basic abilities, skills, and habits which will affect the course of subsequent development. In secondary education the inculcation of knowledge is put in the foreground, but inculcation should take place also through its incorporation into the actual experience of the student. He recommends the American type of comprehensive high school for China's reference. As to higher education, he considers its function as the cultivation of specialized abilities, not the production of specialized machines. His idea foreshadows the subsequent conflict between the concept of general education and that of specialized training in colleges and universities.

Regarding vocational education as it is advanced in *Democracy and Education*, Dewey wants to humanize, liberalize, and intellectualize it. In vocational training not only the skill but also the intelligence is to be developed or cultivated. The student's skill must be so trained that he can intelligently understand what he is about and what the meaning of his operation is. In so doing he will not be a tool of a machine, but its master instead.

In moral education, he makes a distinction between ideas about morals and moral ideas. The latter are to be grasped through living the actual moral life in the school as society in miniature.

Speaking of the Chinese Student Movement in connection with moral education, Dewey earnestly hopes to turn the accidental, sentimental, and negative nature of the Movement into a permanent, rational, and positive one. It is a real corrective advice to the then rather wild movement.

So much for Dewey's Peking lectures on the Philosophy of Education. As for his Nanking lectures on the same subject not much needs to be related. Being more technical, more philosophical, the whole series of lectures can be regarded as a replica of *Democracy and Education* with some retouching here and there. This series of lectures is composed of two main parts. The first is a treatment of education in general. The following five topics are discussed:   *1)* the necessity of education,   *2)* the possibilities of education,   *3)* the means of education,   *4)* the results of education, and   *5)* the criteria to evaluate the results of education.

In Part Two, Dewey takes a philosophical approach to the above-mentioned topics. He defines education as growth and as reconstruction of experience. The subject-matter is interpreted in terms of experience. The method of education is considered as the incorporation of subject-matter into the pupil's actual experience. Dewey holds that all the school subjects from play and work through humanities to sciences should be so taught as to correspond to the different stages of the development of the pupil's experience. The subsequently developed core curriculum and problem-solving method have already been foreshadowed in his lectures.

The different educational ideals and aims discussed in *Democracy and Education* are also dealt with in Part Two. Their evaluation and criticism are made in reference to his own conception of education as growth or reconstruction of experience.

Both vocational and moral education are approached from the same philosophical point of view.

Lastly, Dewey makes a special remark on the proper attitude toward the conflict prevailing in China between cultures old and new. He takes a position of compromise and wants the school to cultivate four mental attitudes to deal with the conflict. They are: *1)* open-mindedness, *2)* purposiveness, *3)* responsibility, and *4)* appreciativeness.

To conclude these synopses of the two series of Dewey's lectures on Philosophy of Education, one observation is in point. In both series Dewey never mentions his pragmatic philosophy, although it actually permeates both series of lectures. This should cause no wonder, since in his whole book of *Democracy and Education* he refers to "pragmatism" and "pragmatic" only once each.

2.   Social and Political Philosophy—It is important to remark that apart from the series of lectures on Social and Political Philosophy given in China, Dewey never wrote or spoke systematically on the same subject using a similar title. Here lies the special significance of this series of lectures. Of course, he published before and after its delivery a number of articles and books more or less related to social and political philosophy. But this series of lectures remains as Dewey's sole systematic treatment of the subject.

In his lectures Dewey talks about political and social philosophy as one and the same thing. He never draws a line between the two, although the Chinese title of the series of lectures, if translated literally, should be Social Philosophy and Political Philosophy.

In these lectures Dewey's approach to the subject is something like the following: First, he states social and political philosophy in general terms. Its nature, its scope, its use, and the criteria for the judgement of its value are related one by one.

Then he comes to the problems which social and political philosophy deals with. They are divided into three groups, i.e., *1)* the group of political and legal problems, *2)* the group of problems of knowledge and culture, and *3)* the group of economic problems. Through all his lectures on social and political philosophy Dewey's position represents a third school of thought along with what he terms the idealistic school on one hand and the materialistic school on the other.

According to Dewey, the third school's characteristics consist in the following: *1)* It is experimental. It holds that ideas and theories must be tested by practical application. If the practical result demonstrates that an idea is valid, it can be applied as a guide to social and political activities. *2)* It is specific. It does not resort to sweeping generalizations in the interpretation of social and political phenomena. It is concerned with individual cases in particular situations, and does not advance panaceas or universal laws. *3)* It stresses application of knowledge and intelligence to social change.

From the above-stated features it is obvious that here Dewey also applies his pragmatic method to dealing with social and political philosophy.

When using the pragmatic method to deal with concrete economic, political, and cultural problems, Dewey first criticizes the traditional schools of thought and then advances his own views. Regarding economic problems he condemns both the laissez-faire school and Marxism. Among different socialisms he is in favor of syndicalism, which, he thinks, represents industrial democracy. He even recommends that China keep the good points of her traditional guild system. For the future of China's economy he makes a two-point proposal. Point one is the national development of its important resources—railroads and highways, mineral reserves, forests, and trade roads—to avoid the monopoly of any minority group; and the second point is just the preservation of the desirable aspects of the guild system.

With regard to political problems, Dewey criticizes both the school which advocates the absolute authority of the state and the school which advocates liberalism or individualism. What he advocates is a philosophy of democracy. In a democratic society there would be opportunities for individual development, opportunities for free communication of feeling, knowing, and thinking. The foundation of such a society would be free participation by each member of the society in setting its goals and purposes, and full and willing contribution by each person toward the fulfillment of those goals.

For China, Dewey also suggests some practical measures to realize the ideal of democracy. He does not think it necessary to follow the Western pattern to go through self-seeking individualism and then employ the power of state to equalize society. She may, he thinks, amalgamate these two steps at one stroke. Since in China political individualism has not made headway, traditional paternalism can be turned into the protection of its citizens by a democratic government.

In dealing with cultural problems, Dewey proposes to attach great importance to the authority of science instead of the authority of tradition. He pleads for free thinking and free expression of thought. In addition to a prosperous material life, Dewey advocates a free intellectual life. To fulfill this ideal, he stresses the importance of using education as an efficient tool.

*3.* Types of Thinking—In his lectures on Types of Thinking, Dewey states and criticizes several schools of philosophic method. Four schools are involved. They are: *1)* the Systematizing or Classifying School represented by Aristotle, *2)* the Rationalistic or Deductive School represented by Descartes, *3)* the Empirical or Sensationalistic School represented by Locke, and *4)* the Experimental School represented by Dewey.[7]

Judging by the content of this series of lectures, it is to be noted that this is his first systematic treatment of the subject. As we know, in his previously published works like the articles in *Studies in Logical Theory* and *Essays in Experimental Logic*, *How We Think*, and Chapter 25 on "Theories of Knowledge" in *Democracy and Education*, Dewey had already criticized the

7. Dewey has not mentioned his own name in this connection.

traditional methods of philosophy and had advanced his own position as an experimentalist. But the former cases lack systematic, comparative presentation of the schools concerned, and the latter case is only a chapter in a book giving a brief review of the several philosophic schools concerned. One may say that it is in China that Dewey first developed this subject-matter into a systematic form. It is also to be remarked that shortly after returning to Columbia University from his visit to China, Dewey offered in 1922–23 a course, the syllabus of which is entitled "Types of Philosophic Thought." This syllabus must have been based on his lectures on Types of Thinking. In 1938, Dewey published *Logic: The Theory of Inquiry*. In this epoch-making book Dewey writes another chapter on "The Logic of Inquiry and Philosophies of Knowledge" similar to Types of Thinking and the chapter mentioned from *Democracy and Education*. In view of these facts, it can be said without much risk that, although in terms of content Types of Thinking contains no more material than what appears in Dewey's works concerning the theories of knowledge, it is historically significant because it constitutes an important stage of the development of Dewey's logical thought.

4.   On Ethics—Most of the substance of Dewey's lectures on Ethics is contained in his book *Ethics*, published with James H. Tufts as coauthor in 1908. As the lectures were delivered shortly after the New Culture Movement had begun in Peking and Chinese traditional morality was under severe criticism, Dewey's lectures often refer to the Movement and particularly to Chinese morality. Contrary to what might be expected, Dewey never advances any extreme view with regard to the then prevailing moral revolution. He takes a middle-of-the-road position vis-à-vis the conflict between the moralities old and new. At the end of his lectures, Dewey makes an excellent comparison between Eastern and Western ethical thought. He first states that morality is a function of the environment and varies with it. So it is difficult to judge which morality has more value than another. Then he discerns the differences between Eastern and Western moralities as follows:    *1)* Eastern ethical thought is more concrete, more practical, while Western ethical thought is more abstract and more intellectual;    *2)* Western morality is based upon individuality, while Eastern morality is based on

family;  *3)* Western morality respects the right of the individual, while Eastern morality ignores it.

Out of courtesy Dewey does not explicitly attack Chinese moral traditions, but in his stand for reflective morality, he does provide a weapon for the people involved in the New Culture Movement to do away with a number of old Chinese moral mottoes and practices.

5.   Experimental Logic — Just like the lectures on types of philosophic thinking, Dewey's lectures on Experimental Logic have historical significance. So far as the content is concerned, experimental logic provides no more substantial ideas than Dewey's previously published works such as *Essays in Experimental Logic*, *How We Think*, and relevant articles. But this series of lectures delivered in Nanking on Experimental Logic constitutes what may be called Dewey's first systematic presentation of his School of Logic, since his essays do not form a whole system, and *How We Think* is written more for educational application than for philosophical pursuit.

Experimental Logic has another merit. It is in this series of lectures that Dewey begins to incorporate the much criticized formal logic into his experimental logic system. He finds a place for deduction in his "complete act of thought." Deduction provides a way for Dewey of reasoning out the consequence of a hypothesis to be tested by experiment. This thoughtful incorporation foreshadows Dewey's *Logic: The Theory of Inquiry*. In a sense it can even be said that the latter is an elaboration or a development to culmination of the former. That is where lies the significance and importance of the Nanking lectures on Experimental Logic.

6.   The Other Series of Lectures — Besides what has been analyzed above there are other series of lectures such as "Three Philosophers of the Modern World," "History of Philosophy," and "Modern Tendencies in Education." Owing to the limits of space and their lesser importance, their analysis is omitted.

### Dewey's Influence

Two important institutions were the main centers of Dewey's influence in China both during his stay and after his departure. These institutions were the National Peking University and the National Nanking Teachers College. Both had students of Dewey at their head, viz., Chiang Monlin in Peking and P. W. Kuo in Nanking. Hu Shih, Dewey's greatest Chinese disciple, involved Dewey in the New Culture Movement while the latter was in Peking. In Nanking, Kuo and his colleagues in the Department of Education, especially T'ao Chih-hsing and Ch'en Ho-ch'in, spread the great educator's influence among their own students and followers. Many educational reforms followed as a result of their efforts.

Thus it is accurate to say that it was mainly Peking University which radiated Dewey's influence throughout the country, and mainly from Nanking Teachers College that his influence permeated the whole educational world of China.

Besides National Peking University and Nanking Teachers College, two other important institutions of higher learning helped to extend Dewey's influence throughout China. Both were headed by former students of Dewey: Li Chien-hsun, the president of Peking Teachers College, and Chang Pei-lin, the president of Mankai University in Tiensin. With so many of his former students placed in high key posts, there is little wonder that Dewey was so warmly received or that his teachings were practiced by an ever-widening circle of disciples and friends.

Even before Dewey went to China, the way had been prepared for his reception. *New Youth* magazine, founded by Ch'en Tu-hsiu in 1915, later with Hu Shih as a strong supporter, opened an avenue for new ideas. The *New Education* magazine, established and edited by Chiang Monlin in January 1919, was inspired by Dewey's educational ideas, as stated in Chiang's *Tides From the West*.[8] *New Education*'s masthead actually read: "Stands for Individual Development and Social Progress." The third issue of the magazine was a special issue devoted entirely to Dewey. Hu Shih, Chiang Monlin, and Liu Pei-ming, all of them serving later as Dewey's interpreters, wrote on Dewey's philosophy, ethics, and logic, respectively, to introduce Dewey to the Chinese academic world. Moreover, shortly before Dewey's arrival Hu Shih delivered four lectures on the pragmatic movement, emphasizing Dewey.

8. Chiang Monlin, *Tides from the West* (New Haven, Conn.: Yale University Press, 1947), p. 114.

During and after Dewey's visit, certain national educational organizations also helped to expand Dewey's influence. The China Society for the Promotion of New Education was founded in the same year that Dewey arrived in China by Tsai Yuan-pei, Chiang Monlin, T'ao Chih-hsing, etc., with the *New Education* magazine as its organ. The new education they promoted, as the magazine's masthead indicated, was inspired by Dewey.

The National Federation of Educational Associations was a federation of provincial educational associations with Kiangsu Educational Association as its nucleus. It was very influential, and many educational reforms promulgated by the Chinese government were based on its recommendations.

The Chinese National Association for the Advancement of Education, with T'ao Chih-hsing as its secretary general, was also active in promoting Dewey's ideas in education.

The connection between Dewey and Dr. Sun Yat-sen is a little known fact of modern Chinese history. Sun had encountered psychological resistence to his revolutionary views from the very outset, opponents frequently dismissing them in the words of an old saying: "To know is easy; to act is difficult." In his struggles to overcome this resistance, Sun wrote the book *On Psychological Reconstruction*, in which he advanced the theory that "to know is difficult, but to do is easy." Before publishing his book, Sun conferred with Dewey in Shanghai on 12 May 1919 shortly after Dewey's arrival. In Chapter 4 of his book, Sun referred to his meeting with the American educator, writing: "On the eve of the publication of the first edition of this book, Dr. Dewey happened to be in Shanghai. I confirmed my theory with him. He said, 'We Westerners only think to know is difficult, but no one would think to act is a difficult matter.'" Dewey's own writings support Sun's statement. In his *Letters from China and Japan* Dewey wrote, "Ex-President Sun Yat-sen is a philosopher, as I found out last night during dinner with him. He has written a book, to be published soon, saying that the weakness of the Chinese is due to their acceptance of the statement of an old philosopher, 'To know is easy, to act is difficult.' Consequently they did not like to act and thought it was possible to get a complete theoretical understanding, while the strength of the Japanese was that they acted even in ignorance and went ahead and learned by their mistakes; the

Chinese were paralyzed by fear of making a mistake in action. So he has written a book to prove to his people that action is really easier than knowledge." [9]

Later in his article "What Holds China Back?" published in *Asia*, May 1920, Dewey again wrote about his interview with Sun: "In an evening pleasantly spent with ex-President Sun Yat-sen, he set forth his theory as to the slow change of China as compared with the rapid advance of Japan. It seems some old Chinese sage once said, 'To know is easy; to act is difficult.' The Chinese had taken this adage to heart, so Mr. Sun explained. They did not act because they were afraid of making mistakes; they wanted to be guaranteed in advance against any failure or serious trouble. The Japanese, on the other hand, realized that action was much easier than knowing; they went ahead and did things without minding mistakes and failures, trusting to a net balance on the side of achievement. I am inclined to think the old sage was influential because his teaching was reinforced by effects of the ever-close and ever-thick environment." [10]

In his Chinese lectures Dewey also referred to Sun's theory. In his lecture on ethics, he observed: "To practice means to seek knowledge. A theory must be tested before it becomes accurate. I fully agreed with the great Chinese statesman Dr. Sun Yat-sen, when he said the old saying, 'to know is easy; to act is difficult' has contributed a great deal to the backwardness of China, because under the influence of the saying people have become lazy and hesitant to do anything. It is true that we cannot always anticipate with accuracy the consequences of what we do. But this is no warrant for us to sit idle. The more we try doing something, the more experience we have and therefore the more knowledge we can get. The attempt to get knowledge apart from doing and applying it in a practical situation never will succeed." [11] Here Dewey gave his full support to Sun's theory. Furthermore, in his lecture on the philosophy of education, Dewey again commented on the old Chinese saying: "I heard that there is a Chinese proverb saying 'to know is easy; to act is difficult.' This is contrary to the experimental

9. *Letters from China and Japan*, with Alice Chipman Dewey, ed. Evelyn Dewey (New York: E. P. Dutton and Co., 1920), p. 166.

10. Dewey attributed Chinese habits and ways of thinking to the crowded population.

11. *Five Major Series of Lectures* (Peking: *Morning Post*, 1920), p. 447.

method according to which it is only after we have acted upon a theory that we really understand it. There could be no true knowledge without doing. It is only doing which enables us to possess a new kind of outlook, to organize the facts in a systematic way, to discover new facts. The conclusion is we cannot expect to get true knowledge without acting upon our idea." [12]

Sun's theory of the relation between knowing and acting actually agrees in some respects with Dewey's pragmatic theory of knowledge. No wonder, then, that Dewey so emphatically and repeatedly gave it his blessing. Nor must it be forgotten that at the very time Sun was writing on revolutionary theory, he was also contemplating the reorganization of his own party. Conceivably he gained more self-confidence and encouragement from Dewey's support, and conceivably Sun's followers were strengthened in their resolve to follow their great leader and take the risk of revolutionary activity which led eventually to the Kuomintang's rise to power.

There is no doubt whatsoever that of all Western educators Dewey most influenced the course of Chinese education, both in theory and practice. While his influence on Chinese thought, politics, and society in general is a controversial question difficult to resolve, his influence on Chinese education can be pinpointed and even itemized.

As mentioned before, Dewey's former students at Columbia University held important positions in the Chinese educational world. Chief among these were Chiang Monlin, P. W. Kuo, T'ao Chih-hsing, and Ch'en Ho-ch'in. Chiang did a great deal to extend Dewey's influence after he became Minister of Education in the Nationalist government. Kuo, T'ao, and Ch'en were at National Nanking Teachers College during Dewey's sojourn in China. Kuo was its president, T'ao headed the Department of Education, and Ch'en was a professor of education. They applied Dewey's ideas in their training of secondary and normal school teachers, and these latter, in turn, spread Dewey's influence in the schools where they taught after their graduation. Thus Dewey's influence expanded from the college level down through the middle schools to the elementary schools. Those graduates of Nanking Teachers College who became school inspectors or superintendents likewise carried Dewey's

12. *Five Major Series of Lectures*, p. 198.

influence into administrative areas. With Nanking Teachers College as the radiating center, therefore, Dewey's influence was able to reach the entire country.

Of these disciples of Dewey who were most responsible for spreading his influence in China, T'ao and Ch'en deserve special mention because each developed his own system, taking Dewey's educational theory as his starting point.

The teaching and practice of T'ao Chih-hsing may be said to represent Dewey pushed to extremes.[13] T'ao's contribution to extending Dewey's influence can only be compared to that of William H. Kilpatrick. From his early Nanking days up to his death in 1946 T'ao devoted his life to the cause of educational reform in China. He was the first of Dewey's Chinese followers to develop his own system of educational theory and practice, and the first to seek to extend Dewey's influence from the college level down to the rural school.

T'ao's oft-quoted statement bears witness to the fact that his concept of "living education" was a type of Dewey's own experience-centered education: "What is living education?" T'ao asked. "Living education is life-centered education. . . . Education which has no life-centered work is a dead education. Schools which have no life-centered activities are dead schools. Books without life-centered materials are dead books. People who deal with dead education, dead schools and dead books are dead men." [14]

T'ao also advanced the "Principle of Teaching-Learning-Doing Combination." According to T'ao, teaching is nothing but the art of teaching the students to learn by doing. Only when teaching, learning, and doing are combined as an educational method, practiced in a life situation, can the "living education" be said to exist.

On the practical side, T'ao's experiments at Shao Chuang exemplified Dewey's educational ideas, and helped popularize Dewey's teaching among numerous normal and rural schools.

13. T'ao Chih-hsing later changed his name to T'ao Hsing-chih to show his firmer conversion to the pragmatic philosophy of Dewey. The old name meant "doing after knowing" or "to know in order to do" while the new one means "knowing after doing" or "to do in order to know."

14. T'ao Hsing-chih, "The Text Books Prepared According to the Principle of Teaching-Learning-Doing Combination," *Chung Hua Education Review*, XIX (1930), quoted and translated by Chu Don-chean in "T'ao Hsing-chih and Chinese Education" (Ed.D. thesis, Teachers College, Columbia University, 1953), p. 92.

Dewey and Kilpatrick were so impressed by T'ao's work that on T'ao's death they jointly sent a telegram which read: "We honor Dr. T'ao for his unsurpassed and heroic devotion on behalf of a better education for the common people of China. We who remain must keep alive his memory and his work." [15]

Ch'en Ho-ch'in, another of Dewey's influential disciples, was T'ao's colleague, friend, and follower. Ch'en played an important role in modernizing Shanghai's municipal school system, and later followed up with his work with kindergarten teachers. Through his efforts Dewey's influence reached to the most basic level—the kindergarten and the elementary school. Ch'en's role in promoting Dewey's educational theory and practice was so great that the Communists later forced him to make a public recantation in order to combat Dewey's influence on Chinese education. In his public confession Ch'en declared: "As one who has been most deeply poisoned by his [Dewey's] reactionary educational ideas, as one who has worked hardest and longest to help spread his educational ideas, I now publicly accuse that great fraud and deceiver in modern history of education, John Dewey!" [16]

We will return to Ch'en's accusation later, but there can be no doubt as to the great role he played in spreading Dewey's influence.

It has been mentioned above that Dewey's influence on Chinese education was general and even total. As strong as the statement is, it is a statement of fact and not an exaggeration. We may begin our illustration of this statement by tracing Dewey's influence on Chinese educational theory.

Dewey's philosophy of education dominated the teaching of educational theory in all teachers colleges and university departments of education for many years. His epoch-making textbook on the philosophy of education, *Democracy and Education*, was in general use either as a text or as a work of reference. More than a dozen of his major works were translated into Chinese, and most of their translators were educators, not professional philosophers. There were even several versions of some of these translations.[17]

15. Chu Don-chean, "T'ao Hsing-chih and Chinese Education," p. 23.
16. Quoted and translated by Hu Shih in "Dewey in China," p. 767.
17. The following works of Dewey exist in Chinese translation:

Numerous articles, books, and pamphlets were published to introduce and interpret Dewey's philosophy of education. Some of his sayings, such as "education is life," "school is society," "learning by doing," "education for the needs of life" were known at all levels of the Chinese educational world throughout the whole country, and became oft-quoted clichés. No dissenting views were ever voiced during the time of Dewey's visit nor for many years afterward. Dewey became the highest educational authority in China, and there were many more converts to Dewey in the Chinese educational world than in philosophy.

On the practical side, a number of educational reforms and practices were introduced which reflected Dewey's influence. The following are the salient features of his practical influence:

*1)* Chinese educational aims were reconsidered in the light of Dewey's thought. The first Conference for Educational Investigation was held in April 1919, attended by sixty outstanding educational leaders including Tsai Yuan-pei and Chiang Monlin, all appointed by the Ministry of Education. Dissatisfied with old educational aims promulgated in 1912, which had emphasized military education, the Conference suggested that the aim and spirit of American education should be adopted. The new aim was to be: "the cultivation of perfect personality and the development of democratic spirit." [18] This sounds like the platform of Chiang Monlin's *New Education* magazine, inspired by Dewey.

The Fifth Annual Meeting of the Federation of Educational Associations endorsed the new educational aim in the same year, and even went a step further in following literally Dewey's teaching that "education has no ends beyond itself; it is its own end" by advocating the abolition of all educational aims

---

Democracy and Education, School and Society, The Child and the Curriculum, My Pedagogic Creed (two versions), Schools of To-morrow, Freedom and Culture (two versions), Sources of a Science of Education (two versions), Education Today, Reconstruction in Philosophy (two versions), Ethics, How We Think (three versions), Moral Principles in Education, Experience and Education (two versions). (See *John Dewey: A Checklist of Translations, 1900–1967*.)

18. Shu Hsin-ch'eng, "Chin-tai Chung-kuo chiao-yü shih-liao" [A collection of documents on the history of modern Chinese education], II, 113–20.

and replacing them with a statement of the nature of education instead.[19]

In 1922 the New School System Reform Decree promulgated by the Chinese government made no provision for the establishment of educational aims. Only general principles governing the school system were stated, and this meant the acceptance of Dewey's teaching regarding the educational end.[20]

*2)* The national school system was reformed according to the American pattern. The Federation of Educational Associations proposed the reform while Dewey was still in China and reform had been discussed by a Committee on School System Reform appointed by the Ministry of Education. In 1922 the government promulgated the decree reforming the school system. This decree marked a new era for Chinese education and was the high-water mark of American, particularly Deweyan, influence on Chinese education. The school system was modeled entirely on the American 6–6–3 plan. The general principles of the reform governing the whole system were as follows: *1)* To adapt the educational system to the needs of social evolution; *2)* To promote the spirit of democracy; *3)* To develop individuality; *4)* To take the economic status of the people into special consideration; *5)* To promote education for life; *6)* To facilitate the spread of universal education; *7)* To make the school system flexible enough to allow for local variation.

A glance at this set of principles is enough to tell us that they reflect Dewey's educational philosophy as it is to be found in his writings and in the lectures he gave while in China.

The government's decree was promulgated in 1922 and still governs educational practice in Taiwan.

*3)* Child-centered education was favored in the revision of the curriculum. In 1922 the Federation of Educational Associations met in Tsinan to discuss a thorough revision of the national school system and curriculum. According to Hu Shih, who participated in the meeting, Article 4 of the New Educational System proposed by the meeting reads: "The child is the

19. Shu Hsin-ch'eng, "Chin-tai Chung-kuo chiao-yü shih-liao," p. 20.

20. *Bulletin of the Ministry of Education* (Oct. 1922).

center of education. Special attention should be paid to the individual characteristics and attitudes of the child in organizing the school system. Henceforth, the elective system should be adopted for secondary and higher education, and the principle of flexibility should be adopted in the arrangement and promotion of classes in all elementary schools." Hu Shih rightly observed: "In the new school curriculum of 1923 and the revised curriculum of 1929, the emphasis was placed on the idea that the child was the center of the school. The influence of Dewey's philosophy is easily seen in these revisions." [21] Although the term "child-centered education" did not appear in the National School System Reform Decree, the spirit of a child-centered education permeated the whole system.

After its reorganization by Sun Yat-sen in 1924, the Kuomintang issued its Political Programme. "Promotion of Child-Centered Education" figured in Article 13 of the Programme, and was put into practice by the Nationalists after they established their government in Canton. This meant that child-centered education was favored throughout the country regardless of the political differences between Northern and Southern China.

*4)* The new method of teaching according to the pragmatic theory was promoted. The Fifth Annual Meeting of the Federation of Educational Associations recommended a reform in teaching method with Dewey's ideas as guiding principles.[22] In its meeting in 1921, the Federation urged the extension of the practice of the project method in elementary schools.[23] To help extend the practice of the project method, Dewey's great disciple and the inventor of the method, William H. Kilpatrick, was invited to lecture in China.

*5)* Experimental schools were multiplied. Taking Dewey's Chicago Laboratory School as a model, a number of experimental schools were founded during and after Dewey's visit. The first to be mentioned was the Experimental School of Nanking Teachers College, under the direction of Yu Tzu-yi, a Japanese-trained educator. Yu turned the school into an experi-

21. Hu Shih, "Dewey in China," pp. 765–66.
22. *Education Review*, XI (1919), 108.
23. *Education Review*, XIII (1921).

mental school in which the project method was first practiced and the curriculum organized around it to give effect to the principles of the child-centered school. The school gradually became a model of the Dewey type and attracted visitors from schools throughout the country who came to gain fresh inspiration and learn its method of teaching and curriculum organization. These visitors copied its practices in their own schools, which further helped to extend Dewey's influence over Chinese education.[24]

*6)* Student government as a mode of school discipline was promoted. Dewey spoke in favor of student government in his lectures.[25] Under his influence, the Federation of Educational Associations suggested, in 1920, an outline of regulations governing the practice of student government.[26] In its meeting of 1922, it reaffirmed student government as an objective of school discipline.[27] Consequently, the practice of student government was prevalent in colleges and schools at the time and was carried to such an extreme as even to produce unrest in a number of schools. This unrest was later attributed to Dewey's teaching.[28]

*7)* Literary reform and the adoption of textbooks for elementary schools written in the spoken Chinese language were encouraged. Dewey spoke strongly on behalf of the literary reform initiated by Hu Shih and others.[29] When the Federation of Educational Associations passed a resolution in 1919 on the use of spoken language for textbooks for elementary schools, Dewey praised the resolution and considered the use of "Pai hua" (spoken language) as a textbook medium a great step forward in Chinese education.[30]

In the following year the Ministry of Education amended

24. See Yu Tzu-yi, *Ten Years' Effort of an Elementary School* (Shanghai: Chung Hua Book Co., 1928).
25. See Dewey's speech, "Student Government Organization," *Bulletin of the Ministry of Education* (Oct. 1920), pp. 51–53.
26. *The Record of Chinese Educational Events in the Past Seventy Years* (Shanghai: Commercial Press, 1925), pp. 109–10.
27. *China Year Book* (Peking, Tientsin: Tientsin Press, 1923).
28. Chiang Monlin, *Tides from the West*, p. 124.
29. *Five Major Series of Lectures*, p. 251.
30. *Five Major Series of Lectures*, p. 158.

the Elementary School Ordinance, dropping the item "Kuo-wen" (literary Chinese) in Articles 13 and 15, replacing them with the term "Kuo-yu" (spoken Chinese).[31] The Ministry also ordered that "Pai hua" textbooks should be used beginning in the fall of 1920.[32]

In the same year, the Commercial Press began to publish twenty series of elementary school textbooks written in "Kuo-yu." [33]

In 1925, the Ministry of Education ordered that all the lower elementary schools should use textbooks written in spoken Chinese.[34] In the same year the Association of the Elementary Schools attached to the Normal Schools of Kiangsu, Chekiang, and Anwei met to pass a resolution urging that all textbooks written in literary Chinese be burned to show the country's determination to do away forever with all textbooks in literary Chinese.[35] Since that time, all textbooks for elementary schools have been written in "Pai hua."

From the foregoing, we may conclude that Dewey's influence on Chinese education was beyond any doubt both extensive and profound.

To return to Ch'en Ho-ch'in, the Chinese Communists were not satisfied with his denunciation of Dewey's educational ideas and required him to attack their philosophical base as well. Obediently, Ch'en fired off "three gunshots" of his own at Dewey's pragmatism. According to Ch'en, Dewey's pragmatism consisted of three elements, viz., 1) idealistic empiricism, 2) a biological view of human nature, and 3) a vulgar evolutionist view of society. Ch'en's attack on Dewey's pragmatism is contained in his pamphlet "Critique of the Philosophic Bases of John Dewey's Reactionary Pedagogy," which is a highly technical performance from the philosophic point of view. Judging from Ch'en's previous academic training, it is doubtful, to say the least, that Ch'en is really the author. The pamphlet attacks Dewey from the official Marxist-Leninist standpoint and contains little not already mentioned in similar

31. *Bulletin of the Ministry of Education* (Feb. 1920), p. 7.
32. Cyrus H. Peake, *Nationalism and Education in Modern China* (New York: Columbia University Press, 1932), p. 143.
33. *The Record of Chinese Educational Events*, p. 89.
34. *Bulletin of the Ministry of Education* (Feb. 1925), p. 10.
35. *Education Review*, XVIII (1925).

work by Russian Communists. But it is worth noting that the virulence of the Communist attack on Dewey is one good indication of how great his impact was on Chinese thought and education, and how necessary the Chinese Communists deemed it to extirpate it root and branch.

Thus today it would seem that Dewey's thought is in eclipse in China, not only on the Mainland where his followers have been purged by the Communist regime, but also in Taiwan, whose school system is still functioning under the decree of the Nationalist government which modified and revised the original Reform Decree of 1922.

But for all that, it must be admitted that Dewey's influence is still alive and felt on Taiwan. For instance, in a recent issue of *Education and Culture*, an official publication of the Ministry of Education, Ho Min-lin published an article entitled "The Influence of Dewey's Theory of Teaching Method and Subject Matter upon Chinese Education." Ho writes: "Dewey was a reformer and a foreign philosopher; his educational theory has had a tremendous influence upon Chinese education. Dewey lectured in China between 1919 and 1921 during which time he made a great many constructive suggestions to the existing Chinese educational system and curriculum. Even the present educational system was established also directly or indirectly under his influence. In spite of the fact that his prestige has been rapidly reduced in America, his philosophy of education and his way of thinking are still worthy of study." [36] Since these are the words of an ordinary teacher, they probably reflect the general attitude of the average Chinese educator toward the great American philosopher and educator.

We may well conclude on a note of promise. The Elementary School Teachers In-Service Training Center in Taipei is headed by a follower of the Dewey school, and Dewey's educational philosophy permeates this institution. Hundreds of elementary school teachers have been trained under the influence of Dewey's pragmatism over the past nine years. According to a recent issue of *Education and Culture*, twelve thousand in-service teachers will be trained by the Center on a rotation basis in the next five years. If its present spirit does not change, the outlook for a revival of Dewey's influence is by no means dim. [37]

36. *Education and Culture*, No. 317 (Apr. 1964), p. 18.
37. *Education and Culture*, No. 319 (June 1964), p. 44.

CHECKLIST OF MISCELLANEOUS WORKS

CHECKLIST OF COLLECTIONS

INDEX

# CHECKLIST OF
# MISCELLANEOUS WORKS

"The Angle of Reflection, 1–6," in *The Early Works of John Dewey, 1882–1898*, Vol. III, pp. 195–210. Carbondale: Southern Illinois University Press, 1969.

"Fred Newton Scott," *Oracle* (University of Michigan), 1894, 4 pp.

[Statement], in *Talks to Teachers on Psychology, and to Students on Some of Life's Ideals* by William James, p. 303. New York: Henry Holt and Co., 1900.

"Introduction of the Orator [Nicholas Murray Butler]," *University [of Chicago] Record*, IX (May 1904), 12–13.

"In Behalf of Culture," letter to the editors, *Freeman*, VII (Mar. 1923), 38–39.

"Foreword," in *Studies in Psycho-Expedition* by Feiwel Schneersohn, pp. vii–viii. New York: Science of Man Press, 1929.

[Report of address], *American Hebrew*, CXXVI (Nov. 1929), 125.

[Note on *The Russian Land* by Albert Rhys Williams], in *Impressions of Soviet Russia*, cover. New York: New Republic, 1929.

"Introduction," in *India's Outlook on Life: The Wisdom of the Vedas* by Jagadish Chandra Chatterji, p. 7. New York: Kailas Press, 1931.

"Funds for Brookwood College," *New Republic*, LXXIII (Dec. 1932), 101; "Help for Brookwood," *Nation*, CXXXV (Dec. 1932), 592.

[Communication], in *Twelve Axioms* by Clyde Miller (reissued, 1960?), n.p., n.d. ["Address given before the Greater Cleveland Schoolmasters Club, February 20, 1934."]

"Foreword," in *Seventy Times Seven* by Carl Christian Jensen, pp. vii–x. Boston: Lothrop, Lee and Shepard Co., 1935.

"Foreword," in *Argumentation and Public Discussion* by Angelo M. Pellegrine and Brents Stirling, p. iii. Boston: D. C. Heath and Co., 1936.

"Henry Linville Pension Fund," *Social Frontier*, II (Apr. 1936), 230.

[Statement in Regard to *Capitalism and Its Culture* by Jerome Davis], *New Republic*, LXXXIX (Nov. 1936), 89.

[Tribute to James Hayden Tufts], in *James Hayden Tufts* by Frederic Woodward, T. V. Smith, and Edward S. Ames, pp. 19–23. N.p.n.d., 1942.

[Memorial notice of James H. Tufts], *Philosophical Review*, LII (Mar. 1943), 163–64.

"Message from the Philosopher John Dewey to the Teachers of Perú," trans. Jo Ann Boydston, *Dewey Newsletter*, II (Oct. 1968), 21. [Published originally in *Jornadas Pedagógicas Regionales* (Apata, Departamento de Junín, Perú), 20 al 27 de marzo, 1944, p. 11.]

"Introduction: Greetings to the Urbana Conference," in *Essays for John Dewey's Ninetieth Birthday*, eds. Kenneth Dean Benne and William Oliver Stanley, pp. 3–4. Urbana, Ill.: Bureau of Research and Service, College of Education, 1950.

# CHECKLIST OF MISCELLANEOUS WORKS

"Author's Preface," in *Minshushugi to Kyōiku* [Democracy and Education], trans. Hoashi Riichirō, n.p. Tokyo: Shunjūsha, 1952. [English.]

## Letters, in:

Perry, Ralph Barton. *The Thought and Character of William James,* I, 104; II, 516, 517, 520, 525, 527, 528, 529, 531, 532. Boston: Little, Brown and Co., 1935.

*The Morning Notes of Adelbert Ames, Jr.,* ed. Hadley Cantril, pp. 171–231. New Brunswick, N.J.: Rutgers University Press, 1950.

Buswell, James Oliver. *The Philosophies of F. R. Tennant and John Dewey,* p. 464. New York: Philosophical Library, 1950.

*Thoreau Society Bulletin,* No. 30 (Jan. 1950), p. 1

*The Flowers of Friendship: Letters Written to Gertrude Stein,* ed. Donald Gallup, p. 254. New York: Alfred A. Knopf, 1953.

"Dewey's Letters (1946–1950) to Robert V. Daniels," *Journal of the History of Ideas,* XX (Oct.–Dec. 1959), 569–76.

Frost, Corinne Chisholm. "Texts and Motifs: Reflections of John Dewey. Excerpts from Unpublished Correspondence," *Daedalus,* LXXXVIII (Summer 1959), 549–59.

Dykhuizen, George. "John Dewey: The Vermont Years," *Journal of the History of Ideas,* XX (Oct.–Dec. 1959), 521, 533, 537, 538, 540, 541, 543.

Jaffe, Raymond. *The Pragmatic Conception of Justice* (University of California Publications in Philosophy, Vol. XXXIV), pp. 46, 113. Berkeley, Los Angeles: University of California Press, 1960.

Dykhuizen, George. "John Dewey at Johns Hopkins (1882–1884)," *Journal of the History of Ideas,* XXII (Jan.–Mar. 1961), 105, 106, 107, 112, 113, 115, 116.

Dykhuizen, George. "John Dewey and the University of Michigan," *Journal of the History of Ideas,* XXIII (Oct.–Dec. 1962), 513, 516, 529, 530, 541, 543.

Dykhuizen, George. "John Dewey: The Chicago Years," *Journal of the History of Philosophy,* II (Oct. 1964), 229, 331, 244.

Dykhuizen, George. "John Dewey in Chicago: Some Biographical Notes," *Journal of the History of Philosophy,* III (Oct. 1965), 224, 225, 226, 227, 228, 231, 232.

# CHECKLIST OF COLLECTIONS

C–1. *The Educational Situation* (University of Chicago Contributions to Education, No. 3). Chicago: University of Chicago Press, 1902. 104 pp. [Revised versions of three papers presented to educational organizations.]

C–2. *The Influence of Darwin on Philosophy and Other Essays in Contemporary Thought*. New York: Henry Holt and Co., 1910. vi, 309 pp. [Previously published articles reprinted with revisions.]

C–3. *Essays in Experimental Logic*. Chicago: University of Chicago Press, 1916. vii, 444 pp. [Essays from *Studies in Logical Theory*, with editorial revisions, and essays from journals, in part reprinted and in part rewritten.]

C–4. *China, Japan and the U. S. A.* New York: Republic Publishing Co., 1921. 64 pp. [Reprinted material from the *New Republic*.]

C–5. *Impressions of Soviet Russia*. New York: New Republic, 1929. 270 pp. [Reprinted material from the *New Republic*.]

C–6. *Individualism, Old and New*. New York: Minton, Balch and Co., 1930. 171 pp. [Reprinted articles from the *New Republic*, incorporating considerable new matter.]

C–7. *Philosophy and Civilization*. New York: Minton, Balch and Co., 1931. vii, 334 pp. [Reprints, with revisions, of previously published articles.]

C–8. *Problems of Men*. New York: Philosophical Library, 1946. 424 pp. [Articles from various journals, reprinted, with a new Introduction.]

C–9. *Knowing and the Known*, with Arthur F. Bentley. Boston: Beacon Press, 1949. xiii, 334 pp. [Reprinted articles from the *Journal of Philosophy*, with new material.]

C–10. *Characters and Events*. Ed. Joseph Ratner. 2 vols. New York: Henry Holt and Co., 1929. [Reprints of articles published in various journals.]

C–11. *Intelligence in the Modern World: John Dewey's Philosophy*. Ed., with introd. by Joseph Ratner. New York: Modern Library, 1939. xv, 1077 pp. [Reprinted articles and sections of books.]

C–12. *Education Today*. Ed., with Foreword by Joseph Ratner. New York: G. P. Putnam's Sons, 1940. xix, 376 pp. [Reprinted articles and sections of books.]

C–13. *The Wit and Wisdom of John Dewey*. Ed., with introd. by A. H. Johnson. Boston: Beacon Press, 1949. 111 pp. [Reprinted selections.]

C–14. *John Dewey: Dictionary of Education*. Ed. Ralph B. Winn. Foreword by John Herman Randall, Jr. New York: Philosophical Library, 1959. x, 150 pp. [Reprinted selections from books and articles.]

C–15. *Dewey on Education.* Introd. and notes by Martin S. Dworkin. New York: Bureau of Publications, Teachers College, Columbia University, 1959. 134 pp.

C–16. *John Dewey on Education.* Ed., with introd. by Reginald D. Archambault. New York: Modern Library, 1964. xxx, 439 pp.

# Index

# INDEX

# INDEX